BESIDE STILL WATERS

Also by Gregg Easterbrook

This Magic Moment
A Moment on the Earth

BESIDE STILL WATERS

Searching for Meaning
in an Age of Doubt

GREGG EASTERBROOK

William Morrow and Company, Inc.
New York

It is the policy of William Morrow and Company, Inc., and its imprints and affiliates, recognizing the importance of preserving what has been written, to print the books we publish on acid-free paper, and we exert our best efforts to that end.

Library of Congress Cataloging-in-Publication Data

Easterbrook, Gregg.
Beside still waters : searching for meaning in an age of doubt / Gregg Easterbrook.
p.   cm.
Includes bibliographical references.
ISBN 0-688-16065-4
1. Bible—Criticism, interpretation, etc. 2. Monotheism—Biblical teaching. 3. Spiritual life—Biblical teaching. 4. Christianity—Controversial literature. I. Title.
BS533.E37   1998
220.6—dc21   98-18005
CIP

Printed in the United States of America

First Edition

1   2   3   4   5   6   7   8   9   10

BOOK DESIGN BY BERNARD KLEIN

www.williammorrow.com

For Grant, Mara Rose and Spenser

It is well said that each new child
who comes into the world
proves that God has not given up hope

Is There Anything Left to Believe In?

We live in an age characterized by explosions in knowledge, science, historical insight, sociological articulation, and the education that ought to render us able to make sense of these developments. Far more things are known today than ever before, and with each passing year, vastly larger numbers of men and women possess the advanced learning traditionally considered essential to enlightenment. And yet in many ways we know less than ever, especially about our spirits. Does existence enfold higher purpose? Is there any higher being? Did life have a creator, or did it simply happen through mechanics of chemistry and heat exchange? Are we watched and loved, or alone in a void? Are we each other's brothers and sisters, or strictly self-interest units? On some of the greatest questions, the outpouring of information and education has done little to bring us closer to answers.

Is There Anything Left to Believe In?

And in the standard analysis that dominates Western thought regarding such great issues, middle ground is rare. Hard-hearted postmodernism assumes existence to lack meaning. Closed-minded traditionalism assumes the whole of life, even its blemishes and torment, springs from an omniscient divine plan. In public debate, nihilism endlessly vies with fundamentalism. Each person who thinks about spiritual issues is expected to choose up sides, believing everything or nothing.

Yet millions of thoughtful, skeptical women and men are comfortable neither with traditional dogmatic religion nor with postmodern abdication of faith. They long to know their souls. They wonder whether they are children of molecules or of a Maker. They may have felt a sensation of the sacred, or seen spiritual awareness redeem a troubled life. They yearn for some glimpse of purpose in the work-and-spend of material society, for some sense of connection to a larger whole, for assurance that there are still things worth believing in. But they also find it hard to reconcile the hopeful aspects of faith with the instances in which organized religions have harmed the world rather than helped it; with the flaws in every form of scripture; with the cardinal question of how an all-powerful God could tolerate the suffering of the world.

It is to those who seek the spiritual center—whose hearts are open to higher purpose but whose heads are aware of the many valid objections—that this book is addressed.

YEARS AGO I BEGAN TO WONDER if there is a center understanding of faith, one that emphasizes ideals of meaning and purpose while striving to discard dogma and the infighting of denominations. Many men and women have, of course, wondered the same. Some have tried to seek the center by advocating ecumenical cooperation among the institutional faiths. Others have been drawn to nontraditional interpretations that teach the general principles of faith but shy away from specifics, an impulse seen today mainly in the "spirituality" movements. As a rationalist, I found that my interest focused on whether there are, within the traditional understanding of monotheist belief, correctable errors that would help bring us back toward the center. That is, can a person look the problems of faith directly in the eye, and come away believing?

Seeking the center in this way, I have devoted time to contemplating such issues as whether we can still believe in a higher being, or whether scientific findings show the universe to be self-generated, an engineering scaffold rather than a realm of purpose; whether the wars and repressions staged in the name of religion invalidate the ideals that arise from faith; whether our increasing knowledge of history demonstrates spiritual thought to have begun in mythology or superstition; whether faith is on balance an advantageous force for society. These are the issues that the first section of this book will cover.

And over the years I have wondered what to make of the Bible, on which the Judeo-Christian tradition and considerable portions of Islamic and Baha'i thought are based. The Bible contains errors and contradictions; more importantly, it contains many disagreeable, even repugnant, ideas. Yet the Bible has held so much sway over so many minds for so long that it is hard not to believe it offers a genuine spiritual vision as well. Like many people, I have wondered if there is some way to approach the Judeo-Christian scripture that would accord the Bible the spiritual validity it deserves, while taking into account its errors and the wrongs done in its name. Seeking such a center path to scripture, I came to feel there exists an elemental error in typical comprehension of the monotheist writ, an error that causes us to overlook an aspect of the Bible that has for centuries been hiding in plain sight. This will be the topic for the second section of this book.

Finally, over the years I have wondered if a thread of universalism runs within monotheist thought: a vision of the spirit that would wear down the barriers raised when people call themselves Buddhist, Catholic, Hindu, Jewish, Protestant, Shia, Shinto, Sunni, or by any other denominational name. I came to feel there exists a way to approach the Bible—not some complicated web of revisionism but a fairly straight-line reading based on plain words taken at face value—that emphasizes universal values over the specific contentions of particular faiths. This is the topic for the third section.

Throughout the book, the focus will be the Bible and the core beliefs of monotheism. Eastern spirituality has extensive significance, too, and it may be that there are lost faiths, such as "goddess" doctrine, that are also worthy of contemplation. But whether we like it or not, beliefs grounded in the Judeo-Christian scripture are pivotal to American, European, Latin, and, to a surprising degree, African and Asian cultures. For most men and women of the West, biblical themes are the music that plays on the radio station from which the mind cannot ever really be switched. Biblical spirituality must be fathomed if spirituality is to be fathomed.

Spiritual understanding is often conceptualized as an intensely personal experience. But there is also a common aspect of spiritual thought, in which what matters is what people can agree upon.

Surely much of the feeling of emptiness so many men and women experience in our materially favored age links to a loss of the shared aspects of spiritual hope—not the teachings of any particular faith but to the sense that we're all in it together in the quest to make our lives matter. Of course there will never be unanimity on the particulars of human belief. But we can agree on the need for spiritual concord: for those common ideals, such as compassion and morality, that underlie every faith. These reside at the spiritual center.

Brussels, Belgium
April 1998

Two Notes

GIVEN THAT THIS BOOK will propose a new understanding of Western scripture, some readers may ask, "Why isn't the author a doctor of divinity or a defrocked priest or a professor of something unpronounceable?"

People with such backgrounds have composed many illustrious works on spiritual issues. But the specialist view is only one of many. Through the centuries, insights about belief have come in equal proportion from experts and everyman. The enduring questions of meaning and purpose are open to any inquiring mind.

On a stylistic matter, an increasing percentage of writers embrace "he or she" for the indefinite pronoun. But in the special case of the divine, the construction He or She looks like a failed attempt at a comic touch. And although male allusions to God unquestionably appear in the original versions of the monotheist writ, the uppercase "He" does not. Early Hebrew and Greek testaments lacked any case distinction: theological capitalization is not a matter of scripture, but an invention of the Middle Ages.

The gender, if any, of spiritual entities representing a matter for another day, I have sidestepped the divine chromosome debate by the simple expedient of wording second references to God so as to eliminate the indefinite pronoun. It was surprisingly easy. He, Him, and similar constructions will, however, be employed in quotations, when these usages occur in the original.

Acknowledgments

FOR THE REALIZATION OF THIS VOLUME thanks are due to my colleagues, editors, and friends Riccardo Baschetti, Mary Beth Brown, Michael Carlisle, Joelle Delbourgo, Carey English, James Fallows, Henry Ferris, Kate Forsyth, Erica Goode, Celeste James, Amy Kost, Mark Madden, Cullen Murphy, Shuja Nawaz, Timothy Noah, Harrison Rainie, Sheila Thalhimer, Richard Todd, Ann Treistman, Steven Waldman, and William Whitworth; to my brothers Frank and Neil; and to my wife, Nan Kennelly, who spent five years listening to me say, "I've just thought of something else missing from the Bible."

I am especially thankful to David Holmes, a professor of religious studies at the College of William and Mary, who reviewed chapters of this book for technical accuracy. He is in no way responsible for the opinions that appear in these pages.

Also I wish to express my debt of inspiration to the former University of Chicago philosopher of theology Charles Hartshorne, born in 1897 and still alive at this writing. Hartshorne has spent nearly a hundred years swimming against the tide by composing rational arguments that truth and purpose really do exist: that the search for the spirit ought to be the "organizing principle for human thought." When the life-is-meaningless intellectual fad passes, as inevitably it will, Hartshorne will be recognized as among the century's leading minds.

Contents

I know not what you believe of God,
but I believe he gave yearnings and longings to be filled,
and did not mean all our time should be
devoted to feeding and clothing the body.

LUCY STONE, FEMINIST ORATOR, 1855

Part One

✦

Reasons to Doubt

I repent me of the evil that I have done
unto you.
God, apologizing to humanity about 2,600 years ago
JEREMIAH 41:10

Chapter One

Hope and a Good Joke

*To me the sole hope of human salvation lies in
teaching man to regard himself as an experiment in the realization of God.*
GEORGE BERNARD SHAW, 1909

ONE DAY IN THE EARLY 1990S archaeologists working a dig near
the town of Haifa on the Mediterranean Sea found vestiges of
an ancient human grave with characteristics unusual for its
time period. To picks and trowels the powdery site yielded
the ancient skeleton of a young mother whose arms had been
delicately wrapped around the form of an infant, the two having been buried together after both died, presumably during
childbirth. Tests dated the bones as 100,000 or more years
old, meaning they were interred early in the Pleistocene ice
age: tens of millennia before genus *Homo* knew of controlled
agriculture, writing, or the wheel;[1] long, even, before the cave
paintings of France.

What was striking about the find was that the bodies appeared to have been buried ceremonially. At a time when the
highest achievements of human culture were campfires and
sharpened stones, someone spent many days tenderly fashion-
ing a resting place for two departed souls. Someone, in that
place, surely wept as earth was heaped in over the still forms

of woman and child. Possibly someone uttered the sort of words now called prayer, with eyes raised to the heavens, demanding answers.

Coolly rational modern analysis might say that a prehistoric man weeping over the death of a prehistoric woman and child represented nothing more than the deterministic interaction of hormones governed by genetic codes designed to maximize reproductive strategy, supplemented by a primeval cost-benefit analysis of lowered economic forecasts owing to reduction in the labor force. Any ceremonial aspect, modern analysis might add, was a sociological accretion engendered by mythology and dysfunctional power-structure dynamics, to say nothing of a poor expenditure of resources better devoted to chiseling flint.

Yet the realization that our distant ancestors memorialized the fallen tells us that questions of life and purpose, of meaning and loss, of yearning and spiritual hope, have been in the human family for an unimaginable span of time. Women and men began to wonder about the purpose of their lives, and to reach for a sense of spiritual meaning, seemingly from the moment they began to think.

Stretching as far back as the first written records and likely much further, every culture has evolved beliefs that life enfolds purpose greater than mere satisfaction of want or sustenance of biological need. "We are born believing," Emerson wrote: women and men "bear beliefs as a tree bears apples."[2] Either some divine power made *Homo sapiens* spiritually inclined, or nature did so, through the offices of natural selection. In either case the human heart yearns for a sense of the unseen.

That people believe things does not necessarily make beliefs true. For centuries some people have believed that stones, totems, or secret incantations convey good fortune or bad. People have believed in mythical creatures, and in charms to ward off those creatures. Even in an information age, people ardently hold insupportable beliefs, such as conspiracy theories; or improbable ones, such as astrology; or highly fanciful ones, such as removing money from politics. The very unlikelihood of beliefs sometimes makes men and women cling to them all the more tenaciously. For some people, as Mark Twain observed, conviction may be defined as "Believin' what you know ain't so."[3]

But credence for amulets or alchemy has never grown beyond a minority; most people know flimflam when they see it. Occasional widely entertained beliefs that arise at specific junctures in history, such as the turn-of-the-century fascination with séances, rapidly peak and decline. Controvertible ideas that do manage to find adherents from generation to generation, such as fortune-telling, rarely spread to more than a tiny fraction of the population.

Spiritual yearning, in contrast, has expanded with the passage of time, embedding itself into the consciousness of billions. Specific religions have had their ups and downs, but in no society has spiritual interest expired nor shown the possibility of doing so. Spiritual yearning has cut across every category of human culture, making believers of some of the brightest, most sophisticated people in history.

Perhaps some aspects of faith do originate in fable. But if artifice were the essence of spirituality, it seems inconceivable that over many centuries, so many people would keep falling for the same tricks. A more likely explanation for the historical significance of faith is that people by the millions have sensed that somewhere within spirituality lies an essential aspect of the human prospect.

WITHIN FAITH THERE IS ALSO FALLACY and intolerance. All the world's scriptures contain statements that cannot be true; all religions sometimes attempt to deny reason; nearly all beliefs have generated hostility as well as harmony.

Even if, for example, one reveres the Bible, it would be foolish to assume every one of that scripture's statements are true,
since the Bible shows significant contradictions. A simple example is the two mutually exclusive accounts of the boyhood
of Jesus. In the Gospel of Matthew, there is no Roman census
or donkey journey; Jesus is born at home in his parents' home-
town of Bethlehem.[4] Warned by the wise men about Herod's
plan to kill their singular child, the family flees to Egypt—a
place with harrowing connotations for Jews at the time—and
raises Jesus in that country, returning to Israel only when the
boy has become a teenager. In the Gospel of Luke, Joseph and
Mary do not live in Bethlehem, but must travel there when
the census is being called.[5] During the trip, the baby is born
at an inn, angels appear to glorify the moment with hosannas,
and in one of the highest moments of all the world's writing,
mere shepherds are chosen to receive the child into history.
(The shepherds and the wise men never meet: crèche scenes
are an invention of popular culture.) Afterward Joseph and
Mary return home and raise their boy in Nazareth, rather than
living in exile in Egypt. Obviously, these accounts conflict in
prodigious ways. The presence of contradiction does not disqualify scripture from containing spiritual power, nor, for that
matter, from containing records of actual events: one or the
other Christmas story may very well be historical. But such
imperfections ought to warn us that every organized religion
stands partly on institutionally imbedded error.

More worrisome than contradictions in scripture may be
the notion of faith as the opposite of logic. As Abdu'l-Bahá, a
Baha'i theologian, wrote in 1912, "If religious beliefs of mankind are contrary to science and opposed to reason, they are
none other than superstitions, for the Lord God has endowed
man with the faculty of reason in order that through its exercise he may arrive at the verities of existence."[6] In cautionary
notes such as these, we find even a thinker who worked in the

spiritualist tradition warning against much of what is wrong with traditional monotheism and with many of the unaffiliated new "spirituality" movements: the inclination to assume that to reach for the unseen, men and women need be "opposed to reason."

No one who yearns for the spiritual ought to fear holding up faith to the methods of reason: you can think rationally about that which fails to meet the eye just as readily as about that which does. The traditionalist Swiss theologian Karl Barth, who wrote in the first half of this century, often said he accepted modern critiques of scripture or findings of natural science because he could not understand why any believer would *not* want to know as many details as possible about the reality of faith, even if new discoveries overturned cherished illusions. Trying to sift through the question of what aspects of spirituality are profound and which are traceable to error ought to be seen as a positive exercise, helping us to concentrate on that portion of spirituality that is truly worth believing.

More than fear of reason, the behavior of the faiths offers a harsher bill of attainder against belief. A substantial portion of the horrors of history—inquisitions, oppression, ethnic hatred, wars—has been instigated in the name of the invisible. Spiritual belief continues to serve as a source of animus between the Irish and the English, the Israelis and the Palestinians, the Hindus and the Moslems, the Bosnians and the Serbs, and many other groups. As levels of education rise throughout society, more people come to know of religion's role in past and present barbarities; this knowledge naturally instills a sense of disillusionment. That faiths preach love but generate hate can hardly be seen as a minor shortcoming.

But knowing of the many faults associated with the theory and practice of faith should not make us abandon spirituality as an ideal, any more than knowing the exasperating faults of democracy ought to leave anyone longing to turn back the clock to the Hapburgs. As the age of doubt advances, as greater understanding renders women and men more skeptical of the claims of every institution of thought, we engage the risk that the beauty of spiritual yearning will be overturned along with the blemishes. Wanting to rid ourselves of the mythology and intolerance associated with faith, we risk ridding ourselves of its insights and glories as well.

THE RUSSIAN SOCIAL CRITIC ALEXANDER HERZEN once said he found it amazing that "after all the trials of modern skepticism, there was still so much left in our souls to destroy."[7] Herzen said this not in 1995 nor 1965, but in 1855. Already by that time it was common to think that cynicism and modernity had overturned the hope for higher purpose—and to continue to yearn regardless, since even cynicism privately hopes for an afterlife in which unbelief, too, may be preserved. Nevertheless, the notion that nothing is left to believe in clearly predates our age of doubt.

There are those who argue, and not without force, that the human cause would be served by the cessation of spirituality. We'll all be better off, it is supposed—more level-headed and more accepting of each other—once we admit there is nothing more to existence than chemistry: no help available from above, no tormentor awaiting below. This view traces at least as far back as Rousseau, who thought that a world of high-minded atheists would be a more kindly place than a world of believers: disabused of illusions about the almighty, people would be forced to realize they have only one another to fall back on.

But by the evidence so far, dilution of belief has mainly harmed the modern age. Today nearly everyone feels that character, integrity, and values are in decline. Of course we should not romanticize the past as a time of moral exactitude, for it surely was not, but can it be coincidence that the decline in modern values is happening during the same period in which faith is disdained by intellectuals and educators? Today it is fashionable for thinkers to describe life as pointless or a realm of existential dread: but it is those very people who walk the Earth without any sense that a Maker watches and records their actions who create the conditions that existentialism dreads, whether as street criminals or corporate criminals or soulless leaders of institutions. Renewed emphasis on the spiritual ideals of compassion and community might cause the social conditions that call forth existentialism to decline.

If modern thought is correct, and dread inherent to the human condition, then no new technical device or government program will ever overcome that; but spiritual awareness might. If modern thought is correct, and our bodies are just machines governed by deterministic forces, then our spiritual impulses, capable of transcending the material, would seem to become more important, not less. In this sense the modern age would be served by more faith—of an open, thoughtful nature—not less, especially faith in life as a meaningful experience in which values and moral choices have lasting significance.

Of course it is open to debate whether life carries meaning; whether higher purpose can be discerned; whether a soul or an immaterial awareness exists; whether men and women are born for a purpose or simply born. No one can prove any of these elemental propositions, while firm objections to each can be raised.

Yet as Shaw once argued in a letter to Tolstoy, "Suppose the world were only one of God's jokes. Would you work any the less to make it a good joke instead of a bad one?"[8] Even though we cannot know whether our lives reflect some larger scheme, a renewed sense of spiritual purpose—not of blind acceptance of dogma but of fair belief in the human potential—

may help restore the dream of the common good. The spiritual impulse is essential in that regard. Few things mean more to society than having its members take a hopeful view of the future, for this animates the sorts of actions that improve social circumstances. And few things mean more to the self than a sense of participation in the larger rhythms of life. As humankind faces an uncertain future, it is not quixotic to suppose our prospects will be better if we believe the living enterprise is vested with meaning.

Surely one reason a blurred unease so pervades the modern era is the danger of loss of faith in anything larger than the Land's End catalog. Even as their lives grow longer, manual toil declines, and the material lifestyle steadily improves, ever-larger numbers of men and women feel caught up in a crisis of hope about the human prospect. The modern soul aches; the appointment calendars of psychiatrists and therapists are overbooked; the abundance of the postwar era has brought a striking increase in standards of living, but no increase in the percentage of people who describe themselves as "happy" or "content."[9]

Today huge numbers of men and women enjoy sound incomes, high levels of schooling, and find themselves reasonably in control of their lives. They may not have everything they would like, but do not fear for their daily bread. Advancing health care allows them to worry about their own mortality less than any generation that has ever lived. They may wish society had a more moderate pace, but, being well-informed, are seldom blindsided by change. All these things are obviously to the good; the only problem with modern affluence is that not everyone in the world can experience it. Yet the same people who enjoy these unprecedented material advantages often depict their lives as lacking fulfillment and describe themselves as possessed of diminishing hope for the human prospect.

Perhaps this means no more than that with affluence rising, more people now have leisure time in which to experience feelings of shallowness. Perhaps, as Robert Samuelson has written, contemporary disquiet has its explanation in the media's ever-improving skill at emphasizing things to worry about. But the most likely root cause is decline in the conviction that life carries meaning. At our peril do we relinquish faith: not adherence to any particular religion or denomination, rather to the essential belief that all human beings are each other's brothers and sisters, sharing a Maker who wants us to hold each other's hands. There remains truth at the core of faith, however much detritus has been up around the margins.

A century ago, when Charles Dickens did his writing, his imperative concern, like that of most progressive thinkers, was material poverty, something that dominated the daily existence of the majority of women and men alive in his time. Today material poverty remains, and in the Western nations is inexcusable given that enough wealth now exists to share. But in the United States and most of Europe, no longer do most women and men worry about whether there will be walls to surround them, or go to bed wracked by pangs of hunger. Today they worry about whether there will be meaning to frame their lives, and wake up wracked by pangs of the soul. In the West, spiritual poverty has replaced material poverty as the leading want of our age.

Chapter Two

In Praise of Doubt

Skepticism is the beginning of faith.
OSCAR WILDE, 1891

THE POSTWAR DECADES HAVE NOT BEEN KIND to any type of faith. Faith in government has been shaken by recurrent scandal and by the realization, made plain during the Vietnam War, that even democratically elected leaders can be indifferent to human life. Faith in the family has been shaken by the spread of divorce; faith in the public commons, by crime. Faith in market economics as the engine of a better life has been shaken by corporate executives who lavish millions upon themselves while begrudging twenty-five cents an hour to those who struggle to get by. Faith in the progress of *Homo sapiens* toward a more gentle social order has been shaken by a succession of intellectual theories depicting women and men as mere genetic automatons. Each day's newspaper brings word of some ideal dashed or someone in a position of respect sullied by disgrace. Today people are even suspicious of what the Girl Scouts do with the proceeds from their cookie sales.

Shaken faith is especially pronounced in religious subjects. Though more than three quarters of Americans continue to say they believe in God, by 1995 pollsters found that only 35 percent of adults in the United States considered themselves "religious," the lowest such figure for the century.[1] Despite expansion in several traditionalist denominations, and not-withstanding those "baby boomers coming back to God" stories now obligatory for the Easter Week editions of newsmagazines, through most of the postwar era there has been a decline in the portion of the United States population that regularly participates in worship activities.[2]

The rationalists of the Enlightenment era would have been delighted to hear of a widespread social phenomenon of women and men becoming more skeptical about beliefs and institutions. But they would be horrified to see how far it has gone—for many, beyond questioning authority to believing in nothing, beyond doubting dogma to rejecting meaning. To question is essential to human freedom, and in this regard doubt has many constructive uses. The challenge today is to honor the constructive application of doubt, without allowing purpose and hope to be lost in the process. The question, then: Which aspects of doubt should we esteem, and which should themselves be doubted?

SOME DOWNWARD SLOPE FOR FAITH was inevitable if only because the portion of belief that was grounded in folklore was sure to be overturned. Consider how many of the oldest spiritual notions concerned the heights of the sky, unattainable to the ancients. The chief Babylonian god, Marduk, manifested far above people's heads as thunderstorms. The Norse pantheon lived in Asgard, a celestial stronghold reached by crossing the rainbow. The Greek immortals were ensconced on Mount Olympus. In many polytheist traditions the cardinal deity was called the "sky god," senior to other supernatural beings by virtue of holding the high welkin. Throughout much of the monotheist tradition, references to heaven are employed interchangeably with terminology for the sky. In Genesis, for instance, the Maker summons into being "fowl that may fly above the earth in the open firmament of heaven."[3]

Humanity has now visited "heaven" and found nothing there. Flying machines have coursed the vault of the sky and encountered no corridors of glory, only chemicals interacting with the ozone layer. Sophisticated optical, radio, X-ray, gamma-ray, ultraviolet, and infrared telescopes have looked deep into the cosmos, observing an astonishing magnitude of structure—some 40 billion galaxies at last count—and recorded many examples of breathtaking might, but glimpsed nothing that appears supernatural.[4]

Looking inward, modern knowledge confounds ancient spiritual expectations in similar ways. When our bodies are scanned in tremendous detail by advanced devices such as the magnetic-resonance imager, there appears no organ where the spirit may reside. Brain research increasingly makes consciousness seem a mechanical affair of electrons moving along axons to interact in synapses that control polypeptides, employing processes more numerous, but no more numinous, than what goes on inside a paramecium. A soul may be there, but it has been cleverly concealed.

More generally, in recent decades it has become common to attribute the development of spiritual longing entirely to factors unrelated to the spirit. Some commentators suppose that people envisage a spiritual plane because the notion is drilled into them during childhood, in the form of fables about golden beings or entry into paradise—exactly the sorts of ideas to which the child's mind is plastic. Others maintain that men and women sign on to religion because they feel compelled to do so by threats of damnation, autocratic social structures, or coercive peer pressure. Some theories put forth that spiritual craving is subconscious in origin: our psyches cannot adjust to the inevitability of death, so we compensate by inventing a mythos of glory on the other side. Or we cannot accept a spontaneous origin of life, implying as it does that no loving Maker will ever return to rescue us from our blunders, so we compensate with parables of splendor in the morning hours of creation.

In art and in cultural commentary, science is treated as having invalidated the unseen, or at least as having shown that sophisticated people should not take seriously any theory of human nature that cannot be reduced to mathematical formulas, economics, or DNA. Media coverage of the evolving spirituality movements dwells on the lifestyle quirks of adherents, subtly making sport of the craving for inner peace; the mainstream faiths are depicted as dinosaurs oblivious to an approaching comet. Within the educational establishment, faith has lost nearly all its standing: today it is standard to encounter "religion and mythology" as an academic classification.[5] As recently as 1929 Alfred North Whitehead, holder of a chair in the philosophy department at Harvard University, could end a book with the declaration, "The kingdom of heaven is with us today [through] the love of God in the world."[6] That opinion is surely open to debate, but in the contemporary intellectual milieu, any Harvard instructor who said the same would be regarded as having gone daft, probably even by the faculty of Harvard Divinity School.

Perhaps it will eventually be shown that spiritual longings represent no more than sociological accretions, vestiges of fable, or psychological adjustment mechanisms. Yet today many men and women confuse the awareness that all belief systems contain errors with the assumption that therefore the underlying truths claimed by spirituality must also be in error. Saying that faith has flaws, as it surely does, is entirely different from saying it lacks verity. But contemporary thought increasingly treats the two notions as reciprocal, forming a feedback loop. The more we become aware of flaws in belief, the less we believe; and then the more we scan for collateral flaws, and so on.

YET MUST WE NOT HAVE DOUBTS? Beyond the inability of telescopes to pinpoint the empyrean, beyond deterministic theories of biology or the subconscious, exists an elemental reason why the traditional form of monotheist faith really ought to be in decline: the continuing absence of divine action against evil.

More than 2,000 years ago the Greek philosopher Epicurus called the existence of evil the essential question for human thought, supposing that "Either God wants to prevent evil and cannot, or can and does not want to." As recently as the work of the theologian Paul Tillich, who died in 1965, God's apparent silence in the face of human suffering was taken as the first and highest obstacle to belief. Today both organized religion and the informal spirituality movements often have little to say about the continuance of evil, seeming to consider the topic bad for business. By 1993 *The New York Times*, the nation's best and most thoughtful newspaper, seemed to feel the subject of why evil persists had fallen to such a low significance as to describe scriptural accounts of human suffering as no more than "stories and symbols" that must be sorted out by "post-biblical thinkers," whatever they may be.[7]

This banishes to tertiary status what ought to be *the* issue of spiritual inquiry. How could an omnipotent, benevolent deity exist and not right the wrongs of the world? Surely, at heart, this is *the* issue driving the age of doubt.

From the Hebrew prophets of 3,000 years ago to the young Jesus movement of the first century to the Islamic mystics of the late first millennium, even the most devout believers have fretted about why the divine has not offered immaculate justice and brought daily suffering to a close. Most of the pious of the past maintained that the glorious day of divine justice was due at any moment. Thousands of years later it has not come. Wars and atrocities wrack every generation; evil runs unchecked; poverty and want grind on; inequity between rich and poor remains entrenched; the blameless are taken by accident or disease, while the invidious prosper; hearts are broken by the millions; everywhere is beaming innocence dragged down.

And as the world's population shoots upward, from less than 1 billion in our great-grandparents' era to about 5.6 billion today, the misery experienced by human beings increases by exponential progression. Today people suffer in numbers staggering in historic terms. In this century alone at least 60 million people have been killed by war,[8] more than the total number of people alive worldwide when Moses wandered the Sinai.[9] Today 1.3 billion persons subsist under conditions the World Bank calls "destitution,"[10] seven times the total number of men and women alive worldwide when Jesus walked the dirt byways of the Promised Land, preaching clemency for the poor.

Yet as the weight of suffering presses ever-harder on humankind, and the sum of spiritual need expands, no divine agency steps forward to proclaim: *Enough!* With each year that a spiritual sovereign fails to set our world to right, the case against faith appears to grow. Add to this the many powerful criticisms of belief raised by science, sociology, intellectual thought, and the study of history, and surely we find good reasons for every thoughtful woman and man to entertain doubts. Can a modern, worldly-wise CNN watcher still be a believer?

ON THIS POINT, SKEPTICISM AND DOUBT ARE ALLIES, not enemies, of belief in higher purpose. Only by challenging traditional assumptions can a person come to understand what is truly worth believing. Today we forget, for example, that the Enlightenment revival of skeptical reasoning began largely with the goal of finding a rational understanding of faith. Descartes is usually credited with kicking off the Enlightenment by proposing, in the name of spirituality, the ultimate axiom of skepticism—that all we can be sure of are our doubts.

Descartes supposed that our ability to harbor doubts lets us know that we are thinking; in turn, becoming aware of our thoughts allows us to know we exist. Skepticism thus drives Descartes's celebrated 1637 dictum, *cogito ergo sum*. In his formulation, doubt is not a negative influence, leading men and women toward feelings of meaninglessness. It is instead a source of exultation, confirming that people are vested with the ability to substantiate their consciousness on its own terms.

Like many Greek thinkers and Renaissance minds, Descartes was fascinated by the question of whether mathematics held some lesson about the unseen world. To Descartes, whose specialty was algebraic negative roots, searching for mathematical evidence of primal laws—for example, relationships among roots and sines that always hold regardless of the values inserted—was an exercise that might prove the existence of "first causes," or elemental truth woven into the fabric of the universe. This, in turn, might put belief on a sounder footing than poignant but unverifiable claims of revelation. Descartes's contemporaries and followers had similar goals; Spinoza asserted that the highest ambition of reason was to qualify for "the intellectual love of God"; Thomas Jefferson wrote, "Question with boldness even the existence of a God, because if there be one, He must more approve of the homage of reason."

Jefferson reasoned that the Maker would prefer the devotion that arises from skeptical inquiry to devotion based on rote. From inference such as this arises an obvious speculation: that if humankind did receive the faculty of reason through a divine grant, then God must have surmised that very power would be used to question God. Perhaps, since no Maker can be seen or touched, doubting is the first step toward belief, akin to sprinkling magnetic filings on the larger outline. Today increasing knowledge generates increasingly sophisticated reasons to question faith. This may not necessarily trouble the Maker.

Skepticism no more guarantees wise conclusions than does its lack. Many famous skeptics came to erroneous conclusions. Aristotle thought that a child's traits were inherited exclusively from the father. Einstein rejected the idea that the universe is expanding. Darwin, who drafted the theory of natural selection before the basic laws of genetics were known, entertained the standard nineteenth-century assumption that blood chemicals were the agents of heredity, an idea that would get him laughed out of any contemporary biology department.

Of course if Descartes or Spinoza were alive today, by the standards of our age these renowned skeptics would seem exceptionally devout. Nevertheless, they were harassed by the church authorities of their time. Descartes was called a heretic by Christianity for endorsing the Copernican thesis of heliocentric celestial motion. The man known to history as Benedict Spinoza latinized his birth name, Baruch, in response to excommunication by the Jewish authorities of Amsterdam, who found Spinoza's ideas intolerably tolerant.

GOING FURTHER BACK, SKEPTICISM EXTENDS to the roots of faith. Today many assume that skepticism about the unseen is primarily a modern phenomenon. The reverse is true: many faiths were founded with a quizzical eye toward the divine.

Seven thousand years ago the Sumerians, forebears of the Babylonian religion, supposed that every rock, tree, and similar natural object contained a spirit. Today this strikes us as improbable; it struck people as improbable seven thousand years ago, too. As Samuel Kramer recounted in *History Begins at Sumer*, several extant Babylonian poems, dating to the origins of the written word, are dialogues on whether spiritual claims should be taken seriously.[11] In one a believer and an atheist resolve that since the actions of the gods are unfathomable, there can be no ultimate knowledge, only knowledge as it appears in context. This conclusion is remarkably similar to that found in postmodern philosophy, much of which holds that no pure truth exists that applies equally to all cultures. In another antiquarian Babylonian text, slave and master argue about fairness. The master is forced to defend his position of privilege with the assertion that, since life is voided by death, moral choices may be meaningless anyway. This is not what one would call an unquestioning attitude, and it is 7,000 years old.

In many systems of faith, skepticism and spirituality arose concurrently. Hinduism, which is perhaps 4,000 years old, takes a playful attitude toward the gods, allowing adherents to choose which ones they wish to believe in, while depicting divine figures as embodying a range of qualities from sagacity to roguery. The Romans and Greeks had love-hate relationships with their panoply, gods often depicted as so maladjusted that genus *Homo* seemed elevated by comparison. The ancient Greek religion emphasized spiritual skepticism: the gods would deliberately attempt to trick people for nefarious ends, so one had always to be on one's toes. Buddhism, which is approximately as old as Judaism, is in some ways a faith that actively celebrates doubt. Mainstream Buddhist thinking rejects the idea of divine oversight, finding the machinery of life and suffering so powerful not even a god could resist it. Buddhism is a religion by virtue of concerning the disposition of the soul, but not a religion in the sense of a theory of worship or divine understanding: though it trains priests and builds temples, Buddhism has no deity.[12] For thousands of

years Buddhism has taught its believers to be skeptical of
claims that gods or eternal glory exist.

Skepticism is also found at the beginnings of monotheist
faith. As Jonathan Rowe of the social reform organization Re-
defining Progress noted in 1996, "The basic Jewish and Christian teachings are the true home of the skeptic." Almost
immediately after God and humankind first meet in Genesis,
doubt breaks out. Eve doesn't believe God is telling the truth
about that tree.[13] Adam is suspicious of divine purpose: one of
the earliest things the first man says to his Maker is, "I heard
the sound of you in the garden and I was afraid."[14] Jacob,
among the most ancient Hebrews, meets God at a place called
Peniel and spends a night attempting to wrestle the Maker to
the ground in the physical sense.[15] A mere eighteen chapters
into the Judeo-Christian Bible, Abraham is openly calling
God's plan to destroy Sodom immoral because the righteous
will die along with the wicked.[16] During this encounter, one
of the first consequential dialogues of monotheist theology,
Abraham comes close to taunting God, demanding, "Shall not
the judge of all the earth do what is just?"[17]

Doubt has been the adjutant of faith for as long as records
have been kept. This is as it should be. Wrestling with God
is healthy—and a great workout.[18]

A TELLING DISTINCTION EXISTS, HOWEVER, between the form of
doubt that runs parallel to spirituality and the form prevalent
in contemporary culture. To Descartes, Spinoza, Jefferson, and
other eminent rationalists, reasoned doubt was what lead them
to the kind of faith worth having. Today, in contrast, skepticism is viewed as battery acid to be poured over belief. In the
constructive application: doubt helps us sift through the ore
to find the hidden jewels within. But in its contemporary declination, doubt fixates exclusively on the errors and mumbo-

jumbo of belief, with the goal of demonstrating that it's all errors and mumbo-jumbo.

It is possible that, ultimately, life is bereft of meaning: anyone entering into spiritual contemplation must engage the risk of reaching this null-set conclusion. What is troubling about the contemporary declination of doubt is the assumption that nullity is where skepticism *ought* to lead. As Karen Armstrong has written, one reason faith seems in decline is that "many of us no longer have the sense that we are surrounded by the unseen."[19] The modern declination of doubt seems to take as given that whatever cannot be empirically documented must be cast off. Yet almost everything that makes life worth living is centered on ideals that lack any tangible reality: honesty, morality, cooperation, kindness, compassion. All these are parcel of "the unseen," present around us, attempting to influence us, though no camera can photograph them nor any scientific device detect them.

An example of how doubt can take someone deep into disenchantment, and then back out to renewal of belief in higher purpose, is the nineteenth-century Parisian priest and theologian Alfred Loisy. Ordained in 1879, Loisy became a professor at the Institut Catholique, but was dismissed for questioning the reality of miracles. In 1908, he was excommunicated for expressing doubts about the resurrection. His writings, full of rational skepticism, were placed on the Vatican's notorious *Index of Forbidden Books*.[20] Loisy came to oppose all dogmas of all faiths, and spent much of his adult life being harassed by organized religion as a result.

Today we would expect that someone going through what Loisy did would become embittered, write a scorching book about the pretenses of ecclesiastical insiders, and dedicate his time to complaining on the talk show circuit. What Loisy did, instead, was to advance a profoundly hopeful view of faith. He taught that science, rationality, and historical accuracy should be used not to denigrate belief in the human prospect, but rather to place that faith on firmer ground. For Loisy, as the critic Bruce Chilton has written, the meaning of the world's scriptures "resided in their capacity to transform our collective existence,"[21] holding out the conviction that regardless of whether miracles have occurred in the past, the ultimate miracle—that of universal fellowship—remains possible in the present.

Loisy found this chain of logic persuasive: Even if the origins of belief contain mythology, the impact on the human consciousness of spiritual teachings of love, fellowship, and human kindness is, itself, a miracle. Whether or not the seas parted for Moses, or Jesus raised Lazarus, or Muhammad was called by Gabriel, we need not doubt that somehow the promulgation of faith's ideals of love and morality did, in fact, happen. After agonies of skepticism about the scriptures, years of rejection, and banishment by self-interested religious institutions, Loisy found there was something intensely spiritual in which he could have perfect faith—the ability of men and women to seek higher purpose. Shedding the sophistry enabled Loisy to see that human beings are capable of loving each other: they just haven't yet done a good enough job of it. Doubt had set him free to have faith.

So let's offer two cheers to constructive doubt. Roll your eyes regularly whenever in temple, church, or mosque; question every assumption of every faith; read your Darwin. But do not allow such exercises to prevent you from seeing that, whether divine or spontaneous in origin, the human soul exists and has beauty and purpose.

Chapter Three

Spirit and Society

If sometimes poor people die of starvation, it is not that God didn't care for them but because you and I didn't give.
MOTHER TERESA, 1975

THROUGH MUCH OF THE POSTWAR ERA, an ascendant view has held that spiritual belief should be cast out of public life. To opinion-makers, at least, the faith impulse has come to be associated solely with its negatives: money-craving televangelists, creationists run amok at school-board meetings, New Age infomercials hawking instant transcendence kits. In a representative opinion, the astute political scientist John Mueller of the University of Rochester has argued that the abdication of belief is already benefiting Western Europe, where "the human race has, for perhaps the first time in its history, developed societies that are orderly, moral, and generally admirable, if materialistic; and in which religion plays no important part."[1] Most contemporary editorialists would likely hold with Mueller, or with Rousseau and Voltaire, in viewing spirituality as a reversionary force, one that propels society backward toward customs it were better-served to forsake.

Of course belief has its shameful hours: the repressive theocracy of the Puritans, the burning crosses of the Ku Klux Klan,

24

the systematic anti-Semitism of the old WASP elite, to cite three of many in the American legacy. Yet the notion that faith holds society back overlooks that many nations, including the United States, have been made more progressive and humane by the influence of belief. Without the dreams of the spirit, America might never have come as far as it has.

Believers were the motivating force for the abolition of slavery. English evangelicals led the campaign for the 1807 British outlawing of slavery and for the subsequent commitment by the British Navy to patrol the western coast of Africa to intercept slave traders. In the United States the Second Great Awakening, a spiritual movement that swept much of the country at the beginning of the nineteenth century, provided the first impetus for general demands to free slaves. As Benjamin Schwarz, a fellow of the World Policy Institute, has written, "Between the Revolution and the War of 1812, Virginians freed more slaves than at any other period before the Civil War . . . [because of] evangelism, which characterized slavery not just as an abridgment of natural rights but as a horrible evil."[2] Evangelism of the nineteenth century also argued for women's rights, on the grounds that women were treated as equals by the early Jesus movement.[3] Evangelists fueled the abolition campaign of the 1850s. The first time American churches instituted organized get-out-the-vote drives was not during the Reagan years but in 1860, to support the antislavery candidacy of Abraham Lincoln. When Lincoln stood for reelection against General George McClellan, who opposed the Emancipation Proclamation, churchgoers swung the election by turning out in towering numbers for Old Abe. As the Lincoln biographer David Donald has noted, in 1864, "The support the President received from religious groups was overwhelming . . . there probably never was an election in all our history into which the religion element entered so largely, and nearly all on one side."[4]

That faith played a leading role in the drive for abolition is not an exception: throughout history, spiritual conviction has been at the forefront of pressure for social progress. The fourth-century emperor Julian once complained that Roman society was being shamed because believers took care of the less advantaged while the state would not. "No Jew is ever seen begging," Julian grumbled, "and the Galileans [Christians] support not merely their own poor but ours as well."[5]

Closer to our era, during the depression of 1893–1897, which caused widespread bank failures and unemployment, religious leaders, including the Protestant clergyman Walter Rauschenbusch, founded the influential "social gospel" movement, which emphasized New Testament directives that society be restructured with fairness to the disenfranchised in mind.[6] "Social gospel" advocacy became integral to the establishment of trade unions, child labor laws, public relief programs, and other reforms. Inspired by the philosopher William James—the founder of American pragmatism, whose guiding belief was that the value of an idea is judged by whether it has a beneficial practical effect[7]—believers felt themselves obliged to show that spiritual ideas could improve daily life. Around that time, like-minded spiritual initiatives had similar positive effects in other countries. An example is the Rama Krishna movement in India, a Hindu effort to reform the caste system that began in the late nineteenth century and survives today as an advocate of labor laws and literacy.

By the arrival of the Great Depression, social-gospel thinking had brought sufficient awareness of compassion into American politics that Franklin Roosevelt, as governor of New York state in 1931, would declare, "The test of our progress is not whether we add more to the abundance of those who have much, it is whether we provide enough for those who have little." Roosevelt knew this idea would be easier to advocate politically using spiritual rather than secular rationale, and he turned that knowledge to advantage.[8] Congress was pushed to enact Social Security, the Works Progress Administration, and other reforms that rescued millions of Americans from poverty or workplace abuse, in no small part because so many clergy were promoting "social gospel." Through the Depression years a focal point of forward-looking American politics was Dorothy Day's closely read publication *The Catholic Worker*, which was at once left-wing and unabashedly religious—a refreshing combination sorely lacking from contemporary debate. As John Dewey and other progressives of the time said, the New Deal could not have happened without the support of religion.[9]

NEARER TO THE CURRENT ERA Judaism, Christianity, and Islam were essential to the civil-rights movement of the 1960s. The Southern Christian Leadership Conference was a central organization for civil-rights progress, while many rabbis, ministers, priests, and laity played bold roles in the struggle against color discrimination. Spiritual organizations such as Clergy and Laity Concerned About Vietnam were also influential in opposing the Vietnam War.

Belief took an important role in the dissolution of tyranny in the former Soviet Union, with demands for freedom of worship on the part of Catholics and the Eastern Orthodox Church causing pressure against totalitarian regimes throughout the old Eastern bloc.[10] Faith helped oppose military dictatorship in Latin and Central America, especially under the banner of "liberation theology" advocated by courageous priests and nuns at the cost of their lives.[11] By the mid-1990s, Catholic and Jewish organizations in the United States were taking the lead in pressuring apparel manufacturers such as Nike to eliminate their sweatshops and pay a living wage.[12]

Faith has been the underlying motive for many of history's leading benefactors. Albert Schweitzer often said that he lived and practiced medicine among the impoverished of Africa because of his religious beliefs; thousands of other less-known women and men have engaged in similar lifelong service for spiritual reasons. Throughout American history, faith-based organizations or affiliates such as the Salvation Army have fed and clothed the poor, reached out to criminals, reformed addicts and alcoholics. Today it is common to read in the literature of postmodern deconstruction that the poor are more religious than the upper class because faith dupes the poor through a sociological control structure that encourages them to be passive in this life by promising rewards in the next. A more straightforward reason often explains why the poor are believers: religious organizations help them and intellectuals do not.

Personal-recovery organizations such as Alcoholics Anonymous and Promise Keepers often employ spiritual argument, warning that God is not pleased with anyone who lives dishonorably. Pundits may scoff at Promise Keepers for its revival-like meetings, and feminists may have a point about some of its political statements. But the main effect of Promise Keepers is to encourage men to be honest, responsible, and nonviolent: men, who are the source of most of the world's duplicity, irresponsibility, and destruction. Any form of argument that persuades the typical person toward ethical behavior ought to be welcome, and for many, arguments that include spiritual appeals are most effective in this role.

On a personal scale, the spiritual impulse may draw people from all walks of life into working for social change. Here is a small example from my own sphere of experience. My wife's refugee work often takes our family overseas. When we most recently lived in the United States we belonged to Trinity Church of Arlington, Virginia, of the mainly liberal Presbyterian USA denomination.[13] This particular congregation passed my wife's test of having a woman at the altar and our kids' test of having a wing devoted to kids. It passed my test of having a minister who gave sermons concise enough to remember and use in daily life: the iron law of public speaking being that the less someone has to say, the longer it takes to say it.

Each summer, Trinity sent members to perform volunteer work in rural Guatemala. One Sunday in 1994 regular services were suspended so the returning Guatemala contingent could report. I sat nonplused as a 17-year-old named Andrea Davnie, who baby-sat our kids and whom I'd mistaken for the archetypal sullen teenager, rose to describe her month working with Guatemalan reformers protesting the murder of the human-rights activist Reverend Roberto Vasquez. At the conclusion of Andrea's talk, everyone prayed for the soul and for the cause of Roberto Vasquez.

It might be protested that our church members who went to Guatemala were just outsiders who wasted half their time stumbling around inconclusively in a place they did not really know, and then left. That is true. And did they change the world? No. But the test of personal commitment is not whether you change the world, an impossible expectation: the test is whether you improve something that you do have the power to change, and by this standard people of faith, such as Andrea Davnie, often do admirably well.

Wholly secular influences such as political movements may also inspire people to go to Guatemala and sweat in the sun. But how often, compared to faith? Anyone who travels the poor nations of the developing world or the inner cities or rural backwoods of Western countries quickly discovers that a high percentage of those women and men working in voluntary service are motivated by some form of belief in larger purpose. As Joseph Cardinal Bernardin noted shortly before his 1996 death, many studies have shown that spiritual faith "has a decisive impact on the kind of civic engagement in which individuals participate, particularly engagement in the service of others."[14] Faith tells people to reach out, because every person shares equally in a larger scheme of everlasting significance.

WHEN CONSIDERING THE RELATIONSHIP between belief and the betterment of society, it is essential to remember that most of the bright lights of spirituality have been opposed the status quo. The Hebrew prophets Isaiah and Amos demanded equality for the poor nearly 3,000 years ago. Jesus was a social revolutionary, advocating pacifism, women's rights, acceptance of outsiders, the embrace of lepers, communal economics, and a society-centered care of the poor. Muhammad advocated property rights for women and a formal obligation to give to the poor.[15] Through the Middle Ages, at least, Islam was a liberalizing influence.

William Gladstone, four times prime minister of England during the late nineteenth century, was another spiritual opponent of the status quo. Gladstone employed his devout evangelical faith in arguing for aid to the poor. When he famously declared, "I will back the masses against the classes," Gladstone's religious orientation rendered his views more persuasive in English politics. Today it is common for intellectual commentators to praise Gladstone as the first modern liberal, the person who cleared the ground that FDR would later walk, yet to speak as though Gladstone's religion was some kind of oddball handicap that the great man overcame. Far from it: spiritual belief is what enlightened Gladstone's politics. Gladstone often said that God required him to do as he did. Imagine if his sovereign had been, instead, polling data.

As recently as the glory days of Martin Luther King Jr.'s presidency of the Southern Christian Leadership Conference, belief was seen as a positive political force. Then came *Roe vs. Wade*, the Supreme Court's 1973 ruling that legalized abortion. As the writer Amy Waldman, an advocate of the revival of a "religious left," has pointed out, that pro-life activism against *Roe* took on a moral tenor modeled on the civil-rights struggle caused no end of irritation to opinion-makers. "Wanting the voice of spiritual concern out of the *Roe* debate, many establishment figures began to argue that faith has no business in public life," Waldman has written.[16] Editorialists who jeer at the sight of pro-life protesters outside the White House might instead encourage other public expressions of belief, such as the delegation of religious leaders who called at the White House in 1991 to urge President Bush to postpone the Gulf War offensive.[17] Both such spiritual viewpoints originate from respect for the sanctity of life, a sentiment of which politics can never have enough.

In the aftermath of *Roe*, progressive believers have retreated from the civic sphere, chastened by opinion-makers who deride faith as unsuitable for politics. In turn, a primary reason that religious conservatives have become influential in American politics in the past two decades is that they have been able to expand into the vacuum created by the withdrawal of spiritual progressives. A 1996 survey by the Pew Charitable Trusts found that nearly half of fundamentalists now believe churches should be active in politics,[18] compared to less than a quarter of religious liberals.[19] There is nothing wrong with fundamentalism being politically active: it has important messages to convey about the destructive effects on children of dissolution of the family, the moral complexity of abortion, the folly of shunning values in education. But the voices absent from public debate are those of the millions of people who have strong faith in God but who hold no antipathy to those with views or lifestyles different from theirs. These voices should again be heard. By stepping out of the public square, progressive believers concede politics to those whose beliefs are more restrictive—or to those lobbyists, campaign consultants, and opportunists who believe nothing at all.

Today public assistance, health insurance for the working

poor, aid for developing nations, and similar humanitarian causes are becoming harder to defend politically. One reason is surely that the removal of progressive spiritual belief from the civic sphere has made justice for the poor seem merely a management problem, rather than a moral imperative on which our Maker will judge us.

AT THIS POINT A READER MIGHT THINK "Private spiritual action is well and good, but hasn't the Supreme Court banned faith from the public square?" It is here that confusion arises over the Establishment Clause, the provision in the First Amendment to the Constitution that states, "Congress shall make no law respecting an establishment of religion or prohibiting the free exercise thereof." This clause is today widely misunderstood as prohibiting expression of spiritual belief in public arenas.

James Madison and others responsible for the Establishment Clause were concerned that government not mandate religion, as Britain then mandated the Anglican faith; that government not discriminate against minority beliefs; and that religion not become a justification for political repression, a running theme of Europe's past. Yet Madison did not intend that government be hostile toward belief, only that no faith be compulsory or favoritism expressed.[20] As William Rehnquist, chief justice of the United States, wrote in *Stone vs. Graham*, "The Establishment Clause does not require that the public sector be insulated from all things which may have a religious significance or origin."[21]

The notion that government should show animosity toward belief is a phenomenon of the present generation that can be traced to *Abington School District vs. Schempp*, the 1963 Supreme Court decision holding unconstitutional the recitation of the Lord's Prayer in public schools.[22] That decision was wise, as the form of prayer struck down was compulsory—a clear violation of the First Amendment. Since then, however, many judges have assumed that the precedents created in 1963 require public officials actively to oust belief from daily public life. Recent court decisions have banished nativities and menorahs from public property, even when such displays are privately financed; prohibited the posting of the Ten Commandments on the walls of schools and courts; banned nonsectarian invocations at school ceremonies; held that schools can support after-school clubs on almost any subject except religion; even prohibited moments of silence from classrooms, on the horrifying prospect that during the stillness students might *think* the word God.[23] Such developments have lead Stephen Carter, a law professor at Yale University, to object that courts are now intent on "expelling faith from involvement in the public square."[24]

The essential distinction should be between a secular government, which the Constitution demands, and a secular society, which is not constitutionally mandated. As Joseph Cardinal Bernardin said in 1996, "To endorse a properly secular state, which has no established ties to any religious institution, does not mean we should support a secularized society, one in which faith is reduced to a purely private role."[25]

Like many courts, news organizations have grown to regard faith with aversion. The writer and journalist Cullen Murphy has called belief "the blind spot of American journalism."[26] News organizations do not recoil from reporting on scandal within religion, and the tabloid press is perennially enamored with claims of fresh sightings of the Virgin. But in most cases the media shy away from the substance of spiritual belief—the part that really matters. Even mild public allusion to religion may lead to media derision. In 1996, the Tennessee State Senate passed a nonbinding resolution urging "every citizen to observe the Ten Commandments, teach them to children and display them in their homes, businesses, schools and places of worship." This proclamation had no legal force, and it is hard to imagine what anyone could find objectionable about an outbreak of observation of the Ten Commandments. Nevertheless the Associated Press moved a widely reprinted story with the hyperventilating headline, TENNESSEE SENATE IMPOSES RELIGION.[27]

The mistaken notion that the Constitution demands that faith be expelled from the public square causes some institutions to approach theater of the absurd in the ways they pretend spiritual belief does not exist. For example, in 1996 school-bus drivers in Fayette County, Kentucky, were instructed by county lawyers not to say "Merry Christmas" to children. That year, public-school teachers in Pittsburgh were informed that rather than utter such incendiary words, they should wish students a "happy sparkle season."[28] Dictates such as the "sparkle season" policy are sufficiently silly that they satirize themselves, but the fact that they happen at all indicates a disconnection between reasonable belief and the public arena.

Thinking, for reasons of legal misunderstanding or intellectual fad, that faith should be treated as an ideal *non grata*, many public schools now evade the basic task of educating students about the cultural history of belief. This evasion manifests in ways that are minor—for instance, some primary schools now reword a stanza of "Walkin' in a Winter Wonderland," which in the original reads, "In the meadow we can build a snowman/and pretend that he is Parson Brown," to "and pretend that he's a circus clown," eliminating mention of the existence of persons called parsons[29]—and ways that are not, such as deleting religious studies from textbooks and curricula. Creationists have pressured school boards to buy textbooks granting credence to implausible views about geology and biology; on the tails side of this coin, politically correct factions have pressured many textbook publishers to delete all but the most cursory mention of the role of religion in American culture and history. At the same time as educators and others in public life increasingly treat both the good and bad of faith as better left unmentioned, they bemoan the decline of moral awareness and the ideal of public service: as if these developments were mutually inexplicable.

BEFORE SUBURBS, TELEVISION, AND COMMUTING by private car began to push Americans toward the life of impenetrable isolation that many now lead, churches were centers of community life. Churches can indeed be stultifying influences, especially when they amplify small-town judgmentalism. But faith can also be a primary means of connectedness—for contact with neighbors, for consolation from tragedy, for the celebration of the everyday. One of the most common complaints in the affluent nations of the West is lack of connectedness with community and the rhythms of life. This is an ache that recovery of the spirit might salve. If we suppose that belief in the spiritual meaning of life should be hidden from public view, what do we then share in the commons—sports anecdotes? Comparisons of new clothes and cars?

The contemporary perception that faith ought to be ejected from the civic sphere is among the reasons ordinary life can seem drained of import, since the eternal cycles of birth, adolescence, marriage, childbearing, aging, and death, simultaneously ordinary and extraordinary, are where living purpose is found. As the author Thomas Moore has observed, America's glitz-oriented electronic culture now pays far too much attention to celebrities and fluke events, not nearly enough attention to the everyday circumstances around which the spirit revolves. "Because of this focus on the exceptional," Moore has written, "America is largely starved for the ordinary life of neighborhoods, friends and family."[30]

Neither excessive secularity nor excessive materialism is

new to our age, but today each seems to magnify the other as we suppose that the public aspects of our lives should be stripped of spiritual and metaphysical concerns. Faith exists in opposition to the notion that we have been placed on the Earth simply to accumulate, especially to accumulate at the expense of others. Something must counterweigh the subjugation of humankind to the consumerist cycle of work-and-spend, and that something is more likely to be belief than any law, secular notion, or technical invention.

Spiritual injunctions are unequivocal on this point. The central teaching of Buddhism, for example, is that men and women can never escape the cycle of physical or psychological torment until they stop being obsessed with material things. Everyone knows the warning, "Love of money is the root of all kinds of evil."[31] This biblical verse is frequently interpreted to mean that the desire for riches causes crime. The larger meaning of the verse is that materialism depletes the soul. Just before the "root of all kinds of evil" reference comes the admonition that those whose goals are materialistic "fall into temptation and are trapped by many senseless and harmful desires that plunge people into ruin and destruction."[32] Jesus pointedly cautioned, "Woe to you who are rich, for you have received your consolation."[33] Most people are not rich, but today people by the millions do possess enough means to be materialistic. For them, perhaps most poignant is Jesus's warning, "Do not store up for yourselves treasures on earth, where moth and rust consume."[34]

Spiritual statements against materialism can at first seem to be appeals for men and women to forsake their needs for those of others.[35] That is part of it, but hardly all: equally important is a component of self-interest. Read the injunction from Jesus again: "Woe to you who are rich, for you have received your consolation." If material things are your goal, then *all you will ever have is material things*. In 1991, Pope John Paul II asserted that millions of people in the affluent nations are "ensnared in a web of false and superficial gratifications rather than being helped to experience their personhood in an authentic and concrete way."[36] Read the Pope's statement again: Breaking free of materialism is in your self-interest: it represents a means of achieving selfhood and fellowship with others, accomplishments more important than any material gratification. The soul-draining effects of materialism do as much harm to those who win the battle of acquisition as to those who lose it.

One reason spirituality accentuates the need to serve fellow beings is delightfully selfish—helping others is among life's most rewarding experiences. Decline of belief in higher purpose is one reason contemporary society places declining emphasis on acts of care. We're all either supposed to hire someone for that—at minimum wage, of course—or buy a machine that substitutes. Yet even under good circumstances, lending care to others is essential to the cooperative aspects of life. Caring for and loving others is also constructively selfish, conferring the sort of enduring gratification that never fades.

From the standpoint of society, few developments are more corrosive than reduction in the community's willingness to care for its members. Nevertheless contemporary law, market economics, educational theory, and entertainment all emphasize materialism to the exclusion of the spiritual. Obviously material objects are fun to have. But objects cannot confer satisfaction because in the end, things are only things: inanimate, unknowing. Thoreau noted that a person is well-to-do "in proportion to the number of things that he can afford to leave alone."[37] The sole material items that hold lasting significance are those that have been invested with spirit through some relationship to people—photos, heirlooms, gifts from the beloved or departed.

Belief in higher purpose increases our sense of obligation to fellow citizens: both to love them with our hearts and to aid them with our time and money. While social compassion is hardly exclusive to faith, it flows from the spirit more readily than from any secular school of thought.

INSTRUCTIVE HERE IS THE OLD SENSE in which the words "love" and "charity" were taken as interchangeable. "Charity" once held a much more positive connotation, meaning "the extended hand" more than "a handout." In one of the most celebrated passages of the monotheist writ, modern translators render the operative word as "love." "If I give away all my possessions . . . but do not have love, I gain nothing"; and "Love is patient; love is kind; love is not envious or boastful or arrogant."[38] Older translations rendered the operative Greek word in question, *agape*, as "charity," as in, "Though I speak with the tongues of men and of angels, and have not charity, I am become as sounding brass or a tinkling cymbal."[39] *Agape* in the ancient thinking of the Holy Land meant loving concern for the well-being of others. A revival of this view of charity as synonymous with love would not only benefit society: it would be good for our selfish self-interest, steering us toward fulfilling interaction and fellowship, away from endlessly unsatisfying acquisition.

Today the West's middle and upper classes enjoy more goods and services than did entire global populations of previous centuries, yet people seem to take less and less pleasure from this affluence, finding no lasting satisfaction in their well-appointed homes or high-tech cars or jet-propelled vacations. By compressing higher purpose out of culture, we create the impression that life really does not offer all that much except the opportunity to compile possessions and rack up career points. Market theory, the contemporary paradigm of public thought, reveres economic trading in the absence of any larger guiding ideal and helps lull men and women into devoting their lives to materialism, presenting acquisition as the only test of worth. Market theory is surely the best model for max-imizing production, but do we really want it governing our inner lives too? Such thinking teaches that people deserve whatever they get, be it riches or deprivation. Spiritual think-ing teaches that the greater the material blessing, the greater the obligation to share. Even Nietzsche, the arch-enemy of faith and purpose, acknowledged that "the modern, noisy, time-engrossing, conceited, foolishly proud" fixation on mate-rial acquisition "prepare[s] for unbelief more than anything else," draining the soul in the name of the checking account.

If any material item such as beef or petroleum or computer parts was in as short supply today as is the sense of purpose, it would be headline news. Yet meaning, the most important concern in our lives, is today considered unsuitable for social discourse: perhaps because Nike will not sponsor it.

As Emerson expressed it, "Things are in the saddle, and ride mankind."[40] Everybody knows that money cannot buy happiness: no matter how many things you possess, there will always be someone with more. Despite this knowledge, most people seem trapped in materialism anyway; higher purpose being seen as discredited, they don't know which way to turn. Materialistic fixation, loss of connectedness, shallow lonerism, and other tangents of the modern age seem likely to keep in-creasing, if only because they are encouraged by market forces. Against them stands the promise of the spirit.

AMONG THE WORST EFFECTS OF EFFORTS to compress spirituality out of public life is that while the genuine values of higher belief are today discouraged, the phony, ostentatious aspects continue to flourish. Rarely are there protests against feigned faith-for-show: it is the heartfelt statements of belief that get people upset.

If a politician or celebrity stands up to mumble about being blessed by the Lord, and speaks in a manner unmistakably vacuous and intended for public consumption, nobody minds. If the same person says with conviction, *I really believe* my faith requires me to do this or that, the expression will be condemned as inappropriate. As the critic Michael Kinsley has noted, the effect is to reward religious hypocrisy by classifying phony spiritual feelings as socially acceptable and sincere ones as indecorous.[41]

Suppose a political leader were to speak openly of agonizing about how to mollify interest groups or improve his or her standing in opinion polls: pundits would praise this as brutal honesty. If the same leader were to speak openly of being afflicted by concerns about the religious acceptability of abortion or war or wealth, pundits would insist that such concerns be kept private.

Consider the quandary faced by Thomas Jefferson, who revered Jesus but also scorned the obscurantism of institutional faith. While president, Jefferson spent hours in the old White House using razors to cut from a New Testament accounts of supernatural events he considered unlikely.[42] Ultimately this project led to Jefferson's posthumous *The Life and Morals of Jesus of Nazareth*,[43] a radiant work the normally daring Virginian declined to publish during his lifetime, fearing political opponents would charge him with atheism for depicting Christ as a mortal rabbi.[44]

It can be haunting to think of Jefferson alone in the White House, pouring over a Bible late into the night by lamplight, made or driven to wretchedness by his longing to know which verses should be believed and which should not. Such crises of conscience should be seen as healthy signs, but instead are increasingly viewed as old-fashioned. Just imagine the hubbub if it were reported today that a current president was spending hours snipping paragraphs from a Bible, reassembling here and there, trying to sort out a vision of faith. Conservatism would go ballistic, claiming sacrilege; liberalism would be appalled that a president was taking faith seriously enough to wonder what to believe.

Society would be better served by leaders who sit up into the night contemplating whether some planned act will be spiritually acceptable, than by those concerned only about poll results and budget statistics. We should wish upon the public sphere more agonies of conscience.

YET SINCERITY BALANCED UPON FAITH is now considered suspicious; insincerity, acceptable social convention. No better argument for atheism exists than the torpid ceremonial prayer that accompanies the opening gavel of each day's deliberations of the U.S. Congress: empty words delivered in a somnific monotone as members and staff shuffle about, obviously paying no attention. Countless public events still begin with prayers—sessions of legislatures and parliaments, graduations, county fairs, ceremonial dinners. Usually no one cares, providing the prayer is clearly synthetic and for show, challenging no one's thoughts. When the occasional heartfelt prayer slips into public utterance, that is what is deemed objectionable.

An example was the 1993 case of Bishop Knox, principal of a public high school in Jackson, Mississippi, who was fired for allowing a student to read a twenty-one-word nondenominational prayer over the public-address system.[45] Knox is a politically liberal African American, who explained that he felt students needed to be reminded that values cannot develop without awareness of higher purpose. That is, Knox endorsed *genuine* spiritual sentiment. This was what made the prayer unacceptable.

Hearing of Knox's firing brought to mind the memory of Christmas Eve, 1968. On that day the first Apollo spacecraft went into orbit around the Moon, and broadcast salutations back to the world. As grainy black-and-white images of the rockbound lunar surface passed through view, astronauts Wil-

liam Anders, Frank Borman, and James Lovell read from the
Genesis story: "In the beginning, God created the heavens and
the Earth, and the Earth was without form and void . . ."[46]
The words crackled, as if from the effort of crossing the void.
A cramped metal capsule, heated and pressurized to sustain
life, flew above a distant surface of frigid lifelessness, carrying
with it the first sound of breathing ever there heard.

Yes, the Genesis account is a spiritual text, and whether it
is true is a matter for contention. And yes, selection of this
account favored Judaism, Christianity, and Islam, which honor
Genesis, over the creation stories of other faiths. Yet reading
the most familiar of creation stories from the heights above
the Moon challenged listeners to turn their thoughts toward
issues at the nexus of life: *Why are we here? What caused existence
to begin? Are we alone or are there others like ourselves? Do we exist
for a purpose?*

At the time, some commentators suggested that the astronauts' reading of the Genesis story only reminded men and
women how negligible they are when juxtaposed against a cosmos of unfathomable age and magnitude. As an adolescent I
thought the reverse; the event should remind people of the
significance of the living enterprise. Physical aspects of the
universe, the cold rocks and luminous suns, can never be more
than mere things. The consciousness struggling to survive on
the Earth, and perhaps elsewhere, has the potential to fill those
billions of galaxies with meaning.

Today it is inconceivable that NASA would permit the
reading from space of the Bible, Talmud, Koran, or any statement touching on purpose or belief. Too thought-provoking—
too sincere. If the first vessel were now arriving above the
Moon, we would certainly enjoy better camera work, but for
audio would be treated only to a recitation on planetary geology, or a lawyer-written plea for budget increases, or hear the
astronauts report, "The view is, uh, really, uh, something."

Year by year we withdraw the spiritual from our public lives and then wonder why those lives appear to reflect a diminution of hopes and ideals.

RENEWAL OF THE LINK between spirit and society seems desirable because in our era of runaway isolation—when people all over the developed world eat, read, watch, and do pretty much the same things, but isolated from others—faith speaks to that part of the human experience that is shared.

Rousseau worried that spirituality would drive civic society apart, causing men and women to presume they bore no obligation toward others because God would provide. Today's video mania and market forces have community-shattering effects that would have left Rousseau pining for the good old days of the church bell pealing in the village square. Meanwhile interest-group polarization of politics magnifies our differences; the explosion of specialized lobbying encourages citizens to think not as members of communities but as constituents of fragmented units that prosper by sabotaging other units; the well-to-do retreat into gated developments, escaping community in the literal sense.

When Jews come together to celebrate Passover, or Christians to recite the Nicene Creed, or Muslims to commemorate Muharram, or members of other spiritual interpretations join for similar purposes, they may engage in ceremonies whose symbolism can be challenged.[47] But they are celebrating something *shared:* shared past, shared present, shared aspirations. Society needs more sharing to counter the ache at its center. And it is no small side benefit for society that the sharing of spiritual belief usually leads people toward virtue.

Indeed, the very act of sharing the spiritual impulse may be what gives belief its power. The philosopher Martin Buber, who died in 1965, proposed that the manifestation of God that really matters is not the burning bush, but what occurs between human beings, person to person.[48] That is to say: Any-body can witness divine power simply through kindhearted spiritual encounters with others. The readily available mira-cles of the faith might do for communities what technology, economics, and government cannot. Because of that, belief should look outward to society, not exclusively inward to the self.

Chapter Four

Taking the Opium

God offers to every mind its choice between truth and repose.
Take which you please; you can never have both.
EMERSON, 1841

OFTEN THE MOST COMMON MISCONCEPTIONS are the least justifiable, and into this category falls the notion that faith is a tranquilizer: a numbing concoction of milk and honey designed to blunt awareness of the wretched wrongs of life. Belief in higher purpose, Karl Marx famously wrote, serves as "the opium of the people." For many in the generations since Marx's day, his declaration summed up the case that faith is sedative for those who would escape the clamor of their own thoughts. But those who use Marx's quote rarely cite the sentence that comes before it, as it is inconveniently sympathetic: faith, Marx also said, is "the sigh of the oppressed creature, the heart of a heartless world, and the soul of soulless conditions."[1] Though Marx surely considered spirituality a cultural artifact, he also asserted that the crux of his criticism was not opposition to faith but "a call to abandon a condition which requires illusions," namely man's inhumanity to man.

No one can deny that there are cogent reasons to ask whether belief arises partly from the wishful desire to shut out the unhappy aspects of day-to-day circumstances. Yet those who imagine spirituality to be a soothing drug have it backwards. People do not long for the unseen because they are blind to the horribleness of life: they seek faith *because of* the horribleness of life. Faith has been struggling with the harshness of the world far longer than any other discipline of thought.

Injustice, tragedy, loss, material want, captivity, illness of the body or mind, heartsickness, or the pure longing of the soul enters into almost everyone's existence at some point. For many people such tribulations are not rare events but dominant aspects of daily life, occurring not singly but in combination. People reach out to faith and spirituality not to avoid the pain caused by such problems, but in the hope of finding some larger meaning within the context of the hardship that is often humanity's lot.

Of course there are some who march off to places of worship or spirituality conferences in automated fashion, and there repeat whatever they are told by authority figures in vestments or yarmulkes or, increasingly, saffron robes. But every walk of life contains its unreflective faction. A certain percentage of university professors march off to class every morning and there docilely repeat whatever the authority figures in their specialties reward people for pretending to believe.[2] Yet the existence of lock-step academic factions does not cause us to consider college education to be an opiate.

And of course a percentage of people turn to spiritual doctrines because they wish the contented feeling of assuming glory in the sweet hereafter, and prefer not to think about what happens if that isn't true. But, keeping the analogy, a percentage of people turn to ironic cynicism because they seek the complacent feeling of assuming they will never stand before a Maker, and prefer not to think about what happens if *that* isn't true.

Though many aspects of spiritual awareness arise from joyful meditation on the human promise, the longing of the spirit is as likely to be activated by the knowledge that life contains distress and must inevitably end. A genuine spiritual opium would divert believers with inebriation, libido, and dance: exactly how some of the old pagan creeds, such as Baal worship, functioned.[3] Most modern visions of faith have the opposite orientation, forcing the frightful into our minds. As Pope John Paul II has noted, the whole point of human culture is to ponder the mystery of life, and that cannot be accomplished without contemplating death.[4] If faith were truly an opiate, surely it would not demand rumination on your own demise. Yet all avenues of spirituality lead us to this ultimate question.

As the nineteenth-century French scholar Ernest Renan noted of Jesus's beliefs, whether we can be sure they were true is not necessarily the first question, compared to whether spiritual focus kept Jesus serene in the face of suffering: "His dream rendered him strong against death and sustained him in a struggle to which he might otherwise have been unequal."[5] The same obtains for every person: belief is not about cerebral sedation but about preparing the self for something to which it might otherwise be unequal.

LET ME OFFER ANOTHER EXAMPLE from the everyday sphere of Trinity Church of Arlington, Virginia. In 1995 one of the finest souls of the congregation, a man named Thomas Nelson, died in a boating accident, leaving a wife and children. He was young, responsible, and prudent; one evening he was among us, and when the sun rose again he was not. Nelson had gone sailing on the Chesapeake Bay. The mast of his small vessel swung about in a gust, striking his head. Nelson fell into the waters unconscious and drowned. A friend, resting below deck when this happened, came up to find the sail flapping free. He cried out, but Nelson had already departed this life.

As a community, Trinity Church was shaken by the abrupt loss of a faultless human being. Attending the memorial service, I thought: *This is what it must have been like in the days when faith was forming,* ancient days when sudden deaths were not the rarities they are now. On a regular basis someone would have been with the community one hour, gone the next. Laments must have been continuous. As must have been the yearning to know, *Gone where?*

After Nelson's death, members of Trinity went to church not to be mollified by promises of milk and honey but to try to figure out what life means, to express their shock against its unjust loss, to challenge their Maker for allowing such a tragedy. In weeks to come the church's clergy preached some discomfiting sermons about the injustice inherent in life, while adding extra sections of "wrestlers" classes designed to discuss such questions as why God stands by as the good die. It seems unlikely any form of secular counseling service could have handled the community trauma any better, nor come any closer to answering the ultimate question that pulled at the heart of everyone who had known Nelson: *Will I see him again?*

Can anyone believe the surviving members of this family approach spirituality as an opium to make them insensible to their loss? Rather they approach as seekers, wanting to know the meaning of the lives their loved ones lost, and whether those souls continue in other forms. Faith cannot ban affliction from life and it may not necessarily hold the desired answers. But without the spirit, answers are not possible.

No ONE DOUBTS that at least some of the inclination to turn to faith in times of trial is a legacy of prehistory. In ancient times, all religions mixed their contentions with folklore, social rituals, and displays of legerdemain, some of it directed toward fathoming death. Ancient faiths claimed to control fertility, farm yields, or military success, as well as to adjudicate the soul; to this day the traditionalist interpretations of monotheism assert that God is in total control of all daily events, from the outcomes of wars to the final scores of football games. In this sense, spiritual belief carries a greater heft of assumptions than ideas such as fortune-telling or astral charms, and so would be expected to play more on our minds even in a skeptical age.

The late-nineteenth-century English anthropologist James Frazer, author of the landmark *Golden Bough* series chronicling archaic mythology, has had a pervasive influence on modern thought in this regard. It was Frazer's thesis that parallels between monotheism and folklore demonstrated that both were grounded in make-believe. To many early twentieth-century thinkers, Frazer's work was Exhibit A that belief had been disproved. Frazer thought cultural history could be divided into three phases: mythological ignorance, followed by religious faith, culminating with pure reason, a utopian third stage not quite yet in view. "The human race is slowly crawling out of the magic mode up to and through the religious," he wrote, "and will finally emerge in the sunlight of science and rationality."[6] It is an entertaining twist that *The Golden Bough*, which at the time of publication was seen as an antispirituality treatise, has in recent decades become the source authority for New Age fascination with mythology. A striking percentage of the material recounted in the popular literature of mythology is essentially a rewrite of Frazer, with the appeals to rationality deleted.

But does the fact that spirituality must once have leaned on primitive ideas mean contemporary belief is merely a remnant of ancient indoctrination? It is telling that modernity, which is obsessed by the new, cannot free itself from spiritual beliefs that number among the oldest aspects of human culture.[7] Society has emphatically eliminated much that men and women had been elaborately indoctrinated to believe. Most nations have eliminated monarchy, an idea ground into people's brains for centuries. The nations of the former Soviet bloc rejected communism, which employed the most intense and psychologically sophisticated propaganda campaign in the history of human culture. Women and men of developing nations are beginning to reject feudalism, an idea propped up by thousands of years of harsh social reinforcement. Worldwide rejection of monarchy, feudalism, and communism, along with today's general suspicion of all institutions of authority, should be seen as welcome indicators of the mind's power to overcome vestigial effects of cultural indoctrination.

Yet as people reject many ideas drilled into the heads of previous generations, interest in the possibility of higher purpose endures. While people have been quite happy to abandon their belief in rule by kings, commissars, or *zamindars* (Hindi for feudal land baron), they seem much less content about abandoning belief in the presence of spiritual meaning.

That spiritual seeking has carried on through long catenas of social change is an indication of its primal status in the human essence. Thus, even though elements of propaganda are certainly present in the history of faith, skepticism should not reject spirituality for this reason. Rather, skepticism should be employed to help discard those beliefs that trace to folklore or politics, keeping those beliefs of genuine merit. As G. C. Lichtenberg, an eighteenth-century German philosopher, phrased the graduation from indoctrination to spiritual choice, "First we have to believe. Then we believe."[8]

ONE REASON SPIRITUALITY ENGAGES thoughts of mortality is that men and women crave a counterweight to fear of death. Sometimes it is said that this indeed proves faith to be a narcotic. Yet the fact that people ask spiritual questions because they wonder about death does not show they have been brainwashed. It shows they are thinking clearly.

It is easy to imagine that long ago, as *Homo sapiens* developed self-awareness, our ancestors experienced both sorrow over the deaths of others and terror about the realization that they would someday perish, too. Our earliest ancestors could not have imagined any way to render themselves exempt from the finality of death: it was all they could do to survive a single day. But our ancestors might have longed to believe that somewhere there existed a form of life without end, freed from toil and fear; and they might have guessed that such a life would center on the spirit rather than the material body.

If monotheist belief originally formed partly out of fear of death, it did so in a manner different from that commonly assumed today. Today the standard supposition is that in prehistory, people flocked to faith to be told they would prosper in a blissful afterlife. But spiritual immortality is a relatively "new" concept. Belief arose many centuries before notions of afterlife.

The Old Testament says nothing about heaven as a destination for human souls.[9] Heaven is depicted as reserved for God and the angels, preexistent entities who never experienced temporal life and have always lived in the spirit world. In other ancient faiths, the immortal realm was exclusive to the gods or to a chosen few with special achievements. In Norse mythology, for instance, the main incentive to take up the sword was that only warriors qualified for immortality in Valhalla.[10] Across the spectrum of the ancient religions, the notion of an eternal hereafter available to any believer is nearly unknown.

When Jesus began to speak of an afterlife in which any good woman or man could be rewarded with immortality for tribulations on Earth, he was expressing a fundamentally new idea about theology. So new, in fact, that Jesus often referred to immortality simply as "life," suggesting temporal existence to be the dream and spiritual existence the reality. To "enter into life" was Christ's phrase for what comes next after the righteous person's earthly trials end.[11]

Some who dismiss faith as a means of psychological compensation for fear of death trace Jesus's popularity to his new notion of afterlife. The German philosopher Ernst Bloch, who died in 1977, proposed that admirers were drawn to the rabbi from Nazareth not because they wanted to live righteously, but because they wanted to live forever.[12] In Bloch's view, the promise of an afterlife was the most successful sales pitch in the annals of spiritual marketing: but no more than that.

In turn, to suppose that death brings oblivion may seem a modern notion, forged by the postwar pandemic of doubt. As the contemporary poet Mark Strand has phrased it, parents should teach children they

> live between the two great darks,
> the first with an ending, the second without one[13]

Yet the notion of death as oblivion is an idea of long standing. Writing in the eighteenth century, Voltaire rejected any belief in either a joyful afterlife or frightful perdition, declaring life "a point between two eternities."[14] Many ancients, including the Hebrews, ascribed to this view. During Old Testament times it was believed that upon death the souls even of the righteous would be consigned to Sheol, an underground darkness that, although not exactly oblivion, was hardly paradise. In Sheol, the soul would no longer think or feel. For the ancient Hebrews, the only sense in which "immortality" could be obtained was via continuance of the family line. It was for this reason that in old desert times, it was considered unspeakable to die childless: your deactivated soul would go to the everlasting dark of Sheol, while no remnant of your flesh would be left in the living world. This age-old fear of childlessness is one that contemporary natural-selection theory would find forward-thinking, as human genes seem quite determined to reproduce themselves and are now commonly described by biologists as conceptually "immortal" in the sense that after you die, your DNA continues to live in your descendants.[15]

Hell, in turn, is no more an original spiritual concept than heaven. Satan existed in the Old Testament accounts, but to tempt and torment the living, not to carry the unfortunate dead away to fire. To the Old Testament mind, regular life already held so much punishment that hell represented something of an overkill. Most scriptural mentions of hell as the concept is currently understood originate with the New Testament, often emerging from the mild lips of Jesus.[16] From the standpoint of theology, it was almost as if when Christ extended to every person the chance for eternity in peace, it was necessary that he also add a prospect of eternity in torment, to focus minds on the new choice.

Regardless of whether the notion of death as oblivion is ancient or current, this view contains its own contradictions, among them the preoccupation with horror of death that is a common element in modern literature. If neither glory nor judgment occurs when life concludes, then why worry about death, whose inevitability you can do nothing to change? To be granted life, you must accept its end. In cosmic terms you've only got a blip in which to experience the smells and tastes of existence. So why waste a single precious minute of your one chance at life wringing your hands about the fact that you will surely die? By this I do not mean not to look both ways before crossing the street. But the obsessive fear of death, so central to modern thought, becomes hard to fathom if oblivion is our certain lot. If the universe is pointless and your own passing means nothing anyway, it's hard to see why you should bother to "rage" against this destiny, as the poet Dylan Thomas suggested. Nothing is accomplished by going out disconsolate, other than making your own final years miserable.[17]

Lines of thought like this that can lead us to suppose that while the origins of spirituality may have been linked with human dreams of a rejoinder to death, far more was going on than psychological adjustment mechanisms jazzed up with fancy words and incense. The forms of faith that have survived over the centuries are the ones that urge people to look their own mortality in the eye and ask uncomfortable questions. This is a sophisticated message, not a preserved superstition.

PERHAPS, THEN, THE OPIATE OF FAITH exists as some other kind of cognitive legacy. Freud, for instance, maintained spirituality to be a neurotic delusion. He wrote with acerbity in 1927, "Devout believers are safeguarded in a high degree against the risk of certain neurotic illnesses. Their acceptance of the universal neurosis spares them the task of constructing a personal one."[18] In other words, believers are crazy in the clinical sense. Freud's notion that people with faith embrace a "universal neurosis" because it "spares them the task of constructing a personal one" is a particularly low blow. This means the kind of men and women who believe in higher purpose have not only lost their marbles but are too lazy to come up with their own original dementia which, presumably, would be more entertaining for the therapist.

Freud's notion of faith as psychosis was sufficiently persuasive to the intellectual mainstream that until the year 1994, the American Psychiatric Association formally classified strong religious commitment as a "disorder." Here is a poignant metaphor for an age of doubt. Psychiatrists were trained not merely to decline to believe but to consider mentally ill those with powerful beliefs. That spirituality might be grounded in some genuine human need—only a crazy person could think that!

Searching for an appropriately dismal explanation for the "universal neurosis," Freud theorized that in the mists of pre-history, men routinely murdered their fathers. Such crimes were committed to gain what biologists now call alpha-wolf status—to become the top male, with command of the hunt and the first choice of females. Once established as prehistoric leaders, the murderers experienced guilt and began to venerate their dead fathers as contrition. Along the generations, venera-tion of dead fathers became conflated into a belief in a single, almighty Father who was still alive (that is, never murdered) in an unseeable otherworld. "The psychoanalysis of individual human beings," Freud wrote, "teaches us with quite special insistence that . . . at bottom God is nothing other than an exalted father."[19]

Substantiation of the father-murder theory has never been found, however, either in anthropology or the study of con-temporary aboriginal peoples.[20] Freud's insistence that faith was clinical delusion caused him to split with his protégé Carl Jung, who believed spirituality was a cardinal part of the human soul. Jung wrote in *Memories, Dreams and Reflections:* "Whenever in a person or a work of art an expression of spiri-tuality came to light, Freud suspected it and insisted it was repressed sexuality. I protested that this hypothesis, carried to its logical conclusion, would lead to an annihilating judg-ment upon culture. 'Yes,' he assented, 'So it is, and that is just a curse of fate against which we are powerless to con-tend.'"[21] Jung called Freud "a tragic figure" because he de-voted his life to study of the psyche yet closed his mind against an essential aspect of that psyche, the longings of the spirit.[22]

THEN AGAIN, PERHAPS SPIRITUALITY sedates the mind by preventing it from recognizing an existential nullity at the core of life. Existentialism, a leading aspect of contemporary thought, counsels that each human being stands utterly alone. The universe is indifferent to human fate, offering no justice and containing no larger purpose; creation is no more than a chance assembly of vibrating atoms. Having faith is senseless, there being nothing to believe in save one's own self. History has no direction. One might hope to advance his or her own circumstances, but society itself is beyond hope: so corrupt and repressive that anyone who tries to engage society in a meaningful way will simply be driven mad by its awfulness. There is no good and perhaps not even any evil—only a lot of people you'd better beware of. The emptiness espoused by existential thought is expressed in a line in Samuel Beckett's *Waiting for Godot:* "Nothing happens, nobody comes, nobody goes, it's awful."

The leading advocates of existentialism, such as Beckett and Jean-Paul Sartre, grew up during the horrors of the trench warfare of World War I, then in adulthood experienced the runaway evil of Nazism; small wonder they found the living condition a mockery of what faiths promise. As many social circumstances have improved in recent decades, existential thinking has become less reflexively bleak, acknowledging that human dignity is possible and even incorporating a grain of optimism about the ability of the individual to seize his or her own fate. As the British novelist Anita Brookner has said, the new existentialism is "about being your own hero, without the sanction and support of religion or society."

Though they may not use the term, a significant fraction of the postwar generation carries some form of this modified existentialist outlook. As with many consequential ideas, few people have actually read the books, plays, and treatises on which existentialism is based; but then not many believers have actually read the Bible or Koran, either. Ideas function in a kind of food chain. First a small hub of thinkers offers new interpretations through writings hardly anyone ever reads; gradually the ideas work their way into public commentary, pop culture, and academia; eventually they become parcel to the structure of day-to-day thoughts. Two centuries ago, even well-educated skeptics might have laughed aloud at the existentialist contention that existence is an indifferent vacuity, devoid of purpose. Today, it is fair to suppose, a plurality of American and European opinion-makers would agree to some variation on that statement; sliding down the food chain of thought, so would millions of other women and men.

Yet existentialism can serve as a pharmaceutical with much the same numbing effect Marx ascribed to faith. If you believe that life is meaningless or society irredeemable, you're off the hook for fighting for reform or caring for others. A theory of inherent, inalterable solitude may represent an excuse to withdraw from fellow beings and their concerns; it might equally plausibly be a pretext for feeling superiority over them. Beckett aided the French resistance in World War II, so his existential convictions did not prevent him from seeking to better the world his art decried. But it seems doubtful whether many of today's proponents of the life-is-pointless view would even bother to drop a farthing in the Salvation Army can. Richard Dawkins, who holds a chair at Oxford University and has become a leading proponent of meaninglessness theory, has written that "in a universe of selfish genes, blind physical forces and genetic replication, some people are going to get hurt, others are going to get lucky, and you won't find any rhythm or reason for it."[23] How convenient that someone who has himself gotten "lucky," winning a privileged position in life, sees only a callous universe—not any lack of social commitment by persons of privilege—responsible for the hurts of others. If faith sedates some of its adherents against the world, existentialism can represent a complete anesthesia.

Chapter Five

Spirit and Science

The modern mind is selectively skeptical. We have no problem believing the entire universe came out of a pinpoint. But if told 5,000 brunches once came out of a basket, we confidently exclaim, "That's impossible!"

FROM THE PLAY *Abide for Me Many Days*,
EDMUND ROSE JAMES, 1992

AT LEAST SINCE ARISTOTLE, faith and reason have been perceived as locked in conflict. Standard to this debate is the assumption that while belief in the spiritual requires a person to accept dreamlike ideas, reason deals only in hard increments of objective data. But is this really so? Let's consider a few things contemporary science finds credible. Suppose you accept the Big Bang theory of the origin of the universe, as I do. Here is what you believe, roughly according to the "inflationary Big Bang" model proposed by the physicist Alan Guth of the Massachusetts Institute of Technology.[1]

You believe that once, probably around 15 billion years ago, all the material of the cosmos—*all* the material from a universe of 4,000,000,000,000,000,000,000,000 stars at last count[2]—was contained in an area no larger than a basketball and possibly smaller than an atom.[3] You believe that "when" the incipient cosmos resided in this plenum, time as we use the term did not exist. The plenum was neither old nor new; such terms lacked definition.[4] You believe that the genesis material from which our reality was made may have come from matter being hypercompressed from another universe or may have been a quantum fluctuation without any palpable origin, the entire universe having been "created virtually out of nothing," as *Scientific American* once phrased it.[5]

You believe that as the starter's gun sounded, the universe expanded from a pinpoint to cosmological size in seconds, with space itself "inflating" many thousands of times faster than light.[6] As the expansion occurred, the universe drew unthinkable quantities of energy and mass from intangible sources whose specifics can only be guessed at, the entire firmament perhaps deriving its reality from a cryptically named "false vacuum." You believe that during the early moments, the material of creation was 100 trillion times denser than water and ablaze with light shining so energetically that it could shatter atoms. What would later become matter existed in a state with the charming name "quark-gluon plasma."[7] Probably you're not totally clear on what a quark-gluon plasma is, but then, neither are most Ph.D.s.

Next, you believe that within as little as a few seconds after the initial fireworks, subatomic particles recognizable to modern understanding began to unbuckle from the inexplicable proto-reality, generating matter and antimatter. Immediately these commodities began to collide and annihilate themselves back out of existence, vanishing as mysteriously as they came. The only reason our universe is here today is that the unbuckling of particles was ever-so-slightly uneven, its yield favoring matter over antimatter by about one part per 100 million. Owing to this, when the stupendous cosmic annihilation drew to a close amidst sundering energies beyond comprehension, a residue of standard matter survived, and from that remnant formed the galaxies. In some ways this represents the most enchanting aspect of Bang thinking: that in the beginning there was not only enough stuff to make an entire universe compressed into a pinpoint or even into a vacuum, there was enough potential to make 100 million universes. But most of the raw material was wasted during construction, and now, ahem, we don't know where it is.

Believing in the Big Bang is a smart idea, because current evidence weighs heavily in favor of this hypothesis.[8] Yet it is impossible to avoid pointing out that nothing in spiritual thought can hold a candle to the fantastic character of Big Bang reasoning. Surely if this description of the origin of the universe came from the Bible or Koran rather than the Massachusetts Institute of Technology, the Bang would be scoffed at as preposterous mythology.

And what else might today's level-headed scientist believe? Under the heading of quantum electrodynamics, she or he believes matter not only sprung from nothingness during the Big Bang, but continues to do so. Even in a vacuum subatomic particles endlessly pop in and out of existence, forming a short-lived haze called "quantum foam."[9] Some researchers have suggested quantum foam has no physical components, but consists of sheer mathematical permutations. Other quantum theories support the view that matter contains nothing "ponderable," with heavy rocks and hard bones ultimately based on no solid substance. Still other current theories assert that something called the "cosmological constant" prevents gravity from collapsing the universe. This force is postulated to be so strong that it may propel the galaxies away from the cosmic center at speeds that increase essentially forever, yet no test has so far observed any cosmological constant at work in local space. Related theories hold that seemingly empty space crackles with "quintessence" or "vacuum density" (what a delightful phrase!), potent forces that in effect arise from nothing.[10] Theories such as these may someday be verified, but they make assertions about water from stones quite pedestrian by comparison.

Next consider "superstring" theory, a proposed explanation for aspects of the formation of mass. The superstring hypothesis asserts that there are at least ten dimensions, though six are unobservable because they are "folded" into probability structures millions of times smaller than atoms. Developed during the 1980s by researchers, including Edward Witten of the Institute for Advanced Study at Princeton, superstring theory was an instant hit with the establishment media. *The New York Times Magazine* featured the hypothesis on its cover; *Time* magazine named Witten one of his generation's leading minds.[11] Any person of faith claiming to have glimpsed a single unobservable dimension, the plane of the spirit, would have been treated as a crackpot by the same publications.

Perhaps superstring theory should be taken seriously, though the brain may overheat when asked to imagine a "folded" dimension. The point is that today's rational, skeptical scientists believe a range of things that can sound notably less plausible than a sacred tree in a perfect Garden.

Sophisticated, skeptical women and men from all walks of life, not only science, today hold a range of beliefs that rationalists of prior generations would have considered carnival bunkum. We believe aircraft carrying the population of small towns can vault into the sky supported by nothing more than differential air pressure crossing their wings. We believe space is "curved" and that entire stars roll down the curvature of space to disappear into black holes. We believe we can trust our messages, financial secrets, and love poems to computers whose internal mechanics we barely understand, and of whose whereabouts we may not even be aware. (Do you have the slightest idea where the computers that run the Internet are located?) We believe the elements in our bodies come from stars that exploded eons ago.[12] We believe lambs can be cloned and DNA from fish can be recombined into tomatoes.

The contemporary mind finds such things easy to believe *because they have no meaning*. Items like the expansion rate of baryons at the beginning of time, or the lift-over-drag coefficient required by a Boeing 747, can be arcane without activating skepticism because they are mere data points lacking any larger significance. The contemporary ethos accepts the wildest claims that rest on a purely mechanistic basis, while rejecting the mildest claims in favor of meaning. Think there are six unobservable "folded" dimensions? Give that man a chair at Princeton. Think God knows our hearts? Get that man a psychiatrist!

Most Big Bang proponents, for example, readily acknowledge that the initial condition they describe could not work under known physical law. But, they add, within the genesis plenum different physical laws were in command, and under those laws it is fair to assume that which defies the mind.[13] Perhaps there were once different physical laws; given that *something* made the universe, some majestic and perhaps strange era may have come before all else. Yet when physicists call on imagined physical laws, it is merely a matter of semantics as to whether they are invoking a supernatural explanation. Modern thought finds supernatural circumstances acceptable when claimed in the name of science but unacceptable when claimed in the name of the spirit.

In Oscar Wilde's play *Salome*, a world-weary Roman official scoffs that spiritual men and women "will only believe in things they cannot see." Faith clearly does require acceptance of something that the eyes cannot confirm. Modern science likewise believes in unseen and unknown forces. But what scientists believe means nothing, and in the age of doubt, that makes the claims credible.

"KEEP THAT WHICH IS COMMITTED to thy trust, avoiding profane and vain babblings and oppositions of science falsely so called," the New Testament exhorts in one of the Bible's rare references to science.[14] (In the original Greek the reference cautions against *antithesis gnosis*, which might mean science, might mean secular rationality, or might mean the Gnostic Christian schism.)[15] This verse helped establish what is, by now, a commonly held assumption that one can either be a believer or a rationalist but not both.

Throughout the centuries of religious hostility toward science, some subsets of thinkers always maintained that knowledge of the physical world is favorable to faith—especially if new knowledge overturns dogma. Siddhartha Gautama, the Buddha, preached in favor of rationality 2,600 years ago.[16] Deism, the Enlightment-era philosophy ascribed to by many of the founding minds of liberal democracy, held that the more one knew about the natural world the better for faith, because proof of the Maker resided in the subtlety of nature. The eighteenth-century poet Alexander Pope summed in hopeful tones the view that science and spirituality could join:

> Nature's laws lay hid in night; God said
> *Let Newton be!* and all was light.[17]

In recent decades the idea that science and spirituality need not conflict has gained some in the world of faith.[18] The mid-century theologian and Christian martyr Dietrich Bonhoeffer said that the ascent of science simply meant people no longer needed to look to religion to answer questions about the natural world; now they could answer them for themselves.[19] In 1996 Richard Harris, an Anglican bishop, declared that "Darwinian theory is not only compatible with belief in God but I find it enriches and deepens my understanding of how the Lord creates."[20] That same year Pope John Paul II gave selection theory a hesitant recommendation, calling evolution "more than just a hypothesis."[21] The geneticist Francisco Ayala of the University of California at Irvine, a former president of the American Association for the Advancement of Science, said in 1997, "Acceptance of evolution is essential to the credibility of faith, and that acceptance is beginning to come."[22] Outside fundamentalist circles, religious endorsement of natural selection theory may eventually become the norm.

Big Bang thinking has also begun to pick up spiritual backing. The hypothesis was first proposed in 1927 by Georges Lemaître, a Belgian astronomer. When Lemaître published his conjecture that the present universe began with the detonation of a "primordial atom," prominent scientists resisted the idea in part because a discrete moment of creation was exactly what Genesis preached.[23] Astronomers were suspicious that a breakthrough in cosmology could come from Lemaître, who was both an astronomer and the abbé of a Catholic monastery. Yet the ability of priests to create and be comfortable with revolutionary scientific ideas—recall that the basic science of genetics was pioneered by the monk Gregor Mendel—ought to suggest that spirituality and rationality need not repel each other.

Other aspects of modern cosmology are not as hostile to faith as generally assumed. Quantum mechanics, which suggests that matter and energy seem to arise from nothing, has overlays with spiritual thought. The New Testament assertion "By faith we understand that . . . what is seen was made from things that are not visible"[24] would fit right in with state-of-the-art quantum theory, provided the "by faith" part was crossed out. Augustine's contention that reality began *ex nihilo*, "out of nothing," is not that far from quantum thinking either. The enigma of what set the Big Bang in motion seems amenable to Aristotle's contention that temporal existence was called forth by a supernatural "unmoved mover," or

Thomas Aquinas's related contention that existence began at the behest of a "prime mover."[25] Parallels between spiritual thought and Big Bang theory might simply be coincidental. Still, it is worth noting that natural cause-and-effect can explain the development of stars, planets, perhaps living creatures; it cannot yet explain the initiation of the process that brought about the firmament in the first place.

IN 1860 THOMAS HUXLEY, the first public proponent of Darwinism, boasted, "Extinguished theologians lie about the cradle of every science as the strangled snakes beside that of Hercules." The nineteenth-century conception that science and faith are opposed arose when several important ideas impacted on public awareness as assaults against belief, principally the theory of geology advanced by Charles Lyell and the evolutionary theory propounded by Charles Darwin and Alfred Russel Wallace. Geology distressed the prelacy because Lyell's main accomplishment was to show that the Earth is extremely old, though most church doctrine held that it had only recently been forged: the Irish bishop James Ussher's dictum that the world was formed precisely 4,004 years before Jesus's birth was taught as fact at Oxford as late as the eighteenth century. Evolution unnerved church institutions by asserting *Homo sapiens* descended from primates (not from monkeys, a common misconception),[26] while scripture taught that women and men had no forebears.

Why should any believer be unsettled by contentions that Earth is an ancient planet with evolving life? Demonstration of a world eons old might have been received as proof that some Maker fashioned creation with care. Demonstration of a shrewd natural mechanism allowing organisms to respond to environmental change, and capable of keeping the biosphere alive for immense spans of time, might have been seen as evidence of a larger scheme.

If the universe does not exist solely to support genus *Homo*, but may host a multitude of life—surely the more life, the more cheer for God—then scientific evidence of the great, slow movements of evolutionary time, or of the unfathomable age of the firmament, should represent no obstacle to spiritual conviction.[27] If anything, they render such conviction more important, for if the stars stretch to the boundary of infinity, what could give this immense enterprise more meaning than to fill it with consciousness? As Martin Luther King Jr. once said, "As marvelous as the stars is the mind of the person who studies them." One self-aware mind, in its unpredictable complexity, may be more fascinating to God than an entire galaxy of inanimate objects.

But it was surely not as allies of spiritual meaning that Lyell and Darwin were received. Next came Einstein, who would be widely misperceived as having shown that the universe generated itself, in deterministic fashion. This perception arose though Einstein's work had nothing to do with the origin of the universe. When the Big Bang hypothesis was proposed, the master pronounced himself skeptical, in part because his own relativity theory assumed a static, bounded universe without expansion. Though Einstein would assert that "much in the stories of the Bible could not be true," he also called himself a believer in a Supreme Being, once saying, "The more I study science, the more I believe in God."[28] Asked whether the ideas of relativity theory undercut spiritual thought, Einstein replied, "Relativity is a purely scientific matter and has nothing to do with religion one way or the other."[29] Perhaps because Einstein's work was the most prominent of several twentieth-century ideas challenging the classical Newtonian universe of direct causation, he was misperceived as also challenging the classical God.

The division in public judgments about Darwin and Wallace points to how science, as an establishment, came to favor those whose work was seen as eroding faith. Darwin stands among the best-known names of history; Wallace remains unsung, though both devised evolutionary theory at the same time. Darwin achieved famed partly because he possessed sterling connections as a member of the English aristocracy.[30] Wallace tumbled to obscurity partly because he was born poor, made a negligible living as a tutor, and never acquired social contacts. Perhaps equally important, the two diverged on the issue of belief. Darwin had little, which caught the intellectual mood of the times. Wallace was a believer who defended spiritual ideas; he speculated that because sentience is unique to genus *Homo*, it developed by some means other than adaptation. As the historian Richard Milner has written:

> With insects or birds, [Wallace] was even more rigorous than Darwin in applying the principles of natural selection. But he questioned its efficacy for humans. If early hominids required only a gorilla's intelligence to survive, Wallace asked, why had they evolved brains capable of devising language, composing symphonies and doing mathematics? Although our bodies had evolved by natural selection, [Wallace] concluded, *Homo sapiens* has "Something which he has not derived from animal progenitors, a spiritual essence or nature that can only find an explanation in the unseen universe of spirit."[31]

Wallace being sympathetic to faith, the scientific world reserved its praise for Darwin. The English intellectual establishment essentially blackballed Wallace for his endorsement of spiritualism; in the end only Darwin remained Wallace's friend, pulling strings to arrange a pension for Wallace when he slipped into poverty.[32] Around the time that Wallace was losing the battle to win support for his views, Asa Gray of Harvard University, then America's leading biologist, was saying he saw no conflict between natural selection and religious belief. Gray, a strong supporter of Darwin, supposed that the precision of evolution demonstrated the presence of a law-giver.[33] Gray's views were lost in the sauce, too. The antifaith interpretation of natural-selection theory deeply affected intellectual debate; the profaith interpretation, almost not at all.

BEYOND THEIR INTRINSIC IMPORTANCE, one reason theories such as natural selection and relativity made such a claim on the Western mind was that they were thought to put the church to rout. Endorsing science became not only a matter of appreciating rationalism but of repudiating belief. Wole Soyinka, the Nigerian playwright who won the Nobel Prize for literature in 1986, has recalled driving his parents to despair by telling them that astronomers' findings about the expansion rate of the universe had caused him to discard religion. "I cannot recall which came first, the rejection of Christianity itself or the rejection of its creation myths," Soyinka has written. "Any of several creation myths, that of my own Yoruba people for example, appeared to me just as valid."[34] Reasoning that if all creation stories seem equally valid then none are, Soyinka renounced belief, acquired a strong interest in science, and not inconsequentially, declared himself a pessimist.

Yet many contemporary researchers find spirituality compatible with scientific knowledge. A 1997 poll by Edward Larson of the University of Georgia, published in the journal *Nature*, found that roughly 40 percent of working physicists and biologists hold spiritual beliefs, a much higher figure than might have been guessed.[35] The Nobel physicist Charles Townes, chief inventor of the laser beam, is a lifelong churchgoer who describes himself as a "nondoctrinaire" believer. Townes says he prays daily and feels the Bible has "no strong conflict with contemporary science, unless you insist on taking scripture literally." Francis Collins, head of the federal National Human Genome Research Institute and co-director of the team that found the gene for cystic fibrosis, describes himself as a "serious" believer who attends church regularly and has worked in missionary hospitals. John Polkinghorne, president of Queens College at Cambridge University, worked for twenty-five years as a physicist before being ordained as a priest. He says believers "do not have to close their minds, nor are they faced with the dilemma of having to choose between ancient faith and modern knowledge. They can hold both together." As the Nobel biologist Christian de Duve of the University of Louvain in Belgium says, "Many modern scientists are violently atheist, but there is no sense in which atheism is enforced or established by the findings of science. Unbelief is just one of many possible personal views."

Herbert Benson, a research cardiologist at Harvard Medical School, has even proposed that evolution will be proven to have encouraged spiritual conviction. Benson argues that believers are more likely to recover from illness, because faith induces a state of calm in which the body's healing mechanisms are more effective.[36] Benson thinks research will eventually show *Homo sapiens* is "wired for God"—that emotional strength brought on by faith helps people overcome life's challenges, while the faithful do a better job of caring for family groups: two factors conferring an edge in the evolutionary contest for the propagation of DNA.

THE IMPRESSION OF FAITH as bested by science turns in part on common misunderstandings of the scientific method.[37] The principal activity of the physical sciences is to establish that events have material causes, then to seek to understand those causes; this is entirely different from disproving the existence of meaning. As the philosopher Karl Popper proposed, scientific truth must turn on claims that can be falsified.[38] That is, if Einstein predicts that the speed of light is the same for all observers, then light-speed had better test out as the same no matter what the frame of reference, or the theory is falsified.

Such rational filters cannot apply to spiritual claims, for which there is no direct observation, only opinions and degrees of evidence.

God may not exist, but no science can prove this, in the same sense that most negatives cannot be proved. As the empiricist John Stuart Mill wrote in 1874 in *Three Essays on Religion*, the supernatural can neither be proved nor disproved by scientific process.[39] Miracles claimed by the world's various faiths may or may not have happened: most likely we will never know, because all statements about events of the far past are based on inference, rendering them fundamentally speculative. Those who suggest that scientific analysis refutes the possibility of past supernatural events misconstrue what the scientific method can show. In this regard the accomplished social critic Wendy Kaminer of Radcliffe College has asked, "Why is believing in the healing power of crystals any more or less inherently ridiculous than believing God talked to Abraham?"[40] But assertions of crystal cures are falsifiable in the present: if energy refracted through minerals can heal, let's see a controlled clinical study that demonstrates the effect. As there is no way to falsify the past, historical spiritual claims fall into a different category of logic.

Modernism further assumes that science has put faith to pasture by refuting the possibility of supernatural intervention, the miraculous then representing the firewall between rationality and spirituality. No physical miracle has occurred during the twentieth century. But does this mean someone of scientific bent must posit that no supernatural influence exists or can exist?

Many objections to the possibility of the supernatural boil down to "that's impossible!" This is an odd argument to encounter from the research world, which itself has confronted "that's impossible!" as a reproach of evolution, continental drift, relativistic time dilation, the heliocentric solar system, atomic fission, and other advances in knowledge. Nevertheless, stripped to the essentials, many forms of rationalism today hold that since no one can detect the soul or document any spiritual plane, these things must be impossible.

By the same reasoning, gravity is impossible. Obviously gravity is there, its effects quantified so precisely as to guide the space probes now moving among the outer planets, several astronomical units from Earth. But no scientist has ever been able to detect the gearing by which the force of gravity operates. No wave, impulse, field, or other mechanism of attraction shows up in tests to determine what holds the moon in orbit or makes apples fall. When Isaac Newton first proposed that planets are bound in their motions by a real but imperceptible force, he was lampooned by the Cartesians, the leading rationalists of the day.[41] Newton, the Cartesians said, was fouling science with occult claims. An invisible force sufficient to hold an entire planet in its grasp? That's impossible! (Cartesian opposition to Newton's theory of gravity is delightfully described in the book *Three Scientists and Their Gods* by Robert Wright.[42])

Nor is there, so far, a full explanation for another unseen aspect of physics, the subatomic "strong" force. Positively charged protons are packed close together in the nucleus of atoms. Because like charges repel, the protons ought to push each other away, causing matter to disintegrate. Exclusively within the nucleus of atoms, something overcomes the normal repulsion of paired charges—and lucky for us it does, or we could not exist. But though the strong force surely exists, its means of operation has yet to be explained.

Like gravity, the spirit surely is present, even if its mechanisms defy detection. Like the strong force, spiritual awareness gives women and men powerful abilities, even absent any verified material basis for them. Aren't both these spiritual and physical forces miraculous in their own ways? The nineteenth-

century German sociologist Max Weber wrote that the "disenchantment of the world" could be traced to the repudiation of
the supernatural.[43] Once we are convinced that there is nothing unseen, that which is seen may also lose its sense of magnificence. This need not be the end result of the application of
the scientific mind to the question of belief. Reason might lead
us instead back toward wonder.

AT TIMES SCIENCE ITSELF has employed the same arguments now
used to disparage spiritual claims. Scientists of the seventeenth
century, for example, derided as folklore reports from the European countryside that flaming rocks were falling into farm-
ers' fields. Rocks from the sky: That's impossible! The
existence of meteorites was not then understood. As the contemporary astronomer John Lewis has written, generations of
scientists resisted the idea of meteorites on the assumption
that "anything not already understood in physical terms must
be superstitious nonsense."[44]

Many similar examples show scientific figures confidently
asserting "impossible" somethings now taken for granted. The
late-nineteenth-century Austrian physicist Ernst Mach, for
whom the Mach number is named, professed that researchers
were wasting their time discussing the atom because it would
always be far too small to be manipulated.[45] John Rayleigh,
who in 1904 won the Nobel Prize for discovering the element
argon, declared, "I have not the smallest molecule of faith"
that there would ever be heavier-than-air flight.[46]

Through history, what now seems normal would often have
appeared impossible or even supernatural. Ptolemy would have
called the Sears Tower mythology. Faraday would have scoffed
at the idea of ships that weigh 90,000 tons and launch aircraft.
Copernicus would have supposed that physical law would bar
the idea that an entire city could be destroyed by a few pounds
of radioactive material; might have called radioactivity itself

impossible, since this invisible effect was not discovered until three centuries after his death. People are walking around whose hearts have been discarded and replaced, which Kepler would have considered witchcraft. Teenagers think nothing of computers that could store the entire contents of the library of Alexandria on a few small discs, which Pasteur would have considered forbidden by limits of physics. Human beings reside far from the knowledge threshold: what one generation may perceive as miraculous may seem mundane from the standpoint of subsequent knowledge.

When scientists appear as short-sighted as pastors or bishops sometimes have been, they may only be engaged in turnabout. Every researcher knows that organized religion has caused grief for individual scientists by repressing free thought, and added to the sum of human suffering by holding back developments that would benefit society. And faith has hardly rushed to make amends: for instance, it was not until 1992 that the Vatican finally apologized for the arrest of Galileo.[47]

An important 1964 book by the historian Richard Hofstadter, *Anti-Intellectualism in American Life*, documented ongoing reasons why scientists and others rationalists should be uncomfortable with faith: mainly bully tactics used by the religious right to pressure schools to fire those who taught evolution, Marx, Marcuse, or similar subjects. Hofstadter's work was intended as a defense of academic freedom but in many quarters taken as blanket disapprobation of spirituality, causing many of the teachers and professors responsible for educating the Baby Boom to react viscerally against faith.

Today the force against which scientists react viscerally is creationism. Dogmatic creationists comprise only a small percentage of believers. Contemporary Catholicism is conservative but not creationist, an important distinction; Judaism, the mainstream Protestant denominations, and most of Islam have

long since stopped contending that the world was formed over-
night or contesting the validity of the fossil record.[48] But creationists make noise out of proportion to their numbers and
often employ the vocabulary of anti-intellectualism. "Creationism is an incredible pain in the neck," says John
Houghton, a leading contemporary physicist and also a devout
believer who writes articles on the value of prayer. Confronted
by creationism, many scientists overreact, thinking they must
scorn all of faith if they are to cast aside its creationist cohort.

Beyond a valid interest in repelling the creationists, some
of today's scientists disdain belief owing to another form of
turnabout, a self-interest calculus not unlike that once employed by the priesthood. Through history, the prelatures of
many faiths have used intimidation and haughty comportment
to maintain their perquisites. Scientists now possess roughly
the same high status once accorded religious officials, and
sometimes present themselves as above judgment or seek to
confound the public with blather, seeming to maintain their
status with the same sorts of psychology priests once used.
That both priests and scientists routinely refer to those outside their guilds as "laypersons" is a telling overlap. Just as the
old religious priesthood set itself up for a fall by attempting to
discredit empirical reason, the new scientific priesthood may
experience a similar loss of position if it goes too far in trying
to discredit spiritual ideals.

The National Academy of Sciences suggested in 1981 that
"religion and science are separate and mutually exclusive
realms of human thought." Yet there is no reason science and
spirituality must stand as opposing superpowers, each wishing
the other's destruction. Both, after all, are truth-seeking disci-
plines. In recent decades, much of literature and philosophy
have succumbed to postmodernism's claim that all beliefs are
conditioned by social context, leaving nothing "true." Science
and spirituality continue to pursue the Enlightenment vision of

truth proven solely through reference to itself. Perhaps these two fields of thought have so often been at each other's throats precisely because they sense a linked destiny. Far from contesting each other, in generations hence the scientist and theologian may seek each other's solace.

RISING UP FROM THE FINDINGS OF MODERN RESEARCH is a strange kind of homage to meaninglessness. The new view depicts absence of meaning as a legitimate, even welcome, interpretation of the human prospect. That human existence lacks purpose is now thought comforting; that it may bear meaning is what discomfits.

For instance, the Nobel physicist Steven Weinberg of the University of Texas says that "what we are learning about physical law seems coldly impersonal and gives no hint of meaning or purpose." Concluding his popular 1977 book on cosmology, *The First Three Minutes,* Weinberg wrote, "The more the universe seems comprehensible, the more it also seems pointless."[49] Though Weinberg went on to contend that "people can grant significance to life by loving each other, investigating the universe and doing other worthwhile things," his endorsement of an empty view of existence has been cited far more often than his qualification about the chance to add meaning.

The zoologist Richard Dawkins of Oxford University has phrased the matter almost in a rapture of insignificance. In 1995 he wrote that the world is "neither good nor evil, neither cruel nor kind, but simply callous: indifferent to all suffering, lacking all purpose."[50] Reflecting this new conventional wisdom, Jessica Mathews, head of the Carnegie Endowment in Washington, D.C., declared in 1996 that men and women should accept that "human life is a cosmic accident with no purpose."[51] Mathews's statement begs for the rejoinder: Perhaps your life is a meaningless accident, but not mine!

Physical laws surely are impersonal. Does this mean their outcome is nothing but a cosmic fluke? Christian De Duve, the molecular biologist, says, "Some scientists have become masochistic on the question of meaning, as if what they want is to find proof that life lacks purpose, and take delight in speculation that life is meaningless."[52] Alan Dressler, an astronomer at the Observatories of the Carnegie Institution in Pasadena, California, says, "Many scientists seem to be on a crusade to run down human worth, because they think this will destroy the arrogance that leads to religious intolerance. But it also makes science soulless. Much of the antiscience mood in the country today stems from the perception that by venerating meaninglessness, science has become inhuman."[53]

Some portion of the popularity of pointlessness thinking may be attributed to what the novelist Robert Musil called the tendency of Western society to undergo "periodic bursts of revulsion against itself."[54] And some may be the product of a burden of sorrow: Given all the lives lost in humanity's savage wars, isn't it almost better to believe the heartbeat is pointless? Pointlessness theory may also appeal to the age of doubt as rebuttal to religious obduracy of the past: Take that, you vicars of the consistory who harassed Galileo! And in some ways the view may simply represent a culmination of the bleak arcs of philosophy and social theory.

"The universe we observe has precisely the properties we should expect if there is, at bottom, no design, no purpose, no evil and no good, nothing but pointless indifference," Dawkins of Oxford has asserted.[55] Yet this is emphatically not the universe we observe. The universe we observe has roiling friction between the just and the iniquitous, the loving and the callous, the forgiving and the vengeful, the evil and the good. The universe we observe has meaning and needs more.

AT THE FORWARD EDGE OF BATTLE over meaning versus pointlessness is a word that glances tangentially from the evolutionary debate, *design*. Is there evidence in nature or the cosmos of

intelligent input, or can all results be explained by spontaneous processes? The Nobel biologist Jacques Monod of France
devoted a powerful 1972 book, *Chance and Necessity*, to arguing
that everything about the living world may be explained without recourse to higher powers. "Man knows at last that he is
alone in the universe's unfeeling immensity, out of which he
emerged only by chance," Monod concluded.[56] This judgment
reflects the main current of twentieth-century intellectualism,
which runs strongly against design.

In a typical position, the paleontologist Stephen Jay Gould
of Harvard University has argued that enough is now known
about evolution to assert that it operates without any outside
influence; the many imperfections in biology, Gould thinks,
such as the weak lower backs of *Homo sapiens*, demonstrate
there is no flawless Maker standing behind the process. But
only a narrow reading of theology would lead one to assume
that either God's works are perfect or no God exists. And
the autonomous mechanical aspects of natural selection hardly
disqualify a role for the unseen: as selection theory continues
to account for adaptation of species and for their descent, but
not for the origin of life, the prospect of divine latency remains
real. Numerous findings show evolution an astute, judicious,
almost beautiful force: not only bringing into being a lush pro-
liferation of diverse living things, but equipping them to respond to the inevitability of ecological change. The sagacity
of evolution might result from spontaneous forces, but might
also testify to higher influence. The biologist Francis Collins,
a leading proponent of Darwinian theory, says he is "unaware
of any irreconcilable conflict between scientific knowledge
about evolution and the idea of a creator God. Why couldn't
God have used the mechanism of evolution to create?"

Because there is proficient natural law, it does not necessarily follow that there must be a lawgiver. Noteworthy here,
however, is that the universe exhibits many physical constants

that seem fined-tuned to life. Research suggests that had some constants of natural law been slightly different, only the lightest elements could have formed—meaning no carbon, oxygen, or minerals, and hence no organic life.[57] If initial conditions of the Big Bang had been such that gravity were only about 1 percent stronger, the incipient universe would have collapsed back on itself. Had gravity been about 5 percent weaker, stars would have been unable to coalesce, leaving the cosmos an icy dominion of colossal dust clouds. Chance might explain auspicious physical law, but only long-shot chance. Lawrence Krauss, a physicist at Case Western Reserve University, has estimated that our universe had about the same odds of possessing exactly the right density for the formation of galaxies and stars as the typical person has of guessing the precise number of atoms that make up the sun.[58] Our universe behaves as if someone or something once imposed a rule structure that could lead to life, and then said "Go!"

As physicists have become aware of the many fundamental natural constants that appear fine-tuned to favor life—this is called the "anthropocentric" dilemma—meaninglessness theory has felt imperiled. In response it emphasizes a new idea in cosmology, called "multiverse" theory: that there are vast numbers of universes, with many differing sets of physical laws. The physicist Andrei Linde of Stanford University since the 1980s has been supposing that existence is eternal and "self-reproducing," through successions of Big Bangs: billions or even an infinite number of firmaments might exist, with chance alignments of physical law resulting in some being habitable and others barren.[59] Linde's idea might be right, and has a hopeful, almost-supernatural implication that existence in some form will last forever; but since the multiple universes assumed by theories like this cannot be observed, such ideas rest on the fringe of plausibility. The physicist Charles Townes notes, "Perhaps life and the universe are inclined toward anthropocentric features for reasons of structure we do not yet know. But I see a strong possibility intelligent design is present. To get around the anthrocentric universe without invoking God may force you to extreme speculation about there being billions of universes. Positing that essential features of the natural world are explained by billions of variables that cannot be observed strikes me as much more freewheeling than any of the church's claims."

Some opponents of the notion of design in nature argue that such thinking represents the fallacy of reading of human concerns into nonhuman events. The reasoning goes like this: Of course the circumstances of this universe make organic life possible, if not we could not be here to talk about it, therefore auspicious natural law cannot be employed as evidence of a Maker. This reasoning might be true, but seems a little like saying: Of course there are giant stone faces on Mount Rushmore or tourists wouldn't go there to take snapshots; just because there are giant stone faces hardly proves there was a sculptor.

The dichotomy of pure chance versus perfect divinity as the only explanations for existence propels thought away from constructive medians and toward the extremes of creationism or life-is-pointless. As de Duve has written, "Many who reject the view of a meaningless universe would not be driven to creationism if they were not given the impression they had no other choice."[60] The astronomer Alan Dressler phrases the challenge this way: "We have given up our old belief that humanity is at the physical center of the universe, but must come back to believing we are at the center of meaning."

Consider that the universe as observed is not necessarily one whose only state is heartless killed-or-be-killed. Nature does include pitiless forces such as predation; at a glance the found world may seem, as Hobbes called it, an indifferent "war of all against all." Yet forces that appear altruistic exist in nature as well, an example being the relationship between the sugar maple and surrounding plants. Research in the Adirondacks has shown that during dry spells, sugar maple trees use their deep roots to draw up groundwater.[61] Rather than consume all the water themselves, the trees discharge it to sustain surrounding small plants such as goldenrod. The plants are not making conscious choices, merely responding to their genes: in this case, the water transfers seem to improve the function of the maple's leaf stomata. But the relationship established is not some exercise in shivering pointlessness; its effect is collaboration for the mutual good.

Human beings observe the tiger that gores the antelope and, falsely believing this to be the way of all flesh, imitate such conduct in everything from business to statecraft to their love lives. In this way, by looking only at the bad or random in nature, pointlessness theory can be justified. Perhaps society instead should study the sugar maple and the goldenrod: understanding that we need not prosper at each other's expense, but may all prosper together. Scientific findings suggesting unselfish or cooperative influences in nature are an important new field, one in which major discoveries may be due. They lend cause to hope that women and men will eventually learn to emulate the cooperative rather than the predatory. This, too, encourages the search for the spiritual.

Life is so complex, resplendent, and majestically constructed that it is difficult to believe the living world results solely from aimless chemical reactions and random blunders. At the same time society can be so cruel and unjust that it is difficult to believe the living world is functioning smoothly under an omnipotent divine plan. The likely explanation for our existence is neither chance alone, nor purpose alone, but some blending of the two. Perhaps we are an accident: we appear to be a result.

THERE MUST BE SOME MIDDLE-GROUND explanation for existence that would incorporate the percipient points of the scientific skeptic, while sustaining a vision of faith. Essential to this middle ground would be the understanding that meaning can be present regardless of whether our origin was divine or autonomous.

Consider a straightforward reading of the two leading explanations for the existence of life: Either life was created with the aid of some higher power, or was not.[62] If the former is correct, existence clearly has purpose. If the latter is correct, then purpose might have been lacking when the spark of biology was struck, but has been acquired since.

This idea will be restated later, but is worth previewing here because it is cardinal: *If God made life, then life has meaning. If God did not make life, then life has meaning.* Whatever the antecedents of the human heartbeat, people are here and have thoughts, wants, needs, souls, and longings. Existence is in every way infused with purpose.

How Doubt Became Compulsory

*A man full of faith is one who has lost the
capacity for clear and realistic thought.*
H. L. MENCKEN, 1922

ONE REASON THERE SEEMS A LACK of healthy give-and-take about
spiritual issues in contemporary public life is an evolving view
that belief is best understood as a personal idiosyncrasy,
vaguely akin to private sexual preferences: not to be insulted,
of course, but better left unmentioned. For example, recent
years have seen increased media coverage of the political and
sociological questions raised by religion and spirituality, but
little discussion of what the various faiths actually believe, a
topic increasingly seen as a private matter.

What is at work here is the evolution of doubt: from the
tenuous, fearful doubt of the Middle Ages; to the confident,
hopeful doubt of the Enlightenment; to the hostile, null-set
doubt of existential philosophy; to a sort of low-voltage, postmodern doubt in which the longings of the soul are seen as
just another of the meaningless defects with which our species
is born, like baldness or color blindness. In its way the emerging view of faith-as-a-quirk represents a worse snub to spiritual hope than advocating the dissolution of religion: implying
as it does that a topic about which huge numbers of people

say they care deeply actually is too minor to be worth arguing about. Somehow, to the age of doubt, almost all cultural and political beliefs have become equally valid, while virtually all spiritual belief has declined to equal invalidity.

PERHAPS MANY PEOPLE now prefer to regard spiritual longing as a private quirk to minimize the ache they feel in their own souls. Alternatively, women and men may feel pressured to reject faith, to wear what the modern world sees as a badge of smartness. During the Enlightenment, educated women and men signaled their rationalist character to each other by endorsing science and rejecting suffocative religious dogma. Today everyone is expected to endorse science, making compulsory doubt a credential of intellect. As, through the postwar era, education has replaced birth circumstances as the great dividing barrier of Western life, the educated have come to perceive themselves as having a proxy interest in the notion that faith is just an idiosyncrasy: disdaining belief has become not just a philosophical position but a way to communicate that one is in the know.[1] As the Supreme Court Justice Antonin Scalia protested in 1996, today those who adhere even to mainstream faith are presumed "simple-minded."[2] To the ethos of value-neutral postmodernism, nothing more clearly signals lack of mental powers than maintaining belief.

In its contemporary guise, this assumption traces its roots to the 1925 Scopes trial, the national sensation in which a Tennessee schoolteacher received a token fine for expounding Darwin in defiance of a state law. John Scopes's penalty was later overturned, and the law in question was repealed. Thus freethinking triumphed when religion and evolution clashed. But the negative interpretation of the Scopes trial—that it showed believers to be opponents of thought—has always been more popular than the positive one.

At the trial the populist champion William Jennings Bryan,

arguing for the prosecution, squared off against the high-brow champion Clarence Darrow, who defended Scopes. News dispatches of the time, notably those filed by H. L. Mencken, depicted Bryan as a toplofty dunce, Darrow as a gleaming knight of intellect.[3] *Inherit the Wind,* a popular play based on the trial and a favorite of high-school drama societies, adapted the same view. In years since, the phrase "Scopes monkey trial" has become a cultural code for ridiculing faith, a shorthand assertion that spirituality is the province of provincials.

Bryan was wrong to oppose the teaching of evolutionary biology, but as the Northwestern University historian Garry Wills has written, public understanding of the event, especially that which traces to Mencken, distorts Bryan's motives.[4] Shortly before the Scopes trial, Bryan had returned from a revival tour of Germany, where he had been horrified by incipient Nazism. In Germany, Bryan had heard the lingo of Social Darwinism, a discredited theory then popular with the left as well as with facists.[5] Bryan feared that the Nazis would use natural-selection arguments to justify oppression of those declared genetically inferior, exactly as they did. Knowing that Social Darwinism was Bryan's true concern puts the Scopes trial into an entirely different context, a context missing from perennial representations of the event as one in which Bible-beating hayseeds ran amok.

Since the Scopes trial, the notion that spiritual belief means failure of intellect has implanted in American thought. An example comes from the magnificent 1948 novel of mid-American life, *Raintree County.* A character declares that although the teachings of faith "affirm the sacred and eternal," anyone who believes the supernatural actually exists has fallen for "a primitive conception which retards rather than assists religious feeling."[6] The reader is given to understand that it is this sort of sophistication that sets the character apart from lesser minds around him. More recently the same point was made in the

1992 cult novel *Snow Crash* by Neal Stephenson, in which a character declares, "Ninety-nine percent of what goes on in churches has nothing to do with spirituality. Intelligent people notice that sooner or later and conclude that the entire 100 percent is bullshit, which is why atheism is connected with being intelligent in peoples' minds."[7]

It goes without saying that if someone could invent an inanity barometer—a sure path to riches—and mount the device by the door of any church, synagogue, or mosque, it would register incessantly, like a stock ticker. But an inanity barometer would have a flickering needle in any place where *H. sapiens* gathers. All human institutions generate foolishness. When we hear of silliness afoot in schools or universities, we don't say that people should therefore refuse to become educated; if we are told that every job is at times absurd, we don't say that no one should work; if we hear of blunders in government, we don't say, well, let's have anarchy. Yet commonly encountered in opposition to faith is reasoning that reduces to, "Since all beliefs contain errors, the thoughtful person should believe nothing."

THE ASSUMPTION THAT FAITH equals the failure of the mind has some vivid justification in the many historical attempts by religion to subdue free thought, and not only through the Inquisition. The French philosopher Denis Diderot was jailed in the eighteenth century for making the sensible point that the persistence of evil shows that the world is not operating under a perfect divine plan; his jailing became, itself, evidence of the persistence of evil. When in 1835 a German professor named David Strauss published one of the leading nineteenth-century works of theology, *The Life of Jesus Critically Examined*, a book maintaining that Christ's supernatural acts were "historical myth," he was fired from his post and barred from university teaching for the remainder of his life.[8] (Today Strauss would likely be barred from major-university employment *unless* he asserted that faith is mythology, but that's another matter.) Further back, the Middle Ages philosopher William of Occam was forced into hiding merely for endorsing nominalism, a hypothesis that truth exists only as groupings of words, not in any independent sense; church authorities found this view offensive to scholasticism, Thomas Aquinas's theory that absolute truths could be ranked like risers on a stairway to God.[9] Many other past examples show organized religion opposing the use of the mind.

Yet there is also a history of faith and intellect as confederates. Descartes thought the highest use of rationality was the clarification of faith; Muslim philosophers such as al-Ghazali, born in 1058, helped advance the idea of rational systematics;[10] Newton said the subtle order of nature could prove the existence of God;[11] Jefferson believed the teachings of Jesus were the zero event of history; there are many other examples. Important centers of higher learning, including Brandeis, Harvard, and Oxford, were founded by Jewish or Christian denominations. As the noted Harvard theologian Harvey Cox has written, many universities now desiccated by postmodernism hunger to rediscover "the spiritual traditions that nourished them over the millennia."[12]

And surely it cannot be that thoughtful people should disdain belief because faith lacks cerebral concepts. If anything, the history of spiritual thought is too complex rather than the reverse. The eighteenth-century English wit Anthony Collins summed theological complexity this way: "It would never have occurred to anyone to doubt God's existence if theologians had not tried so hard to prove it." Citing a few long-standing spiritual disputes as convoluted as anything in academic thought makes the point; the 3,000-years-and-running dialectic regarding Talmudic law; the centuries of contention over the hopelessly intricate Trinity doctrine; Augustine's rediscovery of the mysticism of Plato; the scholasticism of Aquinas; labyrinthine attempts of the Jesuits to restore the worldview of Aristotle; ongoing arguments within faith circles about whether orthodoxy, religious relativism, fundamentalism, millennialism, ecumenicism, liberation theology, or any of a dozen other competing mental structures are best for faith. As George Santayana wrote in 1905, "The spirit's foe in man has not been simplicity but sophistication."[13]

Likewise, within the history of faith one can find some of the very notions that anchor the age of doubt. Buddhism and Gnostic Christianity, for instance, have maintained since ancient days that women and men are born into unrelenting woe, foreshadowing the central contention of existentialism. Mary Baker Eddy, the nineteenth-century founder of Christian Science, asserted that physical existence is an illusion in the literal sense; quantum mechanics, which asserts that subatomic particles arise from an illusory void, would come as no surprise to Eddy.[14] Putatively modern phenomena such as career fixation are standard to the history of belief. A remarkable, rarely noticed passage on the latter point occurs during the Last Supper. Jesus announces that one of those present will soon betray him. The disciples take no action to flush out the turncoat. Instead, sensing the end at hand, the disciples begin to argue over their places in history: "A dispute arose among them as to which one of them was to be regarded as the greatest."[15] Christ is about to die, and his disciples are more worried about whether they will get good press.[16] Modern careerism has nothing on this moment.

BECAUSE THE HISTORY OF FREE THOUGHT is entwined with rejection of belief, the notion of doubt as compulsory has been building for a long time. As early as 1580 the French essayist Michel de Montaigne was asking, "How many things served us but yesterday as articles of faith, which today we deem but fables?" Rousseau wrote that humanity was good in essence but corrupted by institutions, prominently by the mind-diminishing effects of religion; he declared faith a foe of the *esprit social*, or civic spirit. The early Christians believed the world would soon end in calamity and taught that people should prepare by making bonds of spiritual harmony with each other, but withdraw from society at large. Rousseau believed humanity could achieve paradise on Earth if people became totally involved in civic life, especially in the reform of corrupt institutions.[17] Faith, Rousseau concluded, impeded this by channeling people toward private contemplation of their souls, rather than toward concern about public progress.

A milestone in association of doubt with intellect was *The History of the Decline and Fall of the Roman Empire*, completed by the British historian Edward Gibbon in 1788. Today these books are looked back upon as a recounting of why Rome faded politically; at the time of publication, their conspicuous element was the thesis that religion triggered Rome's demise. Portions of *Decline and Fall* document how Christianity enervated Roman state power by shifting the focus from administration of empire to infighting over dogma, and weakened Romans individually by causing them to waste their mental energies contemplating scripture.[18] *Decline and Fall* would prove one of the masterworks of Western thought, and implicit in its worldview was the idea that faith is for fools.[19] By the nineteenth century, this view had become explicit. The Russian political theorist Mikhail Bakunin would assert, "The first revolt is against the supreme tyranny of theology, of the phantom of God. As long as we have a master in heaven, we will be slaves on earth."[20]

After the savagery of the Inquisition and centuries of the use of religious differences to rationalize war, no one could be blamed for feeling that faith, once a liberating force, had become an oppressor from which people now required a second liberation. For centuries kings and clergy had maintained that society had an interest in mandating belief. Now a new view emerged that society's interest lay in mandating unbelief.

AS THE MODERN ERA APPROACHED, it grew increasingly common for thinkers to assert that anyone with brain engaged would see life as so bereft of meaning as to represent an irredeemable experience. The nineteenth-century German metaphysician Arthur Schopenhauer, influenced by Eastern writing, constructed a notion of existence surpassing Buddhism in its emphasis on suffering as the essence of life.[21] Schopenhauer thought human desires inevitably clash and that no matter how auspiciously society might be ordered, people would always find things to fight about and always mar each other's lives just enough to prohibit happiness. From this he concluded there can be no contentment, only absence of pain.[22] Schopenhauer equated mental misery with rational self-awareness. To put his views in contemporary terms, he felt that if you are able to maintain a positive outlook, then you must not understand the situation.

Such ideas influenced many consequential figures, among them Herman Melville, author of *Moby-Dick*. Melville's 1852 novel of spiritual doubt, *Pierre*, has characters who declare that "whatever other worlds God may be Lord of, He is not the lord of this, for else this world would not seem to give the lie to Him." Melville spent his life vacillating between belief and unbelief, writing bitterly of churchgoers who never question why God could allow the world to be cruel, but also penning thoughts such as, "I feel that the Godhead is broken up like the bread at the Supper, and that we are the pieces. Hence this infinite fraternity of feeling."[23] It could be said that in ambivalent passages such as these, Melville praised God with faint damnation.

The growing literature suggesting of doubt influenced Søren

Kierkegaard, perhaps the most significant nineteenth-century thinker on faith. Kierkegaard earned a spotty living as a newspaper columnist of no distinction. His serious writing, prominently the book *Fear and Trembling*, did not attract attention until after his 1855 death, as the intellectual mood began to swing toward bleakness. Bleakness could be found in profusion in Kierkegaard, who had been obsessed by anxiety and dread. Typical quotes: "Since my earliest childhood a barb of sorrow has lodged in my heart . . . if it is pulled out I shall die"[24] and "My depression is the most faithful mistress I have known."[25]

Kierkegaard held that trepidation was the only intelligent response to life. Meaning remains possible, but can be glimpsed only after enduring many planes of anguish about the impossibility of truly knowing one's soul. In the end a person must "leap" from doubt to pure spiritual conviction; the phrase "leap of faith" originates with Kierkegaard. Even then, placing yourself in God's hands does not right your life, merely inoculates you against sinking ever-deeper into wretchedness. Kierkegaard was among the first existentialists; his work led to a school of Christian existentialism later populated by such thinkers as Karl Jaspers, Gabriel Marcel, Reinhold Niebuhr, and Paul Tillich. "One must be quite literally a lunatic" to embrace belief, Kierkegaard supposed. This from one of faith's defenders.

The notion that intellect compels doubt reached its logical culmination in Friedrich Nietzsche. Born in 1844, Nietzsche was the patron saint of postmodernism, the phrase "God is dead" originating with him.[26] He denounced faith as an elaborate fraud, asserting that spiritual values such as humility and kindness were bogus "slave morality" causing the "herd" of typical women and men to be meekly mediocre. The *Ubermensch* or Superman, self-confident individualists freed from social conventions and from the fear of acting rightly in the eyes of a Maker, could rule the Earth by sheer will, pursuing power and gratification. To Nietzsche higher purpose was a hysterical joke: life was economics, power structures, and self-gratification, and immersion in these things was good, not bad. As the former White House official Marty Kaplan has written mordantly, owing to Nietzsche, "The educated person knows that love is really about libido, that power is about class, that religion is about fantasy. We are all now Nietzsche's children, shivering in the pointless void."[27]

Nietzsche certainly became free from social conventions, going mad at age forty-five. Many commentators, including the contemporary writer Richard Friedman, have asked whether Nietzsche's derangement shows that facing the silence of God causes insanity: that human beings cannot bear the notion of being alone in the cosmos, stripped of any hope of ultimate redemption.[28]

That Nietzsche's writings were later used by the Nazis may not have been the philosopher's fault. But Nietzsche may be wholly faulted for rendering respectable the antisocial notion that even the best aspects of spiritual conviction—such as conscience and moral compassion—are now to be received as suspicious. It is one thing to argue that faith depends on unverifiable claims, quite another to argue that making people care about each other's hearts and souls transforms them into a subordinate herd. We should all be so fortunate as to live among such a herd.

DURING THE PERIOD WHEN philosophy and literature began to adapt bleak worldviews, much of the world of belief was clouding over, too. By the mid-nineteenth century, sects predicting an imminent end of the world were spreading in the United States and Europe. The best-remembered was Millerism, whose founder, evangelist William Miller, preached that temporal existence would end in flaming terror on precisely 22 October 1844.[29] Thousands of Millerites sold their possessions

and waited in fields to be swept up to the heavens. Even after
the world declined to conclude, doomsday faith grew in popularity. Miller founded the Adventist Church and often praised
the awfulness of life as welcome news, asserting that the descent of the society into privation would force God's hand,
leaving the divine no choice but to bring history to a close.

Picking up this theme, the Gilded Age revivalist Dwight
Moody exhorted believers to root for the downward slide of
events that would summon the Second Coming. A typical
chipper Moody declaration from 1888: "I don't find any place
where God says the world is going to grow better and better.
I find that the Earth is to grow worse and worse." Such disconsolate views would in the twentieth century mutate into "premillennialism," a stance popular on the religious right.[30]
Ronald Reagan was a "premil," saying he saw in the behavior
of the former Soviet Union signs of the approaching end of
the world.[31]

Though most followers of Miller or Moody were political
conservatives, they often "matched the most vehement radi-
cals in describing capitalism's human toll and conditions in
the industrial city," notes Paul Boyer, a historian at the University of Wisconsin.[32] Factories, for example, were seen as the
tools of the devil, drawing people away from healthful agrarian
labor under the dome of God's sky and into anonymous urban
communities where sinfulness could prosper. Early industrial-
ization was infernal in its pollution, abuse of workers, and destructive impact on family life, so perhaps the millennial view
was ahead of its time in this respect: as would later be understood through the World Wars, the Industrial Era did make
possible human combat at a hellish intensity that even the
Book of Revelation might have called extreme.

Concurrent with the development of bleak faith, the nineteenth-century explosion of scientific advances called forth fundamentalism as a countervailing force. Despite the impression

that fundamentalism is age-old, in its modern sense this out-look began only about one hundred years ago, when some tra-ditionalists chose to call their views "fundamentalism" as a contrast to "modernism." The pope was not proclaimed infal-lible until 1870, by a vote of the Vatican Council that came a decade after Darwin's *On the Origin of Species.* "Inerrancy," the comparable Protestant notion that scripture is without fault, did not become a common contention until around that time. By 1910 a hot item in American bookstores was a series of short volumes called *The Fundamentals,* which spelled out the credo of the new, backward-focused form of thought. In 1929 the Westminster Theological Seminary, an intellectual center of fundamentalism, was founded by two professors who re-signed from the mainstream Princeton Seminary, accusing it of buckling under to revisionism;[33] though what was believed at the Princeton Seminary in 1929 would seem today excruciat-ingly traditional. Dazzled by the dislocations of modern thought, fundamentalists of many denominations seemed to calculate that only rigid doctrine could persevere against the expansion of doubt.

Early twentieth-century reformers such as James Conant and William James found themselves diabolic figures to funda-mentalism because the reform impulse held that social prob-lems could be solved and humankind rescued from within, while fundamentalism asserted that grace from above repre-sented society's last hope. As Mark Noll has written, the fun-damentalist Moody Bible Institute denounced many reforms, such as the proposed League of Nations, as tools of the end-times.[34] By the 1930s, some believers were opposing the entire New Deal on the grounds that any attempt to make the world humane would merely forestall Christ's return.[35] By the post-war era, there would almost seem to be a competition between intellectuals and believers to see who could describe the human prospect in the most doleful terms.

THUS THROUGH THE PAST CENTURY, main currents of both secular and spiritual thought both flowed toward a view of human society as hollow, depressive, and about to crash. These sentiments are not unique to the modern era: for thousands of years people have supposed that life is pointless, or that they live in the end-time. What seemed new was the conjunction of bleakness with both the secular and the spiritual embracing disconsolate views.

Gradually this overcast fugue enveloped philosophy, art, and literature. Positivism, the main school of twentieth-century philosophical thought, began to hold that only that which could be confirmed by the eye could be believed: by definition this ruled out concepts such as "purpose," which no one can see. Art shifted from demanding reform to mocking society; surrealism not only sneered at faith but at optimism and good intent. In 1928 André Breton, a prominent French surrealist, would condense his sentiments: "Everything that is doddering, squint-eyed, vile, polluted and grotesque is summoned up for me in that one word, God!"[36] By the postwar period, theorist Michel Foucault declared despotism to be the essence of all institutions. Power politics and the suppression of individuality were not only the objectives of totalitarians, Foucault thought, but of democracies, families, charitable organizations, Nobel Peace Prize winners: everything we foolishly thought commendable was in fact contemptible. Foucault expounded that pain is so central to social organization that no civic order could operate without it: "In its function, the power to punish is not essentially different from that of curing or educating"[37] is a typically upbeat quote. To Foucault, not only was no hope left for the human prospect, there had never been any hope to lose.

By 1961 the historian Daniel Boorstin, a voice of establishment liberalism, would confidently describe God as "not a fact of nature but [a] fabrication useful for a God-fearing society."[38]

Around the same time the influential conservative philosopher Leo Strauss of the University of Chicago was saying roughly the same: writing of faith as something known within the elite minds of academia to be fictitious, but whose pretenses should be maintained as a tool of sociological crowd control.[39] From such cues, most of mass culture began to treat higher purpose as exposed. News anchors, Hollywood producers, and others responsible for the version of culture seen by the typical person might not have known what was really in the works of Kierkegaard or Camus or Strauss,[40] but they did know that big-name thinkers were now employing terms like "fabrication" in the same breath with "God." Doubt became the plankton at the base of the cultural food chain.

When the first half of this century brought such horrors as trench warfare, fascist and communist tyranny, aerial bombardment of civilians, atomic bombing of civilians, the Rape of Nanking, and the Holocaust, bleak trends in spiritual and secular philosophy seemed to have become hideously real. Wasn't what happened at the Sommes or in the concentration camps every bit as catastrophic as anything prophesied in millennialism? Didn't Hitler and Stalin show that Freud and Foucault were right in describing the human psyche as just a sump of baneful compulsion? Didn't the atomic bomb prove that Kierkegaard was right, and one ought to face each morning consumed by dread?

TO THE CHANCE that the gloomy thinkers really were right was added the modernist rejection of the supernatural, even as a contingency. Postwar intellectual consensus held that the parting of the Red Sea must have been mythology; the raising of Lazarus, perhaps a prearranged publicity stunt; the restoration of sight to the blind something that might happen, but not without a well-stocked teaching hospital, a team of wisecracking surgeons, and a small army of insurance adjusters. If the supernatural has been discarded, then the human prospect diminishes further, there being no hope of any outside agency that will come to society's aid, or at least provide moral inspiration.

Today the question of the supernatural is perhaps the deepest divide between establishment thought and popular opinion. Hardly anyone in the contemporary intellectual or opinion-making worlds would hold that unseen powers are possible; whereas polls consistently show that a sizable portion of the American population believes miracles to be genuine events. Views of the supernatural have come to be regarded as mutually exclusive, in the way, say, that a person is expected to be prolabor or probusiness but not both.

This mind-set, too, has a longer heritage than might be supposed. The eighteenth-century philosopher Charles de Montesquieu wrote that tales of divine action were inventions that sprung from human vanity, a view reflected in his adage, "If triangles made a god, they would give him three sides." Rousseau declared in *Letters Written from the Mountain* that assertions of the supernatural should be viewed as antithetical to belief, since they cast spiritual truth into doubt. Denis Diderot wrote in 1769 that by dispelling the supernatural, study of something as simple as a chicken's egg can topple "every theological theory, every church or temple in the world." By the turn of the twentieth century, the literary critic and Christian traditionalist C. S. Lewis would declare that the guiding principal of academia is, "if miraculous, unhistorical."

Yet knowing there are objections to the plausibility of some supernatural claims, while keeping the mind open to the possibility of forces larger than ourselves, is essential to seeking a center ideal of faith. It is much too early in the human rise toward knowledge for anyone to know what can or cannot happen under physical law; what the entirety of creation might hold. To assume that men and women already know everything necessary to grasp the full possibilities of physical law, or can already be sure what the vastness of the cosmos contains, is simple hubris.

Consider that at an earlier stage, Locke, Voltaire, and other thinkers of the Enlightenment opposed belief in the supernatural on the assumption that miracles must contravene physical law. This notion has become implanted in the psyche of doubt, though what may be allowed or barred by physics is far from settled and seems to change with every generation. The Greeks, it's worth recalling, believed that amber was a supernatural substance because when it was rubbed with cat fur, amber could lift certain light objects without touching them. No one then understood static electricity; to Greek sensibilities, only the divine could explain this mysterious effect.[41] Had electricity existed as an economic commodity at the time—an invisible current able to cause heat, light, motion, or death—it would have been described as supernatural.

Because it has become standard to assume that physical law somehow prohibits the metaphysical, today even the best minds may assert that supernatural events cannot have happened, as opposed to saying that no one knows for sure. For example, Jack Miles, among the finest voices in contemporary theology, has written that the Old Testament account of Lot's wife turning to a pillar of salt "obviously has no status as history."[42] Suppose a skeptical rationalist of a bygone century, say Denis Diderot, had been handed John Hersey's *Hiroshima*, with its passages depicting people far from the detonation of the atom bomb being flash-incinerated into columns of ash. From the standpoint of eighteenth-century knowledge, Diderot might have supposed this account to contain violations of physical law and declared that people turned to ash by a distant cataclysm "obviously" had no historical status. To us what happened at Hiroshima seems all too sadly thinkable under the same physical laws. Similarly, aspects of spirituality today thought to contravene physical law may seem explicable in some future light.

THIS IS NOT TO SUGGEST that God would be exempt from physics. It is reasonable to work from the assumption that God is bound into the fabric of physical law, just as we are. But this hardly means the Maker would be prohibited from sponsoring actions that would seem transcendent from our perspective.

On close inspection, few of the miraculous events depicted in the monotheist scripture run afoul of physical law as understood thus far, though many would require knowledge that does not now exist. Walking on water? Germany has already commissioned the construction of magnetic-levitation trains that float on an invisible polarity field and weigh appreciably more than a single person in sandals. No current technology could project a levitation field across open water, but that may be only a matter of time. A levitated train, possible now, would have been droll mythology to rationalists of previous generations.

Those 5,000 brunches from seven loaves?[43] Pretty hard to picture, but perhaps not if there turns out to be something along the lines of teleportation. No one can say whether teleportation is possible—maybe this is where those "folded" dimensions will come in handy—but it would be foolish to assert that just because teleportation cannot be imagined now, therefore it will never be imagined. Just a few generations ago, no one could imagine space-relayed telecommunication.[44]

How about resurrection? Rising from the dead has already been achieved in the limited sense of reanimation following clinical death, a "miracle" that now happens to hundreds of people daily. Today it seems impossible that a person could be reanimated on the third day after the last breath is drawn, but once physicians would have sworn it would always be impossible to bring someone back after any cessation of cardiopulmonary function. Many contemporary biologists think organic life first arose eons ago in accordance with unguided natural forces operating with zero information. If we can believe that life can be started by thoughtless processes possessing no knowledge at all, it should not trouble us to suppose that life might be restarted by someone possessing advanced knowledge.

Viewing scripture from the standpoint of physical law, the Bible's only really disquieting miracle comes during the Old Testament story of God stopping the apparent motion of the sun through the sky.[45] To make the sun appear to hang motionless would mean halting the revolution of the Earth on its axis. A task such as this would demand potency at a breathtaking level, the energy output of the whole stars perhaps being insufficient, as well as phenomenal computational ability to manage the event, because gravitational relationships throughout the solar system would be disrupted. The oceans would need to be kept from flying off into space, and the planet's tectonic plates prevented from cracking under the strain of their angular momentum. Some neat trick would be needed to sustain the moon in its orbit, and there would have to be enough horsepower left over to restart the motion of the zodiac at the end of the demonstration.

That, however, is not the troubling part. This miracle is more disturbing from the standpoint of theology than physical law, because it represents the sort of marvel adverse to God's interest—one we would all be better off disbelieving. God stops the sun in the sky not for any constructive purpose, but so that Joshua's infantry can have extra hours of daylight in which to complete "a great slaughter" of the helpless, including women and children: "And the sun stood still and the moon stopped until the nation [Israel] took vengeance on their enemies."[46]

But though halting Earth's revolution appears so arduous

from the physical-law perspective as to be for intents and purposes impossible, it is not hard to suppose that a being of advanced knowledge might have made the sun seem to hang motionless by supplanting sunshine with another light source. Humanity may soon be able to accomplish this feat. Engineers of the Russian space agency have already tested large mirror satellites that collect sunlight from high-orbit positions above the planet's shadow and beam it to the surface for area lighting during nighttime emergencies. Something along these lines might have given Joshua's army the illusion of the sun hanging in place. This is not to suggest that the divine would employ material technology, only that knowledge beyond ours may enable acts that are consistent with physical law but that would represent miracles from the human perspective.

If God actually did light up the night for Joshua's battalion, we remain mired in the theological puzzle of what to make of a deity who stages such an extraordinary act for the purpose of facilitating a slaughter of the helpless. Leaving that question aside for a coming chapter, here we can conclude that it is haughty conceit for rationalism to rule out the supernatural: in doing so, supposing that engineers of contemporary space agencies can imagine a means to accomplish the suspension of nightfall, but God cannot.

OF COURSE THERE ARE FAIR ARGUMENTS that supernatural accounts in scripture are exaggerated or had their origins in folklore. Yet the idea that the supernatural is impossible is now typically treated as fact, rather than as one of several competing hypotheses. This turns doubt into a rigid new dogma of its own.

Doubt-as-dogma may be reduced to the absurd when it proposes ideas more fanciful than the unseen. Into this category falls a widely reported 1992 theory that during the Mosaic flight from Egypt, sustained heavy winds of natural original, blowing along a straight line, might have separated the waters in an area in the Gulf of Suez.[47] There, by chance, ancient Hebrews found a "parted" sea when they arrived with Pharaoh's army in pursuit. The Hebrews fled across and by chance the winds stopped just as they cleared the far side, drowning their pursuers and leaving behind a mythology of divine engagement. This *might* have happened, but has anyone ever seen heavy winds along the Gulf of Suez blow in an unwavering straight line until the waters separate for the hours required for thousands of people to run across?[48] Yet media organizations reported this contention with full credulity, because its proposed mechanism was natural—however improbable.

In 1995 major news organizations featured an even more credulous report. Two geologists had proposed that when Lot thought he saw his wife become salt, he was running near the Dead Sea, and that area "was full of salt floes that might have been thrown up by surging water to resemble a female outline," in the Reuters version of this story.[49] Reuters quoted one of the researchers asserting in full seriousness, "Here legend is created out of what can now be explained as a simple geological phenomenon." This proposed natural explanation sounds significantly more far-fetched than the supernatural one. If the spontaneous materialization of gender-specific salt floes is a mere "simple geological phenomenon," let's see a videotape of it happening naturally, please.

What really troubles many who reflect on claims of supernatural action is not whether such things are possible on a physical-law basis, but that if past miracles occurred, then the unseen does exist.[50] Jesus may or may not have risen, but if he did, there must be higher power and higher purpose. Once such thought was received as reassuring. To the age of doubt, it is unsettling.

DOUBT WAS ORIGINALLY INTENDED to free people from the repressive effects of institutional dogma and to dilute the nonsense quotient of faith—both desirable goals. In its compulsory form, doubt now goes further to dilute the senses of meaning and morality. If to contemporary thought it starts off being bogus to enter a place of worship and pledge righteousness before a God whose existence cannot be confirmed, it can end up being bogus to pledge righteousness regardless of how that value may be derived. By causing us to doubt that there is higher truth, the runaway modern form of skepticism removes from social conduct both the negative fear of ultimate judgment and the positive desire to stand tall before one's Maker. The latter, it can be argued, has inspired much of human ethical achievement.

Once people made a show of faith for public consumption, harboring doubts in secret. Today we make a show of being too worldly to believe, and privately harbor our dreams of the spirit. Yet faith and modernism are not irreconcilable. Each needs the other more than either will say.

Chapter Seven

Beyond All-or-Nothing

Any genuine philosophy leads to action and from action back again to wonder, to the enduring fact of mystery.
HENRY MILLER, 1947

IN THE MIDDLE AGES, believers often spoke of the "quodlibet," or the compelling spiritual question. Quodlibets of the time covered a range of matters from such elementary concerns as how to love our neighbors as ourselves, to such minutiae as whether items still existed that had been in physical contact with Jesus, this being the Holy Grail fixation. In those days it was considered an essential use of time to spend an evening arguing out the fine points of a quodlibet, even if this did mean people actually discussed such questions as how many angels could stand on the head of a pin.

Today, as the pace of life quickens toward a blur, the time women and men spend on great spiritual issues steadily declines to make room for things that really matter—like watching cable TV or circling the mall parking lot looking for a space. Each hour on Earth is just as priceless as it once was, yet with every passing year the obligation to fritter those hours away on frivolity seems more pressing. Striving to understand the spiritual impulse stands among the most important tasks facing any generation; heartfelt belief may both enrich lives and advance the cause of human morality. Instead we revel in our culture's stupendous output of the superficial. When death approaches, few of us will wish we had spent more of our allotted time chasing money, clothes, careers, movies, sports, or even sex, while we might well long deeply for a few additional hours to reflect on the quodlibets.

One Middle Ages quodlibet that remains fully relevant today is whether faith and reason exclude each other. If they do, there can be no spiritual center; questions of belief will always boil down to all or nothing.

All-or-Nothing structures turn out to be surprisingly prevalent in debates about meaning and purpose. The All-or-Nothing premise is often found within faith: the assumption, for example, that God must either be omnipotent or not exist. The All-or-Nothing premise is common within science: for example, the assumption that if some aspects of the living world have a mechanistic origin, then all must. Beyond this is the foremost All-or-Nothing fallacy: each person must choose doctrinaire belief or empty unbelief, rejecting the center.

Reason and faith are natural companions. One asks us to think with our heads, the other to know with our hearts. Both forms of insight are required for a realized life. How did we come to think otherwise, and stumble into All-or-Nothing?

POSITIONS IN THE SPIRITUAL DEBATE have not always been viewed as automatic antipodes. Early in the Bible's first book, Abraham debates with God about whether it would be just to destroy Sodom if the righteous would die along with the wicked. In this debate the progenitor of the three great monotheist faiths reasons from logic, not revelation.[1] As God is slowly talked down to a smaller and smaller number of righteous citizens required to spare Sodom, rationality prevails.

Many ancient Greek thinkers strove to avoid All-or-Nothing

Thinking. Aristotle argued that the highest realization of men and women before God was the exercise of rationality. By advocating spiritual logic he broke with his pupil Plato, a mystic. Searching for rational validation of the divine, Aristotle studied mathematics, physics, and medicine, at one point spending two years dissecting intertidal life along the shoreline of Lesbos, in an attempt to understand marine biology. Not all of Aristotle's conclusions have worn well: he pronounced that the body metabolized food by cooking it internally, and for some reason became convinced that women have fewer teeth than men.[2] Nevertheless, Aristotle demonstrated that a person could address the unseen by using powers of reason.

Early Judaic thinking was often concerned with combining spirituality and rationality. The thousands of pages of rabbinical commentary preserved in the Talmud and other texts may sometimes dwell on matters quaint today, but most of the material remains relevant in logical terms: how to be fair, how to temper justice with mercy. Christianity was born neutral on the matter of secular reason. Jesus spoke almost exclusively about moral behavior among people and the requirements for admission to heaven. It was only after Christ's death that Christian hierarchies began to respond to political persecution, compete with the Gnostic interpretation of Jesus's ideas, and regulate the antagonisms between bishops that would eventually cause the separation of the Roman and Eastern churches.[3] Aspects of these disputes led the young faith to grow infatuated with abstruse claims regarding Christ's morphology and other issues on the boundary of reason. By the fifth century, when Augustine became the most influential Christian thinker partly by advocating complex plaits of mystical ideas derived from Plato, rationality and belief were seen as warring elements.

Through the Dark Ages institutional religion often opposed independent thought, but as the philosopher Alfred North

Whitehead showed, was not entirely closed to reason.[4] Church-affiliated scholars advanced the idea that God's actions have a logical relationship to divine ends; this rationalist notion stood in opposition to the Greek, Hindu, and pagan Roman religious traditions, which viewed the gods as capricious or inexplicable. Whitehead thought the basic idea that means and ends must be logically coupled was one of the developments that caused the Renaissance. Initially concerned with opening the mind, Renaissance thought would eventually veer toward All-or-Nothing structure.

ONE OF THE EARLIEST SIGNS of Renaissance thinking came in the year 1093 when the Italian prelate Anselm, serving as an archbishop in the British Isles, began arguing that faith could be confirmed solely by the application of logic.[5] Anselm was greatly influenced by the rediscovery of works of Aristotle: volumes lost during the decline of Rome, then unearthed in the eleventh century by Muslim and Jewish scholars in North Africa. Especially of interest was Aristotle's critique of the very Platonic mysticism that Christianity had come to espouse. Anselm found logical arguments for faith more persuasive than mystical casuistry. So he devised an "ontological proof" of God, ontology representing the metaphysics of being. Anselm's ideas came to dominate the spiritual debate of the day, and in a sense they still dominate, however few know Anselm by name, for it was the "ontological proof" that proposed that all spiritual contemplation begin with the assumption that the Maker is omnipotent.

To form his proof, Anselm first declared that God must be the highest imaginable aspect of creation, "that than which nothing greater can be conceived"—*Id quo nihil maius cogitari possit*, a passage committed to memory by medieval doctors of philosophy. Anyone who rejects the idea that God is the highest perfection, Anselm argued, is saying there could be something greater the greatest. Since that statement makes no sense, then the Maker cannot be rejected. Therefore the divine must exist.

Today any first-year student of rhetoric can pinpoint the circularity at the heart of Anselm's argument, which uses definition to mandate its own conclusion. But at the time, to have a high church officer speaking of God not in incomprehensible lingo but linear logic was a breakthrough for human assertion.

Little-known though it be may outside the realm of the philosophy seminar, Anselm's ontological proof defined the basic terms under which the trap of All-or-Nothing thinking came about. The key point is that Anselm's first step was to assume that God must be all-powerful and all-knowing. Many had previously described the divine in Absolute terms: for instance, Boethius, writing in the sixth century, said God embodied "eternal life possessed perfectly." Much earlier Plato had supposed that the divine could not undergo the slightest change, because saying that the Maker changed implies God's prior state was imperfect, and divine imperfection is unimaginable.

But Anselm brought to the conception of an all-powerful God distinctive authority, because Anselm argued from logic rather than revelation. A person might claim to have experienced a vision that God is an Absolute: such avowals may or may not be true, but by definition are impossible for others to evaluate. Anselm's claims rested on reason, and were thereby accessible. Right or wrong, there could be no doubt that Anselm's proof "existed." Anyone could debate the ontological concept of God without getting sidetracked into the enigma of private spiritual epiphany.

In the centuries since, believers have argued with passion that Anselm's approach was right and an Absolute God is real. Skeptics have argued with equal force that Anselm was wrong and no Maker ever was or will be. All the attention has focused

on the ontological aspect of the argument. Overlooked and
accepted as a given has been Anselm's starting assertion that,
if real, God must have an Absolute nature. Anselm's Ontological Proof should really be called Anselm's Assumption, the entirely unproved notion that the Maker simply *must* be all-
powerful.

A FEW GENERATIONS AFTER Anselm's death, Thomas Aquinas
would seem to cement spiritual endorsement of reason through
the 1273 *Summa Theologica*, which spoke approvingly of science.
Building from Anselm's assumption of God as an Absolute,
Aquinas declared the Maker infinite in power, knowledge, foresight, and all other positive qualities.[6] There cannot be more
than one God, Aquinas argued, because then the second divinity might possess some ability the first lacked, and that is
inconceivable as God already has all power. But though he
was a rationalist, Aquinas was also a Dominican monk whose
thoughts never threatened the church: his definition of reason
was usually whatever chain of statements led to the validation
of existing doctrine. Later the Jesuit order would be founded
partly with the charge of advancing the Thomist contention
that reason proved the divine. Through the ages Jesuit scholars would delight in showy citations of laws of motion or ther-
modynamics, till they rivaled the most tedious pretenses of
secular philosophers.[7]

The ontological proof was prominently carried forward by
Descartes, who tried to remove its problem of circularity while
retaining Anselm's assumption of an all-powerful Maker. Notions of human shortcomings, Descartes wrote, cannot come
into existence unless there is an exterior standard against
which to compare women and men, and that standard is the
all-knowing, all-powerful God, "this perfect being."[8] For centuries religious traditionalists have been comforted by the notion that an omnipotent God wields a flaming sword that will

someday strike down apostates. During the Renaissance, rationalists like Descartes were comforted by the notion that an omniscient God ponders the supreme knowledge that will someday strike down ignorance.

Yet despite the efforts of great minds such as Anselm and Aquinas, faith and reason seemed eager to clash. Descartes's contemporary Blaise Pascal strenuously contended that logic could never apply to an all-powerful divine. This view bore credence because Pascal was a mathematics prodigy who invented the adding machine and helped devise probability theory. Pascal, who later in life became a spiritual ascetic, assumed that God was in control of human events, but allowed worldly suffering in pursuit of some unknown divine objective that people would never be able to fathom. In *Pensées* (Thoughts), Pascal wrote, "Reason's last step is to recognize that there is an infinite number of things which surpass it."[9]

Around Pascal's time Thomas Hobbes, that lighthearted fellow who found existence "nasty, brutish and short," declared that the application of reason showed the natural state as created by God was inexpressibly awful. To Hobbes what the Maker had wrought was a world of starvation and disease, of mindless beasts goring each other's flesh: the main rationalization for government, he felt, was to protect citizens from devolving to jungle instincts. Hobbes did not object to faith; he preferred that men and women spend their time in dignified if frivolous ecclesiastic ceremony, rather than stalking each other like animals. But his work set in motion what would come to be a powerful idea in Western thought, especially when existentialism was later added—that to be alive represents a curse rather than a blessing, with the cursed nature of existence suggesting there cannot be meaning or higher purpose.

Building on such ideas, Voltaire—who was horrified both by the hypocrisies of clerics and by mass death during an earthquake in Portugal in 1755—supposed that God's failure to stop natural disasters cast all religious assumptions into doubt. David Hume, in *Dialogues Concerning Natural Religion*, would suppose that religion might exist as a mystery or a contingency, but otherwise declare that no omnipotent God could have created evil. Since evil exists, Hume supposed, this means there is no omnipotence, and without omnipotence there can be no Maker. The assumption spread that a person could side with reason or faith but not both: despite the Enlightenment, All-or-Nothing thought was taking hold.

DURING THE LATER EIGHTEENTH CENTURY the idea of a truce between spirituality and rationality enjoyed a revival. Jefferson, Locke, and others spoke optimistically about "natural religion," or deism. Deists asserted that Hobbes and Hume were wrong to view the world with horror. Arguing the opposite conclusion from the same set of facts, the deists found the natural condition not dismal but so complex and subtly ordered that it must reflect the influence of an unseen intelligence. Most people are naturally good, the deists supposed; human society would not be so corrupt if only it strove to imitate the noble state of nature.

Deism was employed to argue against the divine right of kings, by demonstrating that freedom is the natural condition: the flowers growing where it pleases them to grow. Jefferson's three leading interests in life—democracy, religion, and the horticulture of the commonwealth of Virginia—made a neat combination on this point. The American revolutionary Thomas Paine expressed the manifesto of deism in his 1795 *The Age of Reason*, which held that while we may never know if the Bible is true because scripture was composed by people, nature is unquestionably the product of some larger power.[10] Paine's important subsidiary contention was that supernatural claims are suspicious because they cannot be confirmed, whereas the grandeur of nature is self-evident and can be appreciated through our ordinary senses. This, in Paine's mind, rendered nature the better argument for the divine.

In its day such thinking caused more problems for institutional religion than did secular philosophy, if only because, by virtue of being so clement and reasonable, deism stood a chance of overtaking the formal faiths. Clergy of the eighteenth century were particularly horrified at the deist attempt to characterize the perseverance of evil as the disproof of any divine plan: according to deism, God set the world in motion and then declared hands off, choosing freedom as the highest value but having no idea where freedom would lead. Much as they troubled institutional faith of their time, however, compared to what most contemporary intellectuals believe, the deists were exceedingly devout. If deism were to make a comeback today, the mainstream denominations would welcome it warmly.

Around the same time that deism was struggling inconclusively with organized religion, Immanuel Kant was composing the founding arguments of classical agnosticism, which favors neither belief nor disbelief. His *Critique of Pure Reason*, published in 1781, contended that the existence of a Maker could neither be proven nor disproven by "speculative reason."[11] Thus, Kant concluded, nothing about God can be known in any meaningful way. Kant blew to smithereens Anselm's ontological proof. Yet, significantly, Kant accepted Anselm's premise that God simply must be the greatest possible being, lacking no power. Kant asserted that an all-powerful Absolute could not be touched emotionally by human needs, could not learn from human beings, and thereby could not have "any positive properties known to us." This became the manifesto of agnosticism, in its proper sense—meaning the philosophy that God and people are fundamentally estranged from each other. (In modern usage agnosticism is confused with atheism; they are separate ideas.)

Though Kant's arguments against traditional theology became well known, Kant himself would be widely misunderstood by subsequent generations.[12] Within secular philosophy, it has since become standard to say that Kant "killed theology," and to depict him as someone who totally rejected the spiritual impulse. Yet in his second major work, *Critique of Practical Reason*, Kant wrote that society would be better off believing in God regardless of whether the divine can be proven, because the sense of being watched by an ultimate judge is what causes people to aspire to morality. Evildoers might think they can outwit civil laws, Kant noted, but nobody thinks this of the Maker. *Critique of Practical Reason* further supposed that because few people can achieve complete virtue in this life, there must be another life in which the soul can make "infinite" progress toward the emancipating holy condition.[13] Somehow this portion of Kant's work rarely comes up in postmodern commentary, while his arguments against traditional religion remain popular.

BY THE NINETEENTH CENTURY it grew common for thinkers to reject classical arguments regarding faith and rationality as immaterial to the horrors of modern society. The poet John Keats wrote in derision of those who sat solemnly trying to think their way through the great issues, saying he preferred to live "without any irritable reaching after facts and reason." By Keats's death in 1821, the Industrial Age was spooling up to full throttle. Reason hardly seemed to be saving the world. For the typical wage earner in the eastern United States or most of Europe, rational findings of science and economics were turning life into a regimented hell of pollution, overcrowding, repetitive factory labor, and financial exploitation: a process that, as the English novelist Pat Barker has written, would reach its "nightmarish culmination" with the advent of mechanized general slaughter in World War I.[14]

Around the same time came evolution and geology, theories that, taken together, could be read as showing that if anything Hobbes understated his case against nature. The found world was not just a brutal war of all against all: every creature was furiously attempting to render every other one extinct, as the very continents endlessly crashed against one another in pointless pirouettes of ruin. Nature, to the emerging nineteenth-century view, not only lacked a beneficent Maker but was being revealed as a remorseless generator of meaninglessness. And now humanity was imitating nature's engines of decay by developing the technology of broad-scale destruction.

Around the time of World War I, Freud would seem to establish human nature as a domain not of sweet reason but mania and infantile compulsions. Why would any high-minded deity have implanted such things in the psyche? Alternatively, if the psyche arose on its own, what hope could remain for a high-minded future? Following World War II, Sartre would declare that spiritual faith depressed human autonomy, though allowing that there existed a "God-shaped hope" somewhere deep within the human prospect. Sartre put forth the idea that even freedom, Western culture's crowning virtue, ought to be terrifying, because all freedom confers is the opportunity to choose among equally pointless options. By 1995 Francis Crick, the Nobel biologist who was co-discoverer of DNA, would declare that his work scientifically established there is no soul, that even consciousness is just a mechanist illusion devoid of meaning: "Your joys and your sorrows, your memories and ambitions, your sense of personal identity and free will are in fact no more than the behavior of a vast assembly of nerve cells and their associated molecules."[15]

Faith seemed to have been debunked, while rationality could only give a person more reasons to be despondent. And to any who clung to a vision of higher purpose, there seemed a categorical closing argument: the failure of the all-powerful, all-knowing God to halt the Holocaust against God's own chosen.

As disillusionment overcame secular thought, theology continued its parallel slide toward offering ever-more-arid views of the human prospect. Characteristic were the thoughts of the traditionalist theologian Karl Barth. Horrified by the indiscriminate slaughter of World War I, and then by the rise of Nazism, Barth wrote that women and men were so steeped in evil that society might never be made a decent place, while God would always be "wholly other" to human concerns, offering grace but uninterested in righting the wrongs of a depraved Earth.[16] To Barth, belief was no cure for what ailed the world, just the ejection seat that got you out of the crashing plane. Thus Barth urged people to sustain faith, but for bleak reasons oddly similar to the pessimistic viewpoints prevalent in secular thought.

Negative slopes in spirituality and rationality conjoined with the "God is dead" movement of the 1960s. Believers themselves had begun to ask whether the Maker had in some manner been dissembled: too much time had passed since the prophets without the coming justice predicted by scripture. In 1966 a *Time* magazine cover would ask, Is GOD DEAD? This choice reflected not just Ivy League vogue but a broad reading of conventional thought. *Time* seemed to feel the moment had come to declare higher purpose exposed as a swindle: the magazine allowed, "Even though they know better, plenty of Christians find it hard to do away with ideas of God."[17] *Even though they know better.* Spiritual thought had been divided into All-or-Nothing: you believed the entire spiritual package or rejected all of it.

THE FIRST OPTION, of these two choices, total belief in an Absolute God, can seem a simple matter of self-preservation: If a divinity with all power and knowledge does exist, you would be crazy not to worship such a being. Belief in an Absolute also holds out the ancient hope that at some point, possibly within your lifetime, the Maker will touch Earth and commence the Golden Age. This is among the sweetest of the dreams of the spirit.

There are other, entrenched reasons why the All position holds. For centuries institutional religion has taught that the unseen simply *must* be perfect and omnipotent, presuming this will make women and men more likely to support institutional religion. The prayerbooks, hymnals, sermons, catechisms, liturgy, cantillation, mishna, azan, and evensong of every denomination overflow with references to the utter majesty and total perfection of the divine. Even most spirituality movements, existing as they do to provide alternatives to conventional faith, presume God must be Absolute.

Oddly skeptics helped entrench All thinking, because they prefer to argue against an Absolute God. Claims of divine perfection are open to ready scorn in a suffering world. Few experiences are more likely to engender atheism than reading the morning newspaper, tallying the violence and injustice described therein, then strolling into any place of worship to hear God described as a perfect omnipotent who possesses the capacity instantly to right all wrongs. For the skeptic, an Absolute God is the easiest to reject.

Thus on this point, traditionalism and the age of doubt find commonality of cause: both want belief understood in All-or-Nothing terms because their preconceptions are served. Neither view may ever triumph, but at least traditionalists and the antifaith faction can go down together, hands clenched around each other's throats.

From the believer's standpoint the greatest trouble with All-or-Nothing assumptions is that if the Maker is an Absolute, then human suffering stands as it does because God is completing phase one of a perfect plan that requires history to run exactly as it has. Human existence contains many causes for apprehension, but perhaps the most discomforting is the prospect that the world is as it is because *this is the way God wants the world to be*. And that conclusion flows like milk from a kicked pail out of the surmise that God is an Absolute.

If you believe that God has all power to do anything, and you observe that the world is full of suffering inflicted by men and women against each other, you have little choice but to assume that God wishes this to happen; or perhaps, holding with Barth, that the Maker is so removed from concerns of humanity as to pay no heed to what goes on here, which seems almost as bad. On the Nothing side of the aisle, if you assume that God can only be all-powerful, and observe the world's sorrows, you have no choice but to conclude that the Maker is a fabrication. Combine the evil in the world with the assumption of divine omnipotence, and it is possible to reach no outcome other than the extremes of All-or-Nothing: both equally unappealing for the human prospect.

IN THE EARLY CENTURIES the Gnostics tried to evade the sort of reasoning that leads to total belief or no belief by presuming that the Old Testament figure invoked by Judaism and Christianity was evil and fully intended to vest the world with evil. Gnosticism taught that the matter of which the universe is formed is a trap to imprison the beatific spirit; and since the Old Testament God called forth all matter during the six days of cosmic toil, that Maker is to blame for temporal suffering.[18]

A variety of "dualistic" faiths held similar opinions, including Manichaeism, which began in Persia in the third century.[19] Manichaeans believed the universe was established as a contest between a good deity and a bad one: the challenge was to avoid being pulled into the bad god's gravitational field. Gnostics and Manichaeans asserted that much of the early Bible recounts the grim exploits of the evil god—how else to account for the divine slaughters that took place during the conquest of the Promised Land? Both these ancient denominations were vigorously condemned by Christianity as heresies, partly because by calling attention to God's Old Testament destructiveness, they touched a nerve in theology.[20]

During the middle centuries this line of thought resurfaced in Europe in the Cathar faith. Cathars felt the suffering of the world made no sense if God was all-powerful, and so concluded that the world had fallen under the control of an evil being. Cathar thinking informed the larger Albigensian movement, which spread across the Western continental states of the Middle Ages.

Albigensians were Christians who believed that the material realm had been created by evil forces specifically for the purpose of torment, and that Jesus had come from the unseen good to show the way of escape to pure spirituality. One can imagine how in the Middle Ages with disease and privation universal, society divided into excessive privilege for a few and aching poverty for the rest, one woman in three dying in childbirth[21]—bodily existence might have seemed a curse invented by an evil being. For Albigensians, institutional Christianity only worsened the curse. When the Albigensian movement became popular in France, a Crusade against it was declared in 1206. Papal armies assaulted Albigensian towns, killing unarmed civilians by the thousands. Perhaps the Albigensians were so cruelly suppressed mainly for the banal reason that they represented a rival to the Christian institutional structure. Surely another factor was that their thinking treaded on a theological taboo by questioning whether the divine was flawless.

Yet the "dualistic" notion that God shares some blame for evil is found not just in heresy but scripture. One biblical passage asks, "Does disaster befall a city, unless the Lord has done it?"[22] Another declares, "The Lord hath made all things for himself: yea, even the wicked for the day of evil."[23] Job's

story implies that God engages in détente with Satan, the devil
acting as a sort of contract hire to carry out the Maker's disagreeable tasks.[24] Job's wife, the only family member not killed
during his tribulations, urges her husband to condemn the
Maker as evil.[25] Job answers, "Shall we receive the good at
the hand of God, and not receive the bad?"[26] To Job it seems
ineluctable that if the divine has all power, then the Maker
must sanction human suffering.

TAKING THIS PARADOX INTO ACCOUNT, creative attempts to explain evil without giving up on the notion of an omnipotent
God have long been a goal of theology. Consider the New Testament parable of the tares and the wheat. A rich landholder's
plantation is contaminated when an enemy sows the soil with
tares, a weed. Field captains want to destroy the crop and
start over, but the landholder instructs them to allow both
tares and cereal to germinate: "Let both grow together until
the harvest: and in the time of harvest I will say to the reapers,
Gather ye together first the tares, and bind them in bundles
to burn them: but gather the wheat into my barn."[27] The traditionalist interpretation of this parable holds that both evil
and good will be allowed to advance on Earth; at the end of
time the mess will be sorted out, with evil souls discarded to
hell and good souls gathered to paradise. John Calvin took this
line of thought to its analytical extreme with predestination
theory, which pronounced that an all-powerful, all-knowing
God foreordains suffering and arranges the world such that
there is no escape: unless the Maker chooses a person before
birth as "elect," the person will end up damned regardless of
how devoutly he or she lives. Strange as predestination may
sound, it follows logically from a conception of God as an Absolute in total control of the world.

The most influential attempt to explain evil in the All-or-
Nothing context came from Augustine. By the time Augustine

entered the scene, Jesus had been gone from the Earth more than four centuries. The bright fire of the apostles had faded from the world, and the continuing presence of suffering seemed an ever-stronger argument against the beliefs the Jesus movement espoused. A creative response was required, and Augustine delivered it by popularizing the theory of original sin.[28]

It is important to regard original sin as a theory, because this doctrine comes from early church politics rather than scripture: the Bible contains neither the phrase "original sin," nor any reasonable variation on it, nor any passage describing men and women as born wicked.[29] Some traditionalists insist that original sin can be inferred from the moment when Jesus referred to his listeners collectively as "you then who are evil."[30] But the New Testament word rendered here as "evil," the Greek *puneros*, carries the connotation of "culpable" or "hurtful," suggesting sins committed during life, not an elementary state.[31] When Adam and Eve were expelled from the Garden they received from their Maker the curses of toil, strife, and physical pain, but were not called fundamentally bad.[32]

Augustine's theory of original sin was an attempt to rationalize how the Maker could be omnipotent and yet allow evil: the key assumption was that humanity is "fallen" in its essential state. Even infants, Augustine declared, are sinners from the first breath and remain fundamentally wicked regardless of how righteous they become as adults—an idea with scant biblical support, but one that caught on in the depressing Middle Ages ethos.[33] Because of the fallen nature of humanity, Augustine concluded, people should feel awful about themselves, and find the divine offer of grace fantastically magnanimous: more than we deserve, really. But though grace can be acquired during life, its respite is only enjoyed in heaven. On Earth we should expect no more than endless marching centuries of depravity. Thus the existence of evil does not confute God, and the Maker should not be blamed for failing to end injustice. Rather, praise God for shining any glint of goodness into a despicable world.[34]

Augustine has been decried as history's most illustrious misogynist: had his antifemale sensibilities not become snagged in the early expansion of Christianity, religious attitudes toward women might have evolved quite differently.[35] (By the Reformation, institutional spiritual misogyny was so standard that John Knox, founder of Presbyterianism, could mock the secular English establishment by saying that its men "do that to women which no male among the common sort of beasts can be proved to do with their females; that is, they reverence them.")[36] Augustine has also been decried for suggesting that people should feel ashamed of their sexuality.[37] This contradicts the Garden account, in which sensuality was part of the state of innocence: suggesting that either evolution made the erotic pleasurable for natural reasons, or God made it so as a gift to humanity.

But surely the worst Augustinian influence on human thought was the notion that evil *belongs* in the world. Rather than viewing injustice and suffering as errors to be corrected, Augustine saw them as structural requirements of temporal existence. Thought through, Augustine's position can make an Absolute deity sound worse than ever—for if genus *Homo* was created and immediately fell, we must have tripped over something God placed in our path.

WRACKED BY THE IDEA that an omnipotent God wants the world as it is, many have attempted explanations that break the All-or-Nothing deadlock. The second-century Christian bishop Clement proposed that God implanted "seeds" of goodness in everyone; eventually their blossoms would make Earth exclusively good. Origen, the leading spiritual thinker of the third century, created a stir when he declared that even Satan had the potential to renounce evil and be saved.[38] C. S. Lewis, traditionalist though he was, could not swallow the Augustinian notion that society deserves to be evil, proposing instead, "This is a good world that has gone wrong, but still retains the memory of what it ought to have been."[39] Pierre Teilhard de Chardin, the mid-twentieth-century Jesuit and advocate of Darwin, was so driven to despair by trying to imagine why an Absolute divinity allows suffering that he could conclude only that God had for unknown reasons withdrawn from the immediate sphere of Earth. Teilhard thought the divine no longer aware of human society, instead awaiting a reunion with humanity at the Omega Point, an objective of both physical and spiritual evolution.[40]

Such ideas aside, it seems fair to say that no thinker has satisfactorily answered why an Absolute God would sanction the onward progression of human misery. As the *Encyclopedia of Philosophy* dryly avers, "It is extremely difficult to explain the existence of evil in a world created by a God who is both infinitely powerful and infinitely good."[41] A representative example: in his 1996 book *The Quest for God*, the eminent Catholic essayist Paul Johnson wandered inconclusively around the issue of how an all-powerful God could remain silent, then could offer no conclusion except, "I honestly do not know why God permits evil."[42]

As the parent of three young children, I often hear this debate from a more basic perspective, that of questions such as *Who made God?* and *Why doesn't God stop bad things?* This sample of three has given me the impression that children are natural theologians. But rather than encouraging them to pursue such profound questions as divine toleration of evil, institutional faith channels the young toward pat answers that really didn't make sense to the person who made them up, either. Modernism, in its turn, now channels the thoughts of the young toward pat nihilism. The standard positions of All-or-Nothing preclude the middle-ground ideal: that evil dwells where goodness is faint, and that people and a great but imperfect God, working together, must change this.

Many of history's great losses of faith can be traced to Anselm's assumption that God simply *must* be omnipotent. Voltaire gave up on belief because he could not comprehend how an Absolute could allow earthquakes to crush the innocent. Darwin's adored daughter Annie died at age ten of a childhood disease, as her father wept uncontrollably by her side;[43] after that the preeminent mind of the modern age was unable to conceive of mercy on the part of God, and his faith was vanquished. But then Darwin thought in All-or-Nothing terms: believing his only choice was between rejecting faith or prostrating before a heartless Absolute.

Edward Gibbon, author of *Decline and Fall*, was born before antibiotics and had six siblings, none of whom survived childhood.[44] Having watched sweet brothers and sisters consumed by illness, while no doubt unctuous ministers appeared at the bedside to mumble about the will of God, Gibbon's powerful mind was left to consuming turmoil.[45] If you work from Anselm's Assumption, what can you make of faultless children dying in sorrow while an omnipotent God looks on? Do you assume faith is a sham, or that an all-powerful being exists but is indifferent to the cries of the helpless? Gibbon chose sham. You might too—if All-or-Nothing were really the only choice.

BUT IT IS NOT THE ONLY CHOICE. Spirituality holds many possibilities beyond belief in everything or belief in naught.

The All-or-Nothing way of thinking has arisen owing to fundamental misunderstandings about the content of the monotheist heritage, and about that portion of spiritual traditions having their origins in the institutions of society, especially authoritarian societies.

Hoping to corroborate those assertions, this book will now turn to the subject of the Judeo-Christian scripture. How the Bible itself may be resolved to the skeptical mind is ultimately a more difficult question than how to overcome the objections science or literature raise against faith; there are elements of scripture that pose stronger counterarguments to faith than anything ever enunciated by Freud or Sartre.

Before turning to that next subject, let's pause to make an analogy between the condition of spiritual contemplation today and the condition of scientific thought a few centuries ago.

Just before the dawn of the Renaissance, science seemed to be a spent force, twisted up in the ravings of sorcerers. Then came an outpouring of scientific progress at the moment when an observer might have argued that the whole notion of methodical reason was bankrupt and should be abandoned.

Today belief in higher purpose may seem to be in the same state: tormented by disputes regarding what happened on unknowable days in the far past; riven with contradictions; tarnished by attempts to evade the arguments of the modern age.

Perhaps this signals the arid state of spiritual contemplation—or perhaps it is a sign that the dam is about to burst. Stagnant ideas will finally release their grip on belief, just as superstition released its grip on science at the outset of the Renaissance. Men and women will enter an era in which faith and reason jointly seek the sense of meaning.

Spiritual faith has obvious flaws, but stands as the principal humane force that urges men and women to love one another. The necessity for love unifies all beliefs, cultures, and peoples. The joy caused by love can lend purpose to any life. This is the fundamental evidence of meaning.

Part Two

✦

The Spiritual Journey of God

This is like the days of Noah to me: just
as I [then] swore that the waters of Noah
would never again go over the earth, so I
have [now] sworn that I will not be angry
with you and will not rebuke you.

God, speaking to humanity near the completion of a spiritual
transformation

ISAIAH 54:8–10

Does God Believe?

I find letters from God dropt in the street, and
every one is sign'd by God's name.
And I leave them where they are,
for I know that wheresoe'er I go,
Others will punctually come for ever and ever.
WALT WHITMAN, 1855

WHEN WE READ the wellspring of the Western spirituality, the Bible, we read this book as a chronicle of the human attempt to fathom God. We react to the Bible accordingly: pondering, rejecting, or believing these words that seem to tell us how the spirit appears from the perspective of men and women.

But suppose the Bible is not foremost an archive of how people sought to understand God—but rather of how God sought to understand people. We all know Abraham, Isaiah, Jesus, Mary, Peter, Ruth, and the many other figures of the Bible have stories to tell. Suppose the Maker has a narrative too.* Not simply God's declaration of an infinite divine countenance but a *story*—a progression of events from one to the

---

*This is an idea recently explored by Jack Miles in his 1995 *God: A Biography*, an exceptional, erudite book worthy of the honors it received. Miles approached the Maker as a literary character and confined his examination to the Old Testament. This book asks whether God's story represents something genuine and weighs both portions of the scripture.

other, in which the unexpected happens and many things change.

Viewed from the perspective of women and men, the Bible can be seen as telling the history of hesitant human attempts to make sense of divine action. Viewed from the divine perspective, the Bible can be seen as the history of equally hesitant attempts by the Maker to make sense of the made.

Traditional Western theology sees the wrathful, destructive God of the early Old Testament and the serene, compassionate Maker of the later Old Testament and Gospel books as coequal facets of the same all-powerful and immutable entity. Just why God would have executed the initial phase of devastation and rage, if knowing all along that the phase of forgiveness would later come, is a point on which traditional theology is largely silent, except to say that *Homo sapiens* cannot hope to fathom heaven's larger designs.

But perhaps the explanation is hiding in plain sight, in a Bible that describes the spiritual journey of God—a fantastic story of how the divine was at first harsh, but gradually learned benevolent moderation. When viewed in this way, the Judeo-Christian scripture might become a better argument for higher purpose, and might refresh the case for spiritual conviction by suggesting any person can follow the path once trod by our Maker, graduating from severity to compassionate love.

Traditionalism would say God cannot have a story because the divine has always been exactly the same, always known exactly what comes next, always existed in a supernatural continuum in which past and future are interchangeable. Calvin, for instance, pronounced God both changeless and unchangeable. Aquinas declared the Maker *Qui Est*—He Who Is—omniscient, omnipotent, infinite in every sense, immutable. If such things are assumed about the divine, then there is nothing else to say. God simply acts according to a plan laid down at the beginning of time, and human beings respond: the only story is how people learn about the Maker's requirements, and how they appeal to heaven for leniency.

Yet taken on its own terms, the Bible presents a different picture from the one that traditionalism assumes. For example, despite the popular assumption that the Bible calls God omnipotent, only a few verses, beyond the creation account, attribute ultimate qualities to the Maker; and no biblical passages declare God all-powerful or able to see, much less control, the future. (The next chapter provides details on this point.) Roughly half of the Judeo-Christian scripture elaborately describes a divinity who makes mistakes and errors of judgment; who cannot always bring about desired ends, no matter how much power is brought to play; and who becomes swept up in wrenching spiritual transformations.

Traditionalism further says that the two writs of the Bible were meant for different audiences. The Old Testament is about the emergence of the Hebrew nation, and primarily binds Judaism. The New Testament is about how Hebrew ideas were amended into Christianity, and primarily binds that faith. Though either testament may be of intellectual interest to anyone, each is intended to focus narrowly on a particular subset of society.

That is surely the human perspective on scripture, emphasizing, as human perspectives do, those interpretations that lead to conflict. But when the testaments are viewed from the divine perspective, as if they told a story about God, the picture changes. The Old Testament becomes the account of what happened when the Maker was in spiritual turmoil; the New Testament, the account of what happened when God found spiritual peace. Reading the Bible from the Maker's perspective discards the contentious Jewish-Christian distinction and renders all books of scripture ecumenical: as the chronicle of how God learned constructive spirituality and how each of us, regardless of denomination, might do the same.

No ASPECT OF FAITH challenges faith more than the scriptures themselves. Murder, rape, and atrocity are standard biblical elements, with the innocent slaughtered not just by the evil but by *believers*. Military conquest is promoted. Women are treated as inconsequential or as chattel. Slavery is condoned.[1] (Often cited in southern states during the Civil War era, scriptural nods to slavery are an example of how one may shrink faith to fit the smallness of one's mind.) Children are condemned for the sins of their parents; fathers told to abandon their families; the helpless cursed and slain. It is only because few people, even regular churchgoers, ever read more than small portions of the Bible that organized religion does not have mass defections caused by scripture itself. At face value, portions of the Judeo-Christian holy writ are awful enough to cause the faithful to undergo reverse conversions.

More unsettling than biblical violence is the portrait of the Maker that scripture presents. Far from a benign figure, the God of much of the Bible is fierce and vindictive, insensible to poverty, not particularly concerned with righting wrongs, disturbingly eager to punish, and quite willing to kill the helpless. In all the literature of postmodern cynicism exists nothing so chilling as the God of the early Bible. Compared to the Maker of the early monotheist writ, Sartre was a Jehovah's Witness.

Should the unsettling aspects of the Bible be taken for what they seem? Many believers assume that biblical accounts of children slaughtered, or of God in annihilative rage, are mythological episodes or represent psychological history. Obviously there are reasons to doubt the specifics of some scriptural claims, such as, say, whether Elijah was really carried to heaven by a chariot of fire.[2] Scripture almost certainly contains material not intended to be taken literally, such as the swarm of poisonous locusts with battle armor and human faces who appear in the book of Revelation.[3] Beyond that, scriptures of every faith include contradictions and disputed historical references.

But does the presence in the Bible of disputed material mean the chapters-long depiction of a violent God can simply be assumed away? Sometimes it is argued that in order to get around the angry God of the Old Testament, or the contradictions or other disturbing aspects of the Bible, we should disregard all supernatural claims in scripture, viewing the monotheist holy writ as moral poetry burdened by the equivalent of cosmic typographical errors. When scripture is downsized in this manner, its wisdom continues to hold import. But if it's true that the Maker is just a literary character, or that the metaphysical events of the Bible are imagined—if God's voice truly has never been heard on Earth—then we ought to close the churches, mulch the hymnals, and direct our attention to becoming ethical atheists. Scripture that is only poetry or legend might still form the sociological basis of religions, but there would be no point in treating such a work as canon, much less actually believing any monotheist spirituality that calls on the unseen.

Thought through, what really ought to engage contemplation is the prospect that the Maker's story is genuine and most supernatural events of scripture are true. If God really did kill almost every person and animal on Earth in a flood, or really did massacre those blameless Egyptian babies on Passover night, what does this tell us about the divine?[4] Or if a few blind were miraculously given sight, what message is conveyed to the majority of sightless left unaided?

It is against God's interest that we believe many supernatural events of scripture really occurred, because many suggest that God is vengeful or even sinister. The Maker would be more plausible and more persuasive without the Bible's descriptions of celestial misbehavior. This ought to make us wonder just what those biblical accounts of supernatural errors and hostility are trying to tell us—what we could learn about God's journey if we worked from the assumption that scripture records the divine's struggles, warts and all.

Traditionalism sometimes assumes that the purpose of scriptural accounts of divine destruction is to frighten humanity into righteousness. If so this tactic has not worked. What if, instead, the purpose of such accounts is to show us the spiritual journey of God? In that case, working from the assumption that scripture is genuine would have a liberating effect—for if the events of God's moral enlightenment were real, so too then is the revolutionary message of faith.

HERE IN OUTLINE FORM is God's spiritual journey, the specifics to be explored in the next few chapters:

The Maker begins the Old Testament stern but confident, expecting the best at the Garden. Immediately things go wrong. God responds first with anger, then with an unforgiving desire to wipe out life. After the deluge the Maker experiences remorse, realizing that creation was nearly brought to a close. As the Noachian age recedes, God offers humanity a limited amnesty with many loopholes. In the first "covenant" between the Maker and people, it is promised that heaven will never again exterminate Earth. Otherwise divine anger remains.

The Maker remains in a state of conflict with women and men. God first kills Egyptians, then kills elements of the Hebrew chosen, then kills the military enemies of the Hebrew nation. Often God spares no one, not even the aged, women, or children. The Maker intensely desires worship, and intensely objects to any heterodoxy: people are slain or tormented for the slightest dalliance with idols. At this stage events are fantastic and flashy: parted seas, instantaneous plagues, angels with swords, shouting matches between the Maker and the made. But if you're looking for love, you're looking in the wrong place. Within the first dozen or so books of Judeo-Christian scripture, references to divine retribution are frequent, mentions of divine affection rare.

Through the flight from Egypt and the early centuries of military conquest in the Promised Land, the Maker seems to strive to be what people then expected of deities: showy, demanding, a seeker of Absolute control. Perhaps at this stage God really wanted to assert power; or perhaps the Maker was attempting to be seen in ways men and women would recognize. The result is a God much like the kings and Pharaohs of the era—vindictive, self-obsessed, insensible to poverty and injustice.

Sometime following the centuries of supernatural military atrocities in the Promised Land, which kill thousands but still fail in the sense that Israel remains neither militarily secure nor devout, the Maker becomes introspective. Might and dictum lose their appeal; the divine conscience begins to ache. Having spent centuries attempting to be the domineering Absolute ancient times expected, the Maker now becomes something totally unexpected.

The transforming God asks for substantial change in the character of worship: ostentatious displays such as the sacrifice of animals, previously encouraged, are condemned. God's prophets, formerly militaristic and obsessed with the status quo, begin to speak of the circumstances of the poor and to denounce injustice. The new prophets censure the priestly elite; they even criticize organized religion itself, advocating instead personal relationships with the Maker.

Around this time, supernaturally sponsored warfare concludes, never to resume. In fact, all miracles stop. Divine anger seems to drain away, as the Maker achieves new understanding. The language of heaven becomes tender, God learning to converse softly with women and men. Another agreement between humanity and the divine is offered, this time a covenant of peace: God promises to lay aside the divine wrath forever. A remarkable admission is made when God "repents" to men and women for causing them sorrow.

Divine interest in religion as an institution goes into sharp decline, as the Maker begins to desire something very different from adulation. Requirements for worship almost vanish: by the standards of the age, it can seem that God no longer believes. For the first time God speaks of love, reconciliation, and justice for the dispossessed. This does not mean faith has become a feel-good exercise, as hard tests are still imposed. But now the tests concern morality and the development of the soul, rather than religious formality. Heaven asks for allegiance rather than demanding it.

To understand the next part of the story it doesn't matter whether Jesus was divine or merely a voice for the divine, what matters is the message encoded in Christ's actions. When Jesus appears on Earth, briefly the application of supernatural power resumes. Rather than being expansive and flashy, miracles of the last phase are small and personal: the sick healed, the hungry fed. After Jesus delivers his message, the Maker engages in an action that in conceptual terms was stunning to the ancients, though the context is forgotten now: God offers a sacrifice, reversing the pattern of religion to that point. Through most of ancient religious history, people made sacrifices to heaven; at Calvary, the sacrifice flowed from God to people. Again the institutional question of exactly who Jesus was is not material to this point, because regardless of whether God thought Christianity would ever come about, the notion of heaven making an offering of atonement to people is a theological blockbuster, suggesting a profound rite of passage on the Maker's part.

God concludes the Judeo-Christian testaments by extending unlimited clemency to all persons without conditions. This is the third of three covenants the Bible records: the first a highly qualified, almost legalistic pledge that God will not wipe out humanity; the second a more general promise that God will forswear hostility; the third an unconditional warrant of total forgiveness. God once again believes, only this time in a vision of universal compassion.

This spiritual journey undertaken by God shows a wondrous progression from turbulence to peace, from impetuosity to wisdom, from religious formality to universal tolerance. The conclusions reached—the total embrace of love and forgiveness—are far superior in significance to any conception of physical supernatural power. At the heart of God's story is a narrative of how to learn goodness—exactly what human beings need most to know, in an age of doubt or in any other age.

Unicorns and Lobster

Forgive, O Lord, my little jokes on Thee
And I'll forgive Thy great big one on me.
ROBERT FROST, 1962

ONCE, IN CONJUNCTION WITH MY WIFE'S JOB, we lived in Pakistan. It was before the satellite-dish explosion, when venturing outside the favored nations of the West still offered the compensation of release from television. In Pakistan I spent my evening hours doing what many people say they wish they had time to do: perusing the Bible, Koran, *Upanishads*, the Baha'i *Book of Certitude*, and other founding texts of faith. While reading I would hear the megaphone summons of the *azan*, prayer calls echoing from the minarets that dot Pakistani cities as uniformly as gas stations in the West.[1] The resonance of general prayer lent the impression of reading scriptures as they were read in ancient days: when, if history is any guide, spiritual questions were integral to the course of daily life, rarely far from people's minds.

Studying the founding texts of faith caused me many sensations of discomfort, which I came to feel was the correct response. Spiritual contemplation is not necessarily a sublime experience: at times it ought to make you ill at ease, unless you are completely certain you have always treated others in a way you would be willing to have been judged. Studying scripture also caused me the sensation of having missed something. I kept wondering why I was not encountering passages I "knew" must be there.

Paging through the Koran, for example, one looks in vain for any suras commanding that Muslims make "holy war" or demanding *jihad* in the sense that word is now widely misunderstood, Hollywood having seized on the notion of a sinister "Islamic wave" brainwashed by Koranic mandates for battle. Pious Muslims are taught *jihad fi sabeel-lillah*, which translates to "struggle toward the path of God," not "kill your opponents." *Jihad* in this usage refers mainly to a person's inner efforts to follow the Maker and resist evil; the Koran calls war justified only in response to attack. Of course Islamic tenets have been used as pretexts for aggression, as have Christian and Jewish tenets.[2] But within the Koran itself, the presumed verses ordering destructive *jihad* are not there.

Reading the Bible, I many times experienced the sensation of something missing. Most striking was that a reader can travel all the way from the dark waters of Genesis to those enigmatic seven-headed dragons of Revelation without ever finding a plain-words declaration that God is all-powerful. People assume the Judeo-Christian scripture calls the Maker an Absolute, because every form of traditionalism, from church doctrine to lovely lilting hymns to hi-tech televangelists, asserts this. But browse the Bible looking for the verses that declare omnipotence, and you will not find them.

Don't believe it? The advent of search software for the Bible, Koran, and other scriptures now allows anyone to call up all references on a given topic: doing in a comparatively short time research that, in the medieval era, would have taken a monk an entire lifetime of scholarship. These computer programs democratize theology and demystify access to essential works of faith. They have the special advantage of making it practical to verify what is *not* in a text. The Bible totals 800,000 words, 115 times the length of the United States Constitution. Without some methodical form of scanning, even a specialist could never be certain a particular word or thought was absent. With computers, it is possible to be sure.

Computer scanning shows there is often considerable disparity between what we "know" the Good Book says and what it really says. Here are the results of computer searches of the King James and New Revised Standard Version Bibles, the two most important translations,[3] proceeding from light topics to more serious ones:

THE KING JAMES BIBLE does not contain the word "Christianity," but does have thirty-five references to dragons and six mentions of unicorns. The King James contains more references to "lawyers" (eight) than "religion" (five). Lawyer verses include this gem, "Woe unto you, lawyers! For ye have taken away the key of knowledge."[4] The New Revised Standard likewise lacks the word Christianity, though it cuts the dragon references to twenty-one and makes the unicorns more acceptable by converting them into "wild oxen."[5]

The King James never uses the word "moral," but employs "slay" 117 times. "Moral" does not occur in the New Revised Standard either, though "slay" has been throttled back to a single occurrence. The word "slaughter" is found fifty-six times in the King James, more often than the word "kindness." The word "death" appears in the King James sixty-two times more than "love." The New Revised Standard employs the word "death" 286 times more than the word "mercy." Wine, an ongoing biblical concern, is mentioned 125 times more in the NRSV than "justice."

The King James has only two references to the Messiah, and neither concerns Jesus.[6] The word "Easter" is found only once in the Bible, the words "Sunday" and "Christmas" not at all.[7]

Nor is 25 December referred to: this date, the folkloric European observance of winter solstice, was arbitrarily chosen, there being no hint in scripture about the time of year Christ was born.[8]

New Testament Christmas accounts include a verse declaring that Jesus had to be raised in Nazareth to fulfill an Old Testament prophecy.[9] But Nazareth is never mentioned in the Old Testament, nor are variations such as Nazarene. The Old Testament does contain references to the Nazarites, a Hebrew sect whose members refused wine and never cut their hair. A woman is promised that her son will be mighty if he cleaves to Nazarite vows, and the baby grows up to be Samson.[10] But Jesus was as far from Nazarite as could be. Christ happily took his worldly pleasures from food and drink, joking at his own expense that God's voice on Earth was "a man gluttonous and a winebibber,"[11] a wine*bibber* being someone who never opens a bottle he doesn't finish.[12]

The Bible offers references to witchcraft as fact, fifteen mentions of sorcery, and several occasions on which pagans display supernatural power. (For instance, when Moses attempts to impress Pharaoh by using divine authority to transform a walking staff into a snake, Pharaoh calls forth court sorcerers who merrily transform their own canes into living serpents.)[13] There's even a séance! Saul asks a woman described as a "medium" to put him in contact with the ghost of the patriarch Samuel, who "come[s] up out of the ground" and complains of being disturbed, while the woman frets about getting into trouble because Israeli authorities have outlawed witchcraft.[14]

Biblical verses seem to ratify polytheism. The King James refers to the existence of "gods many."[15] The New Revised Standard makes the reference stronger, "in fact there are many gods." At one point the Maker attends a committee meeting of other deities: "God has taken his place in the divine council;

in the midst of the gods he holds judgment."[16] Such verses prompted early commentators to ridicule the notion that the Jesus movement was monotheist, supposing the Trinity incantation of Father, Son, and Holy Spirit means that Christians worship three gods. As William Phipps has written, "Although Muhammad held Jesus in high regard, he rejected Christianity because he thought it contained polytheism."[17] If nothing else, this is a neat historical turnabout to the way Judaic theology was once perceived. During their rule of the Promised Land, the Romans derided Jews as atheists. The pantheon of old Roman belief could have populated a decent-sized suburb. But Judaism would revere only a single god, which to Roman sensibilities seemed insufficient to qualify as a religion.[18]

NOW LET'S TURN to what the Bible says or does not say on matters that touch on fundamental spiritual debates:

Contradictions

Contradictions pepper any lengthy work, and the Bible is no exception. For example, Genesis describes Jacob as receiving a glimpse of his Maker and marveling, "I have seen God face to face, and my life is preserved."[19] The Gospel of John later asserts, "No man hath seen God at any time."[20]

More substantive contradictions can be found as early as the Bible's opening pages, where there are two differing versions of the creation. In the first God conceives man and woman simultaneously, on the sixth day, "male and female he created them."[21] The Maker inspects the dawn of the temporal firmament and is pleased: "Thus the heavens and the earth were finished, and all their multitude."[22] A few verses later, humanity is inscrutably created again, this time as a men-only club: "And the Lord God formed man of the dust of the ground, and breathed into his nostrils the breath of life; and man became a living soul."[23] Adam commences to tend the Garden, but God decides primal man will be lonely, and so lulls him to sleep and for the second time creates Eve.[24]

Failed Predictions

Since it will never be possible to be sure whether past events recounted by scripture occurred, the exact veracity of biblical history is irresolvable. We can, however, be sure about whether future events that are predicted in scripture later did occur.

The apostle Paul armed a theological time bomb when he predicted, nearly two millennia ago, that the Kingdom of God was about to commence. "Brethren, the time is short," Paul wrote, supposing the end of the ages so close at hand that "they that have wives be as though they had none," meaning the cessation of sexuality.[25] During the Middle Ages, the Catholic church interpreted this declaration as an injunction that priests be celibate. But it is clear from context that what Paul meant was that God's experiment in the temporal world was about to conclude, rendering moot further human reproduction.

A theological nuclear warhead is Christ's prediction that suffering will end within the lifetime of those who heard him teach. Jesus describes to an audience the coming establishment on Earth of a benign Kingdom, then pronounces, "Verily I say unto you, This generation shall not pass, till all these things be fulfilled."[26] C. S. Lewis, a stalwart defender of Christian belief, called Jesus's "this generation" prediction "the most embarrassing verse in the Bible." Traditionalists have tried to get around the reference with ingenious ideas: for instance, by asserting that the disciple John was rendered immortal and still walks the Earth as a representative of Jesus's peer group, meaning that technically Christ's generation has not yet "passed."

Just as a few mistakes do not invalidate the larger points of a book, failed biblical predictions do not disprove the authenticity of scripture: every book extant from the past contains sentences foreclosed by knowledge of subsequent events. But failed predictions do rule out any claim of perfection in holy writ—and by extension they are part of the case for ruling out any claim of perfection on the part of God.

The Insignificance of the Antichrist

Popular culture assumes the Bible predicts that a foreboding entity called the Antichrist will stalk the Earth. Intimations of an Antichrist are a running theme of everything from fundamentalist religious observance to late-night horror movies. Important theologians such as Elaine Pagels of Princeton University have argued that Antichrist thinking grew so prominent in Western culture during the Cold War that the West demonized its political opponents, conceptualizing them not just as adversaries but subhuman fiends.[27]

Yet there are no references to the Antichrist in Revelation, the Bible's book of portents. There is no reference anywhere in scripture linking the Antichrist to Armageddon or similar end-time concepts.[28] (For that matter, the word "apocalypse" is never found in the Bible.[29]) The New Testament refers to the Antichrist only four times, and none of the references carries the suggestion of Satanic force. Instead they allude—without upper case—to those who opposed the incipient Jesus movement.[30] One verse asks, "Who is the liar but the one who denies that Jesus is the Christ? This is the antichrist, the one who denies the Father and the Son."[31] Another says, "As you have heard that antichrist is coming, so now many antichrists have come."[32] In the original Greek, these passages mention only *antichristos*, a word that does not imply mythological force, but merely describes those opposed to Jesus. During New Testament days the world was full of antichrists: they

were normal, mortal, non-satanic people who failed to subscribe to the new faith.

That the notion of *The* Antichrist came to play such a prominent role in the sociology of belief is an example of how far
an idea may be removed from what is supported by scripture.
Shortly after his excommunication in 1521, Martin Luther
began to call the pope the Antichrist, describing him as the
prophesied Biblical beast. Luther could be confident that his
audiences, few of whom ever had the opportunity to read the
Bible, would have no way of knowing how insignificantly
scripture treats the Antichrist. Thus after rebelling against
Catholicism partly on the grounds that Rome was misrepresenting scripture for its political self-interest, the founder of
Protestantism began to do the same. By 1559 John Calvin was
also calling the pope the Antichrist, and Rome was saying the
same back about Luther and Calvin. Many of the religious
slaughters of the Reformation wars were inflamed by each side
pronouncing the other Antichrist, giving an entirely artificial
biblical signification of doomsday to the situation.

Does God Have a Name?

Most people would say God's name is Jehovah. Jehovah is a
word with lovely timbre, but it lacks any scriptural basis,
never appearing in original Hebrew or Greek autographs of the
Bible.[33] Christians began to invoke the name Jehovah during
the Middle Ages. The term's origin is uncertain, but its usage
may have begun as an anglicization of Yahweh, which itself
may have begun as an attempt to render pronounceable the
Hebrew "tetragrammaton," or symbol-name, YHWH.

Scripture embodies confusion about what to call the Maker.
Sometimes the divine is *El Shaddai,* loosely God of the Mountain; sometimes *Elohim,* God; sometimes *Adonai,* Lord; sometimes YHWH. (When Muslims address the Maker as Allah,
this should be seen as merely another possible name, not as

suggesting a different deity. *Al-Lah* is simply the Arabic word for Lord. A Jew or Christian could offer prayers to Allah and merely be using an Arabic term of address, no more calling on a different God than a French speaker calls on a different God when presenting a prayer to *Dieu*.) At several points scripture gives the impression that God wants no name.[34] Asked by Moses to state an appellative, God equivocates with "I am who I am."[35] Perhaps the Maker wishes namelessness because names are bestowed by parents, and according to theology the monotheist deity was never born and had no genitor. A hint of sadness may lie in God's choice of namelessness: a recognition that there are powerful experiences—childhood and learning at the knees of loving parents—the creator was forever denied.

Another possibility also presents itself. In her admirable 1993 book *A History of God*, Karen Armstrong notes that at one point in the middle Old Testament, the Maker pauses to explain that the God asking humanity's allegiance is the same one who was worshipped long ago by Abraham, "as if this were a controversial notion."[36] The God of the early Old Testament age was violent and unforgiving; later, after a spiritual transformation, the Maker became compassionate. Men and women might well have felt perplexed about whether they were interacting with a new divinity, or an old one who had changed.

Homosexuality and Lobster

It is inarguable that the Bible condemns homosexuality; but then it also endorses slavery. Those who today call on scripture as the authority for antihomosexual views presumably would never use the Bible to rationalize human bondage.

Leviticus says, addressing men, "Thou shalt not lie with mankind as with womankind: it is abomination."[37] Sound decisive? Yet the word "abomination" occurs seventy-six times in the King James, on matters as minor as the fact that Egyptians did not raise sheep because they considered wool garments an "abomination."[38] Close to the passage that calls male homosexuality abominable are verses that condemn the eating of shellfish,[39] that forbid the charging of interest,[40] and that declare "Ye shall not round the corners of your heads, neither shalt thou mar the corners of thy beard."[41] It is fair to estimate that more than one traditionalist who denounces homosexuality on biblical grounds has nevertheless shaved before putting on a wool sweater and going out to enjoy a lobster dinner, paying the check with MasterCard.

Not far from the verses that condemn homosexuality are those that prescribe death for insulting your parents,[42] death for being "a medium or wizard,"[43] death for working on the Sabbath,[44] death for adultery,[45] and death for any woman who has sex with animals.[46] (Old Testament patriarchs seemed unconcerned with lesbian relations, but did worry that their women were sneaking off with the unicorns.) Not far from the passages on homosexuality are verses that sanction the abduction of young women for rape[47] or that endorse polygamy—Solomon had 700 wives and 300 concubines, hardly what you'd call a family-values role model.[48] Presumably many televangelists would have strong personal reasons for not wishing to see enforcement of the Bible's mandate of death for adultery. So how can it be that scriptural injunctions such as these are now discarded?

In Judaism, Old Testament passages such as those directing death for work on the Sabbath have been deactivated through rabbinical tradition, most of which holds that the sociological aspects of scripture can be reinterpreted as the times change. In Christianity, significant portions of the Old Testament are deactivated through the words of Jesus or the writings of the apostles, who declare their faith to have moved beyond "the law," meaning the punitive legal system of Moses's day. A primary tenet of Christian theology is that the New Testament amends the Old; were this not so, Christians would be expected to keep kosher. Christian theory asserts that Jesus's ministry supplanted the initial contracts between God and people—including those of the Torah days, written for Moses on stone—with a new covenant "not of letters but of spirit."[49] Multiple New Testament verses explain this as meaning that sins that could not be forgiven in ancient times will now be forgiven.[50]

The New Testament also takes a low opinion of homosexuality, which by Christ's era seems to have come out of the tent, as it were. But here is what the New Testament says on the subject: "For even their women did change the natural use into that which is against nature: And likewise also the men, leaving the natural use of the woman, burned in their lust one toward another; men with men working that which is unseemly."[51] By New Testament days, homosexuality has transformed from an "abomination" to "unseemly." The contemporary Christian who condemns homosexuality as abominable, on the basis of the ancient Mosaic legal code, is speaking from both sides of the mouth.

Of course Christian traditionalists are hardly the only ones who artfully dance around scriptural concepts they would as soon ignore. Many Christian liberals, and many adherents of the new spirituality movements, prefer to gloss over Jesus's warnings about sin and hell. Many modern-day Israelis avert their eyes from the Old Testament injunction, "You shall not wrong or oppress a resident alien, for you were aliens in the land of Egypt."[52]

The Missing Myth

A standard objection to the Bible is that some of its accounts are similar to ancient pagan belief. In the Sumerian poem *The Epic of Gilgamesh*, written perhaps 1,000 years before Genesis, a hero who is warned of a coming global flood builds an ark, then anchors it to a mountaintop when the deluge recedes.[53] Babylonian creation myths hinge on a battle between gods to divide a primordial ocean from chaos into order; in the Genesis account, God must "separate the waters from the waters."[54] In the Greek, Roman, and other ancient religious traditions, women are rendered pregnant by deities. The creation myth of the Baroste peoples of Zambia begins with the god Nyambi living harmoniously with Kamonu, the first man, in a bountiful garden. They fall out when Kamonu begins to kill animals for meat, renouncing his previous existence as a vegetarian: this the god Nyambi finds barbaric. According to Genesis, Adam and Eve in the state of innocence lived as vegetarians. They began to kill animals for food only after the expulsion from Eden.[55]

Yet while overlaps with mythology shimmer through the monotheist scripture, equally striking is the absence of an expected myth—God's myth. As the theologian Jon Levenson has pointed out, the Maker of Judeo-Christian scripture is unique among deities in possessing no creation story.[56] Most ancient religions evinced tremendous narrative interest in how their gods came into existence. The God of Genesis is simply there, no glorious autobiographical saga, in fact no explanation at all. If in ancient days, when people were fascinated by creation myths, someone were going to dream up an illusory faith, inventing the god's origin story might have been the first order of business. Mythological hues of the Bible are counterbalanced partly by this absence of the myth one would most expect to encounter.

Son of God—or of People?

The stately phrase "king of kings" carries an enchanting quality when applied to Jesus: suggesting the world's doddering, egocentric sovereigns would kneel before an unshaven flower child. But the common usage of "king of kings" comes from Handel's *Messiah*, not scripture.[57] In the Bible this phrase occurs only in connection with God or, infuriatingly, to describe secular monarchs such as Artaxerxes.[58] Employing "king of kings" as a designation for Christ is as wrong conceptually as it is in terms of scripture. Few of history's leaders ever bowed to Jesus in the meaningful sense of renouncing privilege to embrace righteousness.

Scripture does use the term Son of Man to describe Jesus, as in his statement, "For the Son of Man came to seek out and to save the lost."[59] "Son of Man" is found about eighty times in the Gospels, in each case spoken by Jesus to describe himself. (Not all gender language in the Bible is amenable to modernity, but this phrase in the oldest Greek copies of the New Testament, *huios anthropos*, could be rendered as Child of Humanity without straining the original.) The cosmic description "Son of God" occurs in the Gospels about 20 times, but usually when others are referring to Christ; sometimes antagonists use "Son of God" as a derogatory reference.[60] Thus Christ's own choice of words for his ministry—emphasizing Child of Humanity over Son of God—places humankind ahead of divinity.

The Scriptures and Poverty

The Old Testament has many references to the insignificance of the average person's lot, while the New Testament offers a passage beloved of opponents of antipoverty programs: After Mary Magdalene pours "a pound of costly perfume made of pure nard"[61] on Jesus, and Judas complains that the balm should have been sold to raise money for charity, Christ snaps back in poor humor, "You always have the poor with you, but you do not always have me."

This statement is often cited to rationalize income inequality, on the grounds that Christ himself viewed poverty as a problem that could never be eradicated. But those who use the quote allude only to the version above, which comes from the Gospel of John. Here is how the Gospel of Mark renders the same exchange: Jesus declares, "For you always have the poor with you, *and you can show kindness to them whenever you wish*, but you will not always have me." Funny how the part about kindness to the poor never gets quoted.

Dysfunctional Families

Nothing ever seen on daytime TV approaches the strangeness of the kinship behavior depicted in scripture: an important point, as it is assumed that the Bible is a preserve of old-time family values.

In one of the Old Testament's earliest accounts Abraham, the founder of monotheism, presents his wife, Sarah, to Pharaoh as his sister. This is done so that Pharaoh will have no compunctions about bedding the beautiful Sarah, while giving Abraham gifts of wealth to obtain the good will of his new lover's "brother."[62] Later Abraham fools around with a slave named Hagar and has a child by her. Sarah, the matriarch of monotheism, demands that Hagar and her baby be killed, and Abraham agrees to murder them personally.[63] Hoping to stage the perfect crime, Abraham abandons Hagar and her baby in the desert, where they are to die and leave no evidence of the murderer's identity. Soon the child is screaming from thirst, and Hagar turns away so that she does not have to watch her baby's last breath. They are saved only when an angel appears and creates a sweetwater spring.[64]

In another story that even daytime talk-show bookers would find extreme, Tamar, daughter of King David, one of the grand names of Hebrew lore, is raped by her brother Amnon. David does nothing: perhaps he was distracted by scheming to have the valorous Hebrew warrior Uriah murdered, so that he can ravish Uriah's voluptuous wife, Bathsheba.[65] Another of David's sons, Absalom, arranges to have Amnon stabbed to death at a drinking party; when this occurs, Amnon's brothers look on and do nothing.[66] David's nephew Joab turns out to be a murderer, too; David covers up Joab's crimes. Greedy for the throne, Absalom drives his father, David, into exile, only to be killed in a counterattack.[67] David ends up weeping in madness over the death of Absalom, though the boy was bent on destruction.[68]

In another heartwarming tale of family values, on the night before the annihilation of Sodom, two angels manifesting as handsome men come to warn the righteous Lot to flee. The Noachian equivalent of gay cruisers appear and demand that the guests, whom only Lot can recognize as angels, be handed over for sex. Lot makes a counteroffer: "Behold now, I have two daughters which have not known man; let me, I pray you, bring them out unto you, and do ye to them as is good in your eyes."[69] Lot is the *righteous* man of Sodom, and he proposes to hand his virgin daughters over for gang rape; horrible in itself, and which in old Hebrew society would mean the daughters could never marry and would be compelled to live their lives as prostitutes.

The Dysfunctional Redeemer

Jesus is thought of as a sentimentalist who asked that the little children be brought to see him. This he did, but Jesus also instructed his disciples to abandon their families. At one point Christ says, "Everyone that hath forsaken houses or brethren or sisters or father or mother or wife or children or lands for my name's sake, shall receive an hundredfold."[70] Jesus further declared, "Whoever comes to me and does not hate father and mother, wife and children, brothers and sisters, yes, and even life itself, cannot be my disciple."[71] One man asking to follow Christ was told not to pause to bury his father who has just died, a severe violation of family honor in Hebrew culture.[72]

Scripture does not say what became of the families of Jesus's disciples—children left without support, women abandoned into a society where remarriage was banned. In the Gospels, after joining Jesus, the disciples never speak of their families again. As Christ shoulders his cross toward execution, women line the streets to lament him, but rather than thank or bless them Jesus calls out, "Daughters of Jerusalem, weep not for me, but weep for yourselves and for your children. For behold the days are coming in which they shall say, Blessed are the barren and the wombs that never bare."[73] Traditionalism interprets this as a prediction of the calamitous Israeli rebellion against Rome that would come a generation after Christ's death. The plain-words reading is that the verse means what it says: Jesus wants women to stop having families.

Was Jesus embittered against the family because he was denied conjugality and fatherhood? If Christ was a supernatural being experiencing temporal existence, then sexual drive and the family-forming instinct might have been quite disorienting for him. Or perhaps Jesus had negative feelings about the family because he was born illegitimate, a deep shame in ancient times.[74] The Bible displays puzzling ambivalence on this point. Twice in scripture Christ is called "Jesus son of Joseph,"[75] the term of address for the offspring of married parents. But once he is "Jesus son of Mary,"[76] which in old desert culture meant out-of-wedlock birth. Mary was visibly pregnant when wed, which to strict old Hebrew thinking meant Jesus was illegitimate even if his parents were married by the day of the birth.[77] Was Jesus called "son of Mary" because of this, or because his father skipped? Traditionalism sees Joseph as a kindly man who patiently taught carpentry to his celestial child. In the version of the Christmas story that entails flight to Egypt, Joseph is on hand until Herod dies, when he accompanies his boy's safe return to Israel. In the version that takes place at the inn, Joseph is present only until the birth, then never mentioned again. In all four Gospels, Joseph seems to vanish from the face of the Earth as soon as Jesus reaches adolescence, though Mary and Jesus's siblings (technically stepbrothers and stepsisters, assuming immaculate conception[78]) continue to appear. Something made the Gospel writers decide to stop mentioning Joseph.

Jesus had other "family issues," as pop idiom would say. For one, Christ's own family fears he is crazy. Jesus grants the twelve disciples the power to exorcise demons, and "When his family heard they went out to restrain him, for people were saying, '[Jesus] has gone out of his mind.' "[79] Christ's mother and brothers appear outside a tent where he is preaching, asking for an audience. Jesus refuses to receive them, proclaiming, " 'Who is my mother and who are my brothers?' And pointing to his disciples, he said, 'Here are my mother and my brothers!' "[80]

When Jesus complained of being denied honor "in his own country and in his own house," he meant in Nazareth, where not only was the crowd "offended in him," no family members appeared to invite him into their homes, the customary gesture of respect for returning kin.[81] Elsewhere when confronted with animosity, Jesus faced it down. But at Nazareth he simply left, the Gospels reporting, "He did not do many deeds of power there, because of their unbelief."[82] That his own family would not turn out for his arrival appears to have hurt Jesus acutely. And though Christ is known to history as Jesus of Nazareth, owing to the desert tradition of associating people's names with towns, by adult choice he should be known as Jesus of Capernaum, that being the city Christ selected as the base of his ministry, after his rejection in Nazareth.

Jesus was not categorically antifamily: he told followers to honor their fathers and mothers, and repeatedly declared that everyone should be loved, relatives included. Yet the prime mover of Christianity, a family-values religion, had strongly conflicted feelings about family: another point at which what is actually in the Bible differs significantly from what most people assume to be there.

HAVING COME THIS FAR on the question of what is really in scripture, we arrive at our destination: the absence of biblical support for the common conception that the Maker is all-powerful.

Computer scans show that neither the King James nor the New Revised Standard Version, the two leading translations of scripture, ever uses the word "omniscient" nor any variation of it. Neither uses the phrase "all powerful" or any direct variation. The King James uses the word "omnipotent" only once, but does so in Revelation, the book even most traditionalists consider subjective.[83] The New Revised Standard never uses the word "omnipotent."

In both Bibles the phrase "all power" occurs only twice: once in reference to Satan, and once in a King James verse where Jesus says, "All power is given unto me in heaven and in earth."[84] In context, Jesus's reference to "all power" means supremacy over the realm of faith; in the New Revised Standard the same verse is rendered as, "All authority in heaven and on earth has been given to me," making clear the reference is to jurisdiction, not omnipotence. The adjectival phrase "all mighty" never occurs in the New Revised Standard. It occurs only twice in the King James, but in passages unrelated to divinity.[85]

The Psalms call God a being "of great power."[86] But "great power" is a very different thing from all power. Compared to people of biblical times, contemporary women and men possess "great power," yet this hardly means we are omnipotent. The New Testament declares that events transpire "according to the purpose of him who accomplishes all things according to his counsel and will."[87] But the ability to act by "counsel and will" suggests that God moves out of purpose, not caprice; in the context of the verse, "accomplishes all things" means "accomplishes chosen goals" rather than "accomplishes anything."

The term of address "Almighty," as in God Almighty, appears around fifty times in scripture, with most occurrences falling in the Bible's oldest books.[88] To the extent the construction God Almighty indicates unlimited power, this usage is the primary instance in which scripture suggests omnipotence.

But does a term of address really tell us much? Through history it has been common for entirely earthbound officials and aristocrats to be known by extravagant honorifics. Kings have been hailed as Excellency and caliphs as Perfect One, but no one supposes such circumlocution proves those in question actually were excellent or perfect. Today male members of the Supreme Court are addressed as Mister Justice; one would be foolish indeed to think this honorific means that the person's thoughts and actions are always just. In Old Testament days the term of address "mighty" was liberally dispensed, often to unsavory characters. Exodus, for example, mocks "the mighty men of Moab."[89] It seems far-fetched to suppose that ancient use of "Almighty" as honorific is a sufficient basis for a theology of omnipotence.

The original Hebrew word translated as "Almighty," *shadday*, does carry a connotation of tremendous power and in the Old Testament is used only to describe God. But it is important to remember that many ancient Hebrew words had broad ranges of meaning. (The Hebrew root word *nasa*, for example, has a primary meaning of "to lift," but throughout the Old Testament is also used to mean to accept, to bear, to exalt, to fetch, to go, to marry, to pardon, and to place.[90]) Sometimes ancient Hebrew vocabulary had both divine and secular connotations. Usually the Hebrew word *'elohiym* meant God. But not always: sometimes this word was an honorific for civilian magistrates; sometimes it carried a pagan connotation; sometimes it was an ordinary adjective. For instance, in an Old Testament verse deriding "the gods of the nations"[91] arrayed against Israel, *'elohiym* stands in for the plural "gods." At the Genesis verse, "Then Rachel said, 'With mighty wrestlings I have wrestled with my sister,' "[92] the "mighty" in Hebrew is *'elohiym*.

If the term of address Almighty is the closest the Bible comes to calling the Maker omnipotent, it is telling that most uses of this phrase fall during the oldest Old Testament books, which employed exaggerated language for many subjects. As scripture comes closer to the present, the phrases God Almighty, Lord Almighty, Almighty Lord, Almighty God, and Almighty steadily fade from use. Starting in the latter Old Testament and continuing on through the totality of the New, all these terms of address combined appear less than two dozen times. And once the New Testament is reached, the Greek original word rendered as "Almighty" is *pantokrator*. This word is less assertive than the Old Testament's *shadday*. It can suggest either tremendous power or alternatively mean "universal sovereign," a phrase having to do with spiritual dominion more than physical might.[93]

Significantly, no constructions of Almighty appear in the four Gospels. So far as scripture records, Jesus never addressed the divine as Almighty, nor ever heard anyone use that term.[94] Christ's term of address for God was almost always Father— *patēr* in the New Testament Greek originals, a word without supernatural undertone.

THE PHRASE "ALL KNOWLEDGE" does appear three times in the King James, but always in contexts unrelated to divinity. For example, from Paul's letter to the Romans: "And I myself also am persuaded of you, my brethren, that ye also are full of goodness, filled with all knowledge."[95] The New Revised Standard employs the phrase "all knowledge" twice, likewise in contexts relating to people, not divinity.

The Psalms declare of the Maker that "His understanding is infinite,"[96] which might be argued as a declaration of omniscience; this is as close as scripture comes to that claim. The word "foresight" appears once in the New Revised Standard, in a context unrelated to God,[97] and nowhere in the King James. The word "foreknowledge" occurs once in the New Revised Standard, and the reference might seem promising: "the foreknowledge of God."[98] But in context the sentence means that when Jesus surrendered to the high priests, Christ knew he would be executed: toward the end, this was something widely known on the streets of Jerusalem. "Foreknowledge" occurs twice in the King James, both times as "the foreknowledge of God."[99] With the exception of these two citations, both of which turn on short-term acumen, neither the King James nor New Revised Standard contains any combinations of words that directly describe God as able to see the future.

In scripture the Maker is unmistakably deemed immortal: all translations employ the formulation "the eternal God"[100] or close variations. The Maker is described as timeless in other ways, for example, "from everlasting to everlasting you are God."[101] But possession of eternal life is not the same as possession of Absolute power. The New Testament promises immortality to every righteous person: surely this does not mean every saved soul will acquire omnipotence. Eternal existence and omnipotence are different concepts, but commonly confused in conceptions of God.

Neither the lyrical King James nor the scholarly New Revised Standard is the bestselling Bible in the United States today. That distinction goes to the New International Version, with more than 100 million copies in print. Preparation of the

New International Version was sponsored mainly by traditionalists, and the volume has been accused of bending words in that cause: for example, where in a key passage the King James declares blasphemers are "in danger of" damnation, the New International says they "must" be damned.[102] Yet not even the New International Version, the leading translation of traditionalist thought, contains the words "omnipotent," "omniscient," or any similar phrasing.[103]

PLAIN WORDS ARE HARDLY THE ONLY WAYS to express a concept. Ideas such as omnipotence or omniscience might be conveyed in roundabout terms. Does the Bible use indirect constructions to call God an Absolute, explaining the lack of direct phrases like "all powerful"?

The Maker tells the prophet Jeremiah, "Before I formed thee in the belly I knew thee."[104] This is arguably the only Bible verse carrying a strong avowal of divine precognition on a point of knowledge that could not be available to men and women. Elsewhere Daniel calls on divine authority to interpret the nightmares plaguing Nebuchadnezzar and pronounces that the dreams mean earthly governments will someday collapse and be replaced by the Kingdom of God.[105] This represents divine precognition but only of a very general sort, since it is not a wild guess to predict that governments will fall. Moreover, as a test case of divine foreknowledge, this verse is at best inconclusive. Perhaps 2,600 years have passed since Daniel's prediction of a perfect Kingdom of God, and the prophecy has not come true, though it may in the future.

Could a verse lauding divine magnificence be interpreted as affirmation of omnipotence? Job hails his Maker as "the Almighty" or "God Almighty" more often than all other biblical figures combined.[106] At one point Job declares to God, "I know that you can do all things and that no purpose of yours can be thwarted."[107] If there is an assertion in scripture that the

Maker is Absolute it is Job, not God or Jesus or the apostles, who makes it.[108] But then, Job's views on everything are extreme; the quoted statement comes just before Job tells God, "I despise myself."[109]

A few scripture verses suggest the divine to be changeless, a quality often linked with notions of omnipotence. For instance, the Old Testament says, "I am the Lord, I change not."[110] But in context this verse expresses the idea that God is not fickle, having long-term goals and extended horizons. Straightforward reading of the Bible shows the Maker changing on several occasions—offering different covenants, for example, or first endorsing and then later condemning the sacrifice of animals. As Martin Buber wrote, the divine identity statement normally rendered as the immutable-sounding "I am who I am" can also be translated from the original Hebrew as "I shall be who I am."[111] (Verb tense in ancient Hebrew is often ambiguous.) Seen in its fullness, scripture makes greater sense if the Maker is more concerned with "shall be" than with "am," since God undergoes several philosophical transitions before arriving at serenity.

Could divine perfection be understood as a gauge of omnipotence? Deuteronomy says of God, "his work is perfect;"[112] the Psalms say God's "way" and "law" are "perfect, reviving the soul."[113] But the original Hebrew adjective translated as perfect, *tamiym*, means "unblemished" or "having integrity" as much as it means "incapable of error." When Jesus offers the admonition, "Be perfect, therefore, as your heavenly Father is perfect,"[114] the Greek word used in the original scripture, *teleios*, means "completed" or "fully realized" rather than "incapable of error." The sort of perfection called for here—moral rectitude—is accessible to any person, the very reason Christ hopes everyone will achieve it. Elsewhere, Jesus tells a young man that he can become "perfect" (*teleios*) by selling all his possessions and giving the money to the poor.[115] Christ means that this act will cause the man to become fully realized spiritually—not to become an omnipotent deity incapable of error.

The Old Testament acclaims the Maker as "the high and lofty one who inhabits eternity, whose name is Holy."[116] This verse is sometimes cited by traditionalists as an enunciation of divine omnipotence. But however grand, the qualities "high and lofty" are different from omnipotence. The Old Testament uses the same Hebrew root words to describe the planting of a tree on a "high and lofty" mountain.[117] No one would suppose this means that the mountain is omnipotent.

SAYING GOD IS NOT ALL-POWERFUL is entirely different from saying the divine is not "of great power." The Maker may well be wise, strong, expansive, able to do that which human minds would find miraculous. God could be much more than mortal while still representing less than the sum of creation; possessed of great power but not all power; able to influence but not control events.

Replacing the assumption of omnipotence with the ideal of a great but not Absolute deity could help point the way to a more buoyant, credible vision of spirituality. People on the All side of the faith debate would not have to keep telling themselves that everything happens for a reason, when it clearly does not—life is rife with accidents, misfortunes, and tragedies sufficient to bring tears to the divine eyes. People on the Nothing side of the debate would not have to keep telling themselves that everything happens for no reason—the living world glows with splendor and purpose, every day producing moments of meaning.

If God is less than Absolute—has experienced problems, encountered obstacles, made mistakes—higher purpose could still be present, even if our tarnished world is situated considerably east of paradise. That is, there might still be something to believe in.

Chapter Ten

Infinite, Yes;
All-Powerful, No

Men reverence one another, not yet God.
HENRY THOREAU, 1849

IT MIGHT BE SUPPOSED that the very first sentence of monotheist scripture declares God to be all-powerful. This passage announces that the Maker called the firmament forth from nothing, commanding into existence the celestial light by which the universe would be illuminated. Surely any deity present at the genesis itself must be omnipotent. If scripture does not declare God all-powerful in direct or indirect phrases, perhaps the frame of the biblical story itself conveys this information.

Someone or something, somehow, did bring the firmament into being. But is the making of a universe necessarily a display of omnipotence? Whether omnipotence must have been present at the genesis moment is as good a starting point as any for contemplating whether, as an analytical or logical matter, it would even be possible for the Maker to have all power.

In the secular scientific model of the Big Bang, no knowledge, influence, or authority of any kind sired the universe. Not only was omnipotence not required: *nothing* was required. The genesis just happened, unbidden and unguided. Creation began with zero guidance or design, a condition reflecting the reverse of divine might.

Of course, secular science looks for explanations that discount the supernatural. But if physicists' current theories about the Big Bang are even a tiny bit right—far less than half right—the genesis was not an event in which a magic wand was waved. Mechanical, deterministic forces must have been present too, accounting for at least some of the outcome. This hardly rules out the divine as an important force of the creation: its impetus, perhaps. But a reasonable body of scientific evidence suggests that natural forces were at work in the genesis of the universe, implying, at least, that this most exalted of all physical tasks was not necessarily accomplished through pure supernatural power.

Here resides another All-or-Nothing structure in contemporary thought: the typical assumption that creation began either entirely as a result of omnipotent power, or entirely as the result of purposeless physical forces. There is a third possible explanation: that our universe reflects from some confluence of natural and supernatural.

Though physicists have proposed highly detailed models of natural forces in the initial seconds of existence, none has yet offered a cohesive theory on the more basic point of what *caused* the Big Bang. Something obviously did: that creation happened is a certainty. And there are few theories regarding why the physical constants of the Big Bang favored our present universe: why it became a stable firmament capable of supporting organic life, rather than, say, collapsing into an inert topography of black holes. As chapter five noted, such theories as exist on this point boil down to an unsatisfying, "Well, we got lucky."

Even the most relentlessly mechanistic explications of the Big Bang hold that numerous features of the universe transcend any reality we can now see. All-or-Nothing analysis would say that beyond our four-dimensional atom-based reality lies either divine omnipotence or some purposeless, pointless contraption of pure physics. Suppose instead there lies beyond our visible reality a creator God who was able to exert a positive influence over the genesis, but not necessarily control it in an all-powerful fashion. Perhaps one of the Maker's roles is to exist through the unimaginable blur of matter and energy that precedes a universe, supplying the thought or impetus (or Logos, if scripture can be believed[1]) that brings the new firmament about.[2] A fantastic perspective? Something inexpressibly fantastic did occur at the beginning of this universe. The question is: did that fantastic event just happen or was it vested with purpose?

Einstein once noted that it should be possible for a system to have both finite properties (such as a fixed beginning at a specific time) and infinite properties (such as the ability to exist forever). He was referring to the universe, but couldn't such a chain of logic apply to the divine as well? God might be finite in some respects (unable to exert absolute control over a universe of 40 billion galaxies), infinite in others (able to exist outside normal time and space).

Traditional theology asks us to believe that the Maker has total power in every category; everything arises from the supernatural. Modern physics asks us to believe that in all of creation, there is no supernatural influence of any kind, just vibrating atoms and interacting fields. It is the median possibility—that the universe reflects both physical forces and higher purpose—that ought to engage us. And along this median it is possible to think of God as mighty and wise beyond human ability to comprehend, yet not necessarily omnipotent.

SUPPOSE, AS SUGGESTED EARLIER, that God exists within the sovereignty of physical law. This does not mean that God eats vegetables, wears pajamas, or has to look up things in the encyclopedia. A Maker defined by physical law might be incalculably majestic; sagacious and capable in ways men and women can barely guess at; infinite in scope and eternal in character. A God circumscribed by physical law might be capable of pondering the lives and hearts of every living being; might be able to assimilate the imperceptible, such as our thought and prayers; might have extensive power to affect nature, including in ways that we would view as miracles. A physical-law deity might be able to love to a limitless degree, given that even mortal women and men have already established that love transcends the physical. And a God bounded by physical law might possess the ability to move consciousness, at death, from the corporeal to a spiritual domain.

Traditionalism counters that physics cannot bind the Maker, because God lies outside the plane of corporeal forces. The more likely explanation is that God dwells in aspects of existence not yet understood. Physical law has plenty of room for the immaterial. A leading puzzle of quantum mechanics, for example, is that subatomic particles sometimes jump from A to C without passing through B, just the sort of ethereal maneuver that might aid a spiritual being.

Assuming the Maker is somewhere within physical law is less implausible than assuming God exempt from the forces observed, and therefore represents an assumption in favor of faith. But if God is restricted by what is physically possible, the Maker would have to accept many limits on power. First let's consider whether it would be possible for God to foresee the future.

For theoretical physicists, it is a kind of game to attempt to imagine whether any form of time travel or future viewing could ever happen.[3] Given the confines of what is known about physical law so far, most scientists would say that no form of time travel or time viewing can be possible, because only the present exists.[4] Contemplation of time movement raises so many paradoxes—if you went back into the past and prevented your parents from meeting, wouldn't you instantly cease to exist and therefore not be able to do what you just did?—it is hard to imagine how the universe could function, were time itself pliant.

The physicist Kip Thorne of the California Institute of Technology has proposed what is so far the only (extremely theoretical) physical system for time-manipulating. Thorne's mechanism could access the past but never the future, and would require the existence of "wormholes," cosmic passageways that pop open whenever needed in *Star Trek* episodes, but have yet to be observed by any real-world experiment. Thorne's time machine would require power exceeding the output of many stars, and might have the unwelcome side effect of crushing the time traveler into packets of quantum probability. Based on this, Thorne has written, it may be that no time-manipulating or time-viewing apparatus could ever be built, even by an "infinitely advanced" society.[5]

Merely because men and women cannot envision overcoming time by use of physical technology hardly means the same goal might not be accomplished with powers unknown to us. But just as physical restrictions seem to foreclose knowledge of the future, theological restrictions might as well. Suppose God could see forward in time. If this were so, as the philosopher Charles Hartshorne has argued, then the Maker would be "qualified" by this knowledge, composing today's actions with future consequences already known.[6] In this schema God could not be a true Absolute: prescience would shackle the divine, forcing the Maker to execute only those acts that bring about what has already been foreseen.

By way of analogy, Hartshorne, who taught mainly at the University of Chicago, reasoned that Plato knew his writings would have an impact on future generations, but could not have known what the impact would be. Had Plato possessed divine foresight, his actions would have been qualified by knowledge of his own future impact. That is to say, if Plato changed his mind about the views expressed in his *Republic*, he nevertheless would have been compelled to write the work exactly as it is, because he would already know, from having seen the future, that he did so. Thus, Hartshorne concluded that knowing the future would have changed Plato from a possessor of free will to an automaton.[7]

Using similar logic, the eighteenth-century theist William Tennent, a minister who in 1726 founded the college that became Princeton University, argued that there cannot be both human free choice and divine knowledge of the future. Divine foreknowledge would mean that people have no options, their decisions "already" having been made before they make them. Therefore, Tennent contended, God either lacks the power to see the future, or deliberately refuses to employ it.

Steps of reasoning enlarge this point. Suppose God does see the future: if so, divine misjudgments become incomprehensible. Why did the Maker put that tree in the Garden, already knowing that the first people would reach for the fruit and ruin everything?[8] Why did God flood the Earth, already knowing this would fail to end human sin? What reason would God have for testing Abraham by asking him to raise a dagger to his son's throat, if heaven already knew how Abraham would react?[9] What reason would God have for staging the forty years of Mosaic wandering through the desert, if heaven already knew the Hebrews would revert to paganism in the Promised Land anyway? Why let Jesus die on the cross, already knowing who would believe and who would not?

HERE SOME WOULD RAISE the "mysterious ways" argument. Several systems of monotheist theology hold that God, possessing Absolute power over events, engages in actions that appear inexplicable but have a purpose only heaven can comprehend. It may be said, for example, that God does abhor evil and could bring perfect peace to the world, yet allows suffering for some purpose that human intellect cannot penetrate.

Early in the history of Christian thought it was commonly assumed that world events, however agonizing, were directed toward a holy conclusion the Maker had carefully laid out, and that it would not be long until the logic of the divine plan was made plain. By the middle centuries or so, when the serene Kingdom had not appeared, church officials began attributing the continuing anguish of the world to this "mysterious ways" thesis. This represents, however, a line of speculation for worldly philosophy, since neither the phrase "God works in mysterious ways" nor any close variation is found in scripture.[10] (Not even the word "mysterious" appears in the King James or New Revised Standard Bibles.) The mysterious ways argument may have had its origin in the sociology of pastoral counseling. Asked by a grief-stricken parent or spouse why a benevolent Maker could sanction the tragedies of daily life, pastors or rabbis would say sympathetically, "God works in mysterious ways." This response effectively blunted the inquiry, and over time became a tool of the clergy trade.

Some theologians have supposed that an Absolute God might stage bits of theater such as the Mosaic wanderings, or Abraham's almost-sacrifice, as a means of imprinting messages for future generations to ponder. But any Maker able to see the future would already have known that the message of Abraham's act would be rejected by the overwhelming majority of those to come in future generations; would already have known that the ordeal in the desert would end badly for the chosen. Divine actions would become not just "mysterious" but inconsistent with the Maker's stated goals.

Plain-words reading is always most revealing, and on this point scripture usually presents divine motives not as mysterious but linear and coherent. In the Old Testament, God offers the Hebrews a straightforward reason for forcing them to spend that awful generation lost in the desert: because the Maker was "testing you to know what was in your heart, whether or not you would keep [my] commandments."[11] God *did not know* if the Hebrews would remain loyal under duress, so a trial was arranged. Nothing mysterious here—yet an action unnecessary for an omniscient being who already sees what the future holds.

PERHAPS THE STRONGEST ARGUMENT against divine knowledge of the future is that such perception would not only "qualify" but actively *control* God.

If the Maker sees the future, that vision is meaningful only if what is foreseen is certain to come to pass. If the future can change, then foreseeing it would not amount to much; what is observed would represent conditional images with no more staying power than a dream. But if the foreseen future is certain to occur, even God is merely an actor in a play whose plots and dialogue are controlled by still-higher offices. If, for example, the Maker knew that the snake would demean Eve, yet possessed no option but to leave the first woman alone by that tree because the bite of the fruit was already foreseen, then God had no free option at the Garden. And how could a deity concurrently be omnipotent yet unable to alter a course of action?

Since this question is essential, let's state it a second way. Suppose that when Moses stood on Mount Nebo above the Promised Land,[12] contemplating that place he would never enter, God looked into the future and saw that the new Hebrew kingdom to be founded in that storied place would be corrupted theologically and conquered in turns by the Assyrians, Babylonians, and Romans. If that vision of the future was *certain* to come to pass, then even the divine effectively would be powerless in the present—unable to do more than act out a script that inevitably led to the destruction of the very ancient Israeli society God was trying to nurture.

And if the Maker knows the certain outcome of the future,

God might be eternally bored. Imagine already knowing all events, for an endless quantity of time; a fate akin to endlessly watching network television. As the philosopher of science Karl Popper once wrote, the Maker "seems to have thought that a live universe with events unexpected even by Himself would be more interesting."

But why argue physics or theory? Scripture itself explicitly states that God does not see the future. Consider:

IN THE BEGINNING, GOD WAS UNSURE. The Maker places two trees in Eden, one whose fruit grants awareness of the distinction between good and evil, the other whose fruit bestows immortality.[13] If Adam and Eve keep their hands off the first tree, perhaps they will be allowed to taste of the second. God seems uncertain about whether the first people will break the first rule. It is precisely because the Maker does not know how they will respond that the test is staged. What jumps off the pages of the Eden account is how little heaven anticipates what transpires there. As soon as men and women enter the Garden, God is surprised by the outcome. Surprise ought not to be a major factor in the life of an omniscient, prescient Absolute.

God brings the animals to Adam to have them named and seems to take pleasure in hearing what cognomina the thinking ape will choose for his fellow creatures.[14] Wouldn't an omniscient God already know the names Adam will select? After observing that Adam is lonely, God decides to create woman.[15] How could a divinity who knows the future not already be aware that a solitary creation would be lonely? The woman and man are warned not to eat from the tree of good and evil because "in the day that thou eatest thereof thou shalt surely die."[16] They eat anyway and do not die.[17] Was God bluffing? Was the Maker unaware that mortals could be exposed to the bittersweet distinction between right and wrong, and continue to live?

Here is what occurs after Adam and Eve taste the fruit, become aware of being naked, and hurry to make clothing:

> They heard the sound of the Lord God walking in the garden at the time of the evening breeze, and the man and his wife hid themselves from the presence of the Lord God among the trees of the garden. But the Lord God called to the man and said to him, "Where are you?"[18]

Where are you? God doesn't already know that Adam and Eve are hiding? Adam shows himself and attempts to make a chatty excuse about his sudden interest in fashion. The Maker replies, "Who told you that you were naked? Have you eaten from the tree of which I commanded you not to eat?"[19] Doesn't God already know the children have broken the only rule they were given?

For their offense, Adam and Eve are expelled from Eden. Standing with the first people at the Garden portal, about to consign them to misery "until to the dust you shall return,"[20] God condemns humanity to war, hard toil for daily bread, pain in childbirth, and personal acrimony. God decrees gender hostility, proclaiming, "I will put enmity between you and the woman, and between your offspring and hers; he will strike your head, and you will strike his heel."[21] Then the Maker offers this remarkable declaration:

> The Lord God said, "See, the man has become like one of us, knowing good and evil; and now he might reach out his hand and take also from the tree of life, and eat, and live forever."[22]

Regardless of whether the Maker was addressing other spirits or using the royal plural in this statement, astonishment is the unmistakable sentiment. God had not planned for what has happened: and is not handling the situation particularly well, either.

In the ages that follow, people will long for a second chance, and so will God. Much of the monotheist faith tradition concerns whether Maker and made can reestablish what both once fumbled away at the Garden. However the progress of this quest is viewed, the plain-words reading of the statement at the Garden gate is that it discloses restrictions on divine power. Eve's reach for the fruit has upset the applecart, and God did not know this was coming.

When the first man and woman are expelled from paradise, the Eden experiment ends in fiasco. With it should end any notions of the Maker as able to see the future, or impose control on human events. A garrison of angels is posted at the Garden portal, so that no one can behold the place where the Maker was humbled by the rejection of the first divine offer to humankind. Yet Eden itself is preserved. Why? Perhaps so that men and women can return if innocence is regained. Perhaps so that God can stroll among the evening breezes and ponder what went wrong.

Traditionalism holds that the Maker knew the Garden experiment would come to woe but went ahead anyway to create an object lesson of human failing.[23] But this means God wanted humanity debased—an unfit thought for any parent. The divine-plan explanation is equally curious because heaven is also harmed by the turn of events at Eden. Adam and Eve are hardly the only ones to lose something important in the shadow of that tree. The Maker loses any claim to true Absolute status by asking for obedience and being defied; loses any claim to omniscience by composing a plan that backfires. And in a sense God, too, loses innocence at the Garden, because it is there that divine anger begins. That divine anger will build for many centuries and later fill the Maker with shame: perhaps even leave God nostalgic for the days of Eden when neither humanity nor heaven had anything to apologize for.

INTIMATIONS THAT GOD lacks knowledge of the future continue throughout scripture. Cain murders Abel. God confronts the assassin and asks, "Where is Abel thy brother? . . . What hast thou done?"[24] If the Maker had knowledge of the future, God would have known long before Abel was born that Cain's blood would end up crying out to heaven. Does God mean to torment Cain by asking a question to which the answer is already known, or does this exchange signify surprise?

Cain and Abel have additional significance to the omnipotence debate because the first murder was precipitated when God praised Abel, a shepherd, for alms of lamb, while slighting Cain, a farmer, for an oblation of grain: "And the Lord had regard for Abel and his offering, but for Cain and his offering had no regard. So Cain was very angry and his countenance fell."[25] (For some reason we never learn, in ancient Old Testament days the "sweet savor" of burning animal flesh was exceptionally pleasing to heaven, although later God would emphatically renounce the sacrifice ritual.) Furious that his benefaction has been rejected while Abel's was praised, Cain lures his brother into a field and kills him.

At this early point in the human saga, the world is uncomplicated. There exist only a few people to watch over, and their activities are confined to simple pastoral exertion. Yet the Maker fails to anticipate that the heavenly preference for offerings of animal flesh will be seen as playing favorites—a pernicious influence to introduce into a family or society. That God did something ill-considered in no way absolves Cain's barbaric response. But as Ronald Hendel, a professor of religious studies at Southern Methodist University, has argued, divine favoritism in the matter of Abel and Cain leaves the Maker guilty of "an immoral act."[26]

Awfully harsh? Yet this must be true under the classicist conception of an Absolute who knows the future—because in that case God would have been fully aware that favoring

Abel's oblation would trigger a murder and begin the human descent into violence. Conversely, if a nonomniscient God did not realize that the divine preference for animal sacrifice would provoke such an extreme response, the Maker would bear no guilt regarding Abel's death, but would later experience remorse. This seems to happen when God says to Cain in agitation, "What have you done? Listen; your brother's blood is crying out to me from the ground!"[27]

Divine surprise, suggesting lack of foreknowledge, is the essence of the renowned passage in which God debates with Abraham about sparing Sodom.[28] This audience begins with God approaching Abraham's tent pitched in "the oak groves of Mamre" and thinking aloud about the divine plan to obliterate Sodom: "The Lord said, 'Shall I hide from Abraham what I am about to do?'"[29] One would suppose an Absolute deity who sees the future would not need to ponder whether to conceal an act, already knowing what would be decided. Informed of the plan, Abraham reminds his Maker that even a wicked place may harbor a righteous minority. By the end of a remarkable colloquy, God has been bargained down from fifty to ten virtuous citizens as the requirement for sparing of Sodom.[30] Confronted with human reason, the Maker at first seems annoyed, then restless, and then finally impressed. Gaining confidence, Abraham becomes so bold as to employ sarcasm at God's expense: "That be far from thee to . . . slay the righteous with the wicked. That be far from thee!"[31] God seems stung by this line: since, with the Flood, the Maker has already shown willingness to slay indiscriminately.

The encounter in the oak groves of Mamre, a haunting forgotten locale, is one of the great moments in the unfolding of human spiritual assertion. By the conclusion of this colloquy, God has implicitly acknowledged that human thoughts must be considered in the search for the meaning of existence. Equally important, this conversation shows that the divine cannot make perfect plans or know the future: after hearing Abraham's arguments, God alters a planned course of action.

A similar point of evidence comes from the Maker's dialogues with Jonah. After the encounter with the whale (in scripture the "fish"[32]), Jonah is directed to enter the sinful city of Nineveh and announce that God will soon destroy it. On hearing this news, the citizens convert to righteousness: "When God saw what they did, how they turned from their evil ways, God changed his mind about the calamity that he had said he would bring upon them."[33] That the populace of Nineveh would convert to virtue comes as a pleasant surprise, so the divine mind changes. Here scripture plainly depicts the Maker as unknowing of the future and revising actions in reaction to unanticipated human conduct.

In some ways it can seem amazing that thousands of years after scripture spelled this out, men and women still have difficulty grasping the idea that God is anything other than an omniscient Absolute. But at least that mental block is not new: Jonah could not deal with the thought of his God as less than all-powerful, either. The notion of God being changed by unexpected events so disoriented Jonah that after the city of Nineveh was pardoned, Jonah flew into a fury and announced he would kill himself, fearing he would be mocked for predicting a divine action that was called off.[34]

IF GOD IS UNABLE to see the future, this should not be understood as any kind of failing on the part of the divine: simply as a reflection of physical law. Asking if a divinity can see the future is a little like asking if an explorer could see anything by looking south of the South Pole. There is no south of the South Pole and thus nothing to be seen. Most likely there is no formed future: no one with any amount of power can see that which does not yet exist to be seen. As Hartshorne has written, "God does not already or eternally know what we do tomorrow, for until we decide, there are no such entities as our tomorrow's decisions."[35]

Contemporary physics supports the notion of an unknowable future in ways other than casting doubt on time travel. "Chaos" theory, a blend of physics and mathematics, so far has upheld the idea that even tremendous amounts of data about subjects such as weather patterns cannot make possible precise forecasting on matters as mundane as how long a rainstorm will last.[36] (In chaos theory, general predictions are easy; precise forecasts impossible.) Philosophers of previous centuries have supposed that by knowing the exact location, speed, and direction of every iota of matter in the universe, an omniscient God could know the future by calculating how matter will interact. Instead the Uncertainty Principle, a fairly well-confirmed postulate of quantum physics, holds that it is impossible to know simultaneously the location and velocity of the building blocks of matter: one or the other can be known but not both at the same time. If something along the lines of chaos mathematics and the Uncertainty Principle bind a physical-law God, the divine might have a profound understanding of the general directions of events, but would never be able to possess specific foreknowledge of the next minute of the universe, let alone the eons to come.

Scripture shows God as unable to see the future in a number of ways: among them are surprise, changed plans, and regrets. Consider this passage that precedes the Flood. Human society has grown baneful in a way the Maker did not expect:

The Lord saw that the wickedness of humankind was great in the earth, and that every inclination of the thoughts of their hearts was only evil continually. And the Lord was sorry that he had made humankind on the earth, and it grieved him to his heart. So the Lord said, "I will blot out from the earth the human beings I have created—people together with animals and creeping things and birds of the air, for I am sorry that I have made them."[37]

God is *sorry* to have made humankind. Such a statement would make no sense for a deity able to see the future. If omniscient, long before breathing life into Adam and Eve, the Maker would have known the consequences, good and bad. In the same passage, God declares that *I will blot out from the Earth the human beings I have created.* But this assuredly does not happen: there will be survivors. If divine prescience were possible, the Maker would already know that the future called for human beings so numerous it would be they who threatened to blot out the Earth. What, then, is the point of this unfulfilled threat?

Here is the first of several instances in scripture in which God will feel remorse, contrition, or repentance—emotions that apply to one's errors. A typical later instance: God chooses Saul to be the Hebrew king, but Saul becomes corrupt and destructive, and soon "The Lord was sorry that he had made Saul king over Israel."[38] It makes little sense to be "sorry" about something that you have known from the beginning of time you would do.

In the "wickedness of humankind" passage above, where the New Revised Standard translates the key sentence as, "And the Lord was sorry that he had made humankind on the earth," the King James renders the same phrase, "And it repented the Lord that He had made man on the earth."[39] The Hebrew word used in the oldest copies of Genesis is *nicham*, which can mean either "to repent" (a choice generally favored by whomever penned the King James) or "to feel sorry" (usually used by modern translators).

Obviously men and women sometimes do that which they know in advance they will regret. People behave this way because they are imperfect. If God takes actions even knowing regret will follow, the Maker must be imperfect as well. The words "perfect" and "regret" do not belong in the same sentence: an Absolute, flawless, future-seeing God could scarcely "repent" of anything or commit any act for which to feel "sorry." But an evolving God might well encounter such emotions.

UNDERSTANDING THAT THE DIVINE may be majestic and powerful yet incapable of omniscience about the physical world offers an approach to the larger question of whether the Maker might be incapable of omnipotence.

In many ways the Judeo-Christian Bible is a chronicle of the frustration of God: of the divine's repeated inability to realize the ends sought. The Maker is unable to persuade Moses's people to abandon pagan idols; unable, despite centuries of supernatural military assistance, to keep ancient Israel secure against its neighbors; unable to command piety even from divine favorites (King David arranges the murder of the Hebrew patriot Uriah in order to steal his wife, while Solomon, builder of the First Temple, spends his old age worshipping icons because this pleases his cherished harem[40]); unable to come up with any enunciation of eternal truth, even when spoken by heaven's own child in human form, that cannot be misused. At no point other than the initial creation account is God depicted willing the course of events exactly to the divine liking.

The likely reason for this absence of omnipotence is that omnipotence is not possible: that omnipotence cannot be achieved under physical law, as viewing the future cannot be achieved. This constraint is analogous to the riddles that Sunday-school pupils use to irritate teachers—Can God make a mountain so heavy it cannot be moved? Can God make a tree so tall nothing could fly over it? These apparently vexing questions are actually sophism, because a "mountain so heavy it cannot be moved" is a non-thing, and even unlimited power cannot make a non-thing. Even for a supernatural deity, omnipotence may fall into the category of non-thing, never attainable. Biology shows that as organisms move up the ladder of sophistication, they acquire more autonomy relative to natural forces. But no living thing comes close to being able to do whatever it wants relative to the Earth. Relative to the cosmos, it may be no different for God, in whose image we are told we dwell.

For many centuries commentators have supposed that the Maker could do anything—including make Earth perfect—but declines to exercise omnipotence so as to allow human free will. This traditionalist view seeks to explain how God could be omnipotent and silent against suffering. Yet the existence of illness and natural disaster deflates the idea that the Maker has all power but declines to use it. An omnipotent God could easily restrain those natural forces that kill people in manners unrelated to moral volition or the preservation of choice; and also kill vast numbers of animals, which presumably are neither good nor evil.

Consider the eighteenth-century Portuguese earthquake whose death toll turned Voltaire against faith. What possible end of "free will" was served by allowing this aimless calamity to claim innocent villagers and their children? Events like earthquakes slay the righteous and the ignominious indiscriminately, just as illnesses make no good-bad distinction among victims. And much as human beings generate evil toward each other, illnesses and natural disasters are the primary cause of earthly suffering. Around 60 million people have been killed in twentieth-century wars, a horrible testament to human depravity; through the same period about three billion people, or 50 times as many, have died from diseases, the existence of which do not serve free will in any way.[41] In the last decade an average of 22,000 people per year have been murdered in the United States, another depraved result for which human evil can be blamed. Through the same period about three times as many Americans annually have died in accidents, and most accidents are just that—strings of value-neutral happenstance unrelated to separating the good from the bad.

If an omnipotent, all-knowing divinity existed, that being could protect Earth from diseases, natural disasters, and accidents without placing any restraint on exercise of free choice. An Absolute should be able to regulate tectonic plates such that they do not shift beneath populous areas; be able to manipulate upper-altitude winds such that tropical storms do not gather into cyclones; be able to adjust viruses so they do not mutate into lethal agents; execute other actions that would dramatically decrease the suffering of the world yet allow women and men full grant of moral choice.

A world without earthquakes, floods, disease, or plane crashes might still be a perilous place—one of rapes, repressions, wars, and other evils wrought by free will—but there would be no more indiscriminate, means-nothing demise. Divine intervention to end disease, natural disaster, and accidents would fit easily into a free-will sphere. After all, Adam in the Garden was no zombie. He was free to make decisions, have experiences, create art, invent things: but safeguarded from natural harm. Existing in a place where dangers were precluded through the intervention of the divine, Adam and Eve nevertheless made, according to Judeo-Christian belief, the most consequential free-will decision of all time.

Here, in the standard spiritual debate, an All-or-Nothing sluice gate appears, funneling thought toward two equally unpleasant channels. One is deciding to believe that, for "mysterious" reasons someday to be made clear, an omnipotent God *wants* people to die of AIDS or in tornadoes or in car wrecks. How often do we hear people say "it was God's will" that a relative or friend die young? A figure of speech, to be sure, but taken at face value, one that means an Absolute deity actively desires certain tragedies: roughly what organized religion says on this point.[42] The only other avenue of escape from the All-or-Nothing structure on this point is to renounce belief as a fraud, assuming that men and women die terrible deaths because no higher being cares or ever will.

But shaking free of classicist assumptions leaves a third possibility, that of a God who is real but less than omnipotent. Perhaps it is simply not possible for a large planet to move around a star, with heat rising up from the radioactive decay of its spinning core, without plates of rock occasionally shifting and shaking the surface. Perhaps it is simply not possible for weather cycles to provide rain for crops and wind for sails without fronts occasionally aligning into hurricanes. Perhaps it is simply not possible to have the miraculous complex gift of organic biology without cells occasionally malfunctioning into sickness. Perhaps there may be some genuine being who carries the ideal of higher purpose, but whose magnificence does not extend to the ability to do "anything," any more than there could ever be a way to make a mountain so heavy no one could lift it.

IF THE MAKER IS POWERFUL but not all-powerful, then the afflictions of history and of daily life could be seen as neither staged theological tribulations from on high nor as dismal proof that life lacks meaning; rather, as mistakes to be corrected. The suffering experienced across the ages could be seen as showing neither a heartless God nor a morally empty universe; rather, that neither the Maker nor people have yet found the means to control the forces of nature that cause suffering, or to create the good society that can be.

The greatest tragedy of human social history is that so much of the misery men and women have experienced has been totally unnecessary, having been caused by other people. *Homo sapiens* furiously generate for themselves many of the problems of life; we need only learn virtue to take the world a substantial step toward paradise. All-or-Nothing thinking carries us to despondency or cynicism on this point: it forces us to believe either that an omnipotent Maker assents to the evils of human behavior, or that no one will ever hear our cries for relief. The third possibility—of spiritual power that is real but not in omnipotent control—gives us cause to hope that morality can best savagery within the human soul, and the course of history turn favorable.

SUPPOSING THAT THE MAKER is genuine but less than Absolute gives us cause to hope, as well, that there may be more divine encounters in the human future, though the time-scale may be long.

Consider another possible natural constraint for God: that the Maker is great and wise but cannot override physical law such as the light-speed barrier. Einstein showed that essentially all the energy in the universe would be required to push a single atom faster than light, and experiments support this notion, making the light-speed "barrier" one of the strongest consensus areas of twentieth-century physics. This limit appears to govern everything, including nonmaterial energies such as electromagnetism. Someday someone may discover a loophole, but today it seems that if you wanted to take one scientific principle to the bank, the light-speed barrier would be it.

If the Maker is constricted by the speed of light, God might seem *sloooowwww* by human reckoning. Why? Suppose the divine is large enough, as a consciousness or spirit, to incorporate some significant portion of the firmament. Our galaxy alone, the Milky Way, is 100,000 light-years wide. This means that if God's consciousness were everywhere in our galaxy, a divine thought originating at one end of the Milky Way would take 100,000 years to fill the Maker's awareness.

Today a leading objective of computer-chip design is to shrink the gaps between circuits to speed up processing. Even though the electricity inside computer chips moves at light speed, and though microchip "gates" are already too small to see without a microscope, the time required for electricity to travel between circuits reduces the number of operations per second a chip may perform. In 1989 the most powerful computer processors accommodated about one million transistors per chip. By 1998 the best chips had been shrunk so much that 32 million transistors could be etched on, increasing processing speed. Chip manufacturers hope to be able to pack as many as a billion transistors onto microprocessors by the early twenty-first century, employing gates that require only a single electron to function.[43] Fastness is the objective.

If the speed of light represents a functional barrier to information moving across computer chips that take up mere inches, imagine what an obstruction it might be to a consciousness stretching throughout an entire galaxy. By our standards of scale, the Maker's mentation may be *sloooowwww*. The thoughts produced by a vast, leisurely divine consciousness might be of singular value: perhaps the means to eternal truth. Yet such a deity would have notable limitations, especially when interacting with rapidly evolving societies such as ours, composed of many small minds working on small problems but doing so relatively fast.

Scripture provides tantalizing suggestions that our Maker is by character *sloooowwww*. Among the enigmatic aspects of monotheist writ is that once, millennia ago, God was engaged on a daily basis in the lives of a small group of seekers in a desert. Since then, with billions more human souls crying out for solace, the divine has not been an active presence. All-or-Nothing thought gives two equally unsatisfactory explanations: either God has a perfect plan that requires millennia of divine indifference to suffering, or God is a fraud. Constraints of physical law might offer a third, more encouraging, possibility.

In a galaxy of 100 billion suns, *Homo sapiens* is unlikely to be the sole thinking race in need of guidance. Keeping tabs on the Milky Way alone would be an enormous undertaking, even for a being possessed of fabulous power. To borrow an analogy from the writer on cosmology Timothy Ferris, suppose there were an atlas that devoted just one page to each solar system in our galaxy and that contained 1,000 pages per volume. This cosmic reference work would run to 100 million volumes— more books than the Library of Congress. "Merely to flip through the atlas at the rate of one page per second would require more than 10,000 years," Ferris has written.[44]

Given the vastness of the galaxy, to say nothing of the far larger universe in which it travels, a God limited by physical law might expend considerable time on transits between worlds, or on whatever technique is used to shift the divine focus. This is not to suggest that the Maker zooms around in a spaceship, only that the supernatural consciousness might be dampened by the sheer vastness of the firmament, especially if the light-speed law binds the unseen. If, say, after observing that the initially pacifist and nondoctrinaire Jesus movement had begun to spread through Asia Minor, God had decided to disengage from human affairs to perform a quick status check of the rest of the galaxy, it might be thousands of years before the divine attention returns here. What might be expected is exactly what scripture reports—relatively brief periods when God is present, alternating with extended periods of absence.

Perhaps it is God's goal to visit each thinking culture sometime early in its phase of civilization. On arrival the Maker might plan on remaining for centuries, since with planets hundreds or thousands of years apart even at light speed, celestial transit times are long. The Maker might dwell with fishermen along the shores of Galilee for a while, or watch over the first crops of the Euphrates Valley, or appear to the Clovis people as they fashioned the first chalcedony arrow points, or observe the first cave paintings being rendered beneath ancient France. Cyclical appearance of a supernatural consciousness might, among other things, account for evidence from paleontology that evolution is quiescent for long periods, then accelerates in bursts of development not, so far, clearly linked to natural causes such as environmental change.[45]

But from the moment of arrival in any place, God would anticipate an eventual departure to some other world crying out for grace. At each world where intelligent beings think for themselves, the Maker would attempt to imagine what acts or statements would have lasting positive impact. Communication attempts might run the gamut from triumph to catastrophe. Before departing God might leave messages intended to supply guidance during the centuries or millennia that the society will be left on its own. Chief among them might be an admonition to learn morality and kind accord so that the divine, which must be absent, will be well pleased upon return. This is roughly what the Judeo-Christian scripture describes, and it syncs with physical law.

SINCE NO ONE CAN BE SURE whether the supernatural exists, no one can know whether or not it has physical-law aspects. Owing to this, on the question of omnipotence, reasoning by analogy (that is, from logic alone) may be more persuasive than reasoning from physics or scripture. Consider, then, some analogies to the possibility of an Absolute divine.

The first analogy is the "omnipotence" currently enjoyed by the United States. America of the late twentieth century is to the world roughly what God is to humanity in classicist theology. No one thinks that the United States can do "anything," but its surplus of power, compared to other nations, comes close to the surplus of power, compared to men and women, that traditional thinking ascribes to the omnipotent divine. American wealth roughly equals that of all other industrial nations combined; American culture has more global influence than all other cultures combined; in the post–Cold War era, American military power arguably exceeds that of all other nations of the present and past combined.

But does this mean the United States can impose its will, or even get its wish? America is "omnipotent" compared to Cuba, Iraq, and other nations, yet such countries routinely defy Washington. The prospect of being in the target grids of America's cost-no-object nuclear bombers does not seem to faze lesser nations, any more than the prospect of being hit by a bolt of holy lightning fazed the ancient Hebrews.

When the "omnipotent" United States does attempt to impose its will, involvement seldom goes as planned. Actions may be misunderstood, as was the case with the American role in Panama. Actions may backfire, as did American entanglement in Iran. Despite intense effort, actions may simply fail, as did American presence in Vietnam. Even huge margins of power and knowledge, backed by threats of dreadful retaliation, seem insufficient for the United States to exert dominion over others who think for themselves.

America also attempts to be omnipotent regarding the natural world. Consider attempts to regulate the ecospheres of national parks, as detailed in the fine book *Playing God in Yellowstone* by the naturalist Alston Chase.[46] Various theories of suppressing or not suppressing fires have altered the species mix of trees in Yellowstone, though the point of the exercise was to preserve the mix. Numerous policies on feeding or not feeding bears all share the distinguished feature that the bears decline to stay where carefully drawn plans say they should stay. In the 1990s ecologists decided to reintroduce the timber wolf to the park's expanse, after discovering that such wolves were already reappearing anyway, despite the assumption that they were extinct in the continental United States. If you can find a bookmaker who will take it, place a large bet that the effect of the wolf on Yellowstone will differ from anything that any expert now predicts. Through its Fish and Wildlife Service, Forest Service, National Park Service, and ultimately through its army, the United States government is "omnipotent" relative to the living things of Yellowstone. Yet government managers have proven consistently unable to get their way there.

PERHAPS YOU RESPOND to these analogies by thinking, "Things like international politics and the balance of nature are so complex, it is no surprise that even the United States fails to understand them." Some traditionalist theologians have argued along these lines: that the complexity of modern life is a reason the Maker appeared to women and men only far in the past, hoping to express basic messages when populations were still small and it was more practical to command attention. Think, then, of an analogy to a time when the world was much simpler. Turn your thoughts to the valley between the Tigris and Euphrates: to the kingdom of Sumer seven thousand years ago, long before the events depicted in the Old Testament.

In ancient Sumer the population was modest enough that you could have held a book containing every person's name. Land and resources were plentiful. A warming, agreeable climate was allowing each year to be better than the last. A majestic idea, cuneiform writing, was being developed by scribes wishing to make records of harvests from the newly devised system of controlled agriculture. Many doors were about to be opened.

Suppose you could be teleported back to Sumer, language training supplied in advance: deputized as an honorary omnipotent being. To achieve this distinction, you could take along all current knowledge of science and history. You could take any amount of present-day goods and technology. Medicines with which to cure, making you seem a miracle-worker; gizmos with which to dazzle, making you seem a giver of signs; gifts with which to delight, making you magnanimous (imagine your popularity if you gave California wines to every adult and Frisbees to every kid of ancient Sumer!); military hardware with which to coerce. Take back one modern attack helicopter with guided missiles and spare parts, and you would instantly be the unchallenged deity of the ancient Middle East. People would bow to you everywhere; they would bow to your parked helicopter. By local standards, your awareness of science and history would make you all-knowing, and your technology would make you all-powerful.

Now assume your motives in Sumer are benevolent, your sole goal being to bring righteousness to the antecessor of human civilization. You will shelter Sumer, nurture it, defend it, make it flower, asking in return only that Sumerians practice virtue. Other evolving city-states, you hope, will note the example of Sumer and turn toward goodness as well. The nightmare of human history will be averted. When you re-emerge into the present, you will be returning to the long-dreamt Golden Age: a peaceful world of compassionate equals.

Do you have the slightest confidence that even with the advantages specified here, you could touch Sumer and make it just? Remember, the Sumerians think for themselves. They might misuse your ideas, provoke you to anger, lead you into mistakes with terrible consequences. Are you even confident that, on balance, your intervention in Sumerian culture would be positive, as opposed to triggering some worse sequence of events for world history?

But *aha*, you say: I am me, I have faults, so naturally I would err. God is without faults: the omnipotent Maker could have touched the world of prehistory and made it perfect. And yet we know God did not. If we can be sure of one thing about the human past, it is that the Maker did not apply any combination of power and knowledge that would have prevented human society from experiencing injustice.

Probably God did not because God could not. Even the very greatest may never be certain of achieving desired ends. The Maker might be grand, even infinite, without being all-powerful. This is what scripture, physics, and history all suggest.

Chapter Eleven

Why People Decided to Make God Omnipotent

Man had to gain enormously in confidence be-
fore he could conceive an all-powerful God.
ERIC HOFFER, 1973

REGARDLESS OF WHAT SCRIPTURE or physics or logic may suggest about the character of the divine, Western culture is un-
equivocally saturated with the assumption that God must be
omnipotent: an idea so deeply seated that even those who oppose organized religion rarely challenge this point.[1]

The extent to which the assumption that God simply *must*
be all-powerful came to dominate Western thought is back-
lighted by the absence of critiques of omnipotence from the
heresies so obsessively monitored by institutional faith. Instructive is a thirteenth-century register of heterodoxy compiled by Stephen Tempier, bishop of Paris. The Pope had
become concerned that the University of Paris was too liberal
in its training of divinity students. In 1277 he asked Tempier
to compose an inventory of every known heretical supposition:
the list would be presented to university regents as an inventory of thoughts against which they must guard. Tempier was
able to compile no fewer than 219 impermissible theological
propositions, which ranged from the standard blasphemies to
such abstruse concerns as "God is not able to generate things

like Himself because anything that is generated has a beginning based on something else, from which it depends, and for God to generate would not be a sign of perfection."[2] Yet in the bishop's lengthy register falls no mention of anyone contending that the Maker is other than omnipotent or omniscient. The assumption that the divine simply *must* be all-powerful had by the thirteenth century taken over all spiritual contemplation, even heresy.

It is natural to assume that the notion of omnipotence arose from theology, yet culture, politics, and social science were the greater influences. Forces within the development of political institutions, especially systems of monarchy and empire, had a tremendous stake in the intellectual concept of a single entity vested with all power. Omnipotence thinking began in society and then crossed the membrane into spiritual thought.

THE WESTERN CONCEPTUALIZATION of God probably had its origin in the ancient sociology of the Hebrew struggle to unite a persecuted people against stronger antagonists.[3] No one can know, but it seems fair to conjecture that within Hebrew politics of the far past, it would have been appealing to represent God as an omnipotent being able to solve any problem for the chosen. Most of ancient Hebrew theology derived from the Torah, or the Bible's first five books, which with the possible exception of the creation account hardly depict the Maker as a perfect being. But as we know from our own time, what is written in scripture often diverges both from what is assumed about faith in culture and how religious influence is used politically. Seeking obedience and courage from factions that had never been well organized, Hebrew leaders of the far past might have had a robust interest in speaking of God as an omnipotent being.

Ancient Greek thought had many interpretations of the divine, some for and some opposed to omnipotence theory, but

the main current of Greek philosophy favored Absolute notions. For instance, stoicism denied the existence of human
freedom, depicting all outcomes as controlled by omnipotent
forces. To Greek thinkers generally, not only the Maker but
creation itself was immutable. Stars would shine forever, lighting a static universe; new species would never arise, nor present ones fall extinct; physical objects might be rearranged, but
the constituents of matter itself would exist endlessly.[4]

For its part Christianity would begin as a rebellion against
the status quo, especially its materialism and privilege, only
to be subsumed in the year 313 into the power structure of
an imperial Roman society that had long used religion as a
justification of elite advantage. Both the aristocracy of the
Roman Empire and the hierarchy of its Christian state church
found benefit in speaking of the Maker as omnipotent. To the
extent such claims were accepted, obedience to authority
would be more likely. Once Christianity changed from an outsiders' movement to establishment doctrine of what was then
the world's military and cultural hegemony, the invocation of
an Absolute divine supremacy became part of the mechanism
of Roman authoritarianism. Later it would serve authoritarian
rulers in many nations.

Initially, Rome persecuted adherents of the Jesus movement: the apostle Paul and Christ's brother James the Just
were among many executed for refusing to renounce their
faith.[5] When Christian thought nevertheless spread through
the Roman holdings, the young church engaged in disputes
with Gnosticism, Montanism, and other interpretations. As
Elaine Pagels pointed out in her seminal work, *The Gnostic Gospels*, the Christian church at first liberally embraced many
views, but became rigid as it grew into an institution.[6] Officials such as the third-century bishop Irenaeus tried to repel
Gnostic thought by asserting that anyone who deviated from
institutional Christianity would be denied salvation.[7] To back

such contentions, Irenaeus spoke of God as an all-powerful being of whom only a single view was possible.

Once Constantine converted the Roman Empire to the Christian faith, the political value of an omnipotent Maker appreciated significantly. The proximate cause of the conversion was Constantine's victory at the battle of Milvian Bridge, in the year 312, over the army of a rival for the emperor's dais.[8] The night before that engagement, Constantine told his soldiers that he had seen a flaming crucifix in the sky, a portent that victory would be theirs if they fought under the cross. Because Christian sentiment was in crescendo within the Empire—followers of Jesus were admired as principled, unafraid of death, and incorruptible, the latter being the highest personal virtue in the Roman age—the troops roared in approval. This concurrence made a considerable impression on Constantine.[9]

Following the religious conversion of the Empire, Constantine's next cause was the transformation of Rome into an absolute state. Tensions between republican and imperial government were a running theme of Roman history, and Constantine was hardly the only emperor to crave total supremacy: Julius Caesar spent much of his life fighting for dictatorship. But it was Constantine who converted the world's leading power from a polytheist religion with many approximately equal gods to a monotheist faith asserting that one single divinity possessed all power and knowledge. And Constantine sought, himself, the political equivalent of omnipotence.

As regents and sovereigns of many nations, Constantine's progeny would grasp that a theology of omnipotence, asserting the universe to be ordered under an Absolute ruler with all power, could be turned to advantage as an argument for an autocratic state. If the Maker is an Absolute in active control of world events, then God must have chosen whoever wears

the crown and must have intended the favored classes to receive their positions. If the Maker were Absolute, and the state
were affiliated, reformers who opposed the powers that be
would not be arguing only against the politically entrenched.
They would be arguing against *God*. Such reasoning started
the benign Christian faith down the road toward being an in-
strument of state control, a purpose for which political assumptions of omnipotence became central.

SYMBOLIC OF HOW OMNIPOTENCE THEORY became tangled up
with political sociology is a seemingly tertiary event, the
Council of Nicaea, held in 325. Churchgoers may recognize
this name through the Nicene Creed, written at the council
and still recited by several denominations.

Nicaea was Christianity's first conclave as a state religion.
The conference was called to settle a theoretical dispute about
whether Christ was of the same "substance" as the Maker, a
topic of chronic religious discord in the early centuries. The
newly entrenched church hierarchy was embarrassed by public
conflict with a priest named Arius over such fine points as
whether it was correct to speak of Jesus as "in" God or "of"
God. At Nicaea the bishops decreed Christ and the Maker
equivalent, granting Jesus the status of preexistent divinity.[10]
This and subsequent church councils issued elaborate exegeses
that downplayed the simple moral teachings of Jesus in favor
of complicated new church dogmatics; often the ideas endorsed
drew on Plato, whose dense and confuted claims about spirituality seemed tailor-made for incorporation into stifling doctrine.[11] At Nicaea, canon became a contrivance for enforcing
the privileged status of religious officialdom. The historian
Garry Wills has summed the situation exquisitely:

Finding the doctrines of Christ leveled to every understanding
and too plain to need explanation, the [early] Christian priest-

hood saw in the mysticisms of Plato materials with which to build up an artificial system which might, from its indistinctness, admit everlasting controversy, give employment to their order, and introduce to it profit, power and preeminence. The doctrines which flowed from the lips of Jesus are within the comprehension of a child. But thousands of volumes have not yet explained the Platonisms engrafted on them, and for this reason, that nonsense can never be explained.[12]

Having intentionally created incomprehensible positions, the Council of Nicaea then pronounced its stance "orthodoxy," professing anyone who disagreed a heretic subject to damnation. The phantasm of orthodoxy has haunted spiritual thought ever since and often served as the ally of authoritarian structure. Hard on becoming affiliated with an autocratic regime, the church had begun to act as an autocratic regime, demanding allegiance and threatening dissidents. The priest Arius refused to recite the Nicene Creed and for this act of conscience was tortured to death in 336. Following the logic of Nicaea, in 381 the Emperor Theodosius decreed that heresy was not just a theological question but an offense against the state. This criminalized spiritual disputes, turning religious dissidents into political traitors who could be prosecuted by secular courts; never mind that Jesus was prosecuted on a political charge of opposing Roman state power. Theodosius further pronounced that the church could seize the property of heretics, granting Christianity, once persecuted for its beliefs, a financial incentive to persecute others for theirs.

A mere sixty-eight years had passed between what seemed like a noble victory in 313, as benign Christianity subsumed the mighty Roman Empire, and 381, when the same faith had been deformed into a reason to kill opponents and seize property for the enrichment of the privileged. Obviously Jesus, in whose name this was done, would have been aghast: any lingering questions about whether Jesus would have preferred to be known as a Jew or a Christian might have been resolved at this point in favor of Judaism. The conversion of the Roman state to Christianity, once taken by the faithful as a cause for celebration, was in retrospect a catastrophe.

The related pronouncement of orthodoxy as a component of faith both granted a pretext to oppress and was a contradiction in terms. Spiritual orthodoxy does not exist, other than in the limited and essentially irrelevant sense that whatever a group of people decides to agree on becomes orthodox for a particular moment. Throughout the history of monotheism, what represents "orthodoxy" has changed constantly. Sometimes it has meant practicing slavery, sometimes opposing it; it has at times meant polygamy (an ancient Hebrew as well as Mormon practice), at others monogamy; sometimes it has meant believing Christ was human, sometimes divine; sometimes is has meant clergy can marry, sometimes that they cannot; sometimes it has meant salvation by works, sometimes by grace; sometimes it has meant predestination, sometimes an open future; sometimes it has meant baptizing once, sometimes twice, sometimes never, and so on. That is, not even orthodoxy is orthodox. Even Orthodox Judaism, Eastern Orthodox Christianity, and Shia Islam, faiths whose first concern is conforming to the past, have changed at least some positions across the years.

The evolving notion of orthodoxy helps to show how people decided to make God omnipotent. Once heavenly omnipotence came to be seen as a useful tool of the state and of institutional religion, it was necessary to bar dissent against this concept. If God is less than Absolute and struggling to improve the world, then reform of the existing order may be a divine concern. Believers of the early faith tradition struggled against the faults of society and called for a different world; the Old Testament prophets Isaiah, Amos, and Hosea were social reformers, as were Jesus and most of the apostles. But if God is omnipotent, then heaven must want things the way they are. For the politically or economically privileged of the early centuries, depicting God as an Absolute was a way to take the reform element out of religion.

CLAIMS THAT THE GODS sanction the establishment have occurred outside the context of monotheism, too. The Pharaohs aligned themselves with the divine, and from the standpoint of illiterate and powerless Egyptian peasants of millennia past, the Egyptian ruling families may as well have been omnipotent.[13] Mayan royalty claimed godlike status, as did rulers of other ancient cultures. At least from the time of the development of the Hindu caste system perhaps 4,000 years ago, monarchs, princes, landholders, and others favored by the status quo have endorsed any spiritual systematics that can be used to warrant submission by the typical person.

Traditional Hindu social autocracy was not backed by any single Absolute deity, but was supported sociologically by the religious belief that a person could not advance to a higher reincarnation without uncomplaining agreement to the current station in life. A *harijan* (untouchable) or *Sudra* (laborer) must suffer now to be reborn as a *Kshatriya* (warrior or professional) or *Brahmin* (priest or landholder) who bosses others. For Mohandas Gandhi, opposing the religious subjugation of the *harijan*, an idea generated by his own culture, was as important as opposing rule by imperial British culture. Through the centuries, hundreds of millions of Hindus have led lives of impoverished toil so that wealth might be concentrated on an elite of landed families who claimed themselves chosen by the cosmic wheel.

Confucianism and at times Buddhism have also been used to rationalize status quo allocations of power and wealth. To this day some eastern governments market religious notions as sociological pacifiers. Traveling through Nepal in the 1980s,

I observed numerous government-erected billboards reading PERFORM YOUR DHARMA, which for political purposes meant SHUT UP ABOUT BEING POOR. The gap between wealth and poverty in the United States is too wide, but contemporary American society is nevertheless a paragon of fairness compared to such nations as India and China, where people are either helplessly destitute or obscenely well-to-do. The Eastern religions are sometimes held up as enlightened alternatives to monotheism; it is important to remember that in centuries of sociological application, their main impact has been feudal.

MONOTHEISM, HOWEVER, PROVED ESPECIALLY USEFUL as an implement of political regulation. Preaching that there is but a single god, it was ideal for social structures demanding submission to a single leader. As Christian denominations became sociologically entrenched, they acquired incentives to espouse the status quo; in this context, they benefited from encouraging the notion that an all-powerful God sanctioned the distribution of worldly privilege. Numerous Islamic theocracies employed the argument that an omnipotent Maker supports the powers that be, reasoning still found in modern autocracies such as Saudi Arabia. But the omnipotence itself was arising from politics and culture, not any spiritual theory. As the philosopher of theology Charles Hartshorne has written, the notion of an all-powerful divine "is largely an invention of Western thought in the Dark or Middle Ages."[14]

For example, shortly after Christianity became state doctrine, the faith began to perceive an interest in military power that might protect its ensconced position, formulating such force-serving concepts as "just war." Just war is another of the many ideas erroneously believed to be found in scripture, but never occurring there. The Bible knows two attitudes toward human conflict: the merciless bloodshed of the militaristic Old Testament, and the utter serenity of the pacifist

New. Jesus's teachings were entirely pacifist: when soldiers came for him at Gethsemane, Christ stayed his disciples from raising weapons, saying, "Put up again thy sword into his place: for all they that take the sword shall perish with the sword."[15] Pacifism was the reason the young Jesus movement would neither participate in the year 66 Judean rebellion against Rome nor arm to resist the horrors of the Coliseum. Once it became part of a worldly power structure, however, Christianity took up the sword, sponsoring the Crusades and raising armies to stage massacres of religious dissidents. To the extent Christianity endorsed violence, the desire to enact the theory of omnipotence had infected the church itself.

As it grew, institutional Christianity seemed concerned with discouraging women and men from discovering the lack of scriptural foundation for omnipotence theory. This concern often employed the expedient of opposition to scripture. In the thirteenth century, for example, Innocent III issued a decree banning the reading of the Bible in any language other than Latin. In effect, demanding that the Bible be read only in Latin banned scripture reading by anyone outside the elites of society. This might have seemed an especially incongruous restriction since neither testament was originally written in Latin, a language spoken by few biblical figures. William Tyndale, who in 1526 translated the New Testament into English, was in 1536 declared a heretic and burned. His crime? Making it possible for typical men and women to read the scriptures for themselves.[16] Another Middle Ages pope, Paul IV, would in 1559 forbid anyone outside the formal church hierarchy from printing or distributing Bibles: a rule that would have broken the hearts of the early Christians, one of whose causes was to place what they called "the good news" into as many hands as possible. When in 1599 the Vatican published its first *Index of Forbidden Books*, listed among the forbidden was the Bible itself, in English translation.[17]

An obvious motive for attempts to discourage access to the Bible was institutional Christianity's fear that parishioners would realize that scripture never mentions church-favored concepts such as purgatory and indulgences. But making it harder for believers to read the Bible had the added effect of helping ingrain into Western culture the notion that God is all-powerful, the restrictions against scripture access being applied during the very "Dark or Middle Ages" period when arguments of an Absolute divine were being enthusiastically advanced. Popes did not want laity knowing the Bible says nothing about popes,[18] secular leaders seeking the political equivalent of omnipotence did not want subjects knowing that scripture says nothing about an omnipotent God.

By the point in the eighteenth century that falling printing costs began to make Bibles widely available to the public, the assumption of an omnipotent God had sunk deep into cultural consciousness. What the Bible said was no longer the issue; the issue was what the Bible was assumed to say. Assertions about the Absolute God were so common and oft-heard that over the centuries people came to take as given that omnipotent divinity simply *must* be what scripture depicts.

THE DOCTRINE OF THE DIVINE RIGHT OF KINGS exemplifies how deftly omnipotence theory crossed over into political culture. Divine-rights doctrine was championed in the early seventeenth century by James VI of Scotland, who became the first Stuart ruler of England: the King James responsible for the eponymous translation. This doctrine offered regents a device for claiming that the omnipotence of God flowed through them by extension.

The Bible does contain a few lines useful to despots. One of scripture's least attractive passages is this, from the New Testament: "Let every person be subject to the governing authorities; for there is no authority except from God, and those authorities that exist have been instituted by God."[19] This verse, which sounds like the sort of thing written by lawyers for the Nixon Administration, was an oft-quoted favorite of King James, who used it as part of his case for divine-rights theory.

In order for the doctrine of the divine right of kings to confer absolute power, it had to be backed by an Absolute deity. After all, if God were less than omnipotent, how could citizens be sure their king was divinely favored? King James is said to have commissioned the translation that bears his name when, inspecting one of the many competing biblical adaptations of the day, he found that a member of his own court had scrawled in a royal Bible marginal notes about how the divine right of kings could not be justified through scripture. Stating his case for divine-right theory, in 1609 King James made this remarkable declaration to Parliament: "Kings are not only God's lieutenants upon earth and sit upon God's throne, but even by God Himself they are called Gods."

In effect, King James was asserting that divine-rights theory rationalized the personal sanctification of royalty. Not long after James secured his own throne partly through this doctrine, the "sun king" Louis XIV—builder of Versailles, monarch with the dubious distinction of establishing the world's first permanent standing army—employed divine-right logic to convert France into an absolutist state. If God was omnipotent, the sole entity to whom kings answered, then monarchs bathed in the reflected luster of Absolute glory. The alternative notion of the Maker as a wise but not yet fully realized being, a seeker of truth and reform, was the last thing kings wished to promote.

ARGUMENTS RELATED TO DIVINE-RIGHTS LOGIC were employed by many aspiring despots, especially during the Reformation. Martin Luther's 1517 rebellion against Vatican ideology had the unintended parallel effect of inspiring Teutonic peasants to rebel against their political overlords, the regional princes who ruled before Germany was a modern nation. Luther, protected from papal retaliation by these very princes, did not hesitate to say that the heavenly omnipotent had chosen the princes to rule. When a group of poor Germans issued a condemnation of aristocracy called the Twelve Articles, advocating democracy and asserting that "Christ has bought and redeemed us all, the lowly as well as the great, excepting no one"—an impressive grasp of theology for people who until only a few years before had possessed no German Bibles to read—Luther wrote a blistering condemnation, citing the Old Testament sanction of slavery to declare serfdom biblically justified.[20] As the peasant rebellion progressed, Luther issued ever-uglier statements about how princes possessed an all-powerful right to kill those who opposed them. In one tract, *Against the Robbing and Murdering Hordes of Peasants*, Luther cheerfully declared, "Anyone who can be proved to be a seditious person is an outlaw before God and the emperor, and whoever is the first to put him to death does right and well."[21] Note Luther's choice of words, "God and the emperor." In this phrase both are conceived as Absolutes, with the conjectured omnipotence of the divine flowing downward to the scepter of mortals.

John Calvin spoke of God as all-powerful and unchanging, the divine Absolute justifying absolutes of human power. Cromwell said much the same, as did Huldreich Zwingli, who was after Luther the second leading architect of the Reformation. Zwingli began as a reformer, advocating religious freedom and smashing stained glass as representing a waste of money that might have gone to the poor. By 1524 he had become de facto ruler of Zurich and begun to repress dissidents in the name of the new Reformation status quo. Zwingli expelled from Zurich the forebears of the Anabaptist denomination and raised a personal army,[22] an outrageous act for someone claiming the mantle of the pacifist from Nazareth.[23] Luther and Zwingli met once, in 1529, and immediately fell into acrimony over the fine print of dogma. Their meeting, called the Marburg Colloquy, ended with Luther threatening Zwingli's life. This split the Reformation into the Lutheran and Reformed camps, setting in motion the new theological arms race between competing Protestant visions. Thus a mere twelve years were required from the onset of Luther's rebellion against one set of Absolute rules to reach the point at which Reformation leaders began striving to confer upon themselves Absolute status.

Calvinism would go the Absolute argument one better by preaching predestination, which asserted that God not only had omnipotent control over world events but had selected, in advance, the favored and the damned.[24] What better to abet the protection of entrenched privilege than a philosophy that has an omnipotent God actively endorsing the elite of society? Calvinists were asked to bring their children into the world quaking in surrender to authority, the Dutch Reformed Church having parents repeat at infants' baptism that all children are "conceived and born in sin and therefore are subject to all miseries."[25] Obsessed by the notion that the Devil would send agents to sabotage the privileged elect, Calvinism developed the mass psychosis regarding sorcery that would manifest in witch burning in Scotland and Salem. In carrying omnipotence theory to its logical extreme, Calvinism created a Christian reproduction of the Hindu caste system, holding that the poor deserved their status and the favored deserved their favor.

The pattern of conjecturing Absolute power to the Maker, then reflecting that conjecture back on society's ruling class, came full circle in 1870, when the First Vatican Council voted to declare the pope infallible.[26] Papal error had once been a widely accepted concept, even by Catholicism: so much so that a seventh-century pope, Honorius I, could be posthumously declared a heretic.[27] By 1870, institutions of monotheist faith had spent a full millennium talking themselves into believing omnipotence theory. The world's kings and emperors asserted omnipotence by proxy. For a spiritual leader to assert the same was, at that point, a small step.

CONSIDERING THAT SCRIPTURE does not call God omnipotent, but does offer many passages enumerating actions the Maker comes to regret, it would be reasonable to assume the history of theology is thick with discussion of whether God should be viewed as all-powerful. After all, the New Testament's few, abrupt references to Jesus's nature set off centuries of pitched contention on exactly who Christ was and exactly what degree of power he possessed. Yet though the essential character of Jesus has long been debated, relatively few basic questions about the constitution of God appear in Western thought.[28] There have been many challenges to the prevailing doctrines of institutional religion, but few on the question of what the Maker sees or knows.

For instance, Socinianism, a sixteenth-century Italian movement, held that Jesus had no supernatural power, but its adherents still accepted God as omnipotent. When Calvinism was at its oppressive height, a Dutch Protestant named Jacob Arminius began to argue that immoral behavior could cause the predestined elect to fall from their chosen positions. Through the seventeenth century, "Arminianism" came to represent the idea that God has omnipotent power but chooses not to exert its full sway so that people may determine for themselves whose souls will qualify for heaven. Though they might not recognize the name, most people who today practice in the mainstream Western faiths are Arminianists, believing the Maker to be an Absolute who voluntarily keeps some aspects of perfect omnipotence in the scabbard.

Rare in Christianity or Islam, the idea of God as less than omnipotent is found in some interpretations of Judaism. Perhaps this view can be acceptable to Judaic thought owing to the length of Jewish suffering, the chosen having now endured three millennia without the promised reunion between God and the lineage of Ephraim. Or perhaps Judaism can entertain the idea of a less-than-perfect Maker because it was against the Hebrews that so many Old Testament divine misjudgments were directed. Jon Levenson, a leading Judaic scholar, has written that Old Testament tradition sees God not as an Absolute but a "master." In this reading, the Maker cannot become all-powerful until evil is overcome: "God's assumption of mastery is not complete, and the demise of the dark forces in opposition to him lies in the uncertain future."[29] Christian thinking tends to slide glissando past the mistakes and divine outbursts of early scripture, concentrating on the celestial serenity of the New Testament. Reflecting a culture long beset by the trials of the world, and confined to the turbulent Old Testament, Jewish tradition can be more aware of those portions of holy writ that show the Maker as limited or plagued by error.

AMONG GREAT THINKERS, debates are common over the existence or relevance of God, but speculation on the Maker's character tends to fit into All-or-Nothing boxes. Milton, for example, wrote impassioned arguments against the divine right of kings, which he considered a mercenary attempt to extend celestial standing to a contaminated aristocracy. But his advocacy of liberty was always stated purely on civil grounds, with his religious writings assuming God perfect and omnipotent. The point of *Paradise Lost*, Milton said, was "to justify the ways of God to man," showing that the descent of Earth into evil did have a purpose controlled by an Absolute.

Enlightenment thinkers often turned to deism to resolve their doubts about how an all-powerful Maker could sanction human suffering. Deism's primary Enlightenment political position was that society became oppressive because it failed to follow "natural law," under which God's creatures enjoy innate liberty. "Man is born free, and everywhere is in chains," Rousseau wrote in 1762 to open *The Social Contract*. To the deists, God was waiting for women and men to realize they could return themselves to an Edenic state of innocence simply by following the existing example of the natural condition. But even to the deists, God was assumed all-powerful: silent on human affairs through voluntary self-restraint.

Of the major European philosophers, only the nineteenth-century British empiricist John Stuart Mill directly supposed that God might not have every power, though Mill's reasoning was arcane. Mill thought that since the Maker executed a design for the universe during the six days of cosmic toil, this shows that the divine requires means to achieve ends; and since all physical means are constrained, their employment by the Maker demonstrates conceptual limitations. "Every indication of design in the cosmos is so much evidence against the omnipotence of the designer,"[30] Mill wrote. The very fact that Mill's argument was roundabout—what is objectionable about using design to seek ends?—suggests how deeply seated the assumption of divine omnipotence had become.

The only prominent twentieth-century theory that depicts God as real but less than omnipotent is "process" theology. This school of thought, whose first exponent was Alfred North Whitehead, was taught during the 1920s as a way to understand the divine through the application of reason. At that time most academic philosophers endorsed some version of the Kantian view that rationality could never answer questions of the divine, either pro or con. Feeling under siege by arguments based on science or the persistence of evil, serious theologians were beginning to contend that God could be upheld only through mysticism or revelation. The small cadre of process theologians felt differently. "About the age of seventeen, after reading Emerson's *Essays*," Charles Hartshorne would write, "I made up my mind to trust reason to the end." This brought him to "reject the widespread contention that the deepest questions simply elude the rational process," concluding instead that "ultimate concepts have a rational structure that is lucid and intellectually beautiful."[31]

Process theology began with the rationalist assumption that even a supernatural God would be unable to see the future. The Maker would inevitably be taken by surprise by human events, and change in response. Rather than an immutable all-controlling Absolute, God would be a being whose own passage of self-discovery is to some degree dependent upon stimulus from humankind. Hence "process" theology. Hartshorne wrote, "I am deeply convinced that classical metaphysics mistranslated the essential religious issue by misdefining 'God.' It confused the divine fullness with an abstraction called 'the Absolute,' "[32] making it impossible for men and women to think in other than All-or-Nothing terms. Hartshorne's 1983 volume *Omnipotence and Other Theological Mistakes*,[33] published when he was eighty-five years old, may someday be held seminal.

For the process theologians, doubts about God were enriching rather than alienating. "What we need," Hartshorne once wrote, "is to make a renewed attempt to worship the objective of God, not our forefathers' doctrines about him." But process theology never enjoyed academic vogue. During this century, either logical positivism, which denies the existence of metaphysical truth, or analytical theory, which sees ideas as self-referential wordplay, has dominated the elite schools of philosophy; while in public letters, most commentators have raced to some version of God-as-Fraud. Whitehead, a great name in his day, is now often derided in philosophy departments for committing the intellectual taboo of believing God actually exists; Hartshorne's work is discounted as too spiritual, although to traditionalist religion, process theology is quite radical.

A few other thinkers have broached the notion of a less-than-all-powerful Maker. The early twentieth-century American philosopher Edgar Brightman argued that the existence of natural disasters showed that God must be limited in some fashion.[34] In *Mortality and Morality*, Hans Jonas suggested that the horrors of the Holocaust happened because God, who was omnipotent when humanity began, had somehow lost ultimate power.[35] The scholar and Catholic priest Hans Küng has devoted much of his career to protesting the concept of papal infallibility, sometimes noting that infallibility flows from a presumption of an Absolute Maker that may, itself, be incorrect. In a 1994 lecture series at Cambridge University, the physicist and Anglican priest John Polkinghorne supposed that God is almost but not quite omnipotent; the role of chance in systems such as Earth's weather demonstrating, Polkinghorne supposed, something slightly below total power on the part of the divine.[36]

But beyond the small school of process theology and a few other thinkers such as Brightman, nearly all conventional spiritual debate follows the contours of All-or-Nothing. Once traditionalists, for reasons of political and institutional privilege, made God an Absolute with ultimate amounts of all properties. Today revisionists, for reasons of prevailing intellectual winds, make God a nihility with no properties. The ideal of a genuine but unfinished sovereign striving, just as people should, to find truth and inspire virtue seems suspicious precisely because it offers the hope of humane compromise.

AND IN THAT SENSE the current age of doubt owes its origin in no small part to our disappointment in God: to the feeling that the divine has let us down.

God did not stop the trench warfare of World War I; did not stop Hitler or Stalin or Tojo; did not stop the bombs at Dresden, Guernica, or Hiroshima; did not stop atrocities in Algeria, Armenia, Bosnia, Cambodia, China, Korea, Poland, Russia, Rwanda, and elsewhere. God does not feed the hungry nor soothe our heartbreak; God does not even act to obstruct the decline of belief in God. The Maker has failed to be the all-powerful, all-knowing mainspring we have taken it upon ourselves to declare God must be.

Psychologists caution that a common error in the conduct of life is to establish the very conditions under which we are likely to be disappointed. When people assume the divine must be all-powerful, they ask for something that cannot be, and this impossible God is sure to disillusion. We decree that God must represent utter perfection, and then, failing to see perfection in the world, sink into despair. The result is a wall between Maker and made, a barrier to appreciating the good that faith can do.

In some ways the desire to assume the Maker omnipotent reflects human vanity. Somehow it is not enough for us to think that God is great or represents the ideal of larger meaning or carries purpose and love between people. God must be immaculate, flawless, almighty, capable of everything. The desire to worship an Absolute is not humility but a form of self-promotion; *Homo sapiens* think themselves so advanced that only a perfect sovereign could be mighty enough to sit above us. The real-world God of scripture—who makes mistakes, gets angry, experiences inner turmoil—failed to live up to our standards. And so it was necessary for people to make God omnipotent.

Chapter Twelve

God's Shameful Past

*Happy shall they be who take your little ones
[babies] and dash them against the rock.*
PSALMS 137:9

EVERYONE LIKES TO READ the Bible's lovely passages: the sum-
moning of existence itself ("And there was evening and there
was morning" on the first day); the tablets granting law to
the lawless; the sacred poetry of the Psalms; the erotic tenderness of Song of Songs; the star; the angel who appears to not
royalty but mere shepherds to announce, "good tidings of
great joy which shall be to all people";[1] the timeless parables
of the Good Samaritan[2] and the Prodigal Son;[3] the turning of
the other cheek;[4] sunrise on the empty tomb;[5] the eternal wisdom that love "bears all things, believes all things, hopes all
things, endures all things."[6]

There are, as well, extensive sections of Bible that no one
likes to read. Early portions of Judeo-Christian holy writ are
so chock with malice and the glorification of violence that, by
comparison, the Koran seems as benign as the work of Kahlil
Gibran. An all-too-typical passage is quoted above at the chapter heading. The psalm in question addresses Babylon, which
2,600 years ago seized Jerusalem. Rather than wishing Babylon
would renounce imperialism or see the light or any such hu-

mane formulation, the psalmist writes longingly of smashing Babylonian babies against rocks. From where did the psalmist get this barbaric notion? From God, who in Old Testament days was shockingly casual about killing.

If scripture is to be taken at anything approaching face value, its readers must accept that there was a long phase—perhaps several hundred pivotal years of human history—in which the Maker sanctioned or even practiced barbarism, including at times the mass slaying of children, including at times the mass slaying of *believers*. A significant portion of the wickedness of early scripture was not conducted by people in defiance of their Maker, rather by God directly. Gradually, God rose above violence. But the brutality and error that characterize early scripture tell us that heaven had to grow into the benevolent condition we now associate with divinity. It is impossible to understand the evolution of monotheist spirituality unless we acknowledge that the Maker once had more to apologize for than the made.

Consider this passage, which comes as the prophet Elijah leaves the town of Bethel:

> While he was going up on the way, some small boys came out of the city and jeered at him, saying, "Go away, baldhead! Go away, baldhead!" When he turned around and saw them, he cursed them in the name of the Lord. Then two she-bears came out of the woods and mauled forty-two of the boys.[7]

Elijah, a holy man, turned toward small boys and *cursed them in the name of the Lord*. Schoolchildren die in terror and agony simply because they taunted an old man about his dome. God supplies the divine intervention that causes the deaths.

Whether in the ancient days God actually staged this atrocity is not the first question we ought to ask when encountering such verses. No one will ever really know, just as no one will ever really know whether the Sumerians bowed to statues of Marduk, whether the Baal cult really sacrificed infants, or any such disputed item about the far past. What records exist assert that such things happened, and the assumptions become integral to the cultural histories of the peoples involved. Early scripture descriptions of brutal violence on the part of the Maker are integral to the sacred traditions of Judaism, Christianity, and Islam. Encountering such verses we should not first ask what they tell us about biblical veracity, but rather what they tell us about the Maker.

Like so many aspects of theology, the appalling supernatural violence of the early Bible is normally approached on the All-or-Nothing track. Mainstream religious tradition rarely speaks about God's shameful past, a history that seems totally incompatible with concepts of a perfect benevolence. Bad marketing to mention this, a church leader might say: assuming anyone who has seen faith's dirty laundry, which by now fills many baskets, will cease believing.[8] Revisionists, for their part, usually assert that the supernatural atrocities of the Old Testament have a straightforward explanation: that religious history is fraudulent. As Galen Strawson, a modern British philosopher, has said, "It is an insult to God to believe in God, because He has perpetrated acts of incalculable cruelty."

But from the perspective of the spiritual center, grappling with God's early violence is essential to finding a credible form of belief. Knowing the worst about faith can help renew it, by allowing the spiritual seeker to concentrate on those things that are truly worth believing. And experiencing without flinching the full awfulness of what scripture tells us about the Maker's past is essential to understanding what triggered the spiritual journey of God.

WOMEN AND MEN had barely gotten east of Eden when their Maker turned malicious, devastating the world with the Flood.

Sunday school and Hebrew school teachers love to regale

children with the tale of the upright Noah and his virtuous family; of the mysterious divine blueprints for a vessel no desert dweller had ever seen; of the arduous construction of the magnificent ark, as village lie-abouts stood by taunting; of the elaborately assembled pairs of animals; of the darkening sky and crackle of doomsday lightning; of the frightening passage atop a sea that covers the world; of the dove that at last returns with a fresh olive leaf; of the warm favor that awaits the adventurers when they complete their trial.[9]

Pretty much skipped over in the standard Sunday-school rendition is that God generates this tale of struggle and triumph by killing millions of people, plus billions of animals. Children are told about the race to board the ark as the waters rise. They are not told what the young ones embarking up the gangplanks would have heard: the screams of their playmates being left behind. That one of God's earliest interventions in human society was the equivalent of a thermonuclear first strike should be kept in mind whenever assessing the divine story.

Traditionalists try to explain away the savagery of the Flood account by contending that the Maker had good reason to be angry with humanity: "And God said to Noah, 'I have determined to make an end of all flesh, for the earth is filled with violence.' "[10] But this interpretation depicts God both as short on love and a shoddy thinker: *There is too much violence, therefore I will generate substantially more violence.* What the Flood story really seems to convey is that heaven's initial response to humanity was characterized by confusion. Things did not go well at the Garden: mistakes were made, in the contemporary coinage.[11] Things did not go well east of Eden, where Abel fell and God was implicated. Perhaps a show of force will bring *Homo sapiens* around, force so dreadful no sober person could ever defy its possessor again. To make this show of force, God is willing to sacrifice vast numbers of lives.

But human beings do not get the message. Scripture reports
that impenitence begins anew in the generation that follows
repopulation. Like many other biblical accounts, the Flood
story if nothing else precludes any argument that God can see
the future: otherwise, long before sending the forty days of
rain, heaven would have known that this act would not
achieve its stated goal of ending human evil. Instead, when
staging the Flood, God makes the fundamental mistake of supposing that moral problems can be resolved by physical
force—a viewpoint from which the Maker will later repent in
spectacular terms, but not before a phase of divine Vietnamiza-
tion in which error after error is piled upon the initial
misjudgment.

THE TEARS THAT FORMED in God's eyes after the Flood dry
quickly. On seeing Noah's ark back safely onto land, "The
Lord said in his heart, 'I will never again curse the ground
because of humankind . . . nor will I ever again destroy every
living creature as I have done.' "[12] But this is only a vow never
again to kill *everything*: divine killing in general is not pro-
scribed. Just a few generations downstream from Noah, God
will once more be slaying with frightful abandon.

God sends plagues to compel Pharaoh to release his cap-
tives.[13] First the Nile turns to gore, killing all aquatic life.
Next come afflictions of frogs, locusts, and flies sufficient to
destroy agriculture. Then darkness and an epidemic of boils
arrive, followed by the death of all Egyptian cattle. Next is
intense hail that kills anyone caught outside. Finally comes
the awful night of Passover, during which God sends "the de-
stroyer," evidently a ghoulish killer angel utterly unlike the
sweet white-clad Hollywood cherub,[14] to slay the firstborn of
every household in Egypt, except those homes where the blood
of a lamb "without blemish" is dabbed on the front door.[15]
Tens of thousands of children die.

The whole set-piece of the ten plagues calls omnipotence theory into question: a true Absolute might have simply have whisked the Hebrews off, dispensing with the histrionics. More puzzling, however, is that God repeatedly prevents the emancipation of the chosen. Scripture recounts that after each plague Pharaoh decides to release Moses's people, but at each such moment his heart is "hardened" by God, resulting in a new order that the Hebrews stay. God's decision to use supernatural intervention to prevent the early liberation of the chosen was made even before Moses departed to Pharaoh's court. God had told Moses, "When you go back to Egypt see that you perform before Pharaoh all the wonders that I have put in your power. But I will harden his heart, so that he will not let the people go."[16]

Why does God block the release of the Hebrews, ensuring that events build to the Passover atrocity? Traditionalism supposes this was done as a warning to humanity—lives sacrificed now so that future generations will fear heaven and live righteously. The Bible, however, presents a much plainer explanation: God wants revenge. Years before, Pharaoh had ordered Egyptian midwives to kill male Hebrew babies; when they refused, soldiers threw the infants into the Nile.[17] When the Passover is about to begin, Moses is told that "You shall say to Pharaoh, 'Thus says the Lord: Israel is my firstborn son. I said to you, Let my son go that he may worship me. But you refused to let him go. Now I will kill your firstborn son.' "[18] God made no move to prevent the initial outrage against the Hebrew babies, but does use the event to claim a right of blood vengeance. The Maker almost seems to be looking forward to causing Egypt to grieve: "Now I will kill *your* firstborn son."

There is no moral discrimination in the killings God sends against Egypt. Before the lethal hail, Moses publishes this warning: "Every human or animal that is in the open field and is not brought under shelter will die when the hail comes down upon them." Scripture reports, "Those officials of Pharaoh who feared the word of the Lord hurried their slaves and livestock off to a secure place," but those who did not left their animals and slaves in the fields.[19] The purpose is to punish Egyptian government officials. Who does the dying? Their slaves, who had no choice in the matter.

At Passover the lack of moral discrimination is worst, for the victims are blameless children. That murder of children was the essence of Passover is an ugly fact modern observance of this day deletes: imagine how the Western press would treat it if, say, Islam had an annual festival of celebration of a religious massacre of children. When the children are slain, God does not target government officials but massacres the politically powerless as well: "All the firstborn in the land of Egypt shall die, from the firstborn of Pharaoh that sitteth upon his throne even unto the firstborn of the maidservant that is behind the mill."[20] This general vengeance seems to soothe heaven: as the parents watch their little ones die, "There shall be a great cry throughout all the land of Egypt, such as there was none like it nor shall be like it any more."[21] If only that had been the case.

GOD DOES SO MANY APPALLING THINGS in the early Bible that even in summary the atrocities go on as a cantillation, a long chant in monotone. Some of many, in rough order:

Fleeing from Egypt, the Hebrews are attacked by the Amalekites. Moses and Joshua lead a counterattack, Moses's staff held aloft to provide divine power.[22] After every Amalekite dies, God tells Moses, "I will utterly blot out the remembrance of Amalek from under heaven."[23] The Hebrews clash with the king of Bashon, and again divine power swings the tide of battle. Moses's troops stage a My Lai, killing civilians "until there was no survivor left."[24] God sanctions the atrocity.

The Hebrew leader Jacob finds his daughter Dinah raped by a Canaanite from the city of Hivite. The perpetrator's father, Hamor, proposes that his son marry Dinah to avoid war over the crime. The Hebrews are newly arrived in Canaan, and Hamor presents what should sound like an attractive offer to immigrants: "Make marriages with us; give your daughters to us, and take our daughters for yourselves. You shall live with us; and the land shall be open to you."[25] Jacob's sons accept, on the condition that the men of Hivite honor Hebrew religion by being circumcised. They agree: which considering what adult circumcision must have been like 3,000 years ago, indicates either mass insanity or genuine desire for peace.

After the circumcisions, while the men of Hivite were debilitated and "still in pain," Hebrew soldiers "took their swords and came against the city unawares and killed all the males,"[26] including the kindly Hamor. Then they plunder Hivite and seize the children and women as slaves: "All [Hivite's] wealth, all their little ones and their wives, all that was in the houses, they captured and made their prey."[27] This oath-breaking, atrocity, and plunder are not done furtively; God approves. Later Jacob fears other Canaanite towns will retaliate for the carnage. The Maker intervenes: "A terror from God fell upon the cities all around them, so that no one pursued [the Hebrews]."[28] God says nothing to the chosen people about the murders of civilians, but blesses Jacob instead.[29]

Violence in God's name becomes institutionalized when the Maker designates the Levites, a ruthless group obsessed with privilege, as a hereditary priestly class. The Levites are founded by one of Jacob's sons. Nevertheless, Jacob warns, "May I never come into their council; may I not be joined to their company, for in their anger they killed men and at their whim they hamstrung oxen,"[30] *hamstring* in ancient usage meaning to mutilate. Extended verses describe the Levites' requirements for the most expensive fabrics and jewels, plus a demand that the clan receive the community's best animals. The Levites will accept only lamb or "firstlings," meaning veal; after using the animals' blood for sacrificial ritual, they dine on the meat. Other verses detail the feral ritual for the investment of new Levites, which includes draining blood from a live bull and smearing it on aspiring priests.[31]

The Levites show their true colors while Moses is away on a hilltop conversing with God. Aaron, the chief Levite, fashions a golden calf that he instructs the Hebrews to worship.[32] Discovering this, God declares that the chosen people will be entirely exterminated. Moses talks the Maker down somewhat by arguing that the planned act would cause pagans to make fun of God: Egyptians would snicker about the folly of rescuing the Hebrews from Pharaoh, only to slay them all anyway. Swayed by this worldly argument—essentially an appeal to vanity—God relents about the extinction of the Hebrews.[33] But the Maker only agrees that *everyone* among the chosen need not die. Blood vengeance is still desired. So after smashing the golden calf,

> Moses stood in the gate of the camp and said, "Who is on the Lord's side? Come to me!" And all the sons of Levi gathered around him. He said to them, "Thus says the Lord the God of Israel, 'Put your sword on your side, each of you! Go back and forth from gate to gate throughout the camp, and each of you kill your brother, your friend, and your neighbor.' " The sons of Levi did as Moses commanded, and about 3,000 of the people fell on that day.[34]

And each of you kill your brother, your friend, and your neighbor. Moses and the Levites are furiously killing their own, a presaging of the Inquisition and the Reformation wars, during which Christianity would determinedly kill its own. *Kill your brother, your friend, and your neighbor.* After the massacre, Moses singles out for special commendation any Levite who was relentless enough to slay his own children.[35] You read that correctly: Moses praised those who murdered their children to impress God.

DIVINE-SANCTIONED KILLING continues to distend. Two sons of Aaron make a procedural error involving the smoking of fats on the altar. Execution is instantaneous: "And there went out fire from the Lord and devoured them, and they died."[36] The ark of the covenant begins to tip over, and a man named Uzzah reaches to steady it: God kills him.[37] A boy of a mixed Egyptian-Hebrew marriage curses heaven. The Maker appears and announces, "He that blasphemeth the name of the Lord . . . all the congregation shall certainly stone him."[38] Bystanders grab rocks and stone the boy. A delegation comes to Moses to ask why the Hebrews must go without leavened bread. God answers their question with carnage: "The Lord sent poisonous serpents among the people, and they bit the people, so that many Israelites died."[39]

Later, some 250 "princes of the assembly, famous in the congregation"[40] approach Moses to protest that the Levites are expropriating too much wealth. Moses tells the dissidents that if they participate in a joint incense ceremony with the Levites, all will be well. Moses maneuvers the princes to an isolated place, warns his loyalists to duck, and "There came out a fire from the Lord, and consumed the 250 men."[41] The dissidents' families are also slaughtered: the ground splits beneath them, dropping them directly to Sheol. When news of these events gets around, Moses's word of honor to the princes is questioned; God then sends a plague to kill everyone who expresses sympathy with the victims. The Bible lists the death toll from this sequence of supernatural massacres as 14,700 Hebrews, the population of a decent-sized town.

A scene of hellish carnage occurs when Moses discovers that Hebrew men have been joining Moabite women in the ritualistic sex of Baal worship. The Old Testament reports, "The Lord said unto Moses, 'Take all the heads of the people, and hang them up before the Lord against the sun.' "[42] Once again the Levites turn their swords against their neighbors, this time slaying 24,000 of the chosen. Crowds of Hebrew women come to the tabernacle, begging Moses to stop the slaughter. He is unmoved. The bloodbath reaches its culmination when a Levite named Phinehas spots a Hebrew entwined with a Baalim priestess. Phinehas impales both with the same spear, thrusting the blade through the man's chest and into the woman's breasts. The Maker is so delighted by the sheer creative savagery of this splatter-movie touch that "The Lord spoke to Moses, saying: 'Phinehas . . . has turned back my wrath from the Israelites by manifesting such zeal among them on my behalf.' "[43]

Here again the historical verity of the passage ought not to be the first issue. Whether it would be possible for priests to massacre 24,000 people with swords is hard to say, even if the victims did not resist. At the first Sommes, in July 1916, one of the darkest days in warfare, 21,392 British soldiers died; killing them required the firing of 1.5 million artillery shells, plus tens of millions of rifle and machine-gun rounds.[44] The points that matter are that scripture tells us the ancient supernatural equivalent of the Sommes happened, that believers were the victims, and that God was pleased to witness it.

Later Moses sends a regiment to "execute the Lord's vengeance"[45] against the Midianites, a rival in the Promised Land. At Midian, "The Lord had commanded Moses [to] kill every male."[46] After slaying the men of Midian, Moses's troops seize "the women of Midian and their little ones, and they took all their cattle and their flocks and all their goods,"[47] burning whatever they could not carry off. But when the soldiers return to camp Moses is in a foul humor because field commanders spared male infants. Moses orders the returning infantry, "Kill every male among the little ones, and kill every woman who has known a man by sleeping with him."[48] Women and crying babies are then lined up and executed with God's approval. The only ones allowed to live are the attractive virgins: these, Moses announces, the soldiers may keep for merry-making. Not exactly the portrait of Moses taught at Sunday school. Not exactly the way Charlton Heston played the role.

AFTER MOSES LEAVES THE SCENE, divinely sanctioned brutality continues at scandalous length:

Elijah invites 950 priests and priestesses of Baal to a ceremony to declare an armistice. Soldiers spring an ambush: "Elijah said to them, 'Seize the prophets of Baal; do not let one of them escape.' Then they seized them; and Elijah brought them down to the Wadi Kishon, and killed them there."[49] God's own holy man orchestrates an atrocity under the flag of truce.

After the chosen people split into the competing Hebrew nations of Judah and Israel, the Judean king discovers the dionysian delectations of Baalim sexual rituals. God instructs Israel to attack Judah. There is a "great slaughter,"[50] 120,000 Hebrews dying in a single day. Considerable supernatural force must have been applied to kill so many so fast, as the death toll claimed is about the same as that from the atomic bombing of Hiroshima or the firebombing of Dresden by hundreds of heavy aircraft. The Israelis also "took captive 200,000 of their kin."[51]

More divinely approved barbarity comes when a Levite priest stops with his concubine to spend the night in a city controlled by Benjamin, one of the twelve tribes. "While they were enjoying themselves," scripture reports, "the men of the city, a perverse lot, surrounded the house and started pounding on the door. They said to the master of the house, 'Bring out the man who came into your house, so that we may have intercourse with him.' "[52] To appease them, the Levite shoves his concubine out the door: "They wantonly raped her and abused her all through the night until the morning." Released at dawn, she dies on the doorstep.

Discovering the body, the priest shows no concern for the woman's fate but is furious over a property loss, for which he should be compensated under the Deuteronomic Code. Calling on his guild's skill at mutilation, the Levite "grasping his concubine he cut her into twelve pieces, limb by limb, and sent her throughout all the territory of Israel." This is done not to protest the murder but as a way of complaining that the Benjamites have robbed a priest.[53] The other eleven tribes decide to wage a war of vengeance.[54] God appears and directs the battle, in which all but 600 of the Benjamite soldiers die. The Maker then urges the attackers to finish off Benjamite civilians, who are "put to the sword, the city, the people, the animals, and all that remained."[55]

Afterward the victorious tribes realize that one Israeli city, Jabesh-Gilead, did not contribute any soldiers to the operation. God declares that the city must be punished for refusing to support a divinely ordained genocide; not participating in an atrocity, but *refusing* to participate, was the city's crime in the Maker's eyes. So the victorious tribes send a division against Jabesh-Gilead. Commanders are told, "Put the inhabitants of Jabesh-Gilead to the sword, including the women and the little ones."[56] From this second atrocity only 400 survive. Those spared are the best-looking virgins, dragged away for recreation.

Subsequently the victors feel remorse, not over the silenced "little ones" but because the genocide against Benjamin means Hebrew society will be reduced to eleven tribes, breaking the ancestral legacy. The 600 surviving Benjamite soldiers are told that since no respectable father would give them a bride, they should abduct young women to begin repopulating the twelfth house. But where to find a supply of nubile victims? "The yearly festival of the Lord" is about to commence at Shiloh, the sanctuary city where the ark of the covenant resides. The Benjamite men are told, "Go and lie in wait in the vineyards. When the young women of Shiloh come out to dance in the dances, then come out of the vineyards and each of you carry off a wife for himself."[57] Thus elders direct the kidnapping and rape of participants in a divine festival in a sacred place.

ANOTHER FAVORITE SUNDAY SCHOOL STORY is that of Daniel in the lion's den. In Babylon, during the second captivity of Israel, bad people falsely accuse Daniel of crimes. The king throws Daniel to the lions, but because he has faith, God intervenes and the lions purr. Amazed, the king frees Daniel and praises the Maker; a charming tale of resilience and courage.

They don't tell you what happens next: "The king gave a command, and those who had accused Daniel were brought and thrown into the den of lions—they, their children and their wives. Before they reached the bottom of the den the lions overpowered them and broke all their bones in pieces."[58] Even the children of Daniel's accusers are fed to lions.[59] God, present through the scene, makes no move to prevent this.

Boys and girls also delight in the story of David and Goliath: a small man triumphs over a giant, with obvious parallels to the manner in which the young dream of outsmarting adults. As presented in churches and synagogues, the tale always ends when the Philistine giant gets beaned by David's slingshot, the suggestion being that everyone comes to their senses and decides to be friends.

Here is what gets left out: "David ran and stood upon the Philistine, and took his sword, and drew it out of the sheath thereof, and slew him and cut off his head."[60] The enemy soldiers around Goliath break and run; David's battalion pursues and massacres them. David is welcomed back as the hero of the "slaughter of the Philistines," and with God's approval goes on to become a general, then a king, whose primary interest is conquest. A representative moment from David's later career: "David struck the land, leaving neither man nor woman alive."[61] At another point David wants to marry Saul's daughter. Saul is jealous of David's popularity, so names a bride price he assumes will get David killed—the foreskins of 100 Philistine warriors.[62] David takes a unit of his best fighters, kills 100 Philistines, mutilates them, and brings the bloody heap of tissue to the palace.

David commits so many atrocities that the Maker decides he must be punished, and offers this choice: three years of famine for Israel, three years of pestilence for Israel, or David personally spending three months on foot pursued by his enemies. David, founder of the House of David and spoken of today as a glorious patriot, chooses three years of suffering for everybody else: "So the Lord sent a pestilence on Israel from that morning until the appointed time, and 70,000 of the people died."[63] Somehow in church or synagogue they just never get around to the part about David massacring women, mutilating corpses, and calling down an epidemic on the people he was supposedly protecting; nor do they mention God's supernatural assistance in the killings.

Sunday school teachers also eagerly relate the tale of Samson and Delilah, children always taken by Samson's magic hair and the feats of strength. Normally they do not offer much detail about why Samson pulled down those walls: he was using God's power to cause a building to fall on some Philistines, killing 3,000, along with himself and Delilah.[64]

It turns out that Samson's supernatural ability, conferred by the Maker, was used exclusively to kill people. Samson began adulthood by taking a Philistine woman as a wife, not from love or even lust but because "he was seeking a pretext to act against the Philistines."[65] Then Samson invites some Philistines to a feast and makes a wager over a riddle. When

Samson's wife whispers the answer to the guests, this small transgression gives Samson his pretext: "The spirit of the Lord rushed on [Samson], and he went down to [a Philistine city]. He killed 30 men of the town [and] took their spoil."[66] This act is not only murder in "the spirit of the Lord," but doubly shameful because by the standards of the ancient Middle East, feasts were peacemaking events, with the host pledging his honor to guarantee the safety of guests.

Samson then sets fire to the Philistines' crops.[67] They retaliate by killing Samson's father; he strikes back "with great slaughter."[68] In another clash, Samson kills 1,000 Philistines.[69] His annihilative life comes to conclusion when he is lured into cutting his hair by the beguiling Delilah; Samson then asks God that his strength be restored for one last massacre.[70] Throughout the Samson narrative, this man chosen for favor by the Maker is depicted as performing not a single constructive act.[71]

And Sunday school teachers like to depict the story of Job, the woes of a person who is severely tested yet never abandons faith. Overlooked is the degree of heaven-sanctioned killing that makes this tale possible. All Job's children and servants are slain by Satan, who for the purpose of the Book of Job operates with the Maker's authority.[72] After the ordeal ends God showers Job with new wealth and new children—seven sons and three daughters, each strong or beautiful, to replace those slain by a roaring wind from heaven. But the original entirely blameless children, and all their blameless servants, stay dead. They were expendable.

STILL MORE BRUTALITY under the warrant of God is found in the Deuteronomic Code. The code is sometimes praised as the first consolidation of civil law. For example, one regulation specifies that if an ox gores someone to death, the animal must be killed and its meat not eaten. If, however, the ox had already gored someone and the owner taken no special precautions to prevent additional deaths, then the owner must be executed; unless the victim is a slave, in which case the ox owner pays thirty shekels of silver to the slave owner as compensation.[73] Much, it seems, depends on who by the ox is being gored.

Yet however the Deuteronomic Code may have laid the groundwork for what eventually became humanized law, its ancient function was to legitimize brutality. Under the Code, children and grandchildren are punished for the sins of parents.[74] Death is specified for offenses as petty as adolescent bravado: "If a man have a stubborn and rebellious son, which will not obey the voice of his father . . . then shall his father and his mother lay hold on him, and bring him out unto the elders of his city . . . and all the men of his city shall stone him with stones, that he die."[75] The Code specifies death for adultery, premarital sex, and many other offenses;[76] it even specifies that in some cases of rape, the woman be executed.[77]

From the standpoint of divinely sanctioned violence, the worst aspect of the Deuteronomic Code is the codification of the spoils of war, offering incentives for aggression. One section describes conditions for attacking a town. Make peace only if all males in the town agree to become slaves. If these unlikely terms are rejected, then "You shall put all its males to the sword. You may, however, take as your booty the women, the children, livestock, and everything else in the town, all its spoil. You may enjoy the spoil of your enemies, which the Lord your God has given you."[78]

Deuteronomy contains considerable details on the rules by which God's soldiers may abduct attractive women, which must have been a lively subject of discussion in the ranks. As the warrior dragging off a desirable woman, you must first allow her to spend one month with her head shaved (rendering her repulsive by the aesthetic standards of the time), so that she can mourn for her father and mother who, it is presumed, you have just butchered, probably as she looked on. After the month passes, you may do to her as you please. But if it turns out sex with a woman whose family you have murdered is for some unfathomable reason less than fully orgasmic ("if thou have no delight in her"), then she is to be abandoned, not sold for cash. Selling the woman would be considered consumer fraud, given that your rape of her has already insured that no one will ever marry her.[79]

The war-scruples section of the Deuteronomic Code turns out to apply only to "towns that are very far from you"— that is, places to which Hebrew troops are sent solely for the purpose of plunder.[80] Cities in the Promised Land are dealt with much more harshly. On that point are protracted portions of scripture that Judaism and Christianity really, really don't want to talk about. They evince the divine's most shameful hours.

GOD HAS TOLD THE CHOSEN they will be led to a magnificent Promised Land to be theirs forever. But on arrival, the Hebrews discover the Promised Land already populated. The Maker sanctions unlimited atrocity for the purpose of clearing the territory. Many fights commence with divine fervor: "[God] shall thrust out the enemy from before thee and shall say, 'Destroy them!' "[81] Slaughter is to be universal: "As for the towns of these peoples that the Lord your God is giving you as an inheritance, you must not let anything that breathes remain alive."[82]

One of the Promised Land conquests occurs at Jericho. In churches and synagogues around the world, angelic young voices can be heard joyously singing the song about Joshua and the battle of Jericho. Children delight in the tale of brightly dressed men marching around a city blowing trumpets and waving banners. Often boys and girls act out the moment when Joshua orders the soldiers to shout, and the walls tumble down. They are not told what happens next: charging into Jericho, Joshua's soldiers "devoted to destruction by the edge of the sword all in the city, both men and women, young and old."[83] Just before the horns blew, God had appeared dressed as a gladiator, holding aloft a sword and declaring, "As commander of the army of the Lord have I now come."[84] The Maker not only sanctions the butchery "by the edge of the sword" of women and children, but materially participates.[85]

In 1990 *The New York Times* reported archeological evidence suggesting that a Promised Land city had its walls demolished around three thousand four hundred years ago. The story ran under the headline BELIEVERS SCORE IN BATTLE OVER THE BATTLE OF JERICHO;[86] its spin was that the faithful should feel pleased by corroboration suggesting that Joshua's assault really happened. My faith would have been comforted by archeological evidence that Jericho was a total myth. It is not claims of supernatural healing or miraculous love that modern skepticism ought to hold against spiritual belief; rather the credible, historical-sounding violence of the Bible that poses the real obstacle to thoughtful faith. Far better if the miracle verses were the ones that are true, and the massacre verses the ones cooked up.

Later in the Promised Land wars, God helps Joshua's infantry burn the city of Ai. Soldiers lay ambush for civilians who run from the inferno: "And Israel struck them down until no one was left who survived or escaped."[87] Joshua's troops destroy the city of Makkedah: with the Maker looking on, "Joshua and the Israelites [inflicted] a very great slaughter on them."[88] An Israeli battalion assigned to clear out opposition in the Promised Land "Came to Laish, to a people quiet and unsuspecting, put them to the sword, and burned down the city."[89] According to scripture, Laish was undefended.[90] Local cities band together to oppose the invasion, but God leads the defense, and Joshua's men "slew them with a great slaughter."[91] Remnants of the opposing army attempt to retreat. "As they fled from before Israel . . . the Lord cast down great stones from heaven upon them . . . and they died. They were more which died with hailstones than they whom the children of Israel slew with the sword."[92]

After the chosen get a foothold in the Promised Land, Amalek rises again as a competitor state. God instructs Saul, "Go and attack Amalek and utterly destroy all that they have. Do not spare them, but kill both man and woman, child and infant."[93] Saul does this, butchering every "child and infant" but capturing the Amalek king and city's prize livestock, which he carts off as booty. Learning that Saul has infringed the order to "utterly destroy all that they have,"[94] the Maker flies into a rage. Saul cries out in dismay, then takes the Amalek king, whose name is Agag, to the holy man Samuel. Knowing heaven's priorities, Samuel "hewed Agag in pieces before the Lord,"[95] which calms the divine.

Finding its origin in early scripture, the notion that God can sanction imperial conquest has infected every monotheist faith. Christian Europe staged imperial drives through Africa, the Holy Land, and the Indian subcontinent partly under the banner of driving out heathens. God's approval of killing for the purpose of seizing territory in the Promised Land remains theologically operative in contemporary Israeli politics, and is sometimes called on by zealots to rationalize violence. Iran and Iraq try to seize each other's land in the name of Allah. Protestant canon was used to support the theft of land from American Indians, for example, by Cotton Mather, whose *Magnalia Christi Americana*, a widely read book of 1702, preached that

North America was the new Promised Land and that God wished Europeans to kill Indians with the same zeal that Hebrews once killed Philistines.[96]

Consider the 1572 atrocity during which papal infantry assaulted the Parisian public wedding of a Huguenot Protestant leader, slaughtering an estimated 50,000 people, most of them unarmed civilians. Learning of the attack, Pope Gregory XIII held a mass of celebration and ordered commemorative medals struck. Religious medallions to commemorate a massacre of the helpless: try to think of an action that could mock faith more fully. Equal repugnance on the opposite side of the coin was found in events such as the 1650 massacre at Drogheda, Ireland, in which Protestant forces cut down hundreds of unarmed Catholic civilians, Oliver Cromwell calling this killing "the glorious mercy of God."[97] These acts might be argued away as the depravity of wicked men who falsely claimed to love God. But having read the Old Testament, Cromwell and Gregory XIII probably believed they were faithfully carrying out the wishes of their Maker—slaughtering anyone who opposed their vision, just as God had once done.

GOD'S MALEVOLENCE in the Promised Land campaign ought to be a disturbing lesson about what the Maker once was. Karen Armstrong has called the deity of the Bible's first third "brutal, partial and murderous . . . if Yahweh had remained such a savage God, the sooner he vanished the better."[98] Beyond its vehemence, a striking aspect of God's shameful past is that for all the bloodshed and extreme acts, divine intervention in the Promised Land came to naught. Heaven spent centuries flashing supernatural power against the enemies of the Hebrews. When it was over, nothing had been accomplished. The chosen people were still not secure militarily: Assyria conquered Judah, the northern Hebrew kingdom, about 2,700 years ago, and Babylon sacked Israel, the southern kingdom, two centuries later. And ignoring the celestial bluster, most of the chosen continued to defy God. Graven images, licentious Baalim rituals, and other aspects of paganism remained common throughout the Promised Land, even in Jerusalem itself.

God's failure to attain the divine ends for ancient Hebrew society, even through use of unconditional force, stands as another reminder that the Maker is no Absolute whose will converts to fact. But ancient divine violence becomes intelligible, at least, if understood as part of God's learning experience.

Owing to the All-or-Nothing mind-set, trying to make sense of the vindictive early God has largely disappeared as a concern of theology: one either takes the All view that brutal scriptural events were necessary owing to some perfect preexistent plan, or the Nothing view that divine violence in scripture is just another aspect of the sham. But in bygone eras, groping to understand the Maker's rage was a leading concern. In *Antithesis*, one of the first works of comparative religious studies, the second-century Gnostic commentator Marcion wrote that the God of the Old Testament had been so hideous compared to the peaceful deity of the New that they must be two entirely different beings.[99] Gnostic Christianity became estranged from conventional Christianity in no small part over Gnosticism's insistence on pointing out how repugnant and imperfect the early Maker had been. Other spiritual interpretations wrestled with the same dilemmas. The institutional church detested Albigensianism, the Christian reform movement of the thirteenth century, because Albigensians maintained, based on scripture, that Satan must have ruled Earth in the ancient days, with the true God not present until Jesus appeared.

This ancient inclination to contemplate rather than evade

God's shameful past is the correct one, for stories of divine brutality, however unsettling to read, can help explain how divine serenity was formed.

In the ancient days, the Maker behaved as a first-time parent who assumes loud shouts and liberal use of the rod will correct a child. Perhaps the Maker never could have imagined people would be so recalcitrant as to refuse divine orders backed by the threat of death. But *Homo sapiens* seems conditioned to chafe at authority. In every culture, time, and place, nothing has instilled insubordination more effectively than demands for obedience backed by shows of force. The Amorites are efficiently slaughtered, but the Assyrians merely come along to replace them. Baal-worshippers in Moses's camp end up impaled on spears, but a few years later people are undressing each other for Baal rituals anyway. Wise parents learn that force backfires in this way: shouting causes children who shout, hitting causes children who hit, and high-decibel edicts that acts of pleasure be taboo cause children who do those very things the first chance they get. Eventually the wise parent understands that force and intimidation only fortify resistance: persuasion and good examples are what work over the long run.[100]

Thereby God came to realize that violence is not only morally wrong but represents poor strategy, in that it fails to achieve the desired ends. Reflecting on this, heaven renounced violence. Responding to unanticipated human behavior, God began to greaten in unanticipated ways. Contrition came into play: the Maker grew to feel awful about "the evil I have done" to women and men,[101] and to long for the consolation of human warmth. Transformed, the Maker exchanged force for vows of compassion.

The peaceful God who finally manifests, sometimes spoken of by Christians as a New Testament phenomenon, is in every way rooted in ancient Jewish theology, as the divine spiritual transformation begins in the late Old Testament.

But what matters is not which denomination can claim most credit for the emergence of the serene God: what matters is the emergence itself. Eventually love, not obedience, becomes the Maker's objective. And love is a cooperative endeavor, one in which God may need people as much as people need God.

Chapter Thirteen

The Breakthrough Moments

Throw away thy rod,
Throw away thy wrath.
O my God,
Take the gentle path.
GEORGE HERBERT, 1633

ANYONE WHO HAS SLOGGED through the Bible's worst moments, as we just did, should be rewarded with reminders of its grandeur, such as the justly celebrated passage, "And if I have prophetic powers, and understand all mysteries and all knowledge, and if I have all faith so as to remove mountains, but do not have love, I am nothing."[1] Grandeur may also be found in scripture's wry wit, such as, from Ecclesiastes, "All human toil is for the mouth, yet the appetite is not satisfied."[2] Some of what makes the Bible grand is its sagacity, such as "God hath chosen the foolish things of the world to confound the wise; and the weak things of the world to confound the things which are mighty."[3]

Yet some of the most important aspects of Judeo-Christian scripture remain little known or noted, and among them are the moments of divine breakthroughs—when heaven itself advanced toward the light. These form the outline of God's spiritual transformation. This chapter will recount the breakthrough moments in an approximate chronological order.[4]

The Rainbow

Every schoolchild knows that the dazzling diffraction of a rainbow signifies God's promise never to inundate Earth again. But though the symbolism of the rainbow is presented as a sweet pronouncement from a loving friend, it is far from that: rather, it is a prelude to a breakthrough.

Before discovering the noble family of Noah, the Maker was about to conclude the experiment in carbon biology. Recall the pre-Flood verses: "And the Lord was sorry that he had made humankind on the earth, and it grieved him to his heart. So the Lord said, 'I will blot out from the earth the human beings I have created.' "[5] God's threat is never carried to its culmination, for the Maker seems to experience an incipient sense of shame for allowing the idea of total annihilation to enter the divine mind. This is a substantial step: admitting you have once been wrong is a necessary precursor to avoiding being wrong again. After Noah and his family emerge from the ark, God pronounces of the resplendent rainbow, "This is the sign of the covenant that I make between me and you and every living creature that is with you for all future generations."[6] The compact means that God admits it would be immoral for the creator to wipe away what has been created. Human aspirations gain a sacred standing that not even the Maker may deny.

The significance of the rainbow, then, is that God has become willing to offer concessions. At the Garden, God simply issued orders. Now humanity has imposed a condition on the divine: people demand the right to exist as independent forms, whether their Maker approves of their behavior or not. Through the rainbow, God accepts this condition.

The rainbow is the first "covenant" the Maker offers. Others will follow, and exactly how to interpret their sequence is, historically, a sore point between Christianity and Judaism.[7] But the basic fact that God is willing to offer any kind of pledge to women and men is far more important than either the interdenominational squabbles caused or the content of the rainbow promise itself. After the deluge, the Maker begins to feel an inner need to be well thought of by the made. Small in the days of Noah, this yearning by the divine will grow and grow.

Abraham's Blade

Toward the end of Genesis, God orders Abraham to sacrifice Isaac, his son. Approaching the pyre, the boy realizes something is wrong: "Father! . . . The fire and the wood are here, but where is the lamb for a burnt offering?"[8] Abraham ties down his own son without, so far as scripture records, the slightest hesitation or emotional anguish. He raises a knife to slit Isaac's throat, the initial act of Old Testament blood sacrifice, when heaven calls out, "Do not lay your hand on the boy or do anything to him; for now I know that you fear God."[9]

The traditional interpretation of this account is that Abraham was tested horribly, kept loving God, and thereby proved his faith. Why should anyone love a deity that orders the sacrifice of a child? If ever there was time that a person should shout defiance to the creator, it is here. But supposing the future is unknowable, and thus God had no idea whether Abraham would comply or refuse, this event becomes comprehensible as part of the Maker's spiritual awakening. Groping along in the early phase of interacting with *Homo sapiens*, God might have wondered if a person would really drive a dagger into an innocent throat, and what this might say about the nature of power. When heaven stays Abraham's hand, this explanation is given: "For now I know that you fear God." *Now I know*. Up to this moment, God did not know how far a human being—and perhaps how far a deity—would go to favor power over morality. A great deal of divine contemplation will turn on the new knowledge.

The Suspension of the Supernatural

Toward the end of the Old Testament, the divine desire for vengeance fades. As this happens God dispatches the middle prophets—prominently Amos, Hosea, and Isaiah—a group of celestial spokespersons unlike those who came before. They are not warriors, partisans, or even leaders, but teachers of meaning. Concurrent to their arrival, divine influence on human affairs declines sharply—an essential transition rarely remarked on in traditionalist theology. In the later Old Testament, supernatural events change from common to rare; they will resume only briefly in the New. The middle prophets cannot turn rods into snakes or strike anyone dead. Metaphysical truth is the sole arrow in their quivers.

Perhaps the progression from crackling displays of supernatural might to humble preaching of the truth was part of a preexistent plan. A more plausible explanation is that some change occurred in God's point of view. Initially the Maker assumed that exhibitions of divine capability would result in human deference. But people are obstinate, and shows of both force and beneficence went poorly. Manna from heaven? Tomorrow the crowd is hungry again, and griping about the service. Supernatural intervention may achieve the desired physical objective, in the sense that the waters part or the skies are bright with fulguration. But in terms of suasion, the ancient signs and wonders had this unifying aspect: all were failures. Force works only when present; persuasion may linger after the show of force has ended.

Even the apostles had trouble comprehending this aspect of miracles. Consider that the feeding of the 5,000 was meant to show that the rabbi Jesus served with God's warrant. But in

the New Testament account, immediately after this divine intervention, the apostles begin to fret about where their next
meal will come from.[10] Christ finds it baffling that the obvious-
ness of supernatural influence is lost on his own friends: "Jesus
said to them, 'Why are you talking about having no bread?
Do you still not perceive or understand?' "[11] After patiently
reminding the apostles that they started off with seven loaves,
fed thousands of people, then gathered up numerous baskets
of leftovers, Jesus asks again in exasperation, "Do you not yet
understand?"[12] They did not.

One of Rousseau's objections to supernatural intervention
was that since the lame can be made to walk by means others
than miracles, attributing such cures to divine power debases
the divine, whereas focusing on meaning elevates the divine.
Contemplating why supernatural signs and wonders failed to
make people believers, God may have come around to Rousseau's way of thinking. On the practical—curing the sick,
producing the food, dealing with the elements—let people
rule, as ultimately people will acquire substantial knowledge
of the practical. Reserve the sense of the supernatural for
matters of the spirit, where people will always be in want
of assistance.

Once turned away from miracles the Maker eventually grew
irritable about human expectations for the phenomenal. Jesus
several times protested that people demand divine intervention when what they really ought to demand is divine truth.
Asked to heal a man's dying son Jesus does so, but not before
grumbling, "Unless you see signs and wonders you will not
believe."[13]

Arguing solely from truth is hardly a certain formula for
success. But at least in principle, truth can work. And truth,
the Maker may have ascertained, means so much more than
physical power.

The Offer of an Afterlife

Following the horror of Isaac and the blade, God makes it up to Abraham by promising that his descendants will be "numerous as the stars of heaven."[14] Abraham's heirs did become ubiquitous: there are now perhaps three billion of them, the Jews, Christians, and Muslims who mutually call on Abraham as their earliest paternal forebear.[15] By having many progeny, Abraham achieved what in Old Testament days was the highest glory someone could hope for at the end of life—since then scripture said nothing about afterlife for the soul.

By the late Old Testament, God began to discuss with people the notion of eternal spiritual existence. Daniel prophesies that one day, "Many of those who sleep in the dust of the earth shall awake, some to everlasting life."[16] This first discussion of the risen soul occurs within the Hebrew tradition, centuries before Christianity and phrases like "born again." By Jesus's time, God will promise immediate immortality to the upright. There will be no waiting for the end of time and the awakening of those who sleep: at death, the righteous person will ascend directly to bliss.

Though the offer of afterlife sounds like what we think monotheism has always promised, its declaration in ancient days represented a dramatic shift in divine policy. Christ's resurrection, understood today as having to do with atonement for sin, was in the context of its time understood as proclaiming that death had been defeated. Jesus's experience demonstrated that God will now offer eternal life, replacing the oblivion that even the righteous of past generations expected. When Jesus said, "I was dead, and see, I am alive forever and ever,"[17] this is not a boast but an *announcement*, the declaration of a fundamentally better deal that God will bestow.

Possibly spiritual immortality is just an agreeable daydream that Jesus devised and found popular with crowds. But as an indicator of God's thought processes, the idea of afterlife is enormously revealing. Immortality may represent something the Maker decided to extend to human beings after witnessing their suffering and being moved by it.

In the Garden stood the tree of eternal life, of which it was hinted men and women would someday taste. Came instead the Fall, the Flood, the Promised Land wars: heaven went from sheltering life to squandering it indiscriminately. Then something changed in the Maker, who began to speak of a new system of eternal companionship in a place where human spirits would be treasured. Perhaps God had at last felt empathy and could no longer stand to watch something as precious as a soul expire into the void. Or perhaps after centuries of observing joy among men and women, a solitary God became aware of loneliness, realizing a desire for companions in the next life. Whatever the reasoning, toward the end of the Old Testament, God decides the time has come to offer the benefits of the Garden's other tree. This is a sure sign the Maker's thoughts are warming.

The Repentances

Having once "repented" of creating humanity, by the late Old Testament the Maker begins to feel more general remorse. Gone are such sentiments as, "The Lord takes vengeance on his adversaries and rages against his enemies."[18] God begins to regret deliberately causing so many problems for Israel: so much so that at one point the Maker warns, "Look, I am a potter shaping evil against you and devising a plan against you."[19] God sees that rigid demands and phases of retribution have done more harm than good, and begins to dream of nurturing only. Addressing Israel, the Maker speaks of a coming gentle age in which "I [will] build you and not pull you down, and I will plant you and not pluck you up: for I repent me of the evil that I have done unto you."[20]

Twice in these passages, God admits to flirtation with "evil" against humanity; and wondrously for the human prospect, the Maker decides to repent to the made. Absolution is no longer a one-way street: it must not only flow up from people to heaven, but down from heaven as well. God now asks women and men to forgive God.

The poet W. H. Auden wrote, " 'God is love,' we are taught as children to believe. But when we first begin to get some inkling of how He loves us, we are repelled. It seems so cold, indeed not love at all as we understand the word."[21] Through the early centuries of scripture, God's behavior was cold and repellent, indeed outside any human comprehension of the word love. By the time of the repentances, the divine goal is shifting toward love as we understand the word.

Compassion Replaces Anger

That God had to transform from anger to compassion is not some far-fetched modernist notion: the Bible describes this process in detail. Here the Old Testament prophet Isaiah, speaking for God, details the Maker's evolving love in an extraordinary passage that numbers among the most significant, yet little-known, words in the monotheist canon:

In overflowing wrath for a moment I hid my face from you, but with everlasting love I will have compassion on you, says the Lord, your redeemer.

This is like the days of Noah to me: Just as I [once] swore that the waters of Noah would never again go over the earth, so I have [now] sworn that I will not be angry with you and will not rebuke you.

For the mountains may depart and the hills be removed, but
my steadfast love shall not depart from you, and my covenant
of peace shall not be removed, says the Lord, who has compassion on you.[22]

The Maker acknowledges trouble controlling the divine
temper: "in overflowing wrath I hide my face from you." But
now, rather than pouncing on people's mistakes, God vows a
new standard of patience, learning the lesson of the good parent: "So I have sworn that I will not be angry with you and
will not rebuke you." Marvelously, at the moment of this vow,
God feels the tug of nostalgia. "This is like the days of Noah
to me" refers to the last time, centuries before, when God
thought the relationship between people and heaven had been
set right. The sentimental language of this passage suggests
that the Maker spent long years ruminating on "the days of
Noah," wondering why the grand gestures to Noah's generation, like the gestures to Adam and Abraham, went wrong.
But the covenant God offered in "the days of Noah" was full
of loopholes that would permit wrath and violence. Now
comes an entirely different proposition, a treaty of unconditional peace. Replacing the rainbow covenant, which specified
only protection from global obliteration, the Maker offers an
unqualified pledge: God will never again harm people in any
way, nor ever again be angry.

This new promise of harmony must be of great import to
the Maker, for it is stated much more powerfully than the
first covenant. This agreement is defined as one that will out-
last the physical world: "For the mountains may depart and
the hills be removed, but my steadfast love shall not depart
from you." Through this promise God surrenders an aspect
of divine power, namely the ability to work harm.[23] But far
from becoming constrained, the Maker feels liberated by
this vow.

No Retreat from Goodness

A sign of the transcendent significance of the new covenant of harmony is that it is restated several times toward the end of the Old Testament. One important restatement, spoken by Jeremiah in God's voice, includes this pledge to humanity: "I will make an everlasting covenant with them, never to draw back from doing good to them."[24]

Never to draw back from doing good. A short time ago by divine standards, heaven was dropping lethal hail on slave laborers and sending killer angels against helpless babies: the Maker "drew back" from doing good on many occasions. Now a changing God promises this mistake will never happen again. The divine will confine itself to moral action exclusively. Imagine the relief and joy the Maker must have felt, achieving this enlightened breakthrough.

Love Overpowers War

God sheds the epaulets of "commander of the army of the Lord,"[25] never to wear martial costume again. The Maker instead becomes a source of warmth and reconciliation, "gracious and merciful, slow to anger and abounding in steadfast love."[26] God begins to address humanity with tenderness, using images that almost suggest romance: "As the bridegroom rejoices over the bride, so shall your God rejoice over you."[27] Verses grow extraordinary for their hopefulness and sense of celebration:

> My whole being shall exult in my God, for he has clothed me with the garments of salvation, he has covered me with the robe of righteousness, as a bridegroom decks himself with a garland, and as a bride adorns herself with her jewels.[28]

In ancient desert culture, the day of the wedding feast was the happiest of a person's life. For heaven to speak of humanity in such terms both is endearing and confers on women and men a high compliment. Scriptural images of war and trembling are replaced with images of festival and celebration. "Steadfast love and faithfulness go before you; happy are the people who know the festal shout; who walk, O Lord, in the light of your countenance,"[29] the later Psalms proclaim, expressing divine delicacy that would have been hard to imagine a few centuries before.

Because institutional faith does not like to acknowledge the error and brutality in God's past, it is hard for traditionalism to attach the significance due to moments in scripture in which heaven converts to compassion. The Maker is now admitting to needing people as much as people need God. But the kind of exuberant love God now desires is the sort that men and women must offer up of their own volition. To obtain such heartfelt love, the Maker resolves to behave better.

During these moments something deeply spiritual happens to God. Eventually scripture even tells us what: God learned that love "does not insist on its own way."[30] In the early biblical period, heaven emphatically insists on its own way, and lightning bolts are thrown when other ways are chosen. Gradually the Maker drops the requirement that everything be done on God's terms. By touching love, God learns higher knowledge. Scripture describes a divinity who found compassion and "steadfast" love as part of a journey of self-discovery. Such a God seems connately more believable than an Absolute: and more likely to accept an outstretched hand.

Forgiveness of Sins

Believers today take as given that God will absolve the transgressions of anyone who feels genuine remorse. Yet through much of scripture history, sins were emphatically not forgiven. Smiting was axiomatic: death was assessed for small offenses, descendants were penalized for the sins of previous generations. In early scripture, forgiveness was conceptualized as a windfall God extended to only a favored few, and only after they underwent some harrowing trial. Most who sinned were damned regardless of what they did or said later.

Institutional religion does not like to mention that God took many centuries to arrive at the view that forgiveness is superior to punishment. The point at which this divine breakthrough is announced numbers among the most moving passages of little-known scripture. Toward the end of the Old Testament, the Maker declares,

> I will put my law within them, and I will write it on their hearts; and I will be their God, and they shall be my people. No longer shall they teach one another, or say to each other, "Know the Lord," for they shall all know me, from the least of them to the greatest . . . For I will forgive their iniquity, and remember their sin no more.[31]

A new understanding of spirituality is to be written in hearts, not on tablets of stone. Love, not legality, is its essence. There will be no more barriers between men and women and the divine: no need to teach what the Maker is, "For they shall all know me, from the least of them to the greatest." Most important for human aspiration, there will be no more keeping score. The moment a person sees the light, any transgressions he or she has committed will be erased from God's thoughts: *I will . . . remember their sins no more.* Previously an essential reason to "fear" God was that the Maker kept an eternal ledger of sins; now a clean slate is promised to everyone who asks.

Foreshadowed in this Old Testament breakthrough is the New Testament declaration that every person is "set free from all those sins from which you could not be freed by the law of Moses."[32] Historically, this verse has been distorted into a

rationale for anti-Semitism, or at least into a demand that believers no longer be Jewish. But *the law of Moses* is not synonymous with Judaic faith. At issue in this verse is not Judaism
but the ancient statutes of mandatory retribution for sin. The
news that God will "remember . . . no more" the penitent
person's sins annuls the oppressive aspects of old Mosaic
law—for Jews as well as everybody else. God's first pronouncement of universal forgiveness comes in the Old Testament and applies to all people equally.

Forgiveness First

At one point in the Gospels, Jesus is accused of blasphemy
simply for saying the words, "Your sins are forgiven." Doctrine then held that God alone could offer mercy. Rather than
talk of forgiveness, priests and rabbis were then expected to
speak solely of duty and punishment. Among other things, this
was a dandy rationalization for systems of harsh legal punishment. The notion that God alone could forgive also rationalized the keeping of family, tribal, and political vendettas. If
some person, family, or institution wronged you, theologically
no one expected you to forgive: you were justified in staying
angry and seeking vengeance.

The moment in scripture at which Christ is called a blas-
phemer for preaching forgiveness represents another divine
breakthrough, one that can be appreciated if we bear in mind
that, like the Old Testament prophets, Jesus is understood as
the voice for God's thoughts.[33] In this passage, four men carry
their paralyzed brother to Christ, begging for healing. Jesus
pays no attention to the victim's physical condition, instead
looking on the suffering man and pronouncing, "Son, your sins
are forgiven."[34] Factotums of the council have been following
Jesus, hoping to document some slip-up that could be the basis
of a legal charge. Hearing these words to the paralyzed man

they launch into pantomime horror, declaring, "It is blasphemy! Who can forgive sins but God alone?" Jesus answers,

> "Which is easier to say to the paralytic, 'Your sins are forgiven' or 'Stand up and take your mat and walk'?" But so that you may know that the Son of Man has authority on Earth to forgive sins, [Jesus] said to the paralytic, "Stand up, take your mat and go to your home." And he stood up and immediately took the mat and went out before all of them; so that they were all amazed and glorified God.[35]

In this arresting exchange Jesus, speaking for God, playfully taunts lesser minds with the question, "Which is easier to say to the paralytic?" Obviously it is easier to express forgiveness than to heal paralysis, yet society of the period could not make words of forgiveness pass its lips. The Maker's message is: *You may not have the knowledge required to heal him, but surely you know how to forgive him.*

This passage serves partly to announce the revised theological principle that, instead of expecting forgiveness to come solely from God, people should forgive each other. It also shows that heaven has become willing to extend forgiveness at the beginning, not only the end, of spiritual growth. Before learning anything at all about the paralyzed man, Jesus blesses him with unconditional forgiveness. This is a fantastic breakthrough.

The Poor at Last Noticed

In the early Bible the privileges of the elite were a matter of high concern, with many chapters detailing the perquisites of the Levite class. Circumstances for the typical woman and man were of little moment. During the Mosaic wanderings in the Sinai, "much people of Israel died" after being bitten by poisonous snakes sent to punish them merely for complaining of

hunger and thirst.[36] During this period, the Levites were din-
ing on firstlings and wine.

By the latter parts of the Old Testament, God begins to see
the average person as the forefront of the spiritual mission. In
a passage during which the prophet Amos serves as the voice
of heaven, the Maker condemns the corruptions of religious
elites who "lay themselves down beside every altar on garments taken in pledge, and in the house of their God they
drink wine bought with fines they imposed";[37] condemns business interests who "afflict the righteous, who take a bribe, and
push aside the needy";[38] and censures the wealthy who "tram-
ple the head of the poor into the dust of the earth and push
the afflicted out of the way."[39]

The prophet Isaiah sums the new position thus: "For I the
Lord love justice, I hate robbery and wrongdoing."[40] Today
this sounds like a statement of what everyone assumes about
God. But when announced, this was striking new policy.

God on the Side of the Angels

Justly celebrated is the passage in which Abraham argues with
God that Sodom be spared.[41] Rarely added to its recounting is
that Abraham's victory in this debate is canceled out a few
verses later when the Maker destroys Sodom anyway with a
rain of "sulfur and fire,"[42] having failed to find the requisite
ten righteous residents. Four other cities are wiped out for
good measure: Admah, Bela, Gomorrah, and Zeboiim.

When the same situation arises some centuries later, God's
approach shifts remarkably. Recall that the Maker had decided
to destroy Nineveh by sulfur and fire.[43] Jonah, bearer of the
warning to this effect, has set himself up on a nearby hill,
eager to behold the city's obliteration. Jonah feels safely holier-
than-them and plans to enjoy watching Nineveh die in divine
agony. Instead, the citizens of Nineveh mend their ways. The

Maker is flushed with remorse: "And God repented of the evil he had said that he would do unto them, and did not do it."[44]

When this clemency is announced, Jonah is miffed, demanding that the city be torched like in the good old days. God replies, "Is it right for you to be angry? And should I not be concerned about Nineveh, that great city, in which there are more than 120,000 persons?"[45] Twice in a protracted scriptural conversation, God asks Jonah, *Is it right for you to be angry?* Positions have reversed from the Sodom debate; now God argues mercy against the human desire for retaliation. It is a powerful breakthrough.

We might wonder: What is a supernatural being doing out there on the hillside, wasting the divine breath by holding a debate with a mere person, particularly one as disagreeable and stiff-necked as Jonah?[46] The Maker seems to be using this dialogue to come to terms with heaven's own past urge to destroy. Perhaps the question *is it right for you to be angry?* is really intended for God's own ears, for the Maker has only recently come to understand that the answer is *No*. God, at last, is on the side of the angels.

The End of Sacrifice

Early in the Bible, inordinate attention is devoted to the making of sacrifice, especially the burning of animal fats and the placing of fresh blood on altars. As the books of the Old Testament pass, God begins to reject such rituals. Whether from weariness over the butchering of living things, or growing distaste for institutional religion, or gradual awareness that resources wasted on sacrifice might be used for the common good, God renounces sacrifice. Toward the end of the Old Testament, the Maker declares,

> I despise your festivals and I take no delight in your solemn assemblies. Even though you offer me your burnt offerings and

grain offerings, I will not accept them; and the offerings of well-being of your fatted animals I will not look upon.

Take away from me the noise of your songs; I will not listen to the melody of your harps. But let justice roll down like waters, and righteousness like an ever-flowing stream.[47]

In the early scripture, God demanded audible or visible evidence of worship. Later the Maker experienced second thoughts; by the conclusion of the Old Testament, ceremonial devotion is actively denounced ("Take away from me the noise of your songs"), and God no longer asks any physical thing for the divine self. Today the presumption that God wants nothing for the self is standard to all forms of monotheist faith. But the Maker did not start off this way; centuries of spiritual growth were required to reach this breakthrough. To say, today, that God wants displays of worship may be a misreading of the Maker's own spiritual progress: almost an insult, akin to saying God wants publicity.

God Offers a Sacrifice

Whatever may be true about the nature of Jesus, his death possessed significance easily overlooked in modern culture. A basic expectation of both monotheist and other ancient theology was that people must offer physical gifts to heaven. Animals, grains, virgins: the willingness to allow something of value to be destroyed before heaven was the ultimate token of respect. In that context, the countervailing idea that heaven would allow people to destroy something God treasured was revolutionary in a way that is today impossible to appreciate.

Think for a moment on a famous verse usually presented as traditionalist sentiment, but that may be read as reflecting a divine spiritual breakthrough: "For God so loved the world that he gave his only son."[48] Through many books of scripture, it is not at all clear that God loves the world. By Jesus's day, divine love for people has become so strong that it even exceeds love for heaven's own child.

For nearly two thousand years Western culture has been obsessed with the cross as the symbol of Christian denominational affiliation. But this small consideration, which might have meant nothing to Jesus, pales before seeing the cross as the symbol of a sacrifice given by the divine to humankind. The reason people of ancient faiths made sacrifices was to atone for mistakes. With the crucifixion, the Maker extended the same sentiment toward men and women: Jesus's death washing away the sins of the world but also washing away God's trespasses in the process.

God Accepts Humiliation

In Hosea, the Bible's most remarkable little-read book, God instructs the prophet Hosea to enter the temple of Baal and purchase for marriage a Baalim courtesan. This action scandalizes Hebrew society, causing Hosea to become an outcast. The new wife promptly leaves Hosea, preferring the libidinous diversions of her former career. So the prophet returns and purchases her a second time—an opera-*buffa* touch in the ancient context—and continues to offer her unconditional love. By the book's end Hosea has suffered complete personal humiliation and is widely viewed as a fool.

The symbolic meaning of the account is that God has come to want so desperately to join with humankind that heaven will overlook dalliance with other gods—historically, what the Maker detests most—and endure degradation, if that is the cost of reconciliation. Maintaining dignity was once one of God's obsessions; by the time of Hosea, the Maker is willing to accept heckling and public derision to obtain love. In a radiant passage, God resolves to hold back divine pride no matter how badly Israel misunderstands Hosea's gesture:

My heart recoils within me; my compassion grows warm and tender. I will not execute my fierce anger; I will not again destroy Ephraim; for I am God and no mortal, the Holy One in your midst, and I will not come in wrath.[49]

For I am God and no mortal . . . and I will not come in wrath. Of course the divine is "no mortal," yet this is presented as necessary to state: as if the Maker were saying, *Once I allowed myself to act like you, the time has come for me to act like what I really am.*

This remarkable passage continues, "How can I give you up, Ephraim? How can I make you like Admah? How can I treat you like Zeboiim?" (Ephraim, one of the tribes of Israel, was an ancient generic term for Hebrew society; Admah and Zeboiim were among the cities destroyed with Sodom.) Essentially God is saying, "How can I stand to kill any more?"

In the book of Hosea, warnings of the destruction of corrupt societies contrast with images of delicate longing that seem to be taking over God's thoughts. The Maker asks people to "abide for me many days," promising "so will I also be for thee":[50] heaven itself willing to swear a vow of fealty in return for love. Hosea's story closes with a suggestion that someday God and people will start again, in a second Eden:

> I will heal their disloyalty, I will love them freely, for my anger has turned from them. They shall again live beneath my shadow, they shall flourish as a garden. I will be like the dew to Israel. They shall blossom like the vine, their fragrance shall be like the wine of Lebanon.[51]

In the Middle East the finest grapes came from Lebanon; wines made there were once the libation of kings. Here God dreams of sipping such wines with men and women in a new Garden, loving freely, the disappointments of the past forgotten. The Maker who entertains this reverie is a substantially different being from the one who once clapped with virulent glee to watch a spear thrust through a woman's breasts.

Neither Do I Condemn You

When we bear in mind that Jesus is understood as acting out the thoughts of the divine, one familiar Gospel account can be transformed into a vision of the spiritual growth experienced by the Maker.

Local hypocrites drag a woman accused of adultery to Christ, asking him to order that she be lynched[52]—"put up with stones," in the old Mosaic terminology. This represents the sole time in Jesus's ministry that he was asked for authority to kill: to do what God once did often, and with enthusiasm. As the crowd clamors for the woman's life Jesus appears to ignore them, hunching low to the sand and drawing doodles with his finger. Then he utters what may be the most memorable sentence ever spoken:

> Jesus straightened up and said to them, "Let anyone among you who is without sin be the first to throw a stone at her."[53]

One by one the slime-balls slink off. Jesus continues staring into the dirt, oddly absorbed by whatever scribble he is making. Eventually he realizes the accused has been left behind.

> Jesus straightened up and said to her, "Woman, where are they? Has no one condemned you?" She said, "No one, sir."

> And Jesus said, "Neither do I condemn you. Go your way, and from now on do not sin again."[54]

Neither do I condemn you. Another point that might seem obvious, but that scripture treats as necessary to state. Is Jesus confessing that he too could not qualify to throw a stone? Now there would be a bombshell for traditionalism.[55] And what about that business of staring at the ground? Commentators have suggested Jesus was just being absentminded, or trying for a theatrical effect. But perhaps Christ seemed far away because he was, in fact, far away. Perhaps Jesus's thoughts were infinitely far away, with God.

Perhaps when Christ was confronted with calls for the same unforgiving violence that heaven once propounded, this caused God to reflect on the periods of shame in the divine past. Jesus may have lowered his eyes to the ground because at that moment, his Maker was showing him the horrors once staged in the name of faith: explaining how the divine transformation had led to heaven's new vow, "never to draw back from doing good to them."

We cannot know whether, by his own definition, Jesus could have been eligible to lift a stone against the accused; but from scripture we can be absolutely certain God could not have thrown one. That the Maker realized this and acted upon it is the essence of reading scripture through God's eyes. *Neither do I condemn you* is a judgment fully consistent with the end-point of a spiritual journey.

THE BIBLE REVERED BY THE MONOTHEIST FAITHS may contain errors and embellishments. But the underlying epic it describes, of how God attained a beautiful soul, is too unexpected, too dazzling, and too consequential to represent anything less than spiritual truth.

Chapter Fourteen

The Spiritual Journey of God

> *God, I can push the grass apart*
> *And lay my finger on Thy heart.*
> EDNA ST. VINCENT MILLAY, 1917

Of course it is presumptuous, to say nothing of conjectural, to imagine the processes of God's thought. But scripture encodes some of its most important lessons in exactly this form. Human comprehension of the spiritual promise may be contingent in part on imagining the divine experience. Here, then, is an interpretation of what the spiritual journey of God may have been like.

IT HAD ALWAYS BEEN DARK, and darkness was always upon the face of the waters. But I had come to know that the darkness could be made to yield. I studied the nature of light, and when the time was right, spoke four certain words that called the stars into being. Some elements of the unseen remained aligned with the comfortable shadows; others sought the new illumination. The choice was not so easy as it seems.

Now there was evening, and there was morning. After the chaos of formation receded, life began among the fragile things. Consciousness based on physical chemistry seemed improbable: too much hunger and cold and pain in the material world. But life came, and was determined.

For a long time I watched men and women grow their food, fight with their sticks, chase and be chased, hold each other shivering, die in their petty battles, die in the reeds giving birth, die crying and uncomprehending. Yet somehow they could still raise their voices to sing, and I liked to listen.

One day I heard the songs call out to me.

The concord of these melodies was beautiful, for they spoke to my own breast. Women and men sought nourishment for that part of their beings that they could not see or touch, and yet knew to be present. They searched for meaning, just as I; for like them, I too must have a purpose, and like them, long to know what that purpose is.

Two were chosen for instruction. To them I gave everything, yet they disobeyed me on a simple matter. In wrath I cast them from my presence, and strove to cast them from my thoughts as well. Later I wondered if I had handled the matter correctly.

I went anew to the company of people, offering to reveal many mysteries, asking no more than displays of esteem and a certain aroma from the material world that I found pleasing. But the fragile things showed more affection for the dark than the light. Deep in fury, I resolved to return the primordial chaos.

One small hope was left to float on the face of the waters. When the days of destruction had passed with the hope still present, I trembled: I too contained dark, for I had been moved to destroy. I swore a vow never to repeat my error of the deluge, and spoke of this to the men and women. I became aware that I sought their approval.

Next I selected a downtrodden people and commanded them to stand proudly as my chosen. I assumed my chosen would secure respect; instead I saw their children thrown into a merciless river by enemies. Terrible was the vengeance these enemies knew. Shedding the blood of retribution, I felt sensations of satisfaction. I did not like this discovery about myself.

I guided my favorites through a desert toward a better place, giving them law to regulate their morality. But they did not thank me, and boasted of their prowess in inventing their own gods. More rage came over me, and this time I shed blood from the ranks of the chosen themselves. Such was my reasoning: Surely after such appalling display, all will yield to my authority. But they did not. Later I wondered if, had I been in their position, I would find my own actions admirable.

From the fragile things I specified acts of adoration, thinking these would give me pleasure. Lamentations were pronounced in number; aroma rose in billows from altars crusted with precious stone. But whatever satisfaction I sought in worship, I never found.

In the land to which I sent them, my favored found more enemies. I strapped on armor and slew in awful numbers, reasoning that surely afterward every nation would yield to my supremacy. Instead none did. I caused great signs and wonders, bending the very Earth itself to my intent, reasoning that after such display, all would believe. But each miracle, it seemed, only caused people to want another miracle. Plan after plan I made to force the nations to submission or virtue, and every plan failed.

As the killing went on, I began to take offense at the sword. Seeing men and women take pleasure in retribution against the defenseless, I felt revulsion. Then I remembered I had done the same. Ashamed, I turned my face away from the world.

Seeking consolation from others of the spirit plane, I came to see they had been subsumed or had always been illusions of my consciousness. There could be no turning back: now my destiny was tied to those below. I knew I must I find a way with the fragile things, or forever be alone.

In despair and solitude I experienced doubt. I heard myself cursing those below. One day I came to realize the fault was mine, not theirs. Show children brutality, and brutality they imitate. Show them love and they will love.

So I repented me.

I renounced war as ignoble, renounced violence as the seed of new violence, renounced threats as the debasement of whomever threatens. I forsook the feasts and sacrifices, rejecting every manner of homage. Turning my countenance back to the world I offered an affidavit of peace, never again to exercise the fullness of my anger. Before the spheres themselves I spoke this vow: *for I am God and no mortal, and I will not come in wrath.*

And there was evening, and there was a new morning.

Once my spirit knew peace, I determined to speak only in a still, small voice. As the volume of my voice declined I heard new things: the cry of the poor, the call of the oppressed. I left the company of kings and aligned with the humble, for always it is in the least of things where knowledge of the divine resides.

I sent prophets of the new morning. I denied these prophets signs and wonders, but gave them a greater power, that of truth. Now the kingdom for which I longed would be built on that architecture. Punishments would be set aside; all forgiven unconditionally. The everlasting life I knew would be extended to any of good will, for their consolation and my companionship.

When my heart was ready, I sent a teacher to whom I revealed my every thought and fear. As this rabbi spoke even I listened in wonder, for he could lay his hand directly upon the soul. On that day when my teacher resolved to take the suffering of the world upon himself, I knew everything had changed forever. For ages heaven had demanded sacrifices by people;

now people were offered a sacrifice by heaven. How could this message be misunderstood?

Yet the message was misunderstood. My message was used to justify intolerance, and had I not once sanctioned the same? My message was used to justify war, and had I not once blown that trumpet? My message was used to drive people apart, and had I not once favored some over others? I became aware that revelation was falling onto a world whose failings were partly my own fault.

Pondering these things, I began to see faith solely as the manifest of the way women and men treat each other. Words, worship, doctrine, sect, yarmulke or cross or crescent or saffron flowed together and the distinctions ceased to matter.

I became aware that love bears all things, believes all things, hopes all things, endures all things. Touching this higher knowledge, I learned that love does not insist on its own way. For centuries I had tried to insist on mine. Now I abide until each heart is ready.

Then I had a reverie, a dream that there would come a day in which is set to right what once went wrong in the Garden, and I too would receive back my innocence. As my soul rose, I found I could express my entire theology in just these few words: What does the Lord require of you but to do justice and to love kindness and to walk humbly with your God?

Finally I could be certain: I am who I am.

I will wait as long as required.

The story of God's spiritual transformation must represent something primal to the human condition: whether the revelation of a higher being, or a trajectory for social evolution toward morality, or more.

God left the brutal path and became righteous. We can do the same. This is the fundamental message of faith.

Part Three

Reasons to Believe

Somehow people fend off righteousness.
EURIPIDES

Chapter Fifteen

Is God Religious?

*What does the Lord require of you but to do
justice and to love kindness and to walk humbly
with your God?*
                    MICAH 6:7–8

THERE IS WITHIN RABBINICAL TRADITION a story in which a famished beggar comes to the tent of Moses, who orders his servants to bring a spread of food. Eyes wide, the beggar digs in. Immediately Moses sets upon his guest and begins beating him savagely with a cane.

The Maker appears and stays Moses's hand, asking, "Why do you harm this poor man?" Moses replies, "He began to eat without offering prayer. That is sacrilege." God replies, "Perhaps it is a good thing for humanity that I am not as religious as you."

This punchline invariably draws a laugh from congregations, but rabbis and ministers using the tale rarely locate its sentiment on the time-line of theology. God, after all, was not always as enlightened as the story suggests. The Maker of the early scripture tradition might well have joined Moses in thrashing a beggar who ate without pausing to pray: might have struck the man dead, along with his wife and children. For many centuries, God was religious to a fault—pietistic,

humorless, obsessed with sacerdotal correctness. Then, beginning around the middle period depicted in monotheist writ,
the Maker became steadily less religious. By the time Jesus
walked Galilee, God's interest in conventional religion had di-
minished to a fraction of what it once was. Christ would carry
still farther the renunciation of religious formality—acting
out, theology assumes, God's intentions.

If scripture is read as an account of the Maker's spiritual
growth, it is fair to ask whether, by the close of the Bible,
God is still religious, at least in the sense in which the word
is usually used today. Though institutional religion seldom
speaks of this, scripture offers considerable detail of a divine
progression from denomination specifics to embracing universal, ecumenical, nonstructured notions of faith. And though
Jesus is now thought of as promulgating a new binding faith
structure, there exists a cogent scriptural argument that
Christ was not especially religious either, at least in the sense
the word is used today.

FROM A COMPLEX, LENGTHY WORK such as the Bible, little can
be proven conclusively. Before considering whether God
should be thought of as religious, it is necessary to concede
that there are arguments that scripture does enjoin particular
religious views: though by this point, several basic faiths and
dozens of denominational subsets have managed to claim that
the Bible mandates their view and theirs alone.

A good starting point for considering this question is the
little-known fact that the Bible never declares itself to be the
word of God. The Koran calls its text consecrated, "dictated"
by heaven; Judeo-Christian scripture contains no similar statement. The Old and New testaments offer many sections in
which God speaks, but no assertion that other passages are
divinely specified. The closest is this: "All scripture is inspired
by God and is for teaching, for reproof, for correction and

for training in righteousness."[1] This makes scripture divinely animated, but not divinely controlled. One reason Judaic thought has produced thousands of pages of Talmudic commentary is that it has always assumed scripture to be a mortal product including uncertainties that must be interpreted. And despite professions of biblical "inerrancy" fashioned by some traditionalists, no scripture passage labels scripture faultless. "Claims of infallibility made for the Bible seem stronger than any made in the Bible," Charles Hartshorne has written.[2]

As Helmut Koester of the Harvard Divinity School has noted, the idea that scripture itself is divine probably did not arise in monotheist theology until the second century, with the Christian theologian Justin Martyr.[3] Martyr's claim was not that the originals of scripture were ordained by God, rather that the translation of scripture had been divinely touched, so as to spread the Jesus movement out of Galilee and into the larger Hellenic world. Once Justin Martyr made it common among Christians to speak of scripture as divine, over the centuries people gradually came to assume the Bible must call itself the express word of God.

From the institutional perspective, the Bible was not declared the word of God until 1546 at the Council of Trent, an event triggered by the Reformation. Up to that point Catholicism had felt it impolitic to depict scripture as divine in character, owing to the complication of the Bible's many disparaging comments about priests and hierarchical clerical structures. By the time of the Council of Trent, the new Protestant movement was using centuries-old disagreements about the order and selection of biblical books as one of its arguments for a new faith. In response, Trent formalized the Bible into approximately its present format and then declared the text the word of God, pronouncing anathema on anyone who "does not accept as sacred and canonical" the writ so chosen. Thus, the idea that the words of Bible were divinely decreed comes from human minds and was first broached in the context of a political dispute.

THE MOST POWERFUL REASON God might have gradually forsaken religion is also the most obvious: the role of faith in human terrors. Observing the number of people killed, tortured, imprisoned, or hounded in the name of religion, God must have known long ago that something went horribly wrong in the interpretation of messages sent by the divine. Perhaps the Maker is partly to blame for this, having been complicit in the ancient development of religious homicide. But as God evolved away from brutality, it would have been natural to evolve away from religion's engagement in the brutal, too.

Surely one reason adherence to organized religion has declined so precipitously in Western European nations—today only about 10 percent of the British population regularly attends services of any denomination, while in France the figure is only about 15 percent[4]—is the accumulated weight of awareness of how much blood religion has cost in Europe's past. A representative instance: King Olaf Tryggvason, who forcibly converted Norway around the year 1000, went by the motto "All Norway will be Christian or die."[5] Often the horrors of European religious killing were not aimed at distant foes, but were internally focused: French Christians killing French Christians, Spanish Christians torturing Spanish Christians. Crusades were called not just against Muslims—that was bad enough—but against Christian cities considered insufficiently allegiant, for instance, papal infantry slaughtering hundreds of Albigensian Christians in a 1209 massacre at the French town of Béziers, with many of the killings taking place inside the walls of the Church of La Madeleine, where civilians fled for refuge. The Inquisition began generic Christian-on-Christian killing in 1231, three centuries before the Catholic-Protestant split existed. By 1439 the pre-Reformation Council of Florence declared that all non-Christians, including "Jews and heretics and schismatics," would "go into the eternal fire." Soon the Inquisition was repressing Jews: killing or banishing them in Spain; demanding in 1533 that all copies of the Talmud be located and burned; in 1843 recommending that Jews be confined to ghettos, this Catholic expression of anti-Semitism helping pave the way for the hellish mainly Protestant anti-Semitism of the Holocaust.[6]

Worst from the standpoint of general European history was the horror unleashed by the Reformation wars, especially the Thirty Years' War. In all the shameful chronicles of human conflict the Thirty Years' War, which began in 1618, stands out as the low point for combined viciousness and senselessness. Disjointed French, papal, Spanish, and Swedish armies roamed the landscape of what is now Germany, slaughtering Protestant civilians; equally irregular armies of Danes, evangelicals, and Norwegians roamed elsewhere, slaughtering Catholic civilians. Most actions in the Thirty Years' War were not engagements between opposing military units but pure massacres in which infantry charged into undefended towns, hacking women and children to death. In this war of attrition by atrocity, an estimated 7.5 million innocents died, an astonishing loss of life in an area whose population had been perhaps 20 million when the war began.[7] Given the length of the Thirty Years' War and the short life expectancy then the rule, millions of seventeenth-century Europeans lived out their entire days on Earth experiencing no condition other than constant, ruthless, depraved religious combat. Satan could not have done better.

Religious killing remains an ongoing matter. At this writing, Islamic fanatics in Algeria were staging exactly the kind of random civilian slaughters that Christians staged in the Thirty Years' War. In our day Catholics and Protestants plant bombs in each other's pubs in Ireland; Sikhs in India bomb Hindu

airliners, while Hindus fire artillery at Sikh temples; Jews in
the Middle East gun down Muslims at prayer, while Muslims
blow up buses ridden by Jewish pensioners; hundreds of thousands of adults in China and the Koreas grew up as orphans
because their Buddhist parents were slaughtered by Japanese
soldiers egged on by the Shinto priesthood; Sunnis and Shias
assassinate each other throughout the Islamic world; Hindu
Tamils in Sri Lanka fire machine guns at the school buses of
Sinhalese Buddhists, while aircraft flown by Sinhalese Buddhists drop napalm on Hindu Tamil schools. Perhaps many
killings with ethnic or political components would have happened regardless of whether institutional religion had ever
been devised. But often religion has been the spark, not the
extinguisher, of hatred, and it is hard to suppose what faith
can find attractive about that.

Venality within institutional faith might rank as the next
reason God would turn away from formal religion. The Italian
poet Dante described the institutional Christian church of the
Middle Ages as "a sewer of corruption." As money corrupted
faith, so did power. A low point for human spirituality came
in 858, when Nicholas I became the first Christian leader to
wear a crown—the symbol of secular political domination, and
the very adornment Christ stood against by accepting the
crown of thorns. Vatican vendibility of the Middle Ages
should not be seen as a censure of Catholicism, rather as an
indicator of the ease by which any organized faith may depart
from its founding principles. Seemingly from the day the Reformation began, financial and spiritual corruption infected the
new faith, too. English, German, Swiss, and other rulers used
Protestant doctrine to repress citizens as harshly as ever the
Vatican did. On the theoretical level, Protestantism intro-
duced into monotheist thought Luther's unfortunate concept
of *sola fide*, or salvation exclusively by faith[8]—an idea since
employed by generations of hypocrites to justify failure to per-

form good works for others. It might be said that by creating a Protestant argument against the Roman doctrine of good works, Martin Luther inadvertently generated the best philosophical defense of Catholicism.

That so much of spiritual history would end up written as disputes among the doctrines of denominations must have been another influence driving the Maker away from religion. Many of history's most heated dogmatic disputes have involved subordinate matters such as the corporeal nature of Christ—a controversy for which thousands have died over the centuries, and for which, it is likely, Jesus himself cared not one whit. Albigensianism, Anabaptism, Anglicanism, antinomianism, Arianism, Arminianism, Calvinism, Catharism, deism, Donatism, fundamentalism, Gnosticism, "holiness," Lutheranism, Jansenism, Jesuitism, millennialism, monophysitism, monotheletism, montanism, Mormonism, Nestorianism, Oxfordism, Pelagianism, Photianism, premillennialism, Puritanism, scholasticism, socianianism, suppositionalism, supralapsarianism, Thomism, Trinitarism, and Unitarianism are just some of many interpretations of faith that have caused antagonism within Christianity alone.

One consequence of denominational combat is that, although faith is supposed to extend a caring hand, what it often shows the world is a snarl. As recently as the turn of the century it was still common for Protestant leaders to refer to the pope as the Antichrist or the Whore of Babylon.[9] Through the same period it was still common to hear Rome denounce Protestants as heretics: Pope Leo XIII, who died in 1903, called Protestants "enemies of Christian name." In 1991 the Eastern Orthodox Church declared that the World Council of Churches must be "shunned" for adopting a broadminded view of denominational disputes, though the whole purpose of the council's existence is to engender ecumenical harmony.[10] The mutual attitudes held by what ought to be shared-purpose faith institutions might be summed up in a *New Yorker* cartoon that showed one hound saying to another, "It's not enough that dogs succeed. Cats must fail."

As soon as one sectarian vendetta fades, another arises to replace it. It took the General Assembly of the otherwise liberal Presbyterian USA denomination three decades, from 1966 to 1997, merely to pass a resolution recognizing the Evangelical Lutheran Church, Reformed Church in America, and United Church of Christ as "authentic expressions" of Christianity.[11] Harmony seemed to have broken out, but just months later a dispute over doctrine caused the Evangelical Lutheran Church to reject a related agreement to recognize the Episcopal denomination.[12] In 1996 the Southern Baptist Convention formally endorsed as a priority "the conversion of the Jews." However improbable the objective, its announcement gave pause, as "the conversion of the Jews" has often been code for anti-Semitism: the true meaning of this phrase being social isolation, not evangelical suasion.[13] In February 1997 police had to be called to a mosque in Tulsa, Oklahoma, to break up a band of students from Oral Roberts University who were disrupting a Ramadan observance by pounding on the mosque's walls and pretentiously praying for the conversion of those within.[14] (It seems safe to say Jesus would have handled this situation somewhat differently.) In April 1997 the Union of Orthodox Rabbis declared that the Reform and Conservative subsets of their faith are "not Judaism at all, but another religion."[15] That this particular doctrinal dispute was aired at a press conference, rather than in a torture chamber, may at least be some sign of progress.

Shaw once summed the whole matter as "The nearer the church, the farther from God," a put-down few institutional denominations can counter. Just what the denominations and doctrines are doing wasting so much energy trying to wrestle each other to the turf, rather than reaching out to human want and soulful need, is something for which they ultimately may have to answer to higher authority.

FROM HIS CELL in the Flossenbürg concentration camp, the Christian martyr Dietrich Bonhoeffer wrote in 1944 of the need to move toward "nonreligious interpretation of biblical concepts."[16] To the traditionalist this may sound like anything-goes modernism: though Bonhoeffer, a Lutheran minister, was hopelessly religious by contemporary standards, a saintly man who was executed for opposing Hitler, and who said it was the love of Jesus that lent him the strength to go forward in that cause.[17]

What Bonhoeffer meant by "nonreligious interpretation of Biblical concepts" was that faith should advance toward a common spirituality that would soothe rather than envenom human relations. Strains among denominations, Bonhoeffer thought, prevent belief in higher purpose from uniting as a force in opposition to the nihilism of evil. For Bonhoeffer it seemed possible to understand the Bible in a universal, "nonreligious" manner without surrendering any of faith's beauty, moral insistence, or love for God.

How might we find a "nonreligious" spirituality within the Bible? Consider one of the most significant, and surely least known, passages of monotheist scripture: the verses in which God drops the commandments concerning formal religious practice.

This passage begins when a young man asks Jesus what a person must do to attain eternal spiritual existence, the reward Christ sometimes spoke of simply as "life." To this inquiry Jesus replies, "If you wish to enter into life, keep the commandments." There is a follow-up question; the young man asks, as if this were a point of controversy, "Which ones?"

Which ones? Aren't there a famously invariant Ten Commandments? The Gospels record,

And Jesus said, "You shall not murder; you shall not commit adultery; you shall not steal; you shall not bear false witness. Honor your father and mother. Also, you shall love your neighbor as yourself."[18]

Debating which laws mean more than others is a long-standing exercise of the rabbinical tradition in which Christ was educated. But this passage is not just a discourse on priorities. Something wholly remarkable happens: Jesus edits down the Ten Commandments, endorsing only six.[19] Can you name the missing four? These Commandments are left off Christ's list: "You shall have no other gods before me. You shall not make for yourself an idol. You shall not make wrongful use of the name of the Lord your God. Remember the Sabbath day, and keep it holy."[20] The four commandments Jesus cancels are the ones concerning formal religious practice.

Because what is significant about this exchange is what Jesus does not say, the grandeur and import of the passage is routinely missed. Christ, the child of God, has just carefully and consciously deleted some of the Ten Commandments—basic precepts of a thousand years of relations between Maker and made. The commandments about formal religion that Christ passes over are the very ones that the next two thousand years of religious history will argue about most, as though they were still in force.

The lesser meaning of this Gospel passage is that followers of Jesus ought to speak of the Six Commandments. Recent court decisions barring the posting of the Ten Commandments in public places do so on the grounds that this practice advertises Christianity. In theological terms the Ten Commandments advertise Judaism, which, premised on the Old Testament, does sanctify Ten. Christians, for whom Jesus's teachings amend Old Testament writ, have at maximum Six Commandments. And those Six Commandments could readily be exhibited in any public venue without infringing the boundary between church and state, because the Six Commandments concern only moral relations between people, making no reference of any kind to religion.

The greater meaning of the Six Commandments passage is that in these words, Jesus makes clear that his Maker has ceased caring about the specifics of denomination, adoration, or religious formality. Go back and read the Six Commandments verses again. In them is no mention of religious practice, of denomination, of any sort of formal worship. Jesus gives these words as *commandments*, not fuzzy generalized advice.

Exponents of institutional religion instantly change the subject when the Six Commandments passage is mentioned; oddly, opponents do as well. Within the framework of the All-or-Nothing debate, believers in an omnipotent Absolute glide past the biblical areas that suggest the Maker gradually abandoned formalistic stipulations for worship. Unbelievers of the Nothing school glide past the same aspects, preferring those portions of Bible that describe God as a wrathful stickler for exclusionary religious rules. Such verses better serve Nothing thought, since a hyperreligious Maker represents the sort of deity most people would wish were merely mythology. The last thing the Nothing school wants is for scripture to be understood as showing God converting from formal religion to a new role as a broad-minded universal spiritual reformer.

SCRIPTURE INDICATES A DIVINE TRANSITION to "nonreligious" views in other ways. The Bible's early books do dictate specific religious practices. But by the later Old Testament, this changes. The Maker renounces liturgical formalities such as animal sacrifice and sends prophets to denounce the religious officialdom. The ability to communicate with God, once reserved for vested officials (the notion of an intercessionary priesthood was not a Catholic innovation, but found in ancient

Hebrew culture), is extended to everyone in a decentralized manner. Forgiveness, once a perquisite specially held for a few, is extended to everyone prospectively. Those verses in which God criticizes Old Testament religious practice are read by traditionalist Christians as arguments against Judaism. This misses the point: such verses should be read as conveying the Maker's change of heart regarding all forms of religious subdivision, including the Jewish-Christian split.

Of course officials of multiple denominations have been saying for centuries that formal religious prescripts are implanted in the Bible. Yet here too what is assumed to be in scripture may differ significantly from what is actually present.

The Old Testament says a great deal about the Hebrew nation but precious little about the Jewish religion. Nearly all Old Testament references to Judaism occur in two books, Esther and Ezra, where discussion concerns ethnic conflict and political identity more than spiritual belief.[21] In generally accepted translations of the Bible, Old Testament patriarchs such as Abraham, Moses, and Solomon make no reference to Judaism, nor ever hear the word spoken. Had the Maker planned to mandate that women and men choose Judaism, it would have been simple to incorporate into scripture a straightforward verse that reads, "God instructs you to be Jewish." In the Old Testament, no such verse is to be found.[22]

By contrast the New Testament is replete with references to Judaism, the ethos in which Jesus lived. Gospel translators of the Middle Ages labored to avoid some of the Jewish vocabulary that surrounds Jesus in the oldest scripture autographs. For instance, in the original of the Gospel of Matthew, one verse has Jesus being greeted with the Greek phrase *chairo rhabbi:* the King James renders this salutation as "Hail, master!" while the modern New Revised Standard Version makes it "Greetings, rabbi!"[23] Jesus's essential social and personal character was Judaic. There is a popular evangelical bumper sticker that advertises MY BOSS IS A JEWISH CARPENTER. This declaration is enchanting both for the praiseworthy sentiment it reflects, and because in its formulation you are asked to call yourself Christian in allegiance to someone who called himself Jewish.

But though Judaism is often mentioned in the New Testament, Christianity is not. Recall that in all generally accepted translations of the Gospels, Jesus never speaks nor hears the words "Christianity" or "Christian." Major translations such as the King James and New Revised Standard refer to being Christian only three times: not as what Jesus ever discusses or what God ever instructs humanity be, but as what people in the Turkish city of Antioch decided to call the apostles when they arrived to minister.[24] Christ surely did speak about religious forms—his strongest injunctions in this regard, "no one comes to the Father," we will ponder in a moment—but if the Gospels are our guide, said not one word advocating the practice of Christianity.

After Jesus's death, many of those in Asia Minor to whom the apostles preached assumed they were being asked to convert to Judaism, since the carpenter from Nazareth was renowned as a Jewish messenger.[25] One of the practical barriers the apostle Paul faced in his ministry was the reluctance of Gentile men to answer Christ's call, because they assumed this would mean circumcision, a requirement for conversion to Judaism.[26] To allay potential believers, Paul ruled that the young church would not enforce Hebrew circumcision custom ("I have reached the decision that we should not trouble those Gentiles who are turning to God"[27]), a medical policy that as much as any other event started Christianity down the road of becoming a distinct new denomination.

Obviously the New Testament contains references that support the ideals of Christian religion: and that faith would stand as one of beauty, regardless of what ancient texts said about it. What the Bible does not contain is any mandate for Christianity as such. In New Testament theology, the Maker clearly asks that humanity follow the teachings of Jesus: teachings that represent God's own progression away from binding religious doctrine and toward universal embrace. By the final sections of the Bible, writers are calling for humanity to evolve to a universal spiritual condition in which "all of us come to the unity of the faith."[28] In this verse "the faith" is not Christianity per se, it is belief in love and sacred purpose—universal ideals that transcend denomination.

But no matter how the New Testament is read, it contains no plain-words injunction involving denominational specifics. Had the divine planned to mandate that women and men choose Christianity, it would have been simple to incorporate into the New Testament a straightforward verse that reads, "God instructs you to be Christian." Good luck finding any such reference.

WHETHER JESUS HIMSELF INTENDED to set in motion a new religion, reform an ancient one, or move human thought beyond religion as such, nevertheless remains one of the great questions of spirituality. An engaging topic for an evening of cognac and conversion might be what religion Jesus might affiliate with, were he to return to the present day. At least as strong a case can be made for Judaism as Christianity. A dark horse possibility is that Christ would call himself a Baha'i, this being the only major monotheist faith that has never engaged in persecution or started a war. Perhaps, returning today, Jesus would not subscribe to any institutional religion at all, and would give a quizzical look whenever CNN correspondents insisted on asking him about this.

Jesus started off as an adolescent piously questioning elders at the Temple in Jerusalem:[29] he ended up deeply suspicious of religious stipulation, but infinitely hopeful for the human prospect. The rabbi's gradual loss of interest in formal faith can be seen in small ways, such as his rejection of some Hebrew tradition. For example, Christ worked on the Sabbath,[30] and when asked about kosher laws quipped, "It is not what goes into the mouth that defiles a person, but what comes out of the mouth that defiles."[31] Declining interest in religious formalism is seen in larger ways, such as Christ's condemnation of "teaching human precepts as doctrines."[32] That verse is addressed to "hypocrites," Jesus's favorite synonym for the religious elite.

A few theologians have advanced the argument that Jesus expected everyone to "turn to God," in Paul's phrase, but did not mandate any specific religion. For example, the mid-century Jesuit priest and theologian Karl Rahner developed the idea of "the anonymous Christian," which holds that any person (including any atheist) goes on to heaven if he or she led a virtuous life.[33] Rahner liked to cite Jesus's statement, "This cup that is poured out for you is the new covenant in my blood."[34] Traditionalists read this verse as specifically supporting Christianity. Rahner thought that the teaching more plausibly meant that Christ's sacrifice secures divine peace for every upright person regardless of denomination.

The scriptural interpretation of Jesus as "nonreligious" can, however, be broader. At no point until his final days on Earth did Jesus say anything that sounded like an order to start a spiritual movement. Only when he reappeared to the disciples after the resurrection, in the surpassing reflection of Easter glory, did Christ use such words, in an admonishment known as the Apostles' Charge:

> Go therefore and make disciples of all nations, baptizing them in the name of the Father and of the Son and of the Holy

Spirit, and teaching them to obey everything that I have commanded you. And remember I am with you always, to the end
of the age.[35]

The Apostles' Charge is the culmination of Jesus's thought
and ministry: yet this global injunction does not contain the
word Christian, nor the word religion, nor any instruction
about the institutional specifics of any faith. Surely knowing
he was speaking to history, Jesus simply uttered the words
given above and said no more, the Apostles' Charge being the
sentences on which the Gospel of Matthew concludes.[36]

Today the portion of the Apostles' Charge that asks "baptizing into" is often cited as a justification of specific religion.
But although baptism today equates with Christian practice,
that was not its meaning when Jesus invoked the term. John
the Baptist, remember, was a Jewish evangelist who baptized
for the purpose of spiritual renewal, not for conversion to a
new religion. In Jesus's final instruction, "baptizing into"
means into the heart of God, but not into religion as such.

The portion of the Apostles' Charge that asks the disciples
to spread into "all nations" is also easy to misunderstand in
the modern context. During his years of ministry, Jesus spoke
almost exclusively to Jewish audiences. At one point Christ
resisted healing a Gentile girl on the grounds that all Israel
must be healed first;[37] at another point he instructed the
twelve to preach only to Judaic society, saying, "Go nowhere
among the Gentiles, and enter no town of the Samaritans, but
go rather to the lost sheep of the house of Israel."[38] Placing
Judaism first is consistent with the Maker's ancient first interest in Hebrew culture.

But as the end of his time on Earth approached, Jesus became universal in his concerns. For God, an overarching theme
of scripture is the progression from strict religious propriety
concerning a small group, to universal love of all people under

all conditions. Christ seemed to follow the same path. His life began by focusing on the theology of the chosen, but with the passage of time Jesus's interest in denominational formality declined, while his concern for pure spirituality increased. By the moment of the Apostle's Charge, Christ hoped his message would be heard in "all nations." But what he asked that all nations hear is a concord of love, truth, and divine compassion—not religious institutionalism.

Aglow with resplendence of the resurrection itself, Christ might have used the moment of the Apostles' Charge to specify a religion, had that been his concern. Instead he endorsed no particular religion, urging instead that people enter into virtue and faith. These choices are fully consistent with the spiritual journey of God. Are we to think that Jesus meant to mention some particular religion but *forgot?* Are we to think that the Maker spelled out moral obligations with perfect clarity in statements unmistakably labeled Commandments, yet when it came to spelling out religious affiliations, *forgot?*

TRADITIONALISTS SOMETIMES SAY that Jesus could not have mentioned religion because the concept of Christianity did not come into being until the Pentecost. That was the day, about two months after the first Easter, at which the disciples were granted the ability to speak any language, so that they could fan out into the world and report the truths they had seen.[39] Yet scripture accounts of the Pentecost mention neither Christianity nor formal religion. During this magnificent event, heaven touches the apostles with divine fluency, and Peter proclaims to a crowd that Jesus was indeed the Messiah,[40] but nothing is said about starting a new faith. Peter tells the onlookers, "Repent, and be baptized every one of you in the name of Jesus Christ so that your sins may be forgiven."[41] Perhaps this can be interpreted as an injunction to found a new religious institution, but that is a stretch at best. Remember, being baptized then meant being spiritually renewed, not converted.

Some traditionalists further contend that scripture mandates the establishment of Christianity through such usages as the phrase "Lord Jesus," which grants Christ the status of a divinity who should be worshipped. "Lord Jesus" does occur many times in the New Testament—but only once in the Gospels, the books that directly chronicle Christ's life and teachings. This suggests the carpenter was not known as "Lord Jesus" during his life, but acquired that status later. Nor does the rare Gospel use of this phrase occur in Christ's presence: as far as scripture is concerned, Jesus never heard the description.

The root word translated as "Lord Jesus," *kurios*, or "first authority" in Greek, is often employed in scripture to mean God. But at times it is also employed for secular figures: in the "No one can serve two masters" verse, *masters* in the Greek is *kurios*,[42] though "master" here means roughly "employer." To further the ambiguity, sometimes *kurios* means the overblown form of "Lord" used to address princes, military officers, and landholders. In Christ's day, obsequious title inflation was customary: Jesus even made sport of this, declaring, "Not everyone who says to me, 'Lord, Lord,' will enter the kingdom of heaven."[43] Exactly how to render the word *kurios* in application to Christ—whether it should imply divinity or only that Jesus had special status—is sufficiently open to interpretation that the King James Bible has its sole Gospel usage of "Lord Jesus" in one verse, the New Revised Standard at a different verse.[44]

Often it is asserted that the Gospel accounts of Christ's life implicitly mandate Christian denomination by conferring divine standing on Jesus. Again on this point what is actually present in scripture differs from what many assume is there. As the English essayist A. N. Wilson has written, "The Gospels of Matthew, Mark, and Luke never state that Jesus claimed to be God."[45] These three are the "synoptic" Gospels, or those that generally agree. Only the fourth Gospel, John, makes divine claims for Jesus, including quoting Christ as saying, "I came from God and now I am here. I did not come on my own, but he sent me."[46] But even John's suggestions of divinity for Jesus are not conclusive—conceptually, all men and women may have come from the Maker. Elsewhere in the Gospel of John, a speaker addresses Jesus in terms that suggest divine inspiration, not preexistent divinity: "Rabbi, we know that you are a teacher who has come from God."[47] And throughout John, as in all the Gospel books, Christ speaks harshly against blaspheming heaven, but never suggests any such restriction about himself.[48]

Several times during his ministry, Jesus went out of his way to ask people not to discuss his supernatural abilities or speak of him in religious terms. At one point a leper says to Christ,

"If you choose, you can make me clean." Then Jesus stretched out his hand, touched him and said, "I do choose. Be made clean." Immediately the leprosy left him. And [Jesus] ordered him to tell no one.[49]

A similar instance occurs when Jesus brings a twelve-year-old girl back from the dead. Unlike Lazarus, this girl is little remembered, perhaps because we never learn her name. After she rises from her deathbed, Jesus "strictly ordered them that no one should know this, and told them to give her something to eat."[50]

Perhaps this was a clever stratagem on Christ's part, plying on the insight that people will talk most about whatever they are instructed not to discuss. But if the plain-words reading of scripture is what matters, verses such as these tell us that Jesus was striving to avoid being seen as the sort of figure whose veneration could lead to the founding of a new denominational camp.

MORE POWERFULLY, religious traditionalism points to Jesus's declaration, "No one comes to the Father except through me."[51] Even liberal Christian denominations read this verse as determinate, mandating their religion as sole adjudicator of heaven.

Of all biblical concepts, "no one comes" ought to number among the most unsettling to the thoughtful spiritual seeker. Ancient scripture accounts of divine cruelty can be understood as mistakes committed by a majestic but fallible Maker whose own enlightenment was not yet complete. Biblical endorsement of slavery or gender bias can be understood as social philosophy at a different historical stage. And those supposedly vexing miracle accounts are surprisingly easy to get your head around: someday women and men are sure to do things that seem miraculous from the contemporary perspective, such as live on Mars, or live in peace. But the notion that only those who profess Jesus by name are saved ought to give pause. Can the Maker really be saying that with divine anger finally controlled; with the threats of celestial retribution at last replaced with promises of love; with a church pronounced to be wherever two or more gather[52]—after all this progress, one last rigid imperative remains? Jesus, in every other way a nonconformist, seems in the "no one comes" verse to have imposed the strictest doctrinal requirement of all.

The obvious objection to traditionalist reading of the "no one comes" verse is that it means billions of men and women since Christ's day were denied afterlife, however righteous their character. At least another three billion people alive today have never professed Jesus, and most are certain to die without doing so, however ardently missionaries work. Can we really believe God will reject their souls too?

To place the "no one comes" teaching in perspective, it is important not to sentimentalize Christ by viewing him as utterly selfless. Jesus was humble compared to his mission, yet it is hard to read the New Testament without concluding that Christ had some expectation of personal renown. Jesus decreed, "Because I live, you also will live."[53] Christ stated that his spiritual splendor was appropriate "so that the Father may be glorified in the Son."[54] And in words that are fitting but can hardly be read as self-effacing, Jesus declared, "I am the way, and the truth and the life."[55] Many Gospel passages suggest that the longing for human spiritual unison and the desire for personal eminence did battle in Jesus's soul.

Some commentators try to rationalize Jesus's acclamatory sense of the self by supposing that Christ was an unassuming sage who merely spoke his mind, never once suspecting that future generations would venerate him. But you cannot be history's wisest person and a guileless naïf at the same time. If there is one thing Jesus was not, it was ignorant of human nature: Christ knew he was performing monumental works that would leave an imprint on society. There is nothing wrong with the idea that Jesus wanted admiration for those works, which shows only that he possessed a fully functioning human ego. This merely must be taken into account when assessing whether Christ truly meant us to understand that only people professing his name could go up to God. Jesus thought well of himself. Is that the same as saying he would have condemned to the fire those who did not acknowledge him?

Contrast the glorifying sentiment of "no one comes" with another of Jesus's sayings, that his desire was "not to be served but to serve."[56] Contrast it with any of the numerous passages in which Christ urges that people's thoughts be on God or on love of one another, not on Jesus. For instance, "Then [Jesus] took a little child, and taking it in his arms he said to them,

'Whoever welcomes one such child in my name welcomes me, and whoever welcomes me welcomes not me but the one who sent me.' "[57] *Not me but the one who sent me.* What else is that supposed to mean?

Contrast "no one comes" to a New Testament apostolic teaching, "There is no longer Jew or Greek, there is no longer slave or free, there is no longer male and female; for all of you are one in Christ Jesus."[58] Declaring "there is no longer male and female" has an obvious nonconformist quality; granting slaves the same status as free persons was revolutionary when written, too. Other parts of the verse carry meaning that may elude the modern reader. In the milieu in which this statement was made, "Jew or Greek" meant approximately what black or white, Palestinian or Israeli, Korean or Japanese, Catholic or Protestant, Muslim or Hindu means today—segregated, mutually distrustful groups looking for reasons to dislike each other. A call to bring together Jew and Greek meant what the advocacy of brotherhood of Israeli and Palestinian, or of Christian and Muslim and Buddhist, means.

When institutional religion encounters the "Jew or Greek" verse, it stresses that barriers of ethnicity and gender were meant to break down within Christianity. Then why doesn't the verse simply say that? The plain-words reading of the passage is that hatreds and differences would fade away if people adopted the revolutionary spiritual philosophy of Jesus. Of this, there can be little doubt. But the verse does not say that to adopt the philosophy of Jesus, a person must endorse a particular religion. Religion isn't mentioned.

Thus a straight avenue may lead to resolution of the "no one comes" passage. It is that profession of Jesus is a Christian stipulation, reflecting one of the symmetrical paths to God. And it is a fine thing to be a Christian—but Jesus was not.

If Jesus had believed that salvation was premised on formal Christian conversion, wouldn't he have sought that very thing himself? Nor did Christ convert his own disciples into Christians, asking only they "obey everything I have commanded you." Those commands were to love people and to love God, but said nothing about formal religion. If Jesus did not find specific religious affiliation necessary for the salvation of those friends he loved most, what makes us suppose it is different now?

Throughout the Judeo-Christian scripture, most pivotal injunctions are repeated several times in multiple settings. By comparison, "no one comes" is a lone occurrence. Roughly from the Old Testament book of Isaiah to the conclusion of the Bible, the trajectory of scripture is universal. Dozens of directives concern goals of morality, piety, righteousness, and collective love; only a handful speak of religious institutional requirements. If in a very long body of text with many inconsistencies, the preponderance of the evidence points toward universalism, while fragments of evidence point toward exclusionary doctrine, the reasoned approach sides with the preponderance.

Jesus did show the way, the truth, and the life. Could he really have meant, in a single comment among all his teachings, to suggest that billions of people would be denied the embrace of their Maker owing to the protocol they use to seek the spirit? Christ may very well have said "no one comes," but that one sentence hardly overrides the body of his otherwise universalist teaching. Saying this might, after all, have been a mistake: for the scripture is both true and full of mistakes.

TO ADOPT A "NONRELIGIOUS" VIEW OF FAITH does not mean the dissolution of churches, synagogues, and mosques. We need religious institutions to get us out of bed to join the community at worship, to prod us to read the world's many scriptures, to nag us to donate time and money to those in need, to remind us to put our hearts in order because we cannot know on which day we will taste and smell this world for the final time. Phrasing that last concern with memorable simplicity, Jesus noted, "If the goodman of the house had known what hour the thief would come, he would have watched."[59] We need religions to remind us to stand watch for our souls. But we do not need the factious doctrinal structure of institutionalized faith to cause strife between beliefs that ought to cooperate for the common ideals of life.

There are many consequential reasons why men and women should embrace faith in higher purpose and the human prospect. During the postwar era, the broad dividing lines of Western thought have been on subjects like political ideology, social inequality, and racial discrimination. In future generations the broadest divide may be between those who believe life is vested with meaning, and those who think we float aimlessly in Nietzsche's amoral void. Our souls will be better served, and our societies become more humane and equitable, if meaning triumphs in this coming contest.

But surely in that contest our Maker would consider compassion and morality infinitely more significant than religion. Plain words are what matter most about scripture, and among the plainest words in the Bible are those that appear at the chapter head, quoted from Micah, one of the final Old Testament books: "What does the Lord require of you but to do justice, and to love kindness and to walk humbly with your God?" Here we find an unambiguous directive that women and men seek the spiritual; we find no requirement for any particular religion. God wants our feet on the path, but hardly cares what brand of shoes we wear.

Chapter Sixteen

Whom Shepherds Guard

Never has anyone been less a priest than Jesus,
never a greater enemy of forms which stifle faith
under the pretext of protecting it.
ERNEST RENAN, 1863

MONOTHEIST BELIEF IS NOT ONLY about God; for many adherents, Christ is nearly as important. Jesus, an itinerant Jewish pacifist who never owned a thing, never wrote a word, never held any office, and who spent a surprising portion of his brief years knocking back wine in undesirable company, became arguably the most important person who has ever lived.[1] Regardless of whether Christ was divine or mortal or something in between, no one has exerted greater dominion on the human spirit.[2]

Philosophers, factory workers, monarchs, generals, saints, murderers, tycoons, fieldhands, shut-ins, the good and the baneful, the happy and the downhearted, all have been captivated by Jesus's teachings. The revolutionary ideals espoused by Christ have such power that they seize even the minds of conservatives, who hate change. And they are the mores of an uninhibited, antimaterialistic carpenter who shunned the trappings of the world: the dreams of "the king whom shepherds guard," in the marvelous, emblematic phrasing of the hymn. Jesus's sayings are the baseline of advanced human thought: the point from which the highest spiritual aspirations emanate.

Surely the most enduring testament to the sage from Capernaum is that he continues to hold hearts and minds in his gentle grasp, despite the profusion of offenses committed by those who have expropriated his thoughts and his cross. Across the centuries, huge numbers of men and women have been killed, tortured, or repressed in the name of Christ.[3] Still larger numbers have lived lives of hypocrisy while covering their tracks with a pose of supplication to the carpenter. Christianity, in the words of the eminent Duke University scholar and novelist Reynolds Price, "continues to evoke, for millions throughout the world, a history of murderous intolerance so foreign to Jesus's apparent hopes."[4] Yet the appeal of Christ's philosophy remains, often even among the victims of its corruption.

Anyone pondering the trajectory of faith ought to contemplate at least these things about Christ: whether Jesus was real, whether his story should be viewed as an aspect of the larger spiritual journey of God, and which of Jesus's thoughts express eternal truth regardless of what one concludes on the previous two points.

RECENT DECADES HAVE SEEN a lively debate on whether Jesus even existed, with a number of books by credentialed scholars suggesting that Christ is entirely a creature of legend.[5] For instance, Randel Helms, a professor at Arizona State University, has claimed that New Testament accounts of Jesus's existence are mere "Gospel fictions," if well meant.[6] Burton Mack, former professor at the Claremont School of Theology in California, has declared the entire New Testament to be "myth," no more akin to verity than the epic poems *The Iliad* and *The Odyssey*.[7]

It may seem incomprehensible that a globe-spanning religious movement could have been triggered by a nonexistent person dreamed up as the ancient equivalent of a marketing device, given the ranks of incontestably real people who have tried and failed to found faiths. As the discerning writer on theology Kenneth Woodward has noted, the notion that Christ never lived reduces the Jesus movement to "weak tea." That a single cup of weak tea gave rise to a faith of global proportions is a difficult draught to swallow.

As C. S. Lewis once observed, "As a literary historian I am perfectly convinced that whatever the Gospels are, they are not legends. They are not artistic enough to be legends. They are clumsy and don't work up to things properly. Most of the life of Jesus is unknown to us, and no people building up a legend would allow that to be so."[8] That is, if someone had concocted Christ, they would also have invented stories of youthful valor and brilliance. Instead the New Testament says precious little about Jesus's young life or personal self.

It may be no coincidence that two noted twentieth-century believers, Lewis and J.R.R. Tolkien, both knew made-up mythology when they saw it, being authors of their own fables, Lewis's *Chronicles of Narnia* and Tolkien's *Lord of the Rings*. In their mythology, tension builds in a straight line; heroes glisten in the sun; at the conclusion no loose ends remain. That is normally what mythologists concoct; it is not what is necessarily found in scripture. A typical instance comes when the risen Jesus first reappears to the disciples. A good legend maker would have had Christ stage a spectacular entrance, give a glorious speech or be bathed in splendor and light. Instead Jesus simply walks into the disciples' presence, lets them touch him, and then asks, "Have you anything here to eat?"[9] These are the sorts of touches that suggest a genuine account, not myth-building: though if resurrection is possible, it does sound like the sort of experience that would give a person an appetite.

In addition to being far-fetched, claims that Jesus never existed miss a fundamental point: *somebody* had to compose the elevated thoughts that form Christ's metaphysics. By far the most plausible explanation is that these were indeed the thoughts of the person to whom they are attributed.

SINCE IT IS LIKELY that a spiritual philosopher named Jesus did actually live, richer and more important questions are whether the divine aspects of his calling were genuine, and whether some of his sayings about the supernatural are words he actually spoke or were added to scripture later.

For centuries commentators have supposed that Christ was simply a visionary whose supernatural qualities were later accreted onto his story through religious promotion and the doctoring of scripture. Rudolf Bultmann, a leading influence on the current generation of religious scholars, crystallized this view in his 1948 book *Theology of the New Testament*, which calls for "demythologizing" Jesus's life. Bultmann's work essentially asserts that all divine aspects attributed to Christ by the Gospels are make-believe, invented by religious promoters.

In the fifty years since, the notion that Jesus's spiritual power was contrived after his death has turned up in everything from thriller novels to serious works such as the Nikos Kazantzakis book, and later Martin Scorsese movie, *The Last Temptation of Christ*. Through the same period, a goal of "demythologizing" Jesus has taken over mainstream academic theology. To cite two of many examples, Thomas Sheehan, a professor of philosophy at Loyola University in Chicago, has written that there never was any actual Easter, only an "Easter experience" in which the apostles talked each other into believing their cherished leader was not really gone.[10] John Crossan, professor emeritus of biblical studies at DePaul University, has written that "Jesus was not born of a virgin, not born of David's lineage, not born in Bethlehem, [there] was no stable, no shepherds, no star . . . the divine origins of Jesus are just as fictional or mythological as those of Octavius," the Roman emperor who deified himself.[11]

Doubts about Jesus's deeds must be taken seriously. Many aspects of the far past are shrouded in lore, and surely elements of the ancient church could have had motives for puffing up Christ's legacy by attributing to him supernatural or prophetic powers.[12] But doubt can be cast on the doubt, too. The Catholic University historian John Meier, author of *A Marginal Jew*, a three-part biography of Jesus and his era, has noted that there exists about Christ far more textual information than about most secular figures of the period.[13] Yet revisionist commentators often accept as fully historic any document that casts doubt on the rabbi, while disqualifying as mythological whatever writing supports Jesus. For instance, Crossan has ventured, "It is a little sad to have to say so, because it has always been a captivating story, but the [Christmas] journey to and from Nazareth for census and tax registration is pure fiction." His evidence of "pure fiction" is that Roman provincial records suggest the census occurred in the year 6, not at the turn of the millennium as biblical dating maintains.[14] A six-year discrepancy disqualifies a two-thousand-year-old text? But to this school of thought, ancient secular documents are assumed credible because they do not represent larger meaning; since scripture does assert meaning, contemporary doubt would invalidate its content.

In his *Three Gospels*, Reynolds Price notes that "scholars have grown more and more punitive" regarding the evidence they demand before events depicted in scripture can be regarded as genuine, imposing "degrees of suspicion unfamiliar to sober historians of other fields."[15] If the same level of doubt now directed against the Bible were applied to literary scholarship, Price's argument holds, no one would believe any person named Plato ever existed. Doctoral candidates would now be churning out papers asserting that "Plato's" so-called dialogues were actually mythology collected by factions seeking to glorify ancient Greek history.

When contemporary analysts say that the divine aspects of the Jesus accounts are myths, what they really mean is that a substantial number of professors now think this. That is fair enough: the tenured-faculty consensus currently runs strongly toward absence of higher purpose, and this view has as good a chance of being correct as any other. But arguing that an assumption must be correct because professors say so is a circularity. For example the scholarly journal *Bible Review* headlined a 1997 article on the Gospels accounts of Jesus's sayings, SCHOLARS KNOW SOME SAYINGS ARE INAUTHENTIC.[16] The story that followed offered no hard evidence of inauthenticity, only conceptual objections—objections that may carry weight, but hardly justify the verb "know." Asserting something is "known" in the factual sense, because a group of professionals says it is known, is little different from saying the Red Sea must have parted because priests and rabbis "know" it did. This kind of thinking also disregards the many instances in which academic consensus turns out to be wrong. In recent years, for instance, consensus on such closely studied questions as the age of the universe, or whether human evolution centered in Africa or occurred globally, has been overturned almost annually.

In the 1980s, a loose affiliation of scholars from the religious-studies departments of American universities, operating under the name Jesus Seminar, began to stage theatrical votes on whether particular portions of the New Testament were authentic or mythological; in most cases, mythology won. Robert Funk, leader of the seminar, said its work was "for those who prefer facts to fancies, science to superstition,"[17] and that its goal is "the liberation of the non-eschatological Jesus."[18] Making Jesus "non-eschatological" means to reconstitute

Christ as a savant who simply offered memorable observations about life—more like a first-century seminar leader than a Redeemer.

That contemporary professors labor to reinterpret Jesus as an ancient professor confirms, one supposes, that every generation sees itself in Christ's reflection. Otherwise the claim of the Jesus Seminar to exemplify "science" over "superstition" is useful as a reminder of what can and cannot be known on spiritual subjects.[19] When believers declare that they "know" Jesus is the child of God, they are stating faith, for this assertion is impossible to prove. When skeptics declare that they "know" Jesus's spiritual deeds are mythology they enunciate their own article of faith, because this cannot be proven either. Perhaps the doubters are right, and in any case they bear the same entitlement to articles of faith as anyone else. Yet in its establishment of a new ideology, academic revisionism about Christ has become the mirror image of traditionalism: traditionalists declare Jesus's divinity *must* be true, revisionists that it *must not*, when really the most either side can offer is surmise.

A RELATED CONCERN is whether the New Testament was tampered with in the early centuries to distort its portrait of Jesus.

At least some tinkering with scripture must have happened. Ancient copies of the New Testament, for example, vary on where they position the "cast the first stone" account. As Jaroslav Pelikan of Yale University has noted, at one point in the Gospels where the Greek text has Mary reproach the young Jesus with the words, "your father and I have been searching for you in great anxiety,"[20] some scribes copied the sentence as "*we* have been searching for you," to avoid suggesting that Joseph, rather than God, was Christ's father. The most significant scripture revision for which there is physical evidence comes in the Gospel of Mark. In the earliest extant copies this book concludes at verse 16:8, where an angel guarding the empty tomb announces that Jesus "has been raised, he is not here," news Mary Magdalene and two friends find so disorienting that they run away in "terror and amazement."[21] Slightly later copies of Mark continue on to verse 16:20, recounting how the risen Jesus tells the disciples, "Go into the world and proclaim the good news," then ascends to heaven.[22] The twelve auxiliary verses are sufficiently disputed that the *New Oxford Annotated Bible*, a leading scholarly text, gives them separate listing.[23]

But the probability that at least some changes have been made since the original New Testament documents were drafted has, during the postwar era, been expanded into a larger claim that vast portions of the Bible are doctored. Analysts have suggested, for instance, that Gospel statements such as "Therefore the Jews started persecuting Jesus" were not found in the most ancient texts, but inserted later to make a rival faith sound bad.[24] By the early 1990s the influential Jesus Seminar was asserting that "no more than 18 percent of the sayings attributed to Jesus were uttered by him," the balance being doctored statements spliced into scripture for various nefarious purposes.[25]

Contentions that the Gospels were doctored are not based on physical evidence of splicing or deletions: rather they are linguistic or textual in nature, meaning that they are based on pure conceptual analysis. There exists no "smoking scroll," no early Gospel manuscript that differs significantly from any in use today. Of the approximately 5,000 oldest Greek editions of New Testament books that have been found, all are identical or differ only in immaterial respects such as copying errors.[26] By the third century there were an estimated 24,000 duplicates of various New Testament books in existence, and with the exception of the final twelve verses of Mark, these ancient scriptures are in substantive agreement.

The broadest conceptual objection to the Gospels is that they all were originally created as embroidery on a still older document called Q (from the German *quelle*, for "source").[27] The hypothesized Q might have been an account, written just after Jesus's death, of his moral sayings only, with no mention of supernatural acts or claims. The Gospel writers, who might have come one or more generations after Christ, might have worked from the older Q account, quoting Jesus's beautiful thoughts but then dreaming up nonsense about guiding stars and heavenly hosts and inserting the inventions to make Gospel scripture sound exalted.[28] That, at least, is the Q hypothesis, now taught as fact, or close to it, in many university departments of theology and religious history.[29]

The trouble with this theory is that no Q or fragment of Q has ever been found; the existence of Q is sheer conjecture, based on linguistic and textual analysis.[30] Many documents from Jesus's age must have been lost, so the fact that no Q has been found hardly proves none once existed. Yet on this point, doctored-Bible thinking veers perilously close to conspiracy theory. In order for every New Testament original that exists to contain the same mythological contamination, while every copy of the genuine Q vanished, someone must have staged a well-organized scripture plot that spanned a hefty chunk of the Western world. Either all four Gospel writers were induced to concoct remarkably similar fantasies, or every one of the copies of their work was intercepted and tampered with later, while every one of the genuine Q texts was rounded up and burned.

Society was smaller then: perhaps a scripture-doctoring initiative was possible. The fifth-century Pope Leo the Great ran an orchestrated campaign to destroy Gnostic writing, and this effort was sufficiently successful that many such texts were lost until the twentieth century.[31] But Leo's enterprise does not qualify as a conspiracy, since papal records speak openly of the operation. If the Bible was doctored to fabricate Jesus's spirituality, that conspiracy was so efficient it even erased all trace of itself.

AND IF THE JESUS STORY was substantively altered by ancient intrigue, the tampering criteria were downright strange. Derogatory remarks about Judaism were inserted into the Gospels, but equally derogatory remarks were let stand about Gentiles, who from a marketing standpoint were Christianity's first big target audience. In one Jesus says, "When you are praying do not heap up empty phrases as the Gentiles do, for they think that they will be heard because of their many words."[32] References to divinity and miracles were inserted to delude future generations; yet errors and contradictions were left for future generations to experience doubt over. C. S. Lewis wrote that it was the contradictions that convinced him the Bible was true, since anyone inventing scripture for the purpose of duping people into a religion would have crossed out discrepancies that cause readers to say, "Hey, wait a minute." Not altered by conspirators were references to Jesus drinking too much,[33] to Jesus's own family considering him unbalanced,[34] to Jesus quaking with fear: as the moment of betrayal approached at Gethsemane, the Gospel of Mark reports, Jesus "threw himself on the ground" and begged God to spare him the agony of crucifixion.[35] Wouldn't our well-run conspiracy have deleted such less-than-godlike passages?

A scripture cabal might have taken the red stylus, too, to a passage written by Paul that addresses the resurrection not as a certainty but as a controversy: "If Christ has not been raised then our proclamation has been in vain and your faith has been in vain. We are even found to be misrepresenting God, because we testified of God that he raised Christ, whom he did not raise if it is true that the dead are not raised."[36] According to the postmodern view, biblical verses regarding the resurrection were concocted years later, then engrafted into scripture for the purpose of inventing a cult. Strangely, bracing honesty about the central claim of that cult was also concocted.

A pivotal element any ancient Bible-doctoring team neglected to alter is the account, common to all four Gospels, in which it is women who discover the empty tomb.[37] In the sociology of the ancient Middle East, testimony by women was considered inherently unreliable: for instance, two male witnesses were sufficient to convict a woman of adultery, while no woman's testimony could convict a man.[38] Even the Gospels concede the low standing of female statements. When Mary Magdalene and other women run to tell the disciples the extraordinary news of the risen Christ, "these words seemed to [the apostles] an idle tale, and they did not believe them."[39]

Given the sociology of the times it is likely that no one doctoring scripture, not even a female conspirator, would have contrived essential passages whose believability depends on the affidavits of women. Yet the Gospels present women as receiving two of history's paramount revelations—first the announcement to Mary that a redeemer is coming, second the news at the empty tomb that death is defeated. These are touches no self-respecting ancient faker would have invented.

THE RESURRECTION OF COURSE is where many forms of doubt about Jesus coalesce. Whether Christ rose is almost always addressed in All-or-Nothing terms, with traditionalists insisting that the account simply must be true, revisionists that it simply must be "an idle tale."[40] Though someday a purely technical means may do what the Gospels assert was done supernaturally after Jesus's death, the rationalist mind has more difficulty grappling with the resurrection than with any other biblical claim. It was for this reason that Thomas Jefferson picked up his New Testament and began physically razoring out verses. Pondering the resurrection, Jefferson realized he had come up against the All-or-Nothing problem, and could not bear to think of the beauty of Jesus reduced to a Nothing.

Today no one can be certain what might have happened in an old Roman tomb in Jerusalem, and no one may ever know. But contemplation of Jesus's reality does not have to dead end at the All-or-Nothing diode of uncertainty about the resurrection. There is a third way to contemplate Christ: as an envoy of a God who is engaged in the process of self-discovery.

Suppose we assume that God is real but not Absolute, a higher being engaged in a process of evolution that includes learning by responding to the world. Then All-or-Nothing assumptions about the rabbi Jesus no longer need define our thinking. Christ might be seen not as the agent of a preexistent all-powerful divine plan, but rather as a companion of God's journey. Perhaps Jesus was in some way divinely enabled; but, representing a Maker neither perfect nor Absolute, Christ was not these things either. Perhaps Jesus did have abilities that would appear supernatural to us, remembering that what is supernatural from the perspective of one level of knowledge may be ordinary from another. Perhaps Christ really did live and then die and then live, assisted by a Maker who does not contravene physical law but simply knows more about it than we do.

Perhaps Christ searched for the words that will bring humanity to ethical kindness and to spiritual growth, just as God searches. Perhaps Jesus thought his actions, words, and sacrifice would send a message of complete forgiveness that could never be misunderstood.

And was wrong about that.

Chapter Seventeen

The One Commandment

Men despise faith because they are afraid it might be true.

BLAISE PASCAL, 1660

DEEP IN SPIRITUAL CONTEMPLATION resides the fear that meaning and higher purpose might be real. Far from offering consolation, this thought can terrify.

For many centuries, men and women have possessed valid reasons for wanting to reject faith. The wrathful, belligerent God of the early scriptures was one any sensible person might hope to have exposed as counterfeit. Historically, the institutions of religion have done at least as much harm as good: demanding that people submit to stifling dogma or theocracy; telling people they are unworthy; telling people the smallest error would land their souls in eternal physical torment.

The modern era has its own reasons to fear that the spiritual might be real. Contemporary science and secular philosophy stake considerable prestige on the notion that there is nothing more to human experience than meets the eye: existence is just whirling electrons and replicating amino acids. Market economics stakes its prestige on the notion that unequal distribution of wealth is perfectly fine. Modern ego stakes its self-regard partly on the notion that nothing can be larger than human aspiration. Conceiving of the firmament as meaningless in some ways enhances human freedom, but only the freedom to be as small and negligible as we wish. A heartless world may be harsh, but at least has a clear rule structure. If there is nothing to believe in, then there is no chance our private hearts will be known; no requirement to perfect those hearts, or extend a hand.

Some people fear the spiritual because they do not want to be loved, or to acquire both the joys and commitments of a community of love: or they tell themselves they do not. Awareness of spiritual love may cause us to wonder if we are capable of responding. God, too, once seemed held back by this inner apprehension, hesitant to embrace love and light.

Fear of the spiritual is not a phenomenon solely of secular thought: it is a running theme in scripture. Because, today, we assume that the Bible is the chronicle of women and men coming to God, we tend not to notice how much of scripture concerns people fleeing from faith, wishing it would go away, wishing it would turn out not to be real.

One of the most common of biblical phrases is the words *do not be afraid.* Spoken some sixty-two times in the New Revised Standard Bible alone, the phrase *do not be afraid* usually occurs in the context of urging that people not close their hearts to the possibilities of existence.

A high percentage of the Bible's injunctions against fear of the spirit came from Jesus. Constantly Christ urged his listeners not to flee from their own better selves. "Do not let your hearts be troubled, and do not let them be afraid,"[1] was a bright thread of Jesus's teaching. Do not fear to give of yourself, do not fear to let go of material possessions, do not fear what other people will say, do not fear to open the soul. Do not fear that life does not matter: "Even the hairs of your head are all counted. So do not be afraid."[2] Many men and women fear spiritual power working personal miracles through kindness, fellowship, or moral attainment. Witnessing the good that is possible among people, they must be told, *do not be afraid.*

In addition to often urging people not to fear belief or meaning, Jesus also urged them not to fear their Maker. From the Old Testament books, Christ's listeners knew that past divine interventions on Earth were often abominable—plagues, floods, smashed walls, casualties everywhere. Thus the righteous of ancient days assumed, and not unreasonably, that when the supernatural chose to manifest, mortals had best run for cover. Glimpsing Jesus walking across the water, the disciples were not filled with happiness or wonder, rather they "were terrified." Christ had to call out to his friends, "Take heart, it is I. Do not be afraid."[3] Hearing the voice of God proclaim, "This is my son, the beloved; with him I am well pleased, listen to him," listeners were not rapt but "overcome by fear."[4] Jesus had to reassure them they were safe in the Maker's presence. Coming upon the empty tomb, Mary Magdalene and her companions were not transported by joy but seized by cold dread. The first words they heard from the angel were, "Do not be afraid."[5]

The traditional Sunday-school explanation of why Mary Magdalene was afraid at the empty tomb, or why the disciples felt terror when they heard the voice of God, is that ancient men and women were rustic, superstitious people alarmed by any deviation from expected routines. A more likely explanation is that the people of Jesus's time had a fairly sophisticated understanding of that part of life that they knew, and were sophisticated enough about theology to consider faith as often the source of anguish as rapture. Traditionalism likes to change the subject from issues such as Mary Magdalene's pulse of fear on realizing that God had recently touched the ground on which she was standing, because traditionalism prefers not to discuss the errors and harms once committed by heaven.

At the risk of quoting Shaw again, he once said, "The problem with Christianity is that it's never been tried."[6] True spirituality would revolutionize human society in a way even the most successful democracy or economy never will. It is only our fear of belief that holds us back.

AS SCRIPTURE PROGRESSES, the miraculous declines. An All-or-Nothing analysis might say that miracles decline either owing to a preexistent divine plan or because the fabricators who were inventing faith ran out of ideas for bogus supernatural claims. A third, center possibility is that God gradually withdrew from shows of force, in part because they cause men and women to fear the unseen.

From the latter part of the Old Testament to the end of the New, physical displays of the supernatural grow steadily fewer and less consequential, while interpersonal displays of the spirit increase in importance. Early biblical miracles were breathtaking—seas parted, the earth hewn up. By the late Old Testament books and throughout the New Testament, those marvels that occur are quiet, personal, and gentle—the sick healed, the hungry fed, the righteous praised by angels. (When angels appear in the early scripture, it is usually to threaten or destroy; later in the Bible, angels manifest to lend spiritual comfort or announce glad tidings.[7]) Through the Bible's second half there are no exhibitions of supernatural intimidation, other than the darkness that covers Earth while Jesus suffers on the cross.[8]

When the modest miracles of later scripture do occur, at several junctures Jesus apologizes for calling on supernatural power, instructing those he has aided not to mention their experience. For instance, Jesus heals a deaf person: the first thing the man hears with his newly functioning ears is Christ's instruction, "Tell no one."[9] Jesus, like his Maker, had come to understand that truth is more important than physical miracles, yet could not bear to be in the presence of someone who was suffering without employing curative power. Recall the dialogue between Jesus and the leper, who asks Christ to "choose" to heal him: "Then Jesus stretched out his hand, touched him, and said, 'I do choose.' "[10] What is miraculous about this exchange is not the physical cure, which today a hospital might effect with synthesized pharmaceuticals, but the interpersonal focus: the human and the divine quietly touching each other.

After Jesus leaves the scene there is one final moment of unambiguous supernatural effect, the Pentecost.[11] Following that, divine intervention ends: the remainder of scripture is philosophy, morality, and chronicles of the efforts of believers. A gentle spiritual path has been charted. People may walk upon it or may turn aside; but there is nothing left to fear.

WE MAY NEVER KNOW the answer to Christ's nature or intentions, but within the record of his ministry are moral instructions of timeless value to every person, even if not one word of any faith is true. And if we think of Jesus as the voice for the lessons that the Maker learned from interacting with women and men, Christ's moral thought can become even more affecting. Everyone is aware of the Golden Rule, the Good Samaritan, and the Prodigal Son. Here are other teachings well worth recalling:

Materialism

A young man from a privileged background asks Jesus, "Teacher, what good deed must I do to have eternal life?"[12] The reply:

> Jesus said to him, "If you wish to be perfect, go, sell your possessions, and give the money to the poor, and you will have treasure in heaven."

When the young man heard this word he went away grieving,
for he had many possessions. Then Jesus said to his disciples,
"Truly I tell you, it will be hard for a rich person to enter the
kingdom of heaven. Again I tell you, it is easier for a camel to
go through the eye of a needle than for someone who is rich
to enter the kingdom of God."[13]

A parallel Gospel account of the same encounter concludes
with these words: "Jesus looked around and said to his disciples, 'How hard it will be for those who have wealth to enter
the kingdom of God!' "[14]

It's just the strangest thing how infrequently these passages
are brought up in religious politics. Equally rare are citations
of similar New Testament injunctions such as, "Keep your
lives free from the love of money."[15] As the theologian Harvey
Cox of Harvard University has noted, contemporary Christianity "slide[s] easily over Jesus's harsh warnings to the rich
and powerful."[16]

Jesus was moved to a physical outburst just once in his life,
when he threw the money-changers and dove-sellers out of the
temple.[17] We can only wonder what Christ would think of
those televangelists whose tube time is dedicated to pulling in
the almighty dollar, 800 numbers flashing onscreen; or those
business people who make a show of claiming Jesus as master,
but devote their lives to accumulation at the expense of others;
or those self-satisfied affluent congregations who nod approvingly to sermons on civil rights or nuclear disarmament, but
would squirm if clergy reminded them that Jesus said, "Give
to everyone who begs from you."[18]

Perhaps Jesus's most lingering injunction against materialism comes in this beautifully economical avowal:

Do not store up for yourselves treasures on earth, where moth
and rust consume . . . but store up for yourselves treasures in

heaven . . . for where your treasure is, there your heart will be also.[19]

Jesus's point was not that people should live in deprivation: we all need some material things. His point is that what you orient your life around will be where you end up. People who chase more of what they already have, money, do so at the expense of what they may forever lack, their souls. Use your time to accumulate material things, and you will end stripped of them anyway. Use what time you are given on Earth for the things that really matter, and you will be allowed to keep those things eternally. Of all Christ's teachings, none is more studiously avoided than this.

Fundamental Goodness

It would be a mistake to think that Jesus adhered to a fuzzy I'm-OK-You're-OK sentimentality. He strongly believed in such currently out-of-fashion concepts as evil and hell. Christ was keenly concerned that sin destroys both its victims and the sinner: "Very truly I tell you, everyone who commits sin is a slave to sin."[20] He did not chuckle, as modernism does, when invoking the word Satan: "I will warn you whom to fear: fear him who, after he has killed, has authority to cast into hell. Yes, I tell you, fear him!"[21] Jesus was anything but value-neutral. To him there were bright-line distinctions between right and wrong, with awful consequences for those who stepped across.

Yet missing from the teachings of Jesus is any reference to original sin or similar concepts.[22] Jesus seemed to view women and men as born good and then corrupted, and he held a high opinion of the human prospect. Quoting the Psalms, Christ remarked, "Is it not written in your law, 'I said, you are gods?' "[23] By extension this argument blankets all humankind: the psalm quoted by Jesus reads, "I say you are gods, children of the Most High, all of you."[24] This is scarcely the logic of original sin. To Jesus the basic constitution of *Homo sapiens*, the plenum on which the soul is struck, was goodness. Christ's attitudes show that whatever bitterness the Maker once felt over the Garden had, by his time, been forgiven and forgotten.

Glory in Goodness, Not Power

In the tumult of early scripture, God seeks laud through worship, might, and magnificence. Toward the end of the Old Testament, the Maker loses interest in such trappings. By the time Jesus begins to preach, heaven sees honor not in power but in kindness. In a magnificent teaching, Jesus tells an audience, "Let your light shine before others, so that they may see your good works and give glory to your Father in heaven."[25]

To some this verse may suggest religious traditionalism, since it includes respectful reference to the Father. But in context the thought is revolutionary. Now *human action gives glory to God*. If God is an all-powerful Absolute, every conceivable homage would already reflect on heaven: what could a mere man or woman possibly do that would glorify a flawless ultimate? Instead Jesus tells us that our Maker benefits from moral human behavior—and it is acts of goodness, not power, that create the kind of glory God now seeks.

Greatness in the Least of Things

Jesus extols the meek, saying they will inherit the Earth.[26] The philosopher Charles Hartshorne felt there was natural-science logic in Jesus's thoughts on that score: "Biology teaches that aggressiveness and hostility are no more essential to evolutionary success than cooperation, parental tenderness and sympathy."[27]

Population statistics support this notion, since in terms of passing genes to offspring, the meek are winning Darwin's contest by a runaway margin. The phrase "survival of the fittest" is commonly misunderstood to mean that nature favors the savage. History surely has not. The Mongols and the Dorians were "fit" in the way people think evolution wants us to be, ferocious and war-obsessed; they did not survive. The Spartans and the Vikings were fierce, unpitying; they perished. The Nazis, who challenged the genetic stream directly, were wiped out with blinding speed by the standards of nature, along with the obsessively fit imperial Japanese. While predator societies have in every case extinguished themselves, which groups have prospered in the sense favored by nature— that is, increased their numbers? The meek, who shall inherit: the coexisters. The numerical majority of the men and women alive today, and who have lived throughout history, have been meek in the positive sense of that word, never harming or taking from others. Once the greedy and bellicose have run their course, who can say what the next order will be? When the meek inherit, they may do so for positive reasons.

Jesus often underscored the quintessence of the least of things, the richness in that which the world seems not to value. Drawn to prostitutes, fisher folk, sinners, and publicans, Jesus spent most of his hours on Earth among the meek or outcast. The unassuming group of misfits Jesus gathered about him became the most influential movement in Western history. "The stone that the builders rejected has become the cornerstone,"[28] he noted of his lowly and yet indomitable friends. This is an important lesson in the distinction between the flashy temporal power that comes from money and status, and the lasting influence that can emanate only from the heart.

God as the Least

In classicist religion, the divine is a colossus: a vast figure of apotheosis on a golden throne that refracts the sun. Jesus did not see things this way, speaking of God in terms of everyday familiarity. Christ addressed his Maker as *Abba*—"father" in

Aramaic, but a diminutive that can translate as "daddy" or even "poppy."[29] And in the sole description Jesus offered of the divine, he said simply, "God is spirit: and they that worship him must worship him in spirit and in truth."[30]

God is spirit. That is how Christ chose to characterize his Maker. And if God is spirit, and every human being contains some spirit—well, you can put the rest together for yourself.

Childlike Wonder

Everyone remembers when Jesus noticed barefoot boys and girls being shooed away from a public lecture: "He was much displeased and said unto them, 'Suffer the little children to come unto me, and forbid them not: for of such is the kingdom of God.' "[31] People learn this account while little, when it seems a gratifying instance of the adult world being censured for insufficient appreciation of the young. But many overlook what Jesus declares next: "Verily I say unto you, Whosoever shall not receive the kingdom of God as a little child, he shall not enter therein."[32]

By this Christ means that men and women should approach spirituality in a childlike manner—feeling, as children do, limitless awe at the human possibility. Enthralled by life, the child's mind wants to believe in love, fellowship, and the realms of all possibilities. The adult mind wants to find excuses not to believe these things. The initial instinct is the correct one. Not childish behavior, but the recovery of childlike instinct, is essential to spiritual progress.

The Sermon

The nineteenth-century orator Daniel Webster, looked back on today as an antediluvian, was in some ways well ahead of the curve: he said Jesus's moral teachings were a better argument for spiritual awareness than any claim of supernatural power. Webster, who often spoke to large crowds in the day before the media age, and thus had some sense of what it must have been like for Jesus to address thousands, was particularly swayed by the Sermon on the Mount, which he considered the ultimate example of elocution. On the night before his death in 1852, Webster said, "Philosophic argument, especially that drawn from the vastness of the universe, has sometimes shaken my reason for the faith that is in me. But my heart has always assured me that the gospel of Jesus Christ must be divine reality, for the Sermon on the Mount cannot be a mere human production."

The Sermon on the Mount runs several thousand words, and some of its messages are confined to their time—such as the advice that people settle lawsuits out of court to avoid debtor's prison, for "Truly I tell you, you will never get out until you have paid the last penny."[33] Within the Sermon is both a lifetime of moral teaching and many expressions of notable wit, including this droll observation: "Woe to you when all speak well of you."[34]

Other aspects of the Sermon today require explanation, among them Jesus's injunction that people not swear either by God or by the hair of their heads. In old desert culture it was standard that only words spoken as vows were believed. Swearing by the hair of your head was appropriate for minor promises, swearing by God for major commitments. Jesus opposed swearing because the use of the infrequent vow of truth means a person's other statements need not be sincere. Do not occasionally make a big show of promising honesty, Christ instructed: simply say yes or no, and always make it the truth.[35]

Beyond its anachronisms, the Sermon on the Mount is unadulterated spiritual beauty. What follows is a compression of this great teaching. In devising it I used only the Bible's own words, but reduced the text to roughly a third its original length, merged parallel accounts from the Gospels of Matthew and Luke,[36] and altered the order of some sayings. Traditionalists will protest that this condensed Sermon on the Mount deletes Jesus's statements about hell and the prohibition of divorce: these references appear in Matthew but not in Luke, leaving fair room for disagreement. Read the Sermon both for moral value and bearing in mind Webster's point about the superiority of truth over supernatural power as a proof of the divine:

The Concise Sermon on the Mount

Blessed are the poor in spirit, for theirs is the kingdom of heaven.
Blessed are those who mourn, for they will be comforted.
Blessed are the meek, for they will inherit the earth.
Blessed are those who hunger and thirst for righteousness, for they
    will be filled.
Blessed are the merciful, for they will receive mercy.
Blessed are the pure in heart, for they will see God.
Blessed are the peacemakers, for they will be called children of God.

Do not judge, so that you may not be judged.
For with the judgment you make you will be judged
And the measure you give will be the measure you get.

If you forgive others their trespasses,
Your heavenly Father will also forgive you.
But if you do not forgive others,
Neither will your Father forgive your trespasses.

You have heard that it was said, "You shall love your neighbor and
    hate your enemy." But I say, "Love your enemies and pray for
    those who persecute you."

If anyone strikes you on the right cheek, turn the other also;
If anyone wants to sue you and take your coat, give your cloak
    as well;
If anyone forces you to go one mile, go also the second mile.

If you love only those who love you, what credit is that to you?
For even sinners love those who love them.
If you do good only to those who do good to you, what credit is
    that to you?
For even sinners do the same.

If you lend only to those from whom you hope to receive, what
   credit is that to you?
Even sinners lend to sinners, to receive as much again.
And if you greet only your brothers and sisters, what more are you
   doing than others?

Love your enemies, do good, and lend expecting nothing in return.
Your reward will be great, and you will be children of the Most High.

You are the light of the world. No one after lighting a lamp
Puts it under the bushel basket but on the lampstand.
In the same way let your light shine before others,
So that they may see your good works and give glory to your Father
   in heaven.

No one can serve two masters;
You cannot serve God and wealth.
Give to everyone who begs from you,
And do not refuse anyone who wants to borrow from you.

Woe to you who are rich, for you have received your consolation.
Woe to you who are full now, for you will be hungry.
Woe to you when all speak well of you.

Beware of practicing your piety before others, in order to be seen
   by them.
Whenever you pray, do not be like the hypocrites,
For they love to stand and pray so that they may be seen by others.
Truly I tell you, they have received their reward.

But whenever you pray, go into your room and shut the door
And pray to your Father who is in secret.
Your Father who sees in secret will reward you.

I tell you do not worry about what you will eat or what you will
   drink.
Look at the birds of the air. They neither sow nor reap nor gather
   into barns,
Yet your heavenly Father feeds them. Are you not of more value
   than they?

And why do you worry about clothing?
Consider the lilies of the field. They neither toil nor spin.
Yet I tell you even Solomon in all his glory was not clothed like one
    of these.
If God so clothes the grass of the field, will he not much more
    clothe you?

And can any of you by worrying add a single hour to your span
    of life?

Do not store up for yourselves treasures on earth,
Where moth and rust consume and where thieves break in and steal.
But store up for yourselves treasures in heaven.
For where your treasure is, there your heart will be also.

Ask, and it will be given you; search, and you will find;
Knock, and the door will be opened for you.

Enter through the narrow gate;
For the gate is wide and the road is easy that leads to destruction,
And there are many who take it.
The gate is narrow and the road is hard that leads to life,
And there are few who find it.

In everything do to others as you would have them do to you.

Do the words of the Sermon on the Mount not, alone, demonstrate that spirituality exists? Somebody, after all, had to
devise these thoughts, and they are not the work of scripture-
doctoring fabricators, *of that we may be certain.*
   The integral harmony of the instruction *In everything do to
others as you would have them do to you* compresses into a single
thought the principal insights of all ethical systematics.[37] Just
thirteen words lay out a formula for a humane world: the
sentence is flawless, irrefutable, bulletproof. The warning
that wasting our lives chasing possessions only results in *moth
and rust* compresses into a single thought everything you need
to know about materialism. The unexpected phrase *Love your*

enemies compresses into three words the essence of compassionate enlightenment. Whether Jesus came from the divine or merely sought it, through these teachings he unmistakably proclaimed spiritual meaning, and that is all that really matters.

The Two Commandments

Earlier it was noted that when asked to specify the commandments, Jesus recited only those six that refer to love and morality, dropping the four articles regarding formal religious observation. In another exchange, Jesus edited the commandments down further. This time Christ was asked a question that is traditional to rabbinical debate, "Which commandment in the law is the greatest?" Jesus replied,

> You shall love the Lord your God with all your heart, and with all your soul, and with all your mind. This is the greatest and first commandment. And a second is like it: You shall love your neighbor as yourself. On these two commandments hang all the law and the prophets.[38]

A person could live an admirable, moral, sacred life by following no rules other than these Two Commandments. In the Two Commandments the divine remains prominent. But what God requires of humanity is not veneration, rather heartfelt spiritual love. Worship, which heaven once asked for, flows from an inferior to a superior. Love is a medium of exchange among kindred spirits, and in the Two Commandments, God seems to embrace men and women as such. In the Two Commandments, Jesus also gives the love of neighbor standing analogous to the love of God. Previous theology had depicted deference to the Maker as an obligation surpassing all others. Now Christ calls people's need for love equal to the needs of God: a revolutionary notion.

The Two Commandments passage is among those that occur in overlaid versions in more than one Gospel. A corresponding telling of this story begins when "a lawyer stood up to test Jesus." Here the Two Commandments are rendered as, "You shall love the lord your God with all your heart, with all your soul, and with all your strength, and with all your mind: and your neighbor as yourself."[39] Naturally the lawyer raises a technicality: "And who is my neighbor?"[40] Jesus uses this opening to tell the parable of the Good Samaritan. Closing the account, Christ asks his interlocutor, " 'Which do you think was the neighbor of the man who fell among thieves?' [The lawyer] said, 'The one who showed mercy.' Jesus said to him, 'Go and do likewise.' " Perfect moral clarity.

Love Becomes the Logos

In early scripture, God does not create the world out of love; we never learn the divine motive, beyond desire for a human race "according to our likeness."[41] Nor are heaven's early interactions with men and women presented with love as a primary concern. The Bible's first use of the word "love" entails brutality—the Maker's instruction that Abraham "Take your son, your only son Isaac, whom you love, and go to the land of Moriah and offer him there as a burnt offering."[42] Abraham is assumed to love Isaac; it's not clear that God does. Through much of the early monotheist writ, love is almost a throwaway expression.

With the passage of time, tenderness becomes increasingly important to heaven. By the late Old Testament, prophets speak of "the abundance of [God's] steadfast love."[43] By Jesus's day, love becomes the *Logos*, the "divine expression," or sometimes simply the Word, on which faith turns. The first use of "love" in the New Testament is among the most revolutionary ideals of the spirit: "I say to you, Love your enemies and pray for those who persecute you."[44] Soon after, to love God and fellow beings is the essence of everything the Maker cares about: "On these two commandments hang all the law and the prophets."[45] As God's spiritual journey proceeds, love increases, while religious edicts grow fewer and commandments decrease. They decrease, in fact, to One Commandment:

The One Commandment

Such was his gift that Jesus simplified the entire structure of spirituality into a single unitary sentence: "This is my commandment, that you love one another as I have loved you."[46]

Because Christ is understood theologically as speaking the thoughts of the Maker, when he enunciates "my" commandment, it means the commandment of God. And what is the One Commandment? *Love one another as I have loved you.* Articulating this last and highest commandment, Jesus adds, again with his use of "my" understood to convey the thoughts of God, "I have said these things to you so that my joy may be in you, and that your joy may be complete."[47]

Once God's love was sufficiently open to question that many would not have wished it; and once the Maker did not seem aware of, much less concerned with, anyone's joy. Now love is the priority and joy the reward: now nothing could be more right or more fulfilling than to receive and pass along the divine sense of love. The Commandments have fallen from Ten to Six to Two to One, and encountering the One Commandment, we find the focus entirely on the humane.

Chapter Eighteen

Armor of Light

Let us then lay aside the works of darkness and
put on the armor of light.
ROMANS 13:12

THOUSANDS OF YEARS AGO, forlorn in a desert, our ancestors dreamed a dream. They dreamed that despair and injustice were not the inevitable conditions of society, but could be overcome by righteousness. They dreamed that life need not be a lonely downhill struggle, but could be uplifted by ideals and warmed by fellowship. They dreamed that death need not bring oblivion, but that the soul might endure, giving purpose to the cosmic expanse. They dreamed that the world need not be a heartless realm of kill or be killed, but could someday be remade into a gladsome Garden. Most of all they dreamed their own existence was not meaningless, to be played out alone and unnoted: rather that somewhere a loving creator wanted and watched them, dreaming well for them in turn.

Perhaps people once dreamed such things to escape the inclemency of a cruel, arduous existence. Perhaps they were tricked into dreaming such things by promoters of mythology. And perhaps they dreamed such things because they are true.

How liberating it must have seemed, millennia ago, for people to envision that existence could someday be made tranquil and benevolent; that the human preoccupation with conflict could be surmounted by cooperation and forgiveness. How liberating to envision that life was not some random biochemical coincidence, but imbued with a transcendent meaning that people and their Maker would eventually discern.

How admirable that our ancestors, who lived short lives of toil and suffering, turned so much of their thought to the ultimate issues of existence; when we today, possessing extended lifespans and every material advantage, engage in spiritual contemplation mainly as a diversion.

If records may be believed, long ago devotional reflection was a much more prominent aspect of daily life than in our age. At a time when day-to-day experience consisted mainly of exertion, illness, and the elements, the search to understand the possibilities of the spirit was among principal topics of discussion. Today we like to suppose our distant ancestors were unsophisticated in their thoughts. It may be that they took more care with the questions that really matter than do we moderns, who imagine our data, productivity, and airs of ironic detachment place us at the vanguard of history.

Yet in the contemporary heart we still dream the things of which our ancient forebears dreamt. In every generation, in every society, women and men have felt the tingle of larger purpose, sensed that something must exist outside the tyrannies of biology and time, yearned for the fulfillment of which they know their souls to be capable.

THE SEARCH FOR SPIRITUAL ENLIGHTENMENT can seem perpetually bogged down in reenactments of disputes about what long-silent voices meant by what they said many centuries ago. This backward focus of faith is its most puzzling aspect. No discipline of science or medicine or engineering could advance if required to base all judgments on reinterpretations of ideas proposed centuries before. The scientist is happy when new understanding overthrows some assumption of the past, because this moves the process one step closer to full enlightenment.

Why should the same kind of openness not hold for spiritual thought? The most pertinent questions of metaphysics are not what was believed in the past, rather what we should believe now. Of this we may be certain: the Maker is not sitting around splitting hairs regarding exactly what was meant by two-thousand-year-old words. God's gaze is fixed forward, as ours should be.

No CONTEMPLATION OF FAITH SHOULD CLOSE with a conclusion, in the logician's sense, of "The proposition that must follow." Belief cannot be carried to a conclusion, only explored. No one can be certain whether God exists, whether people of the past were granted special access to the Maker's meditation, whether the divine will one day touch the Earth again. No one can know when answers to these questions will manifest, if ever.

Yet even with so many questions unanswerable, belief can arrive at axial truths. Such truths may arise from a preexistent divinity; may be formed by an autonomously generated cosmos; may have been compiled by an evolving God; or may be the product of human aspiration. In some ways the last possibility is most alluring, because it suggests people can make something that is eternal—not cities or belongings or software but *truth*—and offer it up to the divine.

Here are a few spiritual truths anyone might accept. They are elemental and unrelated to denomination.

First, heaven asks nothing for itself. Whatever veneration the Maker may once have desired, in its place the divine now yearns solely for human tenderness and virtue.

Second, God had to grow spiritually: from belligerence to

nonviolence, from judgmentalism to tolerance, from enmity to forgiveness, from vehement flame to still waters. If the divine had to go through these stages, it is not surprising that humankind must do so as well.

Third, spiritual compassion holds the potential for resolving the world's ills. A verse of scripture notes, "Love does no wrong to a neighbor; therefore, love is the fulfilling of the law."[1] However conscientious and however carefully written, civic law will never make life fully humane. Though today far from the smallest measure of its potential, love holds out the hope of ending inequality and inhumanity. No purely secular ideal can make that claim.

Fourth, life has meaning. Either meaning was given at the creation or has been acquired since. Whichever the case, higher purpose awaits, calling us to join a magnificent enterprise.

Fifth, everything ineffable can be conveyed in a three-word phrase found in some form in the writs of every faith: *God is love.*

"GOD IS LOVE." One of the richest and most fully realized passages in any spiritual traditional comes from the brief, little-known biblical letter titled First John. The true name, nationality, and gender of the author have been lost to history, but it is believed he or she numbered among the second generation of those who answered the call of the revolutionary rabbi Jesus. The author of First John wrote, "So we have known and believe the love that God has for us. God is love, and those who abide in love abide in God, and God abides in them."[2]

This verse is astonishing both in its buoyant expectation for the human prospect and in its simple factual declaration: "God is love, and those who abide in love abide in God, and God abides in them." For all the toilsome argumentation regarding what various passages of various scriptures might or might not mean, there can be no doubt about what this sentence means: not that God has love or approves of love or preaches love—but *is* love.

If God *is* love, then wherever good will exists, the divine becomes present.

If God *is* love there will always be cause for faith, because men and women can choose to make their world blessed by the way they treat each other.

If God *is* love, then every person possesses the ability to create that which is more miraculous, more prized, and more percipient than all physical forces of the universe combined.

If God *is* love, then each of us already knows where the Maker dwells.

And if *those who abide in love abide in God, and God abides in them,* then regardless of whether any religion or faith is ultimately right, the ability to call down the sacred rests equally with every person in every place.

In the ancient desert, people who by our standards possessed nothing of value and understood little of the world nevertheless learned to give their lives meaning by embracing the spiritual dreams of love and justice. They found higher purpose where it has always been and will always be, within the heart. In this, anyone may believe.

If it is true that a divinity gave us being, then it is incumbent on people to treat each other lovingly and with justice, earning that divinity's grace.

Or if it is true that no divinity exists, then it is incumbent on people to treat each other lovingly and with justice, honoring the life-force they jointly share.

In either case the spiritual promise is the same. This is the fundamental reason to believe.

Notes

[1]Cultivation agriculture is believed to have begun around 10,000 years ago; see "Yang-tze Seen as Earliest Rice Site," *Science*, 17 January 1997. Writing is generally thought to have begun about 5,000 years ago, and the wheel to have become common around the same time. Cave paintings are thought to go back 30,000 years or more.

[2]From *The Conduct of Life* by Ralph Waldo Emerson, 1870.

[3]From *Pudd'nhead Wilson* by Mark Twin, 1894.

[4]The first of the two Christmas accounts begins at Matthew 1:25.

[5]The second of the two Christmas accounts begins at Luke 2, with the famous "In those days a decree went out."

[6]From Abdu'l-Bahá, *The Promulgation of Universal Peace* (1912; reprint, Winnetka, Ill.: Baha'i Publication Trust, 1982).

[7]See Alexander Herzen, *From the Other Shore* (1855; reprint, Oxford: Oxford University Press, 1979).

[8]From G. B. Shaw, *Collected Letters, Volume Two*, ed. Dan Laurence (New York: Viking, 1985).

[9]Polling data on happiness discussed in Robert Samuelson, *The Good Life and Its Discontents* (New York: Times Books, 1996). Some polls find that the percentage of people describing themselves as "happy" has fallen since the 1950s. Samuelson supposes that a decrease in self-reported happiness may stem partly from the fact that the media have gotten better and better at emphasizing things to worry about, thus generating unfocused civic anxiety.

Chapter Two

[1]Surveys discussed in "Saving Souls," *American Demographics*, March 1996. In a 1996 Gallup survey, "organized religion" fell from its traditional first place in public trust to third, behind the military and the police. Members of the clergy slipped from first in public trust to second, trailing pharmacists. Near the bottom of the poll on those holding public trust were—pollsters.

[2]See Roger Finke and Rodney Starke, *The Churching of America, 1776–1990* (New Brunswick, N.J.: Rutgers University Press, 1994). This book points out that one reason church attendance in the United States remains higher than in Western Europe is that American

clergy strive in an entrepreneurial manner to discover to what the flock will respond. Finke and Starke wrote that in the eighteenth and nineteenth centuries, Baptist and Methodist congregations expanded rapidly across the growing United States because they showed good business sense: "Both denominations developed systems that made it easy for gifted laymen to enter the ministry. Those not selected to fill the local pulpit had to seek one elsewhere, typically by starting a new congregation. The result was a free-market competition among preachers."

Today the same entrepreneurial instincts can be seen in the market-driven growth of "megachurches," in the acutely marketing-oriented "spirituality" movements (a suspicious percentage of which have Southern California return addresses), and in the evolving "Next Church," baby-boomer oriented congregations that emphasize pop music and social services intended to generate a community sensibility.

[3]Genesis 1:20, King James Version (KJV), 1611. Most biblical quotations will be from the New Revised Standard Version (NRSV), published in 1989 and generally considered authoritative.

[4]Astronomy has identified objects that are supernatural relative to the ability of current physics to explain them. Some distant quasars, for example, appear to be fairly small regions producing as much power as the 100 billion stars of this galaxy combined. "Nearby" in the Pistol Nebula of our own Milky Way shines a single star that kick outs 10 million times the energy of our sun, which is incomprehensible under current theories of star formation. But objects such as quasars seem supernatural owing to the early state of human knowledge of the cosmos, not because they represents divine latency.

[5]Imagine how journalists would react if educators grouped their work under "media and misanthropy."

[6]From Alfred North Whitehead, *Process and Reality* (New York: Free Press, 1985). Though the view that "The kingdom of heaven is with us today" is awfully hard to defend, by this Whitehead did not mean that the world should be considered a perfect reflection of divine intent. Rather, he was making a point from Christian apologetics: the interpretation that once Jesus offered divine grace to everyone universally, the ability of any men or women to obtain godly love converted the world into a "kingdom" waiting to happen.

[7]See Peter Steinfels, "Beliefs," *New York Times*, 24 July 1993.

[8]Theodore Glickman et al. "Acts of God and Acts of Man," research paper, Resources for the Future, Washington, D.C., 1992.

[9]All ancient population figures are estimates; these come from Colin McEvedy and Richard Jones, *Atlas of World Population History* (New York: Viking, 1978). The population computation for Moses's age is for 1,200 years before Christ, which most historians suppose was the period of the Mosaic flight from Egypt.

[10]See *World Development Report 1996* (Oxford: Oxford University Press, 1996).

[11]See Samuel Kramer, *History Begins at Sumer* (Philadelphia: University of Pennsylvania Press, 1989).

[12]The Buddha, though revered, is simply an accomplished mortal. Nirvana, though sought after, is conceived as a release from the cycle of reincarnation into daily torment, not as a cloud paradise.

[13]Eve's taste test is at Genesis 3.

[14]Genesis 3:10, New Revised Standard Version.

[15]Genesis 30:24–30.

[16]Genesis 18:23–33.

[17]Genesis 18:25, New Revised Standard Version.

[18]Admirable self-control enabled me to resist a joke about the fortune waiting to be made by marketing wrestling-with-God fitness tapes.

[19]From Karen Armstrong, *A History of God* (New York: Ballantine, 1993).

[20]Readers would do well to see Loisy's *The Gospel and the Church* (1902; reprint, Buffalo, N.Y.: Prometheus Books, 1988).

[21]From Bruce Chilton, "The Fundamentals of Fundamentalism," *Bible Review*, December 1996.

Chapter Three

[1]Speech in Palm Springs, California, 24 January 1997.

[2]Benjamin Schwarz, "What Jefferson Helps to Explain," *The Atlantic Monthly*, March 1997. Schwarz further notes that in the early nineteenth century, churches were the American institutions pursuing racial harmony: "Nearly a third of all Methodists in America in 1800 were black . . . blacks and whites prayed together, were baptized in the same ceremonies, were held to the same moral expectations and buried in the same cemeteries." This harmony ended when many denominations split over the Civil War.

[3]See Christine Leigh Heyrman, *Southern Cross: The Beginnings of the Bible Belt* (New York: Knopf, 1997). Heyrman shows that early nineteenth-century evangelism appealed to Southern women partly because it advocated greater roles for women.

[4]From David Herbert Donald, *Lincoln* (New York: Simon & Schuster, 1995). The second half of this citation is Donald quoting from a newspaper of the era.

[5]Quoted in Henry Chadwick, *Early Christianity* (London: Pelican Books, 1967).

[6]Rauschenbusch and others of the early century advocated "Christian socialism," the word "socialism" then having a positive connotation. Should believers advocate something more sweeping? There are oft-remarked-upon parallels between the sayings of Jesus and Marx; the New Testament can be interpreted as supporting a dramatic redistribution of society's resources. See Acts 4:32, where Peter takes pride that in his first community of believers, "no one claimed private ownership of any possessions, but everything they owned was held in common." Somehow the Jerry Falwell set never quite gets around to quoting such passages.

[7]James's theory is spelled out in his 1907 book *Pragmatism*, which remains in press (Buffalo, N.Y.: Prometheus Books, 1997). His *Varieties of Religious Experience* (1902; reprint, New York: Macmillan, 1997) is also relevant.

[8]The "social gospel" both helped render American society more progressive and, by reigning in the excesses of capitalism, prevented Soviet-style communism from spreading to the United States: a double achievement.

[9]See John Dewey, *A Common Faith* (New Haven: Yale University Press, 1934).

[10]Readers should consult George Weigel's excellent *The Final Revolution: The Resistance Church and the Collapse of Communism* (Oxford: Oxford University Press, 1992), which shows how Catholic sentiment exerted much of the final impetus for the fall of the former Soviet bloc.

[11]"Liberation theology" may have been bad economics but it was great politics, as it helped put dictatorship on the run in much of Latin America.

[12]See Richard Appelbaum, "Using Religion's Suasion in the Garment Industry," *Los Angeles Times*, 16 February 1997.

[13]The Presbyterian USA affiliation is regularly condemned by traditionalists as too lib-

eral, since its assembly endorses social activism. But to liberal opinion the denomination's formality, moral strictness, and emphasis on reaching out to God would seem hopelessly traditional. This was a combination my wife and I found appealing.

[14]Speech at Georgetown University, September 1996.

[15]Pious Muslims give a *zakat* of 12 percent of their incomes to the poor, bettering those pious Christians who donate a tithe. The progressive Ismaili denomination of Islam, headed by descendants of the Aga Khan, has used *zakat* to fund health-care and rural school projects throughout the Indian subcontinent.

[16]From Amy Waldman, "Why We Need a Religious Left," *The Washington Monthly*, December 1995.

[17]"President's Bishop Leads Religious Group Opposing Gulf War," *Wall Street Journal*, 28 January 1991.

[18]Many fundamentalists dislike that label, objecting to the cultural insinuation of the fundamentalist as a stick-in-the-mud who refuses to acknowledge modernity. Christian conservatives often prefer the classification "evangelicals," which means those who believe they have an obligation to share their faith, as did the apostles. There exists a small subset of liberal evangelicals, of which former President Jimmy Carter is the leading exponent. Because, however, no such thing as a liberal fundamentalist has ever been observed, in most cases I employ the term "fundamentalist" to describe the conservative church faction. Like all labels, it is unsatisfactory.

[19]"Attitudes on Religion in Politics," survey, Pew Charitable Trusts, June 1996.

[20]Madison had hoped the Bill of Rights would constrain all levels of government, but as part of the compromise to win passage, only the federal government was restricted. States remained free to mandate official faith. Jefferson persuaded the Virginia legislature to "disestablish" the Episcopal church via that state's Statute of Religious Freedom, but other states declined to follow suit, Massachusetts keeping Congregationalism as a formally sanctioned faith well into the nineteenth century. Eventually the Fourteenth Amendment led to the extension of Bill of Rights guarantees to state and local jurisdictions. But until this amendment was ratified in 1868 and interpreted by courts, Americans were not guaranteed freedom of speech, religion, or the press, relative to the states.

Some scholars have proposed that the lead religious clause of the First Amendment, specifying that "Congress shall make no law respecting an establishment of religion," actually was designed to protect entrenched denominations: the reasoning being that the amendment would forbid Congress from ordering the states to cease endorsing religions. See Jed Rubenfeld, "Antidisestablishmentarianism," *Yale Law Journal*, April 1997.

[21]*Stone* v. *Graham*, 449 U.S. 39. Rehnquist was an associate justice when he wrote these words.

[22]*Abington School District* v. *Schempp*, 374 U.S. 203.

[23]The Supreme Court held in 1980 that it was unconstitutional for plaques presenting the Ten Commandments to be displayed in public schools, overturning a Kentucky law that allowed such display if the plaques were purchased with private funds. In 1995 there were two similar lower court cases banning exhibition of the Ten Commandments on the walls of courthouses.

[24]From Stephen Carter, *The Culture of Disbelief* (Garden City, N.Y.: Anchor Books, 1994).

[25]Speech at Georgetown University, September 1996.

[26]"The Media and Contemporary Religion," speech by Cullen Murphy at Saint Ambrose University, April 1994. In this talk, Murphy noted that through the early 1990s *The New*

York Times regularly devoted about the same column-inches to the topic "religion and churches" as it did to "teeth and dentistry." Murphy further said, "There are many reasons the press doesn't get religion, and one is a matter of demographics. The type of people who hold influential reporting, editing, and management positions in journalism . . . are by and large irreligious themselves." Murphy is a member of the group he criticizes, by virtue of being managing editor of *The Atlantic Monthly*.

[27]Associated Press, 23 February 1996.

[28]John Leo, "Bust Those Candy Cane Felons!" *U.S. News & World Report*, 30 December 1996.

[29]Another small example: The cartoon classic *Mister Magoo's Christmas Carol*, shown on network TV annually through the 1970s, contains a song in which Bob Cratchit croons that his family is poor but has "the Lord's bright blessing." Could you imagine that reference today?

[30]From Thomas Moore, "Does America Have a Soul?" *Mother Jones*, September/October 1996.

[31]First Timothy 6:10, NRSV.

[32]First Timothy 6:9, NRSV.

[33]Luke 6:24, NRSV.

[34]Matthew 6:19, NRSV.

[35]John Mueller has written that religious opposition to materialism can be understood in economic terms: "If people become primarily materialistic, they will need the [spiritual] product less. Hence it is sensible for churches to feel threatened by people who stress, and supply, economic well-being as opposed to spiritual uplift."

[36]Reported in "Pope Issues Harsh Condemnation of Materialism," *New York Times*, 3 May 1991.

[37]From *Walden*, Henry David Thoreau, 1854.

[38]First Corinthians 13:3–4, NRSV.

[39]First Corinthians, 13:1, KJV.

[40]From Emerson's "Ode Inscribed to W. H. Channing," 1847.

[41]See Michael Kinsley, "The Culture of Too Much Belief," *The New Republic*, 13 September 1993.

[42]See C. Bruce Hunter, "Jefferson's Bible," *Bible Review*, February 1997.

[43]Jefferson's *Life and Morals of Jesus* remains in press under the title *The Jefferson Bible* (New York: Basic Books, 1991).

[44]Jefferson was hardly the first to attempt such a scriptural rewrite, nor would he be the last. In the second century the Gnostic commentator Marcion published a volume selectively deleting those portions of scripture that made Jesus sound Jewish: Marcion's theory was that Gospel references to Jesus's concern for Old Testament prophecy had been inserted by rabbinical interests scheming to co-opt the new faith. Today the "delete what displeases" philosophy lives on in the academic organization called the Jesus Seminar, which is busily publishing versions of the Gospels that strip out the supernatural.

[45]"Mississippi Principal Dismissed for Approving Prayer," *New York Times*, 7 December 1993.

[46]Genesis 1:1–2. This is the King James wording, as read from Apollo 8.

[47]I choose Passover, the commemoration of a bloody atrocity against children; the Nicene Creed, a stifling bit of dogmatics used to justify persecution; and Muharram, the anniversary of an assassination, specifically to acknowledge that spiritual observances that sound elevated today may have roots in horribleness.

[48]Buber's primary work on this subject is *I and Thou* (1923; reprint, New York: Macmillan, 1974).

Chapter Four

[1]All quotations in this paragraph from Marx's 1844 essay *Contribution to the Critique of Hegel's Philosophy of Right*.

[2]Often it is the top faculty who reflect the least, in accordance with the principle that professors spend their early careers trying to think up new ideas and the rest of their careers trying to prevent anyone else from thinking up new ideas.

[3]The Baal creed of Canaan was marketed primarily via explicit exhibitions in which young priestesses of Ashera, the love goddess, took priests, costumed figures, ceremonial phalluses, and each other—athletic live-sex shows that commentators have for centuries primly referred to as "fertility rites." The modern-day Southern California porn video industry has nothing on ancient Canaanite religious practice.

[4]Speech to the United Nations on 5 October 1995.

[5]From Ernest Renan, *The Life of Jesus* (1863; reprint, Buffalo, N.Y.: Prometheus Books, 1991).

[6]From James Frazer, *The Golden Bough* (1890 to 1915; reprint, New York: Simon & Schuster, 1996).

[7]When Sumerians began the first known use of writing, their society was already organized around temples, religious functionaries, and deities such as Enlil, god of water, and Anu, curator of heaven. The Egyptian pyramids, built perhaps six millennia ago, are primarily religious structures; records indicate the Memphis priesthood was contemplating monotheism as early as 3,000 years ago, about the time the idea appeared in Hebrew culture. Hinduism dates to at least 4,000 years ago; Judaism, Christianity, and Islam nearly as far back, as all trace their origins to the postulated time of Abraham. The Olmec temples of Mexico were built perhaps 3,000 years ago. Zoroaster, founder of the ancestral Persian religion, was born about 2,600 years ago; Siddartha Gautama, founder of Buddhism, about 2,500 years ago. Shintoism dates at least 2,000 years into the past. Mani, founder of the dualistic faith called Manichaeism, was born 1,800 years ago. Of major systems of belief, only the Baha'i and Mormon faiths have been established since the steam engine.

[8]From G. C. Lichtenberg, *Aphorisms*, 1799.

[9]Although there is no straightforward Old Testament mention of eternal life for human beings, a few verses can be interpreted as referring to an afterlife metaphorically.

[10]Valhalla ("Hall of the Slain") was not a place of rest. The Norse believed that through eternity, their warriors would battle each other all day, endlessly experiencing suffering and pain just as in earthly combat. Then, at sunset, their wounds would magically heal, and they would spend every night drinking and feasting in Odin's palace.

[11]See, for example, Matthew 19:17, NRSV.

[12]See Ernst Bloch, *The Principle of Hope* (Cambridge: MIT Press, 1986).

[13]From Mark Strand, "The Continuous Life," in *The Continuous Life* (New York: Random House, 1992).

[14]Voltaire's distressed relationship with religion, cause both of his celebrity and his banishment from France, seemed unresolved when he died in 1778. Voltaire's writings depict spirituality as a trap used to suppress free thought. In his works the clergymen are oily schemers, the free thinkers noble and wise. But then Voltaire never married and produced no children: his arc in life was of the sort that deprived him of links to the future, and would have tended to make him think that on death, all was lost. Late in life,

Voltaire built a small chapel and there erected a sign reading *Deo erexit Voltaire*, "Voltaire built this for God." On the sign "Voltaire" was spelled out in large letters, "God" in small—either a final quip, or a proclamation of unresolved feelings.

[15]There is the possibility that ancient fascination with the idea of afterlife represents precognition of something that will eventually happen to *Homo sapiens*, as it is already vaguely possible to imagine sustaining pure consciousness in immaterial electronic form.

To researchers, human consciousness increasingly appears to be mediated by patterns of electrical information: unless there is an ineffable soul, there may be no barrier to the eventual development of technical systems that sustain consciousness following expiration of the material body. Researchers such as Marvin Minsky, co-founder of the Artificial Intelligence Laboratory of the Massachusetts Institute of Technology, have suggested that chip-based electronics equipment will someday be used to preserve consciousness, generating a sort of artificial afterlife. See Marvin Minsky, *The Society of Mind* (New York: Simon & Schuster, 1988).

Whether long-term preservation of consciousness through artificial means would be desirable or cause psychological distress or even be awful is something that can only be speculated upon today. But if human beings can already contemplate creating a pure-spirit form of existence, it seems impertinent to think that any deity that may exist would not be capable of the same.

[16]The King James Old Testament contains references to the dispatch of the wicked to Tophet, a place of torment sometimes called the Hebrew hell. Neither "hell" nor "Tophet" is found in the authoritative New Revised Standard. For example, the New Revised Standard translates Deuteronomy 32:22 as "For a fire is kindled by my anger, and burns to the depths of Sheol," the place of opaque near-oblivion to which even righteous ancient Hebrews were believed to be consigned after death. (Sheol is similar in concept to the Navajo belief about what happens after death: endless darkness underground.) The King James renders the same clause as "shall burn unto the lowest hell." But in this context the Deuteronomist does not seem to mean something would burn as condemnation, rather that an anger runs unusually deep, even down into Sheol, the deepest place the Hebrew mind could imagine. Usage of the term "hell" in the King James may result from an assumption on the part of Elizabethan translators that hell simply *must* be in there somewhere.

[17]And thus one supposes, by circular reasoning, giving you something to be enraged about.

[18]See James Strachey, ed., *The Standard Edition of the Complete Psychological Works of Sigmund Freud* (New York: W.W. Norton, 1962).

[19]From Sigmund Freud, *Totem and Taboo*, 1913. Freud's hostility to the spiritual ideal may have arisen out of his more basic hostility to humanity itself. He once wrote, "I have found little that is 'good' about human beings on the whole. In my experience most of them are trash."

[20]Freud asserted that his theory would eventually be proven by observations of those aboriginal groups that continue to exist. When Freud wrote, it was fashionable for scholars to claim that aborigine research, then a hot growth area, would back various contentions. Unfortunately for Freud, though research on aboriginal tribes has found many forms of violent behavior, especially regarding women, study has not found any common practice of sons killing and then venerating their fathers. See Robert Edgerton, *Sick Societies: Challenging the Myth of Primitive Harmony* (New York: Free Press, 1992).

[21]From Carl Jung, *Memories, Dreams, and Reflections* (New York: Vintage, 1989).

[22]As Marjorie Rosenberg noted in *First Things*, December 1991, Freud concluded that the highest cerebral achievement to which most people could aspire was to find an object of sexual desire outside the self or family. "This remarkably meager assessment of the human potential certainly bore no relation to Freud's own ambitions," Rosenberg wrote.

[23]From Richard Dawkins, *River Out of Eden* (New York: Basic Books, 1995).

Chapter Five

[1]Guth's idea is called inflation theory. The text offers an easygoing summation of this complex model, which is one of several basic theories contesting for the Big Bang crown. For better resolution of detail, see Alan Guth, *The Inflationary Universe* (Boston: Addison-Wesley, 1997). For a competing theory of creation triggered by "paired particles," see the University of Pittsburgh physicist Ernest Sternglass, *Before the Big Bang* (New York: Four Walls Eight Windows Press, 1997).

[2]Using readings from the Hubble Space Telescope, astronomers now estimate the universe contains at least 40 billion galaxies. Our galaxy, the Milky Way, is thought to contain around 100 billion stars. Multiplying 40 billion times 100 billion generates a rough estimate for total stars in the universe—four sextillion, the lengthy number in the text. Bear in mind that this is the low-end estimate, taking into account only those galaxies discovered so far. The true total of stars in creation may be much higher, if not infinite.

[3]Some "inflation" advocates say the initial universe was less than one ten-billionth of its present expanse. Other Big Bang theorists put the initial condition much tinier, proposing that all the material of the universe came from an area smaller than a hydrogen nucleus, which is thousands of times smaller than the smallest atom.

[4]The initial nonexistence of time is mainly Stephen Hawking's idea. Contemplation of what existence without time would be like usually leads to a headache followed by the desire to change the subject. It does, however, create an opening to quote a memorably goofy line from television's *Star Trek* serials. Data, the android, builds a device that suspends the flow of time. He hands it to Captain Picard and proclaims, "Captain, we can now stop time. But the effect will be temporary."

[5]See John Horgan, "Universal Truths," *Scientific American*, October 1990.

[6]Estimates vary, but models generally have the incipient universe expanding within the first second from an inkblot to an area roughly the size of a galaxy. Not much later it had grown to 100 million light-years across, large enough to contain vast sheets of galaxies, and within millennia grown to at least several times the expanse of that portion of the universe observable with current instruments. Obviously, to accomplish this, higher-than-light speeds would be required. Current theory holds that although matter and energy cannot exceed the speed of light, space itself can expand at essentially unlimited velocity, and this happened during the initial epoch.

[7]In 1995, researchers using a particle accelerator in Switzerland may have created a minute sample of quark-gluon plasma. See "Has CERN Made the Stuff of the Newborn Universe?" *Science*, 13 September 1996. No word yet on whether the Swiss experiment caused another Big Bang to detonate in another dimension, creating a new universe. Some readings of Big Bang theory call this possible.

[8]The principal points of evidence are that the galaxies are receding from one another as if all matter had once been grouped in a single point, then hurled outward; while even the empty parts of space are slightly warmer than absolute zero, suggesting they were once heated by a sensational detonation and have not yet finished cooling off. If you can propose a plausible alternative to the Bang as an explanation for these things, scientific fame awaits you.

[9]Some researchers have detected what seems like quantum foam. The work is described by Steven Lamoreaux, *Physical Review Letters*, December 1996.

[10]At least a "dense vacuum" is easier to imagine than reality without time. Vacuum density might be related to the "cosmological constant," which some theories hold would

have the paradoxical effect of enormous influence on the scale of the universe, but no influence on local solar systems: thus be simultaneously present and undetectable.

[11]See K. C. Cole, "A Theory of Everything," *New York Times Magazine*, 18 October 1987.

[12]Big Bang thinking holds that only the light elements hydrogen (as its isotope deuterium), helium, and lithium were present in the early universe. Long before the age of stable stars such as our sun, these light elements coalesced into sizzling, violent blue stars. Within these stars "nucleosynthesis" forged the heavier elements, including the carbon and minerals on which organic life depends. The violent early stars then detonated into supernovas, releasing the elements that later accreted into planets. That is to say, the material in your own skin and bones originated in an ancient stellar explosion.

[13]For instance, the physicist Andrei Linde of Stanford has written of the genesis moment, "One usually assumes that the current laws of physics did not apply then." (See Andrei Linde, "The Self-Reproducing Inflationary Universe," *Scientific American*, November 1994.) In some Big Bang models, the unknown primordial physical laws combined gravity with all other forces, into the single "grand unified" effect misunderstood in pop culture as some kind of physics of bliss. (Actual grand unification would crush the universe out of existence.) In the "inflation" model of the Big Bang, conjectured ancient physical laws were stacked in favor of the hypothesized "scalar" fields that held incalculable energy potential in seeming nothingness.

[14]First Timothy 6:20, KJV.

[15]Many contemporary commentators maintain that the reference is to Gnosticism, but it is unsettled whether First Timothy was written before or after the Gnostic movement began. The New Revised Standard, probably the best Bible translation, renders this verse as warning neither against science nor Gnosticism but "contradictions of what is falsely called knowledge."

[16]See W. Rahula, *What the Buddha Taught* (New York: Grove Weidenfeld, 1974).

[17]From Pope's *Epitaph Intended for Sir Isaac Newton in Westminster Abbey*, 1728.

[18]Pop spirituality and pop science may embrace each other, an entertaining example of this coming from the Maharishi Mahesh Yogi. In the 1960s, Mahesh became prominent for what he trademarked as Transcendental Meditation.™ His celebrity having faded by the 1990s, Mahesh attempted a comeback by purchasing double-page ads in newspapers announcing he had found a way to meld mantra contemplation with "grand unification" theory, which was then enjoying a run as a media fixation. The ads were brimming with pseudoscientific galimatias about invisible energy auras streaming through the universe. If grand unification theory is what explains the soul, we're all sunk.

[19]See Dietrich Bonhoeffer, *Letters and Papers from Prison* (New York: Macmillan, 1972).

[20]See "Prelates Defend Darwin," *The Guardian* (London), 11 April 1996.

[21]See "Pope Bolsters Church Support for Scientific View of Evolution," *New York Times*, 25 October 1996. The Church has never been happy about selection theory, but never specifically condemned Darwin either. The 1950 encyclical letter *Humani Generis* did say that while evolution is not necessarily incompatible with faith, in popular culture it is employed to undermine notions of the divine.

[22]Interview. If not attributed to a printed source, quotations from living persons come from interviews, and the footnote to this effect will not be repeated.

[23]For instance Arthur Eddington, a leading turn-of-the-century astronomer, called Lemaître's theory "repugnant." The term Big Bang was coined by the astronomer Fred

Hoyle to make fun of Lemaître's idea. Hoyle, an advocate of ethical atheism, devised the "steady state" theory of creation in order to describe how the universe could come into existence without divine influence.

[24]Hebrews 11:3, NRSV.

[25]Thomas Aquinas's first proof of God was that in each instance that change is observed in the natural world, some force produces the action, caused in turn by some other force: but at the outset of this chain there must have been a force that moved itself.

[26]In selection theory monkeys and people shared a common ancestor. At least four million years ago the species lines diverged, sending genus *Homo* and the primate order down separate evolutionary paths. People seem too different from monkeys, chimps, and apes to have descended from them, differing not only in appearance and intellect but in adaptation: primates live only in equatorial conditions whereas people have adapted to almost every climate, and did so before the advent of technology.

[27]In this regard, the book by Richard Friedman, *The Disappearance of God* (Boston: Little, Brown, 1996), proposes a novel resolution to the silence of heaven. Friedman suggests that because the universe is expanding, Earth has literally moved away from its Maker, who dwells within the plenum region where the Big Bang occurred. This is an intriguing notion, but the time scale seems wrong. Earth has traveled a huge distance outward from the cosmic starting point over the 4.5 billion years the planet has existed, but a relatively insignificant distance in the 3,000 or so years since Moses. Friedman's theory represents a sort of a quantum answer to Bishop Ussher. But Friedman is important because he is rare among intellectuals in believing that humanity eventually will reunite with God; and that part of the human task is to prepare for "an impending encounter with the divine."

[28]See Albert Einstein, *Autobiographical Notes* (Chicago: Open Court, 1979). Einstein did famously say that he wondered "whether God had any choice in the creation of the universe."

[29]Among other things, the relativistic notion that there is no "correct" frame of reference in physics became confused in public thought as evidence of the postmodern philosophical idea that there exists no absolute truth.

[30]Darwin's maternal grandfather was Josiah Wedgwood, founder of the Wedgwood china fortune.

[31]Quoted from Richard Milner, "Charles Darwin and Associates, Ghostbusters," *Scientific American*, October 1996.

[32]A fine article on the little-known subject of Wallace's spirituality is Jay Kottler, "Alfred Russel Wallace, the Origin of Man and Spiritualism," *Isis*, June 1974.

[33]Gray's views are well described in Mark Noll, *The Scandal of the Evangelical Mind* (Chicago: Eerdmans, 1994).

[34]Quoted in *The Washington Post*, 9 April 1995.

[35]See Edward Larson and Larry Witham, "Scientists are Still Keeping the Faith," *Nature*, 3 April 1997.

[36]See Benson's *Timeless Healing: The Power and Biology of Belief* (New York: Scribner, 1996).

[37]Among these is the common misunderstanding that unlike faith, science is bleached clean of subjectivity. Scientists are no more objective than any other segment of society. One of the celebrated works of contemporary theory of knowledge is the 1962 book by Thomas Kuhn, *The Structure of Scientific Revolutions*. The first half of Kuhn's thesis, that scientists labor for long periods with one set of theories and then rapidly displace them during a "paradigm shift," is well known. Little known is the second half of Kuhn's analysis, his assertion that science is "a political, not objective, realm."

Kuhn put forth that scientists make subjective calculations about career politics and tailor their ideas to fit fashion—that is, they have the same human weaknesses as everybody else. The very reason there are "paradigm shifts," Kuhn supposed, is that scientific fashion generates bodies of dogma that can only be overcome by the accumulation of dramatic contrary evidence. For example, the scientific dogma of the Earth's crust as firmly anchored to its mantle held on for decades against evidence that the continents slowly drift upon tectonic plates. The age of doubt is well aware of the problem of dogma in spiritual thinking; it is hardly aware of the same in science.

[38]Popper's main work was *The Logic of Scientific Discovery* (London: Routledge, 1992). Popper further supposed no scientific finding can be conclusive because no one can ever be sure there is not additional information yet unknown.

[39]Mill went on to conclude that belief in the supernatural was not justified, but hope for the supernatural should never be ruled out.

[40]See Wendy Kaminer, *Sleeping with Extra-Terrestrials* (New York: Pantheon, 1998).

[41]Newton is commonly misperceived to have discovered gravity. What he discovered were the laws that govern gravity. In the fundamental sense gravity still has not been discovered: scientists have no idea by what physical means this attractive force is asserted.

[42]Robert Wright, *Three Scientists and Their Gods: Looking for Meaning in an Age of Information* (New York: Times Books, 1988).

[43]See John Diggins, *Max Weber: Politics and the Spirit of Tragedy* (New York: Basic Books, 1996). For the declining sense of wonder, Weber blamed organized religion as much as secular doubt. Weber especially castigated Protestantism, which as part of its nineteenth-century intervarsity rivalry with Catholicism liked to lampoon Rome's contention that divine intervention could still be observed on Earth. Life is more interesting if miracles still happen, Weber felt.

[44]From John Lewis, *Rain of Fire and Ice: The Very Real Threat of Comet and Asteroid Bombardment* (Boston: Addison-Wesley, 1996).

[45]Mach was influenced by the development of philosophical positivism, which held that only things tangibly confirmed could be real; and felt the subatomic particle could never be confirmed.

[46]See Charles Townes, *Making Waves* (Woodbury, N.Y.: American Institute of Physics Press, 1995).

[47]The atonement took the form of a statement from John Paul II to the Pontifical Academy of Sciences, at long last retracting the heresy charges against Galileo.

[48]Creationists, for example, may claim that the apparent ancient age of geologic formations is an artifact of different physical laws that prevailed during the Flood: possible in the sense that you can't disprove it, but lacking anything like the body of science that supports other ways of dating the Earth. A 1961 book called *The Genesis Flood* is the writ of such creationism. This work traces its lineage to the 1923 book *The New Geology*, which claimed that physical dynamics of the Flood caused the apparent age of geologic foundations; that claim, in turn, is thought to originate with Ellen White, who helped found the Seventh-Day Adventist movement in the late nineteenth century.

One goofy trend in the affray between science and creationism is the attempt to decorate scripture with scientific-sounding notions. Some creationists now assert that the Genesis reference to primordial "waters" shows the Bible anticipated current research suggesting the early universe was made mostly of hydrogen, chief component of water. Muslim fundamentalists have been known to boast that the fact that the Koran says in one place that a day to God is like 1,000 years, and in another says like 50,000 years, shows the prophet Muhammad understood the relativistic concept of time dilation.

[49]From Steven Weinberg, *The First Three Minutes* (New York: Basic Books, 1977).

[50]From Richard Dawkins, *River Out of Eden* (New York: Basic Books, 1995).

[51]Jessica Tuchman Mathews, "Evolution and Creationism," *Washington Post*, 12 April 1996.

[52]Readers would do well to consult de Duve's *Vital Dust: Life as a Cosmic Imperative* (New York: Basic Books, 1995), which argues that organic chemistry is not some improbable coincidence but likely to evolve given the proper range of temperatures and pressures.

[53]I also commend to readers Dressler's *Voyage to the Great Attractor* (New York: Knopf, 1995), both an engaging detective story of deep-space astronomy and a reflection on why, even in an immense cosmos, human life would remain significant.

[54]From the novel *The Man Without Qualities*, published after Musil's death in 1942 (New York: Knopf, 1995).

[55]Dawkins, *River Out of Eden*. Dawkins is to the late twentieth century what Thomas Huxley was to the late nineteenth, science's leading gladiator against faith. But where Huxley was usually good-spirited, Dawkins is a snob: in a 1992 speech called "A Scientist's Case Against God," he asserted that science has shown there is no evidence to support faith, "and nowadays the better-educated admit it." A fitting title for Dawkins would be Mister Meaninglessness.

[56]From Jacques Monod, *Chance and Necessity* (New York: Random House, 1972).

[57]Discussion of the aspects of the Bang favorable to organic life can be found in John Barrow and Frank Tipler, *The Anthropic Cosmological Principle* (Oxford: Oxford University Press, 1986).

[58]See John Horgan, "Universal Truths," *Scientific American*, October 1990.

[59]See Linde, "The Self Reproducing Inflationary Universe."

[60]Letter to the *International Herald Tribune*, 24 April 1996.

[61]See Todd Dawson, "Hydraulic Lift and Water Use by Plants," *Oecologia*, Spring 1993.

[62]The third possibility is that life originated at some location other than Earth and was transported here by an alien intelligence or an as-yet-unknown natural process. Researchers call this idea "panspermia," and it has received some serious study. The notion, however, begs the question of how life came to exist on whatever world it started.

Chapter Six

[1]Today much of public thought subconsciously divides the world into Harvards and Hayseeds. Harvards may admire the architecture of medieval cathedrals, may find value in social connections made through an exclusive Episcopal parish, but presume anyone who genuinely seeks the spirit plane is a Hayseed whose beliefs originate in educational inferiority. And though Harvards say kind things about the Jewish faith, their concern is for the status of a cultural minority. If Judaism were large enough in numbers to represent an expanding religious force, Harvards wouldn't like that either.

Hayseeds, in turn, may view the Harvards with equal lack of charity, seeing them as oblivious to the salvation of their own souls; and feeling that by declaring faith, anyone can become spiritually superior to a Harvard. H. L. Mencken summed this in his typically magnanimous way: "God is the immemorial refuge of the incompetent, the helpless, the miserable. They find not only sanctuary in His arms but also a kind of superiority: He will set them above their betters."

[2]Speech at Catholic University, Washington, D.C., 23 March 1996.

[3]Mencken's many astringent put-downs of faith include the clever line, "The chief contribution of Protestantism to human thought is its proof that God is a bore."

[4]Gary Wills, *Under God: Religion and American Politics* (New York: Simon & Schuster, 1990). Bryan rejected evolutionary biology but conceded that the Earth must be extremely old, so he was not a creationist as the term is used today.

[5]Social Darwinists, eugenicists, and others of the early century argued that natural selection theory showed that the lower classes should be barred from reproducing. Openly expressed in fashionable circles in the United States and United Kingdom through the 1930s—even the American socialist leader Norman Thomas spoke derisively of baby-making by "inferior stock"—such views helped set the stage for Nazism.

[6]Ross Lockridge, Jr., *Raintree County* (1948; reprint, New York: Penguin, 1994).

[7]From Neal Stephenson, *Snow Crash* (New York: Bantam Books, 1992).

[8]See David Strauss, *The Life of Jesus Critically Examined* (Washington, D.C.: Scholarly Press, 1970). Strauss was fired from the University of Tübingen, then Germany's intellectual center of Christian apologetics, today its center of theological revisionism.

[9]During this dispute Pope John XXII ordered that William be hunted down and killed, while Louis IV, the Holy Roman Emperor, ordered that William be protected. Both pope and emperor are said to have spent countless hours listening to philosophers and theologians present their arguments on whether truth exists independently or is a construct of language. This is the kind of learned question on which no head of state would today expend ten seconds. Of course if William of Occam and Thomas Aquinas lived in today's world, their debate might never have started. Rather than formulate nominalism and scholasticism, they might have called out for pizza and watched *Lethal Bimbo II: The Swimsuit Conspiracy* on cable.

[10]Al-Ghazali's lifework, *The Restoration of the Sciences of Religion*, now reads like orthodoxy but in context of the middle centuries was a bold attempt to reconcile spiritual mysticism with reason.

[11]Newton asserted that the zodiac of the planets, which circle the sun in roughly the same plane, could not have occurred by chance, and showed an aesthetic sense on the part of the Maker. Newton died before his disciple Pierre Laplace could demonstrate that the planets are aligned because they condensed from the same nebular disk. Asked about his mentor's theory of divine origin for the zodiac, Laplace famously replied, "I do not need this hypothesis." This statement later became a rally cry to students of Lyell and Darwin.

[12]See Harvey Cox, "The Warring Visions of the Religious Right," *The Atlantic Monthly*, November 1995.

[13]From George Santayana, *Reason in Religion* (1905; reprint, New York: Dover Books, 1982).

[14]A valuable biography of Eddy is Robert Thomas, *With Bleeding Footsteps* (New York: Knopf, 1994). Growing up in a small town in the nineteenth century, Eddy suffered from constant childhood sicknesses for which medical science of the day could do nothing; she saw a beloved brother die in agony when the local general practitioner bungled his case. Rather than conclude that the problem was the backward state of medical knowledge, she grew up believing illnesses were not actual physical events but illusory trials of the mind, to be resisted with mental power.

[15]Luke 22:23–24, NRSV. The moment is foreshadowed in an earlier verse when, during

a walking journey to their base in the town of Capernaum, Jesus asks the disciples what they had been discussing among themselves. "But they were silent, for on the way they had argued with one another who was the greatest." Mark 9:34, NRSV.

[16]Maybe the *Ephraim Inquirer* will publish an exposé of the disciples' botched security arrangements. Maybe only "the greatest" will get a book tour.

[17]That Rousseau himself lived as a recluse for the second half of his life, refusing to participate in civic affairs or even to raise his own children, all of whom he turned over to orphanages, is not exactly a glowing testimonial to his theories.

[18]A leading modern edition is Edward Gibbon, *The Decline and Fall of the Roman Empire*, ed. J. B. Bury (Dallas: Heritage Press, 1946).

[19]Though Gibbon's opposition to the church was antiestablishment by the standards of his era, by present standards Gibbon was an imperialist, since his final point was that Rome should have fought harder to maintain its empire.

[20]From Mikhail Bakunin, *God and the State* (1871; reprint, New York: Dover Books, 1970).

[21]The Schopenhauer book to read is *The World as Will and Representation* (1818; reprint, New York: Dover Books, 1969).

[22]Schopenhauer advised people to renounce status and possessions, believing only the absence of worldly desire could lead to the absence of mental pain. But like many who have recommended that others renounce the world, Schopenhauer had trouble heeding his own advice. For philosophers of his era, the chief measure of status was not book reviews but public lectures. Schopenhauer is said to have suffered intense fits of jealousy that Hegel's lectures were more popular than his.

That, a hundred years ago, paying customers by the thousands would crowd into lecture halls to listen for hours as figures such as Hegel droned on with incomprehensible lingo tells us a great deal about the last century versus ours. Perhaps, had modern distractions been available, the crowds would have stayed home and watched *Lethal Bimbo III: The Lingerie Plot* on cable. But considering the smaller populations of the day, a thousand people at a public lecture was the equivalent of a philosopher selling out Yankee Stadium.

[23]The quote is from one of Melville's letters to Nathaniel Hawthorne, published in *The Letters of Herman Melville*, ed. Merrell Davis and William Gilman (Boston: Houghton Mifflin, 1960).

[24]From *The Diary of Søren Kierkegaard*, published 1847.

[25]From Søren Kierkegaard, *Either/Or* (1843; reprint, Princeton: Princeton University Press, 1987).

[26]See Nietzsche's *The Twilight of the Idols*, 1889.

[27]From Marty Kaplan, "My Spiritual Journey," *Time*, 24 June 1996.

[28]From Richard Friedman, *The Disappearance of God* (Boston: Little, Brown, 1996).

[29]Miller had first said the end would come sometime in the year 1843.

[30]The etiology of "premillennialism" traces to a debate among end-time believers regarding whether the saved will be lifted up to heaven before Armageddon begins or forced to endure the final trial, seeing Jesus only after the Earth has been reduced to ashes.

[31]Today bleak spiritualism continues in "premil" preaching and writing. One of the best-selling books of publishing history, a 1970 premil treatise called *The Late Great Planet Earth*, takes as its premise that the world has grown so vile that a nuclear war would be an agreeable event: so many people would be massacred that Jesus would take pity and return to offer the parousia to any survivors. Ronald Reagan once called *The Late Great Planet Earth* one of his favorite books.

[32]See Paul Boyer, *When Time Shall Be No More: Prophecy Belief in Modern American Culture* (Cambridge: Harvard University Press, 1992).

[33]Described in *Taking the Bible Seriously* by Benton White, Philadelphia: Westminster, 1993.

[34]See Mark Noll, *The Scandal of the Evangelical Mind*, Eerdmans, 1994.

[35]Since many conservatives now argue that government programs intended to improve society actually make society worse, presumably this would cause a logically consistent "premil" conservative to want more government.

[36]From André Breton, *Surrealism and Painting*, first published in 1928.

[37]From Michel Foucault, *Discipline and Punish: The Birth of the Prison*, 1975. Probably the best summary of Foucault's thinking is *Madness and Civilization* (1961; reprint, New York: Vintage Books, 1988).

[38]From Daniel Boorstin, *The Image* (1961; reprint, New York: Vintage Books, 1992).

[39]See Shadia Drury, *Leo Strauss and the American Right* (New York: St. Martin's Press, 1997), for a good description of Strauss's views on religion and politics.

[40]In informal polls of my Washington, D.C., media peer group, I've found that almost all can identify Kierkegaard as a bleak existentialist, but only one in five knew he was a practicing Christian.

[41]A fine article on how electricity has been understood through cultural history is Jesse Ausubel and Cesare Marchetti, *"Elektron:* Electrical Systems in Retrospect and Prospect," *Daedalus*, Summer 1996.

[42]Lot's wife is recounted in Genesis 19. Miles's quote is from his *God: A Biography* (New York: Knopf, 1995).

[43]There are multiple New Testament accounts of miraculous brunches, one giving 4,000 fed (Matthew 15:38 and Mark 8:9) and the other 5,000 (Matthew 14:21 and Mark 6:44).

[44]The idea for space-relayed telecommunication is generally credited to the physicist and science fiction writer Arthur Clarke, who proposed the concept in 1948. Clarke presumed that communication satellites would be enormous structures in which permanent crews of astronauts labored to maintain fragile antenna systems based on vacuum tubes. At that time, no one could imagine the silicon chip.

[45]This story begins at Joshua 10: the sun halts at 10:12.

[46]Joshua 10:13, NRSV.

[47]John Noble Wilford, "Oceanographers Say Winds May Have Parted the Waters," *New York Times*, 15 March 1992.

[48]Exodus 12:37 asserts that "600,000 men on foot," plus women and children, fled Egypt under Moses. Population numbers for the Bible's early books are generally considered extravagant, so there is no way to know how many Hebrews may have actually fled Pharaoh.

[49]See "Geologists Zero in on Sodom and Lot's Wife," *New York Times*, 17 December 1995.

[50]There is a third-rail possibly, which is that the miraculous events described in scripture did happen but were the result of physical technology employed by beings from other worlds, who were either attempting to communicate with humanity or representing themselves as divinities. It is hard to phrase this possibility without sounding like a bad episode of *The X Files*, but the possibility does bear mentioning.

Assuming as now appears that the universe is around 15 billion years old, there could have been ample time for other beings to evolve to advanced states long before *Homo sapiens* appeared; perhaps to evolve to life as pure consciousness. Advanced beings might have the knowledge required to do things, such as reanimate the dead, that our ancestors would have perceived as divine. Advanced beings might feel they ought to visit other worlds and offer guidance; might encounter difficulties communicating with creatures as recalcitrant as humans; might attempt to impress men and women with shows of force, then retreat to using moral arguments; and might depart, leaving behind a cultural remnant of belief in the supernatural. There is, however, not much more you can do with this line of thought, other than wonder if someday an alien emissary will arrive and confirm it.

Chapter Seven

[1]The dialogue on Sodom begins at Genesis 18:22.

[2]On this factoid Aristotle hung a considerable degree of pop psychology, proposing that extra teeth made men more aggressive. If men are from Mars and women from Venus, in Aristotelian thought the dentists are from Jupiter.

[3]See Elaine Pagels, *The Gnostic Gospels* (New York: Random House, 1979), an outstanding depiction of conflicts between the Gnostic movement and the orthodox wing of the young Christian church.

[4]See Alfred North Whitehead, *Science and the Modern World* (New York: Free Press, 1997). This book was first published in 1925.

[5]Anselm was the archbishop of Canterbury. The job then was a Catholic position; now it is an Anglican post.

[6]See Richard Flew, *The Idea of Perfection in Christian Theology* (Oxford: Oxford University Press, 1934).

[7]An example is Bernard Lonergan, *Insight: A Study of Human Understanding* (Toronto: University of Toronto Press, 1972). This important book by an accomplished early-postwar Jesuit scholar offers 800 pages of mathematical formulas and definitions of terms concerning perception and reality. It is as dense, convoluted, and willfully inaccessible as anything in the corpus of French postmodernism.

[8]From Rene Descartes, *Discourse on Method and Meditations* (1637; reprint, New York: Viking, 1987).

[9]Though dour in persona, Pascal had a flair for snappy lines. For example: "Men spend their time chasing after a ball, or a hare. It is the amusement of kings too."

[10]*The Age of Reason* was written while Paine, who had gone to France to show support for the French Revolution, was imprisoned by the Terror.

[11]See Immanuel Kant, *The Critique of Pure Reason* (Buffalo, N.Y.: Prometheus Books, 1990).

[12]See Jeremy Collins, *God in Modern Philosophy* (Oxford: Oxford University Press, 1960).

[13]See Immanuel Kant, *The Critique of Practical Reason* (Buffalo, N.Y.: Prometheus Books, 1996).

[14]See Pat Barker, *The Ghost Road* (London: Penguin, 1996).

[15]From Francis Crick, *The Astonishing Hypothesis* (New York: Touchstone, 1995). Crick's "astonishing hypothesis" is that the soul does not exist. Like many who embrace the Nothing position, Crick finds other people's lives meaningless, but maintains a high opinion of his own.

[16]A good introduction to Barth's thought is *Word of God and the Word of Man*, republished by Smith Publications, 1958. Barth was deported from Germany in 1934 for speaking against the Nazis, yet he never expressed amazement that God did not intervene to prevent Nazi horrors. To Barth, God had no reason to try to fix the world; the Maker's sole interest was to accept into heaven those righteous souls who endured their earthly trials.

[17]*Time*, 8 April 1966. The full cover headline was "TOWARD A HIDDEN GOD: IS GOD DEAD?"

[18]Though New Age theorists romanticize Gnosticism, its thinking was not always benign. Among other things, the Gnostics taught the elitist notion of a predestined elect.

[19]Mani, the founder of this denomination, combined elements of Gnosticism, Zoroastrianism, and other faiths. Like several founders of religions, Mani was executed for refusing to recant his beliefs, his martyrdom helping spread his ideas.

[20]One reason Augustine had such a prominent profile was that he was a convert from the Manichaean faith, which made the Roman church feel warmly toward him: converts always carrying a higher testimonial value than life-long adherents.

[21]Health statistics for this period can be found in Barbara Tuchman, *A Distant Mirror* (New York: Random House, 1978).

[22]Amos 3:6, NRSV.

[23]Proverbs 16:4, KJV.

[24]See the dialogue between God and Satan that begins at Job 1:7.

[25]Job 2:9.

[26]Job 2:10, NRSV. Job prefaces this remark by telling his wife, "You speak as any foolish woman would speak." The New Testament contains several embarrassing verses about female subservience, but they are peanuts compared to Old Testament sexism. An exception is the Old Testament book of Ruth, which tells a story of female friendship and perseverance. The book even offers a sensitive 1990s guy, Boaz, who tells Ruth she's moving too fast with her sexual advances.

Though preferring to wait until marriage, Boaz is one of the last biblical men to show any interest in sexuality. Lust is a running theme of the Old Testament, exhibited by women and men both; it is entirely absent from the New. By the time of the Jesus movement, hanky-panky seems to have disappeared. Few New Testament teachings concern sexual mores, and carnal attraction seems to play no role at all in the apostles' lives.

[27]Matthew 13:30, KJV.

[28]Though cemented into history by Augustine, original sin theory was not original to him; Tertullian first used the phrase two centuries before. Augustine gained some of his reputation by writing tracts against the Pelagians, Christian reformers who opposed Tertullian's original-sin concept as a corruption of Jesus's message.

[29]Some commentators assert that original sin can be inferred from this statement by Paul, "Just as sin came into the world through one man [Adam], death came through sin." Romans 5:12, NRSV. Others believe original sin is implicit in such references as, "If we say that we have no sin we deceive ourselves." (First John 1:8, NRSV.) But passages like this, which reflect the reality that every person commits trespasses, seem quite different from the contention that people are born in a fallen state of shame.

[30]Luke 11:13, NRSV.

[31]In modern Greek usage, *poneros* carries the lesser meaning of "devious." Elsewhere the New Testament has Jesus use the Greek word *sapros*, which does connote fundamental worthlessness, but in contexts such as this: "Either make the tree good, and his fruit good; or else make the tree corrupt [*sapros*], and his fruit corrupt [*sapros*]: for the tree is known by his fruit." (Matthew 12:33, KJV.) None of Christ's usages of *sapros* refers directly to people. The apostolic letters use *sapros* once of men and women, but in a context different from claims of original sin: "Let no evil [*sapros*] talk come out of your mouths, but only what is useful for building up." (Ephesians 4:29, NRSV.)

[32]Beginning at Genesis 3:15. In the expulsion passage the woman's role in marriage is depicted by God as a curse, not a choice or a requirement of nature; one of the Bible's many little-understood nasty twists. God tells Eve she will suffer pain in childbirth, but

even knowing that, "your desire shall be for your husband, and he shall rule over you." (Genesis 3:16, NRSV.) This marriage-as-curse verse makes matrimony sound like an awful institution into which women would enter only through compulsion; biblical literalists such as the Puritans believed as much.

[33]Followers of the Augustinian line quote passages such as Job 14:4, NRSV, "Who can bring a clean thing out of an unclean? No one can." Supposedly the "unclean" in this reference is the womb (the reference can be disputed), meaning no baby can be born untainted.

Ancient Hebrew belief held menstrual activity to defile: exposed to mother's blood in the womb, on birth each child required immediate cleansing for religious as well as medical reasons. To this ancient discomfort with female reproductive necessity, Augustine added the idea that semen, too, defiles. But though the mother's blood washes off, the father's sperm can never be excised from the child's being, leaving the newborn sinful in nature. Weirdly, Augustine's preoccupation anticipates the contemporary fad of claiming that proclivity to crime is transferred to offspring by DNA from the male (Y) chromosome. In Augustinian view, Jesus was the sole person born free from original sin because he was the only one conceived without transmission of sperm cells.

[34]Because Augustine's literary formulations were tortuous, he is hard to quote. This paraphrase reflects mainly his *City of God*, completed around the year 410. See the edition edited by Donald Knowles (New York: Viking, 1985).

[35]The feminist Elizabeth Stanton supposed in her 1895 book *The Women's Bible* that Christianity did not turn antiwoman until Augustine became the faith's leading figure. Feminist critics have further pointed out that Augustine paid more attention to the writings of Paul than the sayings of Jesus because Paul, like Augustine, was a Roman and a member of the professional class; Jesus was an itinerant tradesman from an occupied state. Paul's moderate aversion to women, amplified through Augustine's active misogyny, helped make Christianity chauvinist. Had Augustine instead stuck to the gender-disinterested Jesus, history might have been different.

[36]From Knox's 1557 *First Blast of the Trumpet Against the Monstrous Regiment of Women*, which goes on at length in this humor.

[37]Augustine railed against sexual expression between men and women because lovemaking releases semen, Augustine's metaphysical guided missile of diablerie. Augustine further viewed male homosexuality as depraved, but seemed unconcerned with lesbian relations, perhaps because no semen is exchanged.

The Cathar movement of the Middle Ages, radical in other ways, agreed with the orthodox Augustine about semen. Cathars believed human sexuality was a trap invented by the bad god. Orgasms felt good but only served to prolong temporal suffering by sustaining the cycle of physical existence; thus Cathars found semen, the visible agent of the orgasm, the most repulsive of substances. Such thinking rings Freudian to the contemporary ear, since today not even traditionalists call sex bad: the question is under what circumstances it may be enjoyed.

For his part Augustine once kept a concubine and, according to his *Confessions*, in the years preceding his conversion to Christianity spent all his spare time and discretionary income striving to get under various skirts. He is a prime example of someone who preaches against sex only after taking care to satisfy his own libido.

[38]See Henry Chadwick, *The Early Church* (London: Penguin, 1993).

[39]From C. S. Lewis, *The World's Last Night and Other Essays* (New York: Harcourt Brace, 1984).

[40]Teilhard is hard to read. Perhaps his most accessible work is *The Phenomenon of Man*,

published posthumously (1955; reprint, New York: HarperCollins, 1980). Teilhard is significant in part owing to his optimism regarding the human prospect and in part because, though a Jesuit priest, he worked as a paleontologist, seeing nothing in natural selection theory to contradict the existence of God. As punishment for endorsing Darwin, Teilhard spent most of his life under a Jesuit ban against speaking in public.

[41]Paul Edwards, ed., *Encyclopedia of Philosophy* (Englewood Cliffs, N.J.: Prentice Hall, 1972).

[42]See Paul Johnson, *The Quest for God* (New York: HarperCollins, 1996).

[43]See Robert Wright's fine *The Moral Animal* (New York: Pantheon, 1994).

[44]Family tragedies like these were staples of life until the postwar era. As recently as the late nineteenth century, a third of children in North America and Western Europe died before reaching age five. Today the figure is well below 1 percent.

[45]Gibbon was tossed out of Oxford when he converted to Roman Catholicism, odium in Anglican Britain of the time. Gibbon's father sent him to Switzerland to be set right by Calvinists. Eager to escape their austerity, Gibbon returned declaring himself a Protestant again, but later suggested in his *Memoirs* that the declaration was for public consumption, as he had ceased believing in any religion.

Chapter Eight

[1]As early as Genesis 16:1 Abraham and Sarah, founders of the Judeo-Christian faith, are depicted as keeping slaves. Elaborate rules for the seizing, trading, and executing of slaves are given in the Old Testament. The New Testament declares at Titus 2:9, NRSV, "Tell slaves to be submissive to their masters and to give satisfaction in every respect." This section continues with an inventory of the duties of a slave, including "not to talk back."

[2]See Second Kings 2:11.

[3]See Revelation 9:7.

[4]The Flood account begins at Genesis 6:11, the Passover account at Exodus 12.

Chapter Nine

[1]Some of what was loudly broadcast from Islamic prayer towers by the *muezzin* was religious devotion, some propaganda and, given the homicidal abandon with which Pakistanis drive, some must have been advice such as "speed up at intersections" and "disconnect your brake lights."

[2]The Prophet Muhammad's successors staged an imperialistic campaign into Europe under the banner of the Koran, stopped in the year 732 by the Frankish king Charles Martel, whose name would later grace a beverage offensive to Muslims.

[3]This book relies on the King James and New Revised Standard translations, most notable of the some 450 English Bibles in print. The King James has the highest poetic achievement, and not just because its Elizabethan prosody reverberates pleasantly in the modern ear. Many touches are timeless, for example Song of Songs 8.6: "Set me as a seal upon thine heart, as a seal upon thine arm: for love is strong as death; jealousy is cruel as the grave: the coals thereof are coals of fire, which hath a most vehement flame." Update the anachronistic *thine* and *hath*, and the power remains the same. But the King James is widely considered to suffer from translation errors, and was composed before access to the scriptural remnants that have come to light since the Middle Eastern archeological boom of the nineteenth century.

The New Revised Standard Version, whose translation was sponsored by the National

Council of Churches, is generally considered the most precise rendering of the Bible. On publication in 1989 this adaptation was criticized by traditionalists as too liberal and by liberals as too traditional, because the NRSV retains conventional gender language. It is sure to yield someday to a Revised Revised Standard.

Many passages conflict between these two essential translations. For instance, the King James renders Acts 10:34 as "I perceive that God is no respecter of persons," an ominous phrase, while the NRSV translates the same as a reassuring, "I truly understand that God shows no partiality." On the other hand, the NRSV translates as "Jesus the Messiah" those Gospel phrases the King James renders as "Jesus Christ." On this point the NRSV is more hard-line than the KJV, since "Messiah" is a loaded phrase theologically, while "Christ" can be read as simply a term of honor.

[4]Luke 11:52, KJV.

[5]Compare, for example, Job 39:9, which in the KJV asks "Will the unicorn be willing to serve thee?" and in the NRSV asks if "the wild ox" will serve.

[6]The Messiah references in the King James are at Daniel 9:25–26 and concern David. The New Revised Standard does not employ "Messiah" in connection with David, calling him instead "the anointed prince."

[7]In biblical times the Sabbath was probably Saturday, though the word Saturday does not appear in scripture either.

[8]December 25th is also the birthday of Mithras, a Persian deity.

[9]At Matthew 2:23. Claims that the virgin birth was predicted in the Old Testament may be based on translation error. At Isaiah 7:14, the KJV says a sign from God will be that "the virgin shall conceive." This choice of words appears to rest on transliterating the Hebrew *almah*, young woman, into the Greek *parthenos*, virgin. The NRSV renders Isaiah 7:14 as, "Look, the young woman is with child and shall bear a son, and shall name him Immanuel." How this phrase may have been mishandled is detailed in a 1988 book by a theologian at Boston University, Paula Frederickson, *From Jesus to Christ* (New Haven: Yale University Press).

A second school of thought about ambiguous Gospel references to prophecy holds that the Gospel authors were not contemporaries of Jesus, but came a generation later. When they sat down to write they employed Old Testament allusions to make Jesus sound like the fulfillment of divine contract. But not being Old Testament experts, they got the references jumbled.

[10]Samson's beginnings are recounted in Judges 13; the famous crew cut is at Judges 16:19.

[11]Matthew 11:19, KJV. In the NRSV translation, Jesus jokes of himself as a "drunkard."

[12]Medieval monks sometimes justified gluttony on the grounds that Jesus endorsed it as an alternative to sexuality. If abbey records can be believed, some medieval brothers each day consumed several pounds of beef and mutton, assorted fowl, pastries, soups, and puddings, washing it down with a gallon of ale (two six packs) plus champagne and flavored brandies.

[13]Exodus 7:9–12.

[14]The account begins at First Samuel 28:7.

[15]First Corinthians 8:5.

[16]Psalms 82:1, NRSV. Ancient polytheist religions assumed the world run by a committee of deities. Here the God of Judaism and Christianity seems to make an appearance before just such an organization.

[17]See William Phipps, *Muhammad and Jesus: A Comparison of Their Teachings* (New York: Paragon House, 1996).

[18]Judaism was excused by Roman colonial administrators from performing the annual ceremonial obeisance to Jupiter. Apparently this waiver was granted because Romans found the Judeans impossible to talk to on religious matters.

Rome's refusal to extend the same waiver to the young Jesus movement began the phase of Christian martyrdom. Many valiant men and women of the young church chose to die rather than make any public gesture to Jupiter, though it can be argued that God would have known what was really in their hearts. Staged in the name of preserving Roman culture, the executions of Christians began the process of transforming that culture, causing Romans to think that a God capable of inspiring such fearless hearts was stronger than anything in their pantheon.

[19]Genesis 32:30, KJV. The encounter begins at Genesis 32:24.

[20]John 1:18, KJV.

[21]Genesis 1:27, NRSV.

[22]Genesis 2:1, NRSV.

[23]Genesis 2:7, KJV.

[24]At Genesis 2:21.

[25]First Corinthians 7:29, KJV.

[26]Matthew 24:34, KJV. Some literalists say that what Christ forecasts in this passage is not really the coming of Kingdom of Heaven but rather the dire consequences of Israel's year 66 rebellion against Rome, and thus the prophecy was fulfilled "within this generation" from the standpoint of some listeners. But this reading is very hard to support from the prior verses, which predict, for instance, "Immediately after the suffering of those days the sun will be darkened, and the moon will not give its light; the stars will fall from heaven, and the powers of heaven will be shaken." Matthew 24:29, NRSV.

[27]See Elaine Pagels, *The Origin of Satan* (New York: Random House, 1995), and Robert Fuller, *Naming the Antichrist* (Oxford: Oxford University Press, 1995).

[28]"Armageddon" is mentioned just once in the Bible, at Revelations 16:16.

[29]Scholars and clergy refer to various sections of the testaments as apocalyptic, but the term derives from commentary, not scripture itself.

[30]At First John 2:18, First John 2:22, First John 4:3, and Second John 1:7.

[31]First John 22:2, KJV. Since case distinctions do not appear in original autographs of the Bible, finding them in translations means less than meets the eye. However, it seems significant that even in the King James rendering, "antichrist" is lower case.

[32]First John 2:18, NRSV. This verse contains another theological satchel charge. In full it reads, "Children, it is the last hour! As you have heard that antichrist is coming, so now many antichrists have come. From this we know that it is the last hour." Needless to say, it was not the last hour.

[33]"Jehovah" can be found four times in the King James but not in the New Revised Standard, whose translation committee rejected the term as having originated with Middle Ages culture. High-brow commentators now generally favor Yahweh as God's name, but this word never appears in scripture either.

[34]God's lack of interest in being named may represent a means of differentiation from the countless named local and regional gods of Old Testament days. "You have as many gods as you have towns, oh Judah," the prophet Jeremiah says sarcastically at Jeremiah 11:13, KJV.

[35]Exodus 3:14, NRSV. Because God's reply in the original Hebrew Old Testament— *Ehyeh asher ehyeh*—may include ancient idiom, there exists a wide range of opinion on how to render into English the phrase traditionally given as "I am who I am." Some translators think the phrase represents a dodge of the question of divine identity and would render into present-day vernacular as "mind your own business."

[36]See Karen Armstrong, *A History of God* (New York: Ballantine, 1993).

[37]Leviticus 18:22, KJV.

[38]Genesis 46:34.

[39]Leviticus 11:9–12.

[40]Leviticus 25:36. This verse forbids charging interest to the poor. At Deuteronomy 23:19–20, believers are more generally forbidden to charge interest to anyone except "foreigners."

[41]Leviticus 19:27, KJV.

[42]Leviticus 20:9.

[43]Leviticus 20:27, this quote from the NRSV.

[44]Exodus 35:2.

[45]Leviticus 20:10.

[46]Leviticus 20:16.

[47]Judges 21:19–25.

[48]First Kings 11:3. Solomon was the first wise Israeli king, perhaps always in agreeable humor because he spends so much time sporting with the thousand royal babes. Also, "Solomon loved many foreign women, along with the daughter of Pharaoh, Moabite, Ammonite, Edomite, Sidonian, and Hittite women." (First Kings 11:1 NRSV.) These multinational flings were in addition to the considerable action back at the palace. Perhaps here we find in scripture an argument that Bill Clinton's amorous diversions actually were in the national interest. After all every American benefits from having the President of the United States in a good mood.

[49]Second Corinthians 3:6, NRSV.

[50]For instance, at Acts 13:39, NRSV, "Everyone who believes is set free from all those sins from which you could not be freed by the law of Moses."

[51]Romans 1:26–27, KJV.

[52]Exodus 22:21, NRSV.

[53]As the science writer Colin Tudge pointed out in his 1996 *The Time Before History*, it is possible that Deluge accounts have a natural antecedent: when glacial dams of the last ice age shattered, there may have been gargantuan floods that seemed from the perspective of the survivors to have covered all the Earth.

[54]Genesis 1:6.

[55]Described at Genesis 9:1–13.

[56]Jon Levenson, *Creation and the Persistence of Evil* (New York: Harper & Row, 1988).

[57]The familiar refrain "King of kings and lord of lords forever" refers in Handel's *Messiah* to Jesus, but in the Bible the phrase is applied only to God, at First Timothy 6:15 and at Revelation 19:16. The First Timothy reference may have seemed, in the King James version available to Handel, to speak of Christ, but the NRSV renders the same passage as applying to God. Careful reading of a confusing pronoun is required.

[58]See First Timothy 6:15 and Ezra 7:12.

[59]Luke 19:20, NRSV. The appellation "king of the Jews" occurs often in the Gospels, but always is said about Jesus by others, usually in a scornful context. Jesus never uses the phrase to describe himself.

[60]"Son of man" occurs eighty-four times in the King James, eighty-two times in the New Revised Standard.

[61]"Nard" at John 12:3 NRSV, "always" at John 12:8, NRSV. In this section falls one of the references that proponents of the doctored-Bible thesis assert must have been spliced into scripture. When Judas says the money should have gone to the poor, the Gospels

interject at John 12:6, NRSV, "(He said this is not because he cared about the poor, but because he was a thief; he kept the common purse and used to steal what was put into it.)"

Doctored-Bible theory presumes that as Christianity was spreading, people looked at the verse in which the traitor speaks up for the poor and thought, "this Judas was not such a bad guy," so the comment about theft was dropped in to answer that opinion. That the verse occurs in parenthesis is supposed to be hugely revealing of tampering: though the parens do not come from the oldest autographs, which have no punctuation. Otherwise, as with other doctored-Bible claims, there is no physical evidence of scripture manipulation, only a conceptual analysis.

[62]Recounted in Genesis 12:10–20.

[63]Abraham agrees to murder after a divine go-ahead: "God said to Abraham, 'Do not be distressed because of the boy and because of your slave woman; whatever Sarah says to you, do as she tells you.'" Genesis 21:12, NRSV.

[64]Recounted in Genesis 21.

[65]Recounted in Second Samuel 11. David accomplishes the murder by directing field commanders to send Uriah to the most dangerous part of a battle, then have all support troops around him suddenly withdraw.

Because the "House of David" is a magical phrase to Judaism, David's behavior remains a subject of debate in Israeli culture. Menachem Begin, former prime minister of Israel, defended the affair with Bathsheba, saying that in ancient times as soldiers went to the field they granted wives conditional papers of divorce in case they were killed: therefore when David was sleeping with Bathsheba while her husband Uriah was in battle, technically this was not adultery. Neat point, but it skips the fact that David sent Uriah to the battle for the purpose of having him murdered.

[66]Recounted in Second Samuel 13.

[67]Recounted in Second Samuel 18.

[68]Recounted in Second Samuel 19.

[69]Genesis 19:8, KJV. The angels save the family by hitting the rioters with a supernatural bolt that makes them unable to see the door of Lot's house.

[70]Matthew 19:29, KJV.

[71]Luke 14:26, NRSV. In a similar vein Jesus's brother, James the Just, says at James 4:4 in the NRSV, "Do you not know that friendship with the world is enmity with God? Therefore whoever wishes to be a friend of the world becomes an enemy of God." (The Book of James was probably written by Jesus's brother, but this has been disputed.)

[72]Matthew 8:22.

[73]Luke 23:28–29, NRSV.

[74]The Old Testament declares that children of illegitimacy "shall not enter into the congregation of the Lord, even unto his tenth generation" (Deuteronomy 23:2, KJV), a stunningly punitive ordinance, even if the purpose is to pressure men into taking responsibility for their offspring.

[75]At John 1:45 and 6:42.

[76]At Mark 6:3.

[77]When Joseph saw that Mary was showing, he "planned to dismiss her quietly" (Matthew 1:19, NRSV), but an angel appeared to instruct him to go through with the wedding. Technically this is all the angel directed Joseph to do. Nothing was said about whether he must remain in the houschold.

[78]Some proponents of the doctored-Bible thesis think the immaculate conception was inserted retroactively into scripture to counter Roman commentators who called Jesus a bastard: this way Mary could have been a virgin on her wedding day even if Jesus was

already born. If that sounds like a convoluted answer to a charge about lineage, it's peanuts compared to what Henry VIII would later do.

[79]Mark 3:21, NRSV. In the King James translation it is Jesus's "friends," not his "family," who attempt to restrain him.

[80]Matthew 12:49, NRSV. Stephen Mitchell has woven much of a compelling book, *The Gospel According to Jesus* (San Francisco: HarperCollins, 1988), around the thesis that Christ was tormented by unresolved feelings toward his mother. This may sound inexcusably trendy—next, perhaps, recovered memory of trauma in the manger. Yet anyone who reads the New Testament with Mitchell's hypothesis in mind cannot help coming away with the haunting sense that there was some powerful loss or pain in Jesus's personal life.

[81]Matthew 13:57, KJV.

[82]Matthew 13:58, NRSV.

[83]In the phrase "the Lord God omnipotent reigneth," at Revelation 19:6 in the King James. In the New Revised Standard this reference is "God the Almighty."

[84]Second Thessalonians 2:9; Matthew 28:18.

[85]First Chronicles 12:21 and Jeremiah 5:16, KJV.

[86]Psalms 147:5, NRSV.

[87]Ephesians 1:11, NRSV. The "him" in this verse is probably Jesus, but in the apostolic letters of the New Testament, Jesus and God usually are treated as interchangeable from the standpoint of divine attribution.

[88]This figure is accurate for the King James, New Revised Standard, and other generally accepted translations. Some fundamentalist translations use "God Almighty" more often.

[89]Exodus 15:15, KJV. King David often called his lieutenants the Mighty Men; see, for example, Second Samuel 10:7, KJV. One of the sad bits of minutia that came out of the 1993 destruction of the Branch Davidian compound in Waco, Texas, was that David Koresh addressed his favorites as the Mighty Men, using the Old Testament custom.

[90]By the standards of the ludicrous 1997 book *The Bible Code*, the presence in scripture of the Hebrew word *nasa* means you can claim the Bible predicted the National Aeronautics and Space Administration.

[91]Isaiah 37:12.

[92]Genesis 30:8, NRSV.

[93]See, for example, Second Corinthians 6:18.

[94]Again this statement applies to generally accepted translations such as the King James and New Revised Standard. Some fundamentalist translations do have Jesus speak the phrase God Almighty.

[95]Romans 15:14. The other instances fall at First Corinthians 1:5 and 13:2.

[96]Psalms 147:5, NRSV.

[97]Acts 24:2, NRSV: "Tertullus began to accuse him, saying: 'Your Excellency, because of you we have long enjoyed peace, and reforms have been made for this people because of your foresight.' "

[98]Acts 2:23.

[99]Acts 2:23 and First Peter 1:2. The second reference, to the apostles being "elect according to the foreknowledge of God," proved among the most pernicious in the Bible, as it is from this slender reed that Calvin hung his predestined "elect" and rationalized numerous political repressions.

[100]For instance, at Romans 16:26 in the NRSV, or the "the glory of the immortal God" at Romans 1:23, NRSV.

[101]Psalms 90:2, NRSV.

[102]Mark 3:29. At another key passage, the Romans 1:27 verse at which the King James

says homosexuals will receive "recompense of their error," the New International asserts they deserve "due penalty for their perversion," a more antagonistic wording.

[103]Other than the term of address "God Almighty," which the NIV uses far more often than competing translations.

[104]Jeremiah 1:5, KJV.

[105]The second chapter of Daniel describes this incident.

[106]More than half of the King James and New Revised Standard references to "the Almighty" fall in the Book of Job.

[107]Job 42:2, NRSV.

[108]Perhaps the only other indirect assertion of omnipotence in the Bible is that shortly after Job says, at Job 42:6, that God can do "all things," the Maker says to some of Job's companions, "My wrath is kindled against you and against your two friends; for you have not spoken of me what is right, as my servant Job has."

[109]Job 42:6, NRSV.

[110]Malachi 3:6, KJV.

[111]See Martin Buber, *On the Bible* (New York: Schocken Books, 1982).

[112]Deuteronomy 32:4, NRSV.

[113]"Way" from Psalms 18:30, NRSV; "law" and "reviving" from Psalms 19:7, NRSV.

[114]Matthew 5:48, NRSV.

[115]Matthew 19:21.

[116]Isaiah 57:17, NRSV.

[117]Ezekiel 17:22, NRSV.

Chapter Ten

[1]Many Bible readers have stopped and scratched their heads over the first verse of the Gospel of John: "In the beginning was the Word, and the Word was with God, and the Word was God." *What Word?* is a common retort. The Greek original term most translators render as "the Word" is *logos*, which has a range of meanings, including word, identity, divine identity, a concept of knowledge, and several other things. Taken at face value this verse asserts that before the universe existed, God had access to some extremely important thought or item of wisdom. Maybe it was the knowledge of how to trigger a Big Bang.

[2]To explain: consider that a leading dispute among cosmologists concerns whether the universe is "open" or "closed." If the universe is "open" then the galaxies, which now travel outward from a presumed point of origin, will continue to do so throughout eternity, the cosmos never reaching any boundary of time or space. If the universe is "closed," then across the eons gravity will overcome the outward flight and reverse the movement of the heavens. All matter will be drawn back to the point where it began, shattering the universe in a Big Crunch—the reverse of a Big Bang.

After reality collapses on itself in a Big Crunch, would there be a recoil that causes a new Big Bang, forming another cosmos? Some theories suggest that the universe endlessly recycles in this manner. But the inconceivable pressures of a Big Crunch would obliterate everything with a material basis, even information: even the leptons and baryons that compose matter would be crushed into an undifferentiated blur. Could the incorporeal, by contrast, endure? If so perhaps one of God's roles is to survive the conclusion of each universe, existing to trigger and guide the next.

[3]Stephen Hawking once supposed that the closest thing to time travel would be a sort of universal reverse-time: as long as the cosmos continues expanding, time will move

forward, but if the universe begins to contract, time will run in reverse, with people living out their lives backward. Hawking later retracted this idea, attributing it to a miscalculation. Owing to Hawking's prominence, his withdrawal of the reverse-universe hypothesis precipitated one of the all-time daffy headlines from the AP: "TIME TO MOVE IN NORMAL DIRECTION, NOTED SCIENTIST DECLARES."

[4]Because of relativistic time dilation—the effect that would cause an astronaut moving at high velocity to age more slowly than the society left behind—perception of time may vary depending on one's circumstances. But this has nothing to do with time travel. Even at relativistic speed, only one sense of what constitutes past, present, and future would be accessible to the frame of each observer.

[5]Theoretical time travel is described in Kip Thorne, *Black Holes and Time Warps* (New York: W.W. Norton, 1994). Do not try this at home!

[6]See Charles Hartshorne, *The Divine Relativity* (New Haven: Yale University Press, 1948). One of Hartshorne's related points was that while we think of our ancestors as defunct and ourselves as crackling with life, their thoughts and actions constantly affect us, whereas nothing we can do will ever affect them.

[7]Whether seeing something in the future means it must come to pass, regardless of what is done in the present, is the flip side of whether going backwards in time can alter the present. Both lines of thought create so many paradoxes that they alone seem to rule out time travel or time viewing.

[8]Though Eve is traditionally depicted as munching an apple, in Genesis the tree's product is simply a "fruit."

[9]Recounted in Genesis 22.

[10]The closest reference is to "mysteries," such as in Luke 8:10, KJV, "And [Jesus] said, 'Unto you it is given to know the mysteries of the kingdom of God.'"

[11]Deuteronomy 8:2, NRSV.

[12]This account begins at Deuteronomy 34:1.

[13]The Garden account begins at Genesis 2:8.

[14]"And out of the ground the Lord God formed every beast of the field, and every fowl of the air; and brought them unto Adam to see what he would call them." (Genesis 2:19, KJV.)

[15]Genesis 2:20–21, NRSV.

[16]Genesis 2:17, KJV.

[17]Proponents of inerrant-Bible theory assert that when God predicted that the fruit would kill Adam and Eve, what was meant was that violating the rule would result in humanity being denied knowledge of immortality, and thus consigned to the cycle of dust to dust. But when God warns of the deadly effects of the fruit at Genesis 2:17, the prediction is clearly that Adam and Eve would die "that day" if they ate.

[18]Genesis 3:8–9, NRSV.

[19]Genesis 3:11, NRSV.

[20]Genesis 3:19, NRSV.

[21]Genesis 3:15, NRSV.

[22]Genesis 3:22, NRSV.

[23]This view is plagued by circular reasoning: the Maker staged the Garden as a means of explaining why people must be required to suffer, but the suffering is necessary to atone for actions mandated by the staging.

In her excellent *Adam, Eve, and the Serpent* (New York: Random House, 1988), Elaine Pagels proposed an alternative reading, that the Eden account celebrates free will by showing that people have been willing to defy God from the start. Pagels believes the Gnostic movement of the early centuries liked the Eden account because it abashed God, whom the Gnostics held culpable for the release of evil. Further, she supposes that among the pernicious effects Augustine had on monotheistic faith was the conversion of the Garden from an allegory of bravado to one of guilt and unworthiness.

[24]Genesis 4:9–10, KJV. It is to this question that Cain makes the chilling reply, "I do not know; am I my brother's keeper?"

[25]Genesis 4:4–5, NRSV.

[26]Quoted in *Bible Review*, June 1991.

[27]Genesis 4:10, NRSV.

[28]At Genesis 18.

[29]Genesis 18:17, NRSV.

[30]The colloquy is at Genesis 18:18–33.

[31]Genesis 18:25, KJV.

[32]The "great fish" arrives at Jonah 1:17. Since whales are mammals, what exactly lunched on Jonah has long been a subject of conversation among Bible votaries, with speculations as far-ranging as the reappearance of an ichthyosaur, an extinct fish of Jurassic proportions. Given that the verse in question says "the Lord prepared a great fish," Jonah may have gotten his ride in a one-of-a-kind creature.

[33]Jonah 3:10, NRSV.

[34]Jonah's bummer over the sparing on Nineveh is recounted in Jonah 4.

[35]See *Omnipotence and Other Theological Mistakes* by Charles Hartshorne (Albany: State University of New York Press, 1984).

[36]See James Gleick, *Chaos: Making a New Science* (New York: Viking, 1987).

[37]Genesis 6:5–7, NRSV.

[38]First Samuel 15:35, NRSV. Saul's ascension to royalty comes during the days when Hebrew society was plagued by warlords ruling as "judges." The Israelis asked God for a king, noting that the nations arrayed against them have kings. The Maker tells the Hebrews they will rue the day they requested a royal house: "[God] said, 'These will be the ways of the king who will reign over you' " (First Samuel 8:11, NRSV), citing confiscation of property, loss of young men in pointless wars, and kidnapping of daughters for the sexual amusement of royal cronies. All these things become daily events under Saul.

The verses predicting Saul's corruption could be said to represent a divine forecast of the future, but it is a general prediction, given that any student of history knows royalty means trouble. Otherwise, again we must ask why a Maker with specific foreknowledge would have selected Saul, if God already knew Saul would be a disaster. Surely this was not done to banish the notion of kings, since the Israelis would have many subsequent monarchs. The Old Testament's explanation God chose Saul because he was unusually tall (see First Samuel 9:2) is hardly reassuring from the standpoint of omniscience theory.

[39]Genesis 6:6.

[40]Solomon's embrace of pagan idols is recounted in First Kings 11:2, which reports the king would do anything for his 700 wives and 300 courtesans because "Solomon clung to these in love." To please the harem, Solomon built shrines for "Chemosh the abomination of Moab, and for Molech the abomination of the Ammonites." (First Kings 11:7, NRSV.) It is not hard to guess that a graying Solomon began to gravitate toward pagan sex-rite theology in order to insure that the thousand royal babes remained in the mood.

[41]*Our Planet, Our Health*, report of the United Nations Development Programme (Oxford: Oxford University Press, 1992). Disease death in the cited figure means premature death; fatal diseases of old age are not included.

[42]Even most skeptics reason from All-or-Nothing in this manner. For example a fine

contemporary book, *Facing the Abusing God: A Theology of Protest* by David Blumenthal (Philadelphia: Westminster, 1993), grapples with the enigma of God's failure to restrain evil and concludes, "God's power is absolute, but God cannot use it absolutely," operating under the standard assumption that the Bible simply must call God all-powerful.

[43]See "Can Chip Devices Keep Shrinking?," *Science*, 13 December 1996.

[44]See Timothy Ferris, *Coming of Age in the Milky Way* (New York: William Morrow, 1988). And remember that there are at least 40 billion other galaxies, averaging roughly the size of ours. To flip at one page per second through a cosmic reference atlas delineating all the stars in creation would appear to require more time than the universe has existed.

[45]See "Does Evolutionary History Take Million-Year Breaks?," *Science*, 24 October 1997.

[46]See Alston Chase, *Playing God in Yellowstone* (Boston: Houghton Mifflin, 1988).

Chapter Eleven

[1]Some schisms of the early centuries, such as the Gnostic movement and Manichaeism, were in their time understood as criticisms of the Judeo-Christian deity, but not in the sense that they challenged the idea of omnipotence. Gnosticism, Manichaeism, and some related "dualistic" beliefs held that the firmament contained both good and evil supernatural forces pitched against each other in combat for supremacy: this contravened the Judeo-Christian notion of one supreme Maker. But even for dualistic faiths, the competing deities were seen as omnipotent relative to humanity, lacking only in the final power to eliminate each other.

[2]Tempier's list appears in Edward Peters, ed., *Heresy and Authority in Medieval Europe* (Philadelphia: University of Pennsylvania Press, 1980).

[3]Most historians now use the term "Hebrew" for the subjects of early Old Testament books. It is thought that Jewish political consciousness did not begin until perhaps the fourth century B.C.E., after the destruction of the First Temple in Jerusalem. Around that period, nationalist identity began to coalesce within the group of desert dwellers linked by fealty to the solitary god Yahweh. Modern Bible translations do not employ "Jewish" as an identity term until the middle Old Testament, several centuries after Moses.

[4]This latter aspect of Greek philosophy is more or less making a comeback in the form of current cosmological theories holding that the universe will expand forever.

[5]James, who seems to have had little to do with his brother (perhaps half brother) during Christ's life, was put to death by Rome in the year 70. This suggests James was either executed as an old man or was much younger than Jesus, which might explain why he plays no role in the Gospel accounts. An alternative explanation popular with biblical deconstructionists is that James headed the Jewish wing of the Jesus movement, and thus was deliberately excised from the Gospels by censors of the early Church. This is possible but, like all doctored-Bible hypotheses, unsupported by any physical evidence of scripture deletions, only by a conceptual analysis.

The fourth-century historian Eusebius wrote that like his brother, James went to death asking that his executioners be forgiven. Paul, a Roman citizen, delayed his execution by invoking the Roman right of trial, and some historians think he wavered at the end. Ultimately Paul's faith rallied and he cast his lot with eternity. Paul was right: the Empire is long gone, and Jesus remains.

[6]See Elaine Pagels, *The Gnostic Gospels* (New York: Random House, 1979).

[7]Today much of what is known about the young Church comes from surviving copies of broadsides various pro- and anti-Christian factions composed against each other. For example Tertullian, a third-century Christian father, gained his reputation penning with-

ering pamphlets assailing heresy. Tertullian was himself then denounced as a heretic when he spoke well of Montanism, a Christian denomination that urged people to renounce material concerns because Christ was about to return and conclude history. (Church policy held that the time of the Second Coming was unknowable.) Orthodox Christianity excommunicated Montanists in the year 177, their real crime being not doctrine but representing a rival to the expanding infrastructure of bishops.

[8]Constantine had some experience in this, having claimed in the year 310 to have seen in the sky a vision of the Roman sun god, traditional deity of emperors.

[9]Though he converted the Empire to the new faith, Constantine himself did not undergo baptism until on his deathbed in the year 337. At the time it was strongly felt that if a person received baptism and then sinned anew, subsequent sins would be doubly offensive to God, who had witnessed and blessed the baptism. Constantine wanted the freedom to continue sinning, for example, by turning on and killing his rival Licinius. So Constantine held baptism in reserve to cleanse his soul in the moment before facing heaven, and from his standpoint the timing worked out perfectly.

Whether you can sin throughout life while planning to convert at the last minute, then have your conversion count in God's eyes, was a regular topic of debate in centuries past. Martin Luther's answer was that the conversion would count, even if you cynically planned it. This is one of the many tenets that endeared Luther to the German princes, who saw in the Reformation a means to escape that cumbersome Catholic notion of salvation by good works, while reserving the right to launder their souls just before death. Probably Jesus would have said that a planned deathbed conversion would count if you genuinely repented from your plan to repent cynically.

[10]The status of Jesus's cellular structure being resolved in Church eyes, further councils, such as Constantinople in 680, debated whether Jesus's thoughts were human or divine.

[11]For example, Plato labored to establish the commendable "epistemological principle," which holds that abstract ideas are more important than physical reality; yet he also thought palm-reading could predict the future. In the early centuries Greek Gentiles assumed there must be a connection between Plato and Christianity, because while Judaism believed existence ended with death, Christianity, like Plato, asserted an everlasting soul. A good source on Plato's spiritual theory is W.K.C. Guthrie, *A History of Greek Philosophy* (Cambridge: Cambridge University Press, 1962).

[12]See Garry Wills, *Under God* (New York: Random House, 1990).

[13]Ancient Egyptian religion briefly transformed from polytheism to monotheism under the pharaoh Ikhnaton, but then reverted to the many-gods view.

[14]See *Omnipotence and Other Theological Mistakes* by Charles Hartshorne (Albany: State University of New York Press, 1984).

[15]Matthew 26:52, KJV.

[16]A fine account of Tyndale's life is David Danielle, *William Tyndale* (New Haven: Yale University Press, 1994).

[17]Eventually the early eighteenth-century Pope Clement XI would go all the way to condemning Bible reading by anyone other than church officials. The ruling sounds like a practical joke: POPE CONDEMNS BIBLE READING. By the time it was issued, Bibles had become sufficiently common that this dictum had little effect, except directly within the walls of Catholic churches.

[18]The word "pope" never appears in the Bible; whether the concept appears is arguable. Catholic thinkers maintain that Peter's administrative position, described in the New Testament, justifies the idea of the papacy. If one views the pope as a movement leader, this argument contains merit. Viewing the pope as someone who rules on what the flock

may believe is iffy on biblical grounds, however, since First Peter 5:1–10, a series of directives to elders, instructs that church leaders must never "lord it over" laity.

[19]Romans 13:1, NRSV.

[20]Democracy, Luther said, would constitute "a piece of robbery by which everyman takes from [the prince] his booty," the booty being the serf's own freedom.

[21]Princes, Luther wrote, should erect statues of peasants impaled on swords, to emphasize that the lives of serfs were worthless. Luther also produced some of history's most venomous anti-Semitic screeds, helping instill in the German consciousness the stygian impulses that would later release the Holocaust.

[22]Anabaptists are commonly misconstrued as predecessors of today's Baptists: their beliefs are better seen today in the Mennonite denomination. Anabaptists were pure pacifists who considered all contact with the state to be corruption, forbidding members from running for office or accepting government employment. Yet Anabaptists did not renounce every worldly trapping. Anabaptist men were renowned for telling prospective love interests that since the Bible says that to enter heaven one must surrender whatever one holds most dear, they would be happy to do young women a favor by helping them lose their virginity.

[23]Later Zwingli, like Muhammad, led a military assault in the name of religion, in his case against Swiss cantons loyal to Rome. His fortune at war was not as good as the Prophet's. Zwingli was captured in the 1531 battle of Kappel am Albis and executed by the Catholic victors.

[24]Agreeing with Luther, Calvin maintained that only divine grace, not moral behavior, was essential for salvation.

[25]The Puritans fled England in order to practice their own spiritual views, but denied the same right to others: the reason Roger Williams founded Rhode Island was that he had been expelled from Massachusetts for questioning Puritan doctrine. The humorist Garrison Keillor has a wonderful line about this, that the Puritans sailed to America "seeking less freedom than was allowed in England at the time."

[26]As the novelist and former priest James Carroll has written, "Bishops at the First Vatican Council sought to bolster a Pope who had just been stripped of temporal sovereignty over the Papal States" by conferring on Pius IX the new distinction of infallibility.

[27]Honorius I was condemned as a heretic for a slip of the tongue regarding "monotheletism," one of the endless variations on the dispute about whether Jesus was mortal or empyreal.

[28]Eastern religions generally do not depict the gods as Absolute, representing them rather as wardens for larger cosmic forces; Buddhism, Jainism, and Sankhya Hinduism deny the existence of deities as the concept occurs in Western thought.

[29]See Jon Levenson, *Creation and the Persistence of Evil* (New York: Harper & Row, 1988).

[30]From J. S. Mill, *An Examination of Sir William Hamilton's Philosophy* (1865). This work contains the lovely zinger, "If a being can sentence me to hell for not calling him [Lord], then to hell I will go."

[31]See *The Logic of Perfection* by Charles Hartshorne (Chicago: Open Court Publishing, 1962).

[32]See *Creative Synthesis and the Philosophical Method* by Charles Hartshorne (Chicago: University Press of America, 1983).

[33]See Hartshorne, *Omnipotence and Other Theological Mistakes*.

[34]See *The Problem of God* by Edgar Brightman, Abingdon Press, 1930.

[35]See *Mortality and Morality* by Hans Jonas (Evanston: Northwestern University Press, 1996).

[36]Gifford Lectures, Cambridge University, 1994.

Chapter Twelve

[1]Luke 2:10, KJV.

[2]The beauty of the Good Samaritan story is self-explanatory, but the context stronger than modern readers may know. After the first Israel, whose capital was Samaria, was overrun by Assyria in 722 B.C.E., its citizens marched into exile and never heard from again—these are the "lost tribes of Israel"—Samaria became a pagan center and yet retained elements of Hebrew culture, which Judaism found incredibly galling. By Jesus's day, Jewish society considered Samaritans a lower form of life. To give the parable the same force today one would tell it to an American audience as the story of the Good Communist, to a Japanese audience as the parable of the Good Korean, to a Polish audience as the story of the Good Jew, to a white American audience as the story of the Good Teenage Black Male, and to an Israeli audience as the parable of the Good Palestinian.

[3]The account begins at Luke 15:11. Just as the word "malaise" never occurred in Jimmy Carter's famed 1979 Malaise Speech, the word "prodigal" never occurs in the parable of the Prodigal Son.

[4]Matthew 5:39.

[5]Matthew 28:1 and elsewhere.

[6]First Corinthians 13:7, NRSV.

[7]Second Kings 2:23–24, NRSV.

[8]Sometimes clergy defend the practice of not pointing out the Bible's appalling sections on the grounds that the mentally unbalanced may mistake such verses as instructions that God wants them to kill. There are cases in which mass murderers have said this.

[9]The Flood story begins at Genesis 6:5.

[10]Genesis 6:13, NRSV.

[11]This phrase has become so common in public debate that a Doric engraving reading MISTAKES WERE MADE should be erected above the main entrance to the White House.

[12]Genesis 8:21, NRSV.

[13]Recounted in Exodus 8–9.

[14]Exodus 12:23.

[15]Exodus 12:5.

[16]Exodus 4:21, NRSV.

[17]Recounted in Exodus 1. At Exodus 2, the baby Moses is placed into a reed basket and pushed into the Nile to escape this fate.

[18]Exodus 4:22–23, NRSV. From here follows what may be the strangest moment in the Bible. The Maker has just ordered Moses to return to Egypt and confront Pharaoh. Inexplicably, God then tries to kill Moses. Moses is saved when his wife, Zipporah, grabs a knife, circumcises their son, and touches the bloody tissue to Moses's feet, which for some reason placates the Maker.

Why God tries to kill Moses (and fails!) has perplexed commentators for centuries. Here are the verses: "On the way, at a place where they spent the night, the Lord met [Moses] and tried to kill him. But Zipporah took a flint and cut off her son's foreskin, and touched Moses' feet with it, and said, 'Truly you are a bridegroom of blood to me!' So [God] let him alone." Exodus 4:24–25, NRSV.

[19]Exodus 9:19–20, NRSV.

[20]Exodus 11:5, KJV.

[21]Exodus 11:6, KJV.

[22]Critics of Islam sometimes protest that Muhammad cannot really have been holy because he led a military assault against Mecca. Judeo-Christian holy men including Moses, Joshua, and David were principally military figures as well.

[23]Exodus 17:14, NRSV. The campaign against Amalek is at Exodus 17:8–15.

[24]Numbers 21:35, NRSV.

[25]Genesis 34:9–10, NRSV.

[26]Genesis 34:25, NRSV.

[27]Genesis 34:27–29, NRSV.

[28]Genesis 35:5, NRSV.

[29]Genesis 35:11–12, NRSV.

[30]Genesis 49:6, NRSV.

[31]For instance, most of Exodus 25.

[32]Recounted in Exodus 32.

[33]Exodus 32:14.

[34]Exodus 32:26–28, NRSV.

[35]Exodus 32:29, NRSV.

[36]Leviticus 10:2, KJV.

[37]Second Samuel 6:7.

[38]Leviticus 24:16, KJV.

[39]Numbers 21:6, NRSV.

[40]This recounting begins at Numbers 16:1, the quotation is from the KJV.

[41]Numbers 16:35, NRSV.

[42]Recounted in Numbers 25, quoting from the KJV.

[43]Numbers 25:11, NRSV.

[44]"Horrors of the Sommes Remembered," *International Herald Tribune*, 1 July 1996. Such a high ratio of firepower to death is not uncommon in war. During the 1945 campaign on Okinawa, American forces expended 150 bullets and 40 bombs or artillery shells for each Japanese soldier killed—fantastically more destructive force than could have been mustered in ancient days with hand weapons.

[45]Numbers 31:3, NRSV.

[46]Numbers 31:7, NRSV.

[47]Numbers 31:9, NRSV.

[48]Numbers 31:14–17, NRSV.

[49]Recounted in First Kings 18, the quotation is from 18:40, NRSV.

[50]Second Chronicles 28:5, NRSV.

[51]Second Chronicles 28:8, NRSV.

[52]Judges 19:22; the account begins at Judges 19.

[53]Judges 19:29, NRSV.

[54]The war is detailed in Judges 20.

[55]Judges 20:48, NRSV.

[56]Judges 21:10, NRSV.

[57]Judges 21:20–21, NRSV.

[58]Daniel 6:24, NRSV.

[59]In the apocryphal Bel and the Dragon, found in some Bibles, a local king believes the stone statue Bel to be a living god. Bel's priests require that "12 bushels of choice flour and 40 sheep and six measures [300 gallons] of wine" be placed within the statue every

night as an offering. The bounty is always gone in the morning, which the king interprets as proof that the idol eats.

Daniel, hero of the lion's den, debunks Bel by finding a trap door the priests use to remove the comestibles for themselves, then scattering ashes around the opening so that our rather dim-witted monarch can see the tell-tale footprints. This story, recounted at Bel and the Dragon 1–22, has a typical Old Testament ending: the king orders the priests *and* their wives *and* their children put to death.

[60]First Samuel 17:51, KJV.

[61]First Samuel 27:9, NRSV.

[62]Recounted in First Samuel 18:25–30.

[63]Second Samuel 24:11–15, NRSV.

[64]Judges 16:25–30. Israeli generals speak of their atomic weapons as "the Samson option" because detonation could obliterate Middle Eastern enemies but destroy Israel in the process.

[65]Judges 14:4, NRSV.

[66]Judges 14:19, NRSV.

[67]Judges 15:5.

[68]Judges 15:8, NRSV.

[69]Judges 15:15.

[70]In one the Bible's throwaway lines of condescension to women, Samson tells Delilah about his supernatural hair because "She had nagged him with her words day after day, and pestered him, he was tired to death" of listening to her. Judges 16:16, NRSV.

[71]Samson's story is Judges 13–16.

[72]The children die at Job 1:19.

[73]Ox liability statutes are detailed at Exodus 21:28.

[74]One of the Bible's enigmatic passages is Numbers 14:18, which in the NRSV declares, "The Lord is slow to anger and abounding in steadfast love, forgiving iniquity and transgression, but by no means clearing the guilty, visiting the iniquity of the parents upon the children to the third and the fourth generation." In other words God is forgiving and vindictive at the same time.

[75]Deuteronomy 21:18–21, KJV.

[76]Most of Deuteronomy 22 describes the death-for-sex punishments.

[77]Portions of the Deuteronomic Code do suggest tentative thinking about justice. The code requires that if a virgin woman engaged to be married is caught in a town or city having sex with someone other than her intended, both the man and woman be executed— the woman because she "did not cry for help" to preserve her honor. Ancient cities were so closely packed, a cry for succor would always be heard; therefore, this reasoning holds, the silent woman must have consented. For sex between the unmarried in the countryside, however, only the man would be executed. The reasoning is that in rural areas there might have been no help nearby to summon, and thus no way to establish whether the woman consented or resisted. See Deuteronomy 22:23–27.

[78]Deuteronomy 20:13–14, NRSV. Critics of Islam sometimes call the religion barbaric because the Koran specifies that a fifth of the spoils of war belong to Allah. Judaism and Christianity contain the same barbarism, Deuteronomy's divine permission to "enjoy the spoil of your enemies."

[79]Deuteronomy 21:10–14, KJV.

[80]Deuteronomy 20:15.

[81]Deuteronomy 33:27, KJV.

[82]Deuteronomy 20:16, NRSV.

[83]Joshua 6:20–21, NRSV.

[84]Joshua 5:14, NRSV.

[85]God the "commander" even gives tactical recon advice. Of a Philistine troop column, "The Lord said . . . 'Go around to their rear and come upon them opposite the balsam trees.' " Second Samuel 5:23, NRSV. A French soldier, Comte de Bussy-Rabutin, in 1648 composed a memorable quip from this verse: "God is generally on the side of the big squadrons."

[86]John Noble Wilford, "Believers Score in Battle over the Battle of Jericho," *New York Times*, 22 February 1990.

[87]Joshua 8:22, NRSV.

[88]Joshua 10:20, NRSV.

[89]Judges 18:27, NRSV.

[90]Judges 18:7.

[91]Joshua 10:10, KJV.

[92]Joshua 10:11, KJV.

[93]First Samuel 15:3, NRSV.

[94]First Samuel 15:15–18.

[95]First Samuel 15:33, NRSV.

[96]Typical quote about Indians, from Mather's book: "The woods must be cleaned of these pernicious creatures, to make room for a better growth." Son of Increase Mather, Cotton Mather entered Harvard in 1685 at age 12, and by his 20s was a nationally known preacher of throwback views. Cotton is remembered for coining the term "American" and for asserting that the Salem witch trials were valid, though by his time even most traditionalists considered the event to have been an outrage.

[97]See Antonia Fraser, *Cromwell: Lord Protector* (New York: Knopf, 1973). Though Cromwell eagerly killed fellow Christians, he was tolerant of Judaism, inviting back to England those Jews whose ancestors had been expelled.

[98]See Karen Armstrong, *A History of God* (New York: Ballantine, 1993).

[99]Some biblical commentators speculate that the New Testament dig against "the profane chatter and contradictions of what is falsely called knowledge" (First Timothy 6:20, NRSV) is a riposte to Marcion's claim that comparative analysis proved the gods of the Old and New Testaments were different beings.

[100]Consider an analogy to human attempts to subjugate through the use of force. During the phase of European colonization of the developing world, the colonizers performed demonstrations of power vastly superior to anything locals could muster. All such demonstrations failed: military objectives were taken and riots repressed, but such acts only left future generations more resistant. Attempts at good will failed too. If the colonial power tried to win over the local citizenry by providing a beneficial project such as a rail line or a power dam, the project would mainly serve to remind that the "supernatural" imperial power could do what the locals could not. Whatever thanks colonial subjects expressed for beneficial projects were not heartfelt but designed to propitiate the distant power until such time as it would go away. Only one feature left behind by the European colonialists was welcomed in a genuine sense: thoughts. Books, ideas, music, philosophy—forms of *persuasion*—took hold. Everything else was rejected and despised.

[101]Jeremiah 41:10, KJV.

Chapter Thirteen

[1]First Corinthians 13:2, NRSV.

[2]Ecclesiastes 6:7, NRSV.

[3]First Corinthians 1:27, KJV.

[4]"Chronological order" is a dicey concept for scripture, since dates of composition for many biblical books have not been firmly established, and may never be. The sequence by which books now appear in most Bibles is probably similar to chronological, but far from reliably so. All manner of theories swirl around what order the Gospels were written in.

[5]Genesis 6:5–7, NRSV.

[6]Genesis 9:12, NRSV.

[7]At the Last Supper, Christ says, "This cup that is poured out for you is the new covenant in my blood." (Luke 22:20, NRSV.) Generally, Christian thinking holds that Jesus's "new covenant" cancels out aspects of Judaism, including the covenant by which God promised the Hebrews a special homeland and special relationship with heaven: two ideas still strongly active in Judaic theology.

[8]Genesis 22:7, NRSV; the Abraham-Isaac story runs from 22:1–14. Some Talmud commentaries interpret Isaac as a grown man who volunteered for the sacrifice out of love for his father. Scripture refers to Isaac simply as "the boy" and gives scant indication of his mental state.

[9]Genesis 22:12, NRSV.

[10]This account begins at Mark 8:14. At several places in the synoptic Gospels (Matthew, Mark, and Luke), the apostles are depicted as amiable bumblers. Only the fourth Gospel, John, presents the disciples as wise or gallant. From this arises a long-standing speculation that the synoptic Gospels were composed by authors not themselves members of the original twelve, who had no incentive to present the apostles in complimentary terms; but that John was written by a person who did serve at Jesus's side and who wanted himself and his friends to find favor with history.

Even John, however, records the difficulty the apostles experienced grasping Jesus's thought. In John 16:29, NRSV, when Christ answers a question directly rather than with a parable, the disciples rejoin in cheerful relief, "Yes, now you are speaking plainly, not in any figure of speech!"

[11]Mark 8:17, NRSV.

[12]Mark 8:21, NRSV.

[13]John 4:48, NRSV.

[14]Genesis 22:17, NRSV. Hard on granting this joyful blessing, the divine reverts to Old Testament bellicosity: "And your offspring shall possess the gate of their enemies," God says at the same verse.

[15]This is a rough estimate, from the *1996 Cambridge Fact Finder* (Cambridge: Cambridge University Press). Such estimates treat nearly all North Americans and Western Europeans as Christians, and nearly all Pakistanis and Indonesians as Muslims, though probably less than half of each of these groups actively practice a religion.

Some theologians call Judaism, Christianity, and Islam collectively the "Abrahamic" faiths, because all claim Abraham as their earliest ancestor. This nomenclature is a nice way of reminding Westerners that Islam is closer theologically to Judaism and Christianity than commonly understood. The term "Abrahamic" is hopelessly ungainly, however. Just try pronouncing it.

[16]Daniel 12:2, NRSV. "Those who sleep in the earth" are the residents of Sheol, the Hebrew netherworld in which the spirit continued to exist abstractly, but consciousness was stilled.

[17]Revelation 1:17–18, NRSV.

[18]Nahum 1:2, NRSV.

[19]Jeremiah 18:11, NRSV.

[20]Jeremiah 42:10, KJV. In the New Revised Standard, "the evil that I have done unto you" becomes "the disaster I have brought upon you."

[21]W. H. Auden, *A Certain World* (New York: Viking, 1970).

[22]Isaiah 54:7–10, NRSV.

[23]Some traditionalist theologians have argued that this verse means God voluntarily abdicated some omnipotence; the interpretation may be called on to explain why the Maker exhibits so much less active involvement in human affairs than millennia ago. But even if God had vowed no longer to use the negative power of destruction, we are still left with no explanation of why a true omnipotent Maker would not be using positive powers to end natural disasters, diseases, and so on.

[24]Jeremiah 32:40, NRSV.

[25]Joshua 5:14.

[26]Psalms 145:8, NRSV.

[27]Isaiah 62:5, NRSV.

[28]Isaiah 61:10, NRSV.

[29]Psalms 89:14–15, NRSV.

[30]First Corinthians 13:5.

[31]Jeremiah 31:31–34, NRSV.

[32]Acts 13:39, NRSV. Overturning the vindictive aspects of old Mosaic law was one of Jesus's priority concerns, and could easily have been so even if he considered himself wholly Jewish.

[33]The ancient Hebrew word for prophet, *nabiy*, can translate roughly to "spokesperson."

[34]Mark 2:5, NRSV.

[35]The account begins at Mark 2:1. The quote, Mark 2:9–12, is from the NRSV.

[36]Numbers 21:6, KJV.

[37]Amos 2:8, NRSV.

[38]Amos 5:12, NRSV.

[39]Amos 2:7, NRSV.

[40]Isaiah 61:8, NRSV.

[41]Genesis 18:20–32.

[42]Genesis 19:24, NRSV.

[43]The account begins at Jonah 3:2.

[44]Jonah 3:10, KJV.

[45]Jonah 4:4, 4:11, NRSV.

[46]Scripture often employed "stiff-necked" as an adjective for the closed-minded or stubborn. The term comes from the use of oxen in agriculture: stiff-necked oxen are ones so ornery that even pulling them by the neck won't make them go where you want them to go.

[47]Amos 5:21–24, NRSV.

[48]John 3:16, NRSV.

[49]Hosea 11:8–9, NRSV.

[50]Hosea 3:3, KJV.

[51]Hosea 14:4–7, NRSV.

[52]The story begins at John 8.

[53]John 8:7–8, NRSV.

[54]John 8:9–11, NRSV.

[55]Just before Jesus goes to John to be baptized, the Gospels report that "John the baptizer appeared in the wilderness, proclaiming a baptism of repentance for the forgiveness

of sins." (Mark 1:4, NRSV; the account continues to Mark 1:11.) Jesus submits, thus receiving immersion to wash away evil. What sin might Christ have needed erased?

Jesus's baptism to remove sin comes in Mark, generally thought to be the oldest Gospel. In Matthew's account of the same event, as Christ approaches the river, an extra exchange occurs: "John would have prevented him, saying, 'I need to be baptized by you, and do you come to me?' But Jesus answered him, 'Let it be so now; for it is proper for us in this way to fulfill all righteousness.' " (Matthew 3:14–15, NRSV.) Perhaps when Gospel writers subsequent to Mark composed their accounts, they felt compelled to offer an explanation of why Christ would have submitted to a ceremony for ablution of sin. But the original question from Mark, of whether Jesus too ached to be born again, hangs over the subject.

Chapter Fifteen

[1]Second Timothy 3:16, NRSV.

[2]See Charles Hartshorne, *Omnipotence and Other Theological Mistakes* (Albany: State University of New York Press, 1984).

[3]Koester cited from *Bible Review*, October 1995.

[4]European figures cited on BBC Radio "Religion News," 25 November 1996. Church attendance figures for France are buoyed by a high rate of observance in the country's growing Muslim population.

[5]See James Reston Jr., *The Last Apocalypse: Europe at the Year 1000* (Garden City, N.Y.: Doubleday, 1998).

[6]See David Kertzer, "Secrets of the Vatican Archives," *New York Times*, 7 February 1998. The last Inquisition, based in Rome, did not formally conclude until 1908.

[7]By proportion to population, more Germans were killed hand-to-hand during the Thirty Years' War than all (non-Holocaust) German combat and bombing deaths during World War II.

[8]Part of Dietrich Bonhoeffer's 1930s campaign against the Nazis was an attack on the notion of "cheap grace" then being promoted by some German Lutherans. This idea roughly held that a Christian could be a Nazi and still be saved, because divine grace, not earthly morality, was all that was required for admission to heaven. Imagining there could ever be Christian "grace" in Nazi behavior was the reductio ad absurdum for the *sola fide* concept.

[9]This is another phrase widely believed to come from the Bible, but that never occurs there. The derivation is from the play *Whore of Babylon* by Thomas Dekker, a contemporary of Shakespeare. The closest biblical word structure is at Revelations 17:5, NRSV, where an evil queen who drinks the blood of saints is called "Babylon the great, mother of whores."

[10]Shunning of heretics is detailed at Titus 3:10. Elsewhere in the New Testament, at Galatians 1:8, practitioners of rival religions are "accursed." In the Old Testament, Hebrews were told that if their brothers, children, or "thy friend which is of thine own soul" should advocate any competing faith, "Thou shalt surely kill him; thine hand shall be first upon him." (Deuteronomy 13:9, KJV.) Think about these uplifting passages the next time you hear that Islam is primitive because the Koran condemns heretics.

[11]In 1997 the Church of Christ, Episcopal, Presbyterian USA, and Reformed denominations voted to recognize one another, formally withdrawing past condemnations of each other's creeds. This represents an ecumenical breakthrough, but the motive was also pragmatic. All four denominations are in decline. The establishment of diplomatic relations

enables clergy of one to conduct services for any other, which will help sustain small congregations struggling to keep their doors open.

[12]See Gustav Niebuhr, "Lutherans Reconsider Episcopal Concordat," *New York Times*, 30 November 1997. Lutherans found themselves uncomfortable with their rival's assertion that Episcopal bishops are part of the "apostolic succession," or an unbroken chain backward to the first twelve disciples. Roman Catholicism also asserts this, and both can't be true at once. Episcopalians claim an unbroken apostolic succession through their relationship to the Anglican church of England, which since its split with Roman Catholicism has technically claimed to be the true Catholic church, even though its members call themselves Protestants. This is yet another source of denominational friction.

[13]Judaism generally does not seek converts, being concerned first with the preservation of existing lineage; it makes no claim to be right for everyone. Christianity and Islam seek conversion, and consider it curious when the honor is declined. Every Christian and Muslim should ponder how he or she would feel if Jewish leaders regularly suggested that Christians and Muslims were damned for failing to convert.

[14]"Christian Students Flail Oklahoma Mosque," Associated Press, 19 February 1997.

[15]Laurie Goodstein, "Only Orthodox is Judaism, Rabbi Group Declares," *Washington Post*, 2 April 1997.

[16]See *Letters and Papers from Prison* by Dietrich Bonhoeffer (New York: Macmillan, 1997).

[17]Bonhoeffer was a leader of the Confessing Church, a small but valorous faction of German believers who denounced anti-Semitism during the Nazi period. Bonhoeffer fled his homeland after Hitler's rise but returned in 1935, saying that to be in Germany working against the Nazis was the "cost of discipleship" to Jesus. Bonhoeffer was arrested in 1943, imprisoned in concentration camps, and during the final days of the war, hanged on direct orders from Hitler, who used his last hours on Earth attempting to extinguish any remnant of purity in the German spirit. Bonhoeffer was surely one of this century's greatest human beings, or as a Buddhist might say, most evolved souls. At the liberation of Dachau, allied soldiers found another Confessing Church leader, Rev. Martin Niemöller. A World War I U-boat commander who grew into an active opponent of Nazism, Niemöller was imprisoned from 1937 to the war's end. Granted the long life Bonhoeffer was denied, Niemöller later became a prominent pacifist and president of the World Council of Churches.

[18]Matthew 19:17–19, NRSV. The parallel retelling is at Mark 10:17–23.

[19]Jesus also alters the Tenth Commandment, "You shall not covet . . . anything that belongs to your neighbor" to the broader "Love your neighbor as yourself."

[20]Exodus 20:3–8, NRSV. The commandments continue through Exodus 20:17, and are listed again, in slightly different words, at Deuteronomy 5:6–21. The Jewish, Catholic, and Protestant traditions each cite the commandments somewhat differently, based on various interpretations of the Exodus-Deuteronomy overlay.

[21]Esther concerns the attempt of a Jewish woman to prevent a king's advisor from killing Jews to seize their property. Ezra is about the desire of a Jewish priest to reestablish Hebrew cultural consciousness, especially the ban on intermarriage, following the Babylonian captivity.

[22]Rabbinical tradition asserts this instruction is found by inference. Perhaps, but not in plain words.

[23]Comparisons from Matthew 26:49. Being a rabbi did not make Jesus one of the religious officials he deplored, as the term then meant "spiritual teacher" more than its current first meaning of "member of the clergy."

²⁴Acts 11:26 notes in the NRSV, "It was in Antioch that the disciples were first called 'Christians.' "

²⁵See, for example, the account that begins at Galatians 2:10.

²⁶Discussion of this problem begins at Acts 15:1.

²⁷Acts 15:19, NRSV. Note Paul's choice of words: his policy was a favor to those "turning to God," not becoming Christian.

²⁸Ephesians 4:13, NRSV. This portion of Ephesians makes many references to belief in Christ, but it is fair to read the passages as universalist. For instance, the next verse following the citation reads, "We must no longer be children, tossed to and fro and blown about by every wind of doctrine."

²⁹See Luke 2:41.

³⁰After he heals the sick on the Sabbath, Jesus is accused of blasphemy: "But Jesus answered them, 'My Father is still working and I also am working.' " This infuriates the temple lawyers even more, "because he was not only breaking the Sabbath but was also calling God his own Father." John 5:16–17, NRSV.

³¹Matthew 15:11, NRSV.

³²Mark 7:7–8, NRSV.

³³See Karl Rahner, *The Content of Faith* (Atlanta: Crossroads Publishing, 1993). A fine summary of Rahner's views can be found in James Carroll, "The Silence," *The New Yorker*, 7 April 1997.

³⁴Luke 22:20, NRSV.

³⁵Matthew 28:18–20, NRSV.

³⁶The version of the Apostles' Charge in the Gospel of Mark is longer and somewhat different, but still lacks any reference to Christianity or religion. See Mark 16: 15–18. Directly after Mark's version of the Charge, Jesus ascends to heaven. Matthew concludes with the Charge itself, never saying what happened to the risen Christ: a subject the Gospel writer appears to consider less significant than Jesus's final spiritual promise.

³⁷See Mark 7:25–29. These verses report an exchange, in metaphorical language, between Jesus and the girl's mother. Jesus's statement "let the children be fed first" refers to Israel. When the Gentile woman offers a witty comeback, Christ is impressed and replies, "For saying that, you may go—the demon has left your daughter." This is one of scripture's signs that Jesus had an active sense of humor.

³⁸Matthew 10:5–6, NRSV.

³⁹The Pentecost is recounted in Acts 2. What happened that day was not the frenzied speech in mindless babble today heard in revival tents under the banner of "glossolalia." The Pentecost miracle was the ability to speak correctly and be understood in any actual language. Revivalists who jabber when they claim to be "speaking in tongues" are engaging in a parlor trick easily exposed. Just ask a question in Greek or Flemish or Xhosa and see if there is a reply.

⁴⁰Acts 2:36.

⁴¹Acts 2:38, NRSV.

⁴²Matthew 6:24, NRSV.

⁴³Matthew 7:21, NRSV. "Lord" in this verse is *kurios*.

⁴⁴"Lord Jesus" is used at Mark 16:19 in the NRSV and Luke 24:3 in the KJV.

⁴⁵See A. N. Wilson, *Jesus: A Life* (New York: Norton, 1992).

⁴⁶John 8:42, NRSV.

⁴⁷John 3:2, NRSV.

⁴⁸See Mark 3:28–29.

⁴⁹Luke 5:12–14, NRSV.

⁵⁰Mark 5:43, NRSV. At another point the disciples demand to know who their leader really is. Jesus asks, " 'Who do you say that I am?' Peter answered him, 'You are the Messiah.' And [Jesus] sternly ordered them not to tell anyone." Mark 8:29–30, NRSV.

⁵¹John 14:16, NRSV.

⁵²Matthew 18:20.

⁵³John 14:19, NRSV. In another indication of pride, an account beginning at John 4:7, Jesus asks a woman to draw him some water from the town well, and when she hesitates, dazzles her by reading her mind. Later in the conversation the woman mentions that someday the Messiah will come, and Christ seems annoyed not to be recognized, asserting, "I am he, the one who is speaking to you." Of the well Jesus comments, "Everyone who drinks of this water will be thirsty again, but those who drink of the water that I will give them will never be thirsty."

⁵⁴John 14:134, NRSV. Other statements to this effect use similar words. For example, when told his friend Lazarus is gravely ill, Jesus responds, "This illness does not lead to death; rather it is for God's glory, so that the Son of God may be glorified through it." John 11:14, NRSV.

⁵⁵John 14:6, NRSV.

⁵⁶Mark 10:45, NRSV.

⁵⁷Mark 9:36–37, NRSV.

⁵⁸Galatians 3:28, NRSV.

⁵⁹Luke 12:39, KJV.

Chapter Sixteen

¹The Gospels contain numerous passages describing Jesus taking food or wine with assorted miscreants. Here is my favorite: "When the scribes of the Pharisees saw that [Jesus] was eating with sinners and tax collectors, they said to his disciples, 'Why does he eat with tax collectors and sinners?' When Jesus heard this he said to them, 'Those who are well have no need of a physician.' " Mark 2:16–7, NRSV.

²Obviously it could be argued that Siddhartha Gautama, founder of Buddhism, was the most influential spiritualist, judged by his impact on Eastern culture; the Buddha also predated Jesus by roughly 500 years. Muslims would of course argue for Muhammad. Coming seven centuries after Christ, his total influence on world culture is lesser; though with Islam currently expanding faster than Christianity, at some future point that calculation may change.

³The phrase Jesus Christ is probably best understood to mean "Jesus the Anointed," as the Greek word *Christos* translates to "anointed." "Christ" is often misconstrued as Jesus's last name. In nomenclature of the period most people did not have last names in the modern sense. Jesus would have been known as "Jesus of Nazareth" or "Jesus son of Joseph" or if his parents separated, "Jesus son of Mary." Calling the religion Christianity, then, worked off Jesus's cognomen. Had his given name been used instead the majority of Western citizens might now call themselves Jesuits, a strange historical thought.

⁴See Reynolds Price, *Three Gospels* (New York: Scribners, 1996).

⁵Many who contest the actuality of Jesus's life cite Flavius Josephus, author of one of the few extant first-century histories of the Holy Land. Though Josephus wrote at length of John the Baptist, he made only brief, dismissive reference to Jesus. How could a first-hand observer of ancient Galilee not feature Jesus, if this person were real?

Josephus, however, was hardly an unbiased source. A general from the Pharisee order, he helped lead the year 66 Israeli rebellion against Rome; after the rebellion failed he switched sides and went to work for the Emperor Vespasian. By the time Josephus began writing histories, he was living in Rome and had adopted Vespasian's patronymic: rendering his objectivity a matter of speculation, given that the young Jesus movement had become a thorn in the emperor's side. Scholarship regarding the far past is often based on whatever documents happen to survive—in most respects, a random sample. Josephus's histories may be good or bad, but approaching his work as a clear window to New Testament days is as if a future historian were to stumble on the memoirs of General Norman Schwarzkopf and try to analyze them as a definitive recounting of the 1960s antiwar movement.

One reason the discovery of the Dead Sea Scrolls excited such interest was the hope that they would provide a fresh means of cross-checking extant documents from the first-century Holy Land. But the Scrolls are fragmentary, and so far their content seems inconclusive. See the excellent Hershel Shanks, ed., *Understanding the Dead Sea Scrolls* (New York: Random House, 1994).

[6]See Randel Helms, *Gospel Fictions* (Buffalo, N.Y.: Prometheus Books, 1995).

[7]See Burton Mack, *Who Wrote the New Testament? The Making of a Christian Myth* (New York: HarperCollins, 1995).

[8]See C. S. Lewis, *Mere Christianity* (New York: Macmillan, 1943).

[9]Luke 24:41, NRSV. This is one of the reappearance accounts. In another, the disciples are out fishing when they first see the risen Christ. Again before any serious talk, their master wants to eat: "Jesus said to them, 'Bring some of the fish that you have just caught. . . . Come and have breakfast." John 21:10–12, NRSV.

[10]See Thomas Sheehan, *The First Coming* (New York: Random House, 1986).

[11]The first part of the quote comes from John Crossan, *Jesus: A Revolutionary Biography* (San Francisco: Harper San Francisco, 1994); the second part from a column by Crossan in the April 1996 *Bible Review*.

[12]Several New Testament writers asserted that the fulfillment of prophecy was the proof of Christ's divinity. A representative passage, the final verse of the Gospel of John: "But there are also many other things that Jesus did; if every one of them were written down, I suppose that the world itself could not contain the books that would be written." John 21:25 NRSV.

[13]See John Meier, *A Marginal Jew* (Garden City, N.Y.: Doubleday, vol. 1, 1991; vol. 2, 1994; vol. 3, forthcoming).

[14]And how do we know it is not the secular records that are wrong? Government documents from the present are not always accurate, so it is hardly immoderate to suppose administrative records of the far past may fall somewhat below the level of impeccable.

[15]From Price, *Three Gospels*.

[16]*Bible Review*, April 1997. This delightful publication could be described as the Bible of objections to the Bible.

[17]From *Parables of Jesus*, Robert Funk, ed. (San Francisco: Polebridge Press, 1988).

[18]From Robert Funk, ed., *Five Gospels: The Search for the Authentic Words of Jesus* (San Francisco: Polebridge Press, 1993).

[19]The Jesus Seminar insists that the burden of proof must be on anyone claiming an event in Jesus's life is true, while the Seminar has no burden to disprove an event, merely to raise a doubt. By this definition the Seminar can only be right and others can only be wrong, since no one can prove the far past, while the Seminar is excused from the equally impossible task of disproof. The Jesus Seminar's self-serving dictum on this point sounds awfully like the sorts of things cardinals used to say during the Middle Ages.

[20]Luke 2:48, NRSV. See Pelikan's afterward to *The Jefferson Bible* (Boston: Beacon Press, 1989).

[21]Mark 16:5–8, NRSV.

[22]Mark 16:9–20.

[23]*New Oxford Annotated Bible* (Oxford: Oxford University Press, 1994).

[24]At John 5:16, NRSV. The Gospel reference most translators render as "the Jews" appears in Greek as *Ioudaioi*. Some translators interpret this as "the Judeans," referring to citizenry rather than ethnicity, Judah being the name for southern Israel under Roman administration. The Hebrew Old Testament word *yehuwdiy*, which some translators render into "Jew," can also mean "descendant of Judah." See, for example, Jeremiah 34:9, at which the KJV translates *yehuwdiy* to "Jew," and the NRSV translates it to "Judean." Either translation alludes to the same group of people; the question is whether the original writers intend such references to be edgy or neutral.

[25]From Funk, *Five Gospels*, more or less the manifesto of the Jesus Seminar. This is a thoughtful work but contains such pixilated moments as, "Like the cowboy hero of the American West exemplified by Gary Cooper, the sage of the ancient Near East was laconic, slow to speech, a person of few words." Jesus was like Gary Cooper? Reach for the sky, Satan!

[26]See Price, *Three Gospels*.

[27]To sum an unsettled subject, the Gospels of Mark and Matthew probably were not written by people named Mark or Matthew, and these authors probably were not eyewitnesses to the events they describe; Luke may have been written by a man named Luke, but probably he was not an eyewitness; John may or may not have been written by someone named John, who may or may not have been an eyewitness.

[28]To sum another unsettled subject, the Gospels are generally considered to have been composed 30 to 60 years after Jesus's death. Proponents of the Nothing school like to date them later, so as to imply enough time had passed that religious promoters could have begun making up the supernatural components. Most but not all scholarship tends to date the composition of the Gospels reasonably close to Jesus's life.

[29]For an excellent synopsis of Q theory see Charlotte Allen, "The Search for a No-Frills Jesus," *Atlantic Monthly*, December 1995. See also *The First Gospel: An Introduction to Q* by Arland Jacobson (San Francisco: Polebridge Press, 1992).

[30]Recently Q theorists began to publish a reconstructed document suggesting what Q might have contained. Proponents have since said that because a Q document has been published, it is no longer fair to call Q hypothesized. But this is like saying that because *Newsweek* published the "Hitler diaries," it is no longer fair to call those diaries an invention. There may once have been a real Q. But publishing a made-up Q does not make that model "real," except in the sense of existing on paper.

[31]Most Gnostic writing had been considered obliterated until, in 1945, a farmer found near the Egyptian town of Naj Hammadi a large earthenware jar containing 13 leather-bound papyrus books buried perhaps 1,600 years ago, to escape Leo's purge. These Gnostic texts included the Gospel of Thomas, an account of Jesus's sayings that may eventually be considered canonical.

[32]Matthew 6:7, NRSV.

[33]Luke 7:34.

[34]Mark 3:21.

[35]At Mark 14:35–36, NRSV. The disciples are told to stand guard, but instead fall asleep. Christ removes himself to pray alone: "Going a little farther, [Jesus] threw himself on the ground and prayed that, if it were possible, the hour might pass from him. He said, '*Abba*, Father, for you all things are possible; remove this cup from me.' "

This is one of the Gospel verses that describe Jesus alone, raising the question of how the writer knew what happened when no one else was present. Nearby at Mark 14:51 falls a reference to an unnamed "young man" who watched the Gethsemane betrayal from the bushes and who, caught by soldiers, escaped by wriggling out of his linen cloth—traditional desert boy's attire—and running off naked. Over the years it has been speculated that this unnamed child happened on the scene trying for a glimpse of the Redeemer, and later grew up into a Gospel author.

[36]First Corinthians 15:14-5, NRSV.

[37]See, for example, the account that begins at Mark 16:1.

[38]Greek originals of the Book of Daniel contain an extra chapter, the Book of Susanna, which most Bibles list under apocrypha. In it Susanna, a beautiful woman who likes to relax naked in her garden, is lusted after by two patriarchs. The elders tell Susanna that unless she sleeps with them, they will accuse her of adultery, for which the penalty is death. Under ancient desert law, an accusation by two men would constitute proof of guilt, no further evidence required. Told this by the aspiring rapists, "Susanna groaned and said, 'I am completely trapped, for if I [refuse] it will mean death for me, if I [consent] I cannot escape your hands.' " (Susanna 1:24, NRSV.) Being righteous, Susanna refuses. The elders promptly arrange her execution.

Daniel saves Susanna by acting as her lawyer, perhaps the first recorded instance of defense counsel. He questions the elders separately, and they give conflicting accounts of the adultery they supposedly witnessed. The story ends with the elders themselves executed for bringing a false capital charge. (Under old desert law, if you falsely accused others of a crime, the punishment they would have received would be imposed on you—an idea to be revived, perhaps, for modern corporate litigation?) Susanna was a favored subject of Middle Ages' painters, as biblical descriptions of her beauty and her dislike for the restrictive convention of clothing provided a respectable excuse to paint nudes.

[39]Luke 24:11, NRSV.

[40]The novelist and biblical commentator Isaac Asimov once expressed contemporary sensibility about the resurrection in these words: "If some of us, in this rationalist age, wish to discount the element of the divine, there remains a connected, nonmiraculous and completely credible story of the fate of a Galilean preacher." The phrase perhaps unintentionally summarizes the postmodern assumption that the *element of the divine* is no longer welcome.

After all, if Christ really was resurrected, then some deity must exist: and modern thought not only questions the divine (as it should) but seems actively distressed by any suggestions of spiritual authenticity. If, somehow, physical proof of a benevolent divinity were produced tomorrow, a segment of the modern intellectual world would be hugely disappointed. Members of the Jesus Seminar would rend their garments and weep.

Chapter Seventeen

[1]John 14:27, NRSV.

[2]Matthew 10:29–31, NRSV.

[3]Matthew 14:27, NRSV. "Were terrified" at previous verse.

[4]Matthew 17:5–6, NRSV.

[5]Matthew 28:5, NRSV.

[6]Shaw also said Christianity should be named Paulism, for the often-taut doctrines of the institutional faith originate with the apostle Paul, not the uninhibited rabbi Jesus. Paul was the one concerned with church procedure and administrative edict, subjects for

which Jesus displayed no interest. And Paul was born a Roman citizen, making him attractive to Roman Christianity, the primary form the faith took for a thousand years. The notion that Paul was the true author of Christianity traces to the German scholar Ferdinand Baur, who raised the idea in the mid-1800s; it was revived by the British essayist A. N. Wilson in his 1997 book, *Paul: The Mind of the Apostle* (New York: W. W. Norton).

[7]Angels become ominous again in the Bible's final book, Revelation, but nothing depicted in Revelation actually happens: the book describes a prophetic dream sequence.

[8]At Luke 23:44.

[9]Mark 7:36, NRSV.

[10]Luke 5:12–13, NRSV.

[11]The remainder of the New Testament does contain small touches of the supernatural. At Acts 5:1–10, a husband and wife agree to auction their land and give the gain to the apostles, but lie about the sale price and keep most of the proceeds for themselves. They fall down dead when Peter confronts them with the truth. Acts 19:11–12, NRSV, reports that "God did extraordinary miracles through Paul, so that when the handkerchiefs or aprons that had touched his skin were brought to the sick, their diseases left them and the evil spirits came out of them." Subsequent verses note the comic efforts of freelance exorcists to duplicate Paul's feat.

[12]Matthew 19:16, NRSV.

[13]Matthew 19:21–24, NRSV. The "eye of the needle" then meant the aperture in a city gate through which sentries inspected those asking for admission after dark. Thus to Jesus's listeners, a camel trying to enter the eye of the needle would be a tragicomic image—the animal sticking its snout through an opening just enough to perceive the city within, but unable to enter.

[14]Mark 10:23, NRSV.

[15]Hebrews 13:5, NRSV.

[16]See Harvey Cox, "The Warring Visions of the Religious Right," *The Atlantic Monthly*, November 1995.

[17]Matthew 21:12.

[18]Matthew 5:42, NRSV. Adoration of money shows on the spiritual left, too. For instance Deepak Chopra, who claims to oppose materialism, relentlessly panders to it. His *The Seven Spiritual Laws of Success* promises "the ability to create unlimited wealth with effortless ease" to anyone who follows its sure-fire seven-part act-before-midnight secret formula.

[19]Matthew 6:19–21, NRSV.

[20]John 8:34, NRSV.

[21]Luke 12:5, NRSV.

[22]The New Testament contains two references to sin at the Garden, though neither is attributed to Jesus. At Romans 5:14, Paul mentions "the transgression of Adam." First Timothy 2:14, NRSV, notes, "Adam was not deceived, but the woman was deceived and became a transgressor." Echoing the Old Testament view that obstetric pain is women's cost of Eve's error, the next verse declares, "Yet she will be saved through childbearing."

[23]John 10:34, NRSV. Of himself Jesus argued that if in Old Testament days even human beings were thought to have divine aspects, why should anyone think it strange a carpenter from Nazareth has divine aspects? See John 10:35.

[24]Psalms 82:6, NRSV.

[25]Matthew 5:16, NRSV.

[26]Matthew 5:5.

[27]See Charles Hartshorne, *The Logic of Perfection* (Open Court, 1962).

[28]Matthew 21:42, NRSV.

[29]Aramaic, derived from Hebrew, was the language of Jesus's life and ministry. *Abba* appears in its Aramaic form even in Greek autographs of the New Testament. Owing to Christ's fondness for this word, bishops of the early church liked to be addressed as *Abba*, which is roughly like a modern English speaker addressing a government official as "Poppy."

[30]John 4:24, NRSV.

[31]Mark 10:14, KJV.

[32]Mark 10:15, KJV.

[33]Matthew 5:26, NRSV.

[34]Luke 6:26, NRSV.

[35]At Matthew 5:33–37, NRSV: "You have heard that it was said to those of ancient times, 'You shall not swear falsely.' But I say to you, do not swear at all . . . Let your word be 'Yes, Yes' or 'No, No.' " Today members of the Society of Friends ("Quakers") still observe this injunction, and will not take oaths.

Article II of the Constitution specifies that someone taking the oath of office either "swear or affirm" to uphold the law. This option was added because some Founding Fathers felt that requiring presidents to "swear" loyalty to the republic would violate the religious beliefs of any careful student of Jesus.

[36]The Sermon on the Mount runs from Matthew 5:3 to 7:27 and from Luke 6:20 to 6:49. I worked mainly from Matthew's version, which is more detailed. Word choices are from the New Revised Standard.

[37]Whether the full course of thought of the Golden Rule was original to Jesus or had already been explored by others is unknown. The most similar anterior scriptural reference is Proverbs 24:29, which instructs, "Do not say, 'I will do to others as they have done to me.' "

[38]Matthew 22:36–40, NRSV.

[39]At Luke 10:25–37, quoted from the NRSV.

[40]The teaching "Love your neighbor as yourself" is known to have originated at least a thousand years before Jesus. The Old Testament offers this admonition at Leviticus 19:18; Jesus surely encountered the verse when studying the Torah. The lawyer's objection reflects on a millennia-old rabbinical debate about who one's "neighbor" is. In conservative rabbinical commentary, neighbor was interpreted to mean those close to you personally or politically. Some rabbinical commentary gave neighbor the broader meaning of "anyone you meet who is not hostile." Jesus expanded this part of spiritual thinking enormously by declaring that enemies, too, should be loved as neighbors.

[41]Genesis 1:26, KJV.

[42]This is the first use of "love" in the New Revised Standard, at Genesis 22:2. The first use of "love" in the King James comes at Genesis 27:4, when Isaac from his deathbed requests "savory meat such as I love." As in the NRSV, this first reference to love is not spiritual.

[43]Isaiah 63:7, NRSV.

[44]Matthew 5:44, NRSV.

[45]Matthew 22:40, NRSV.

[46]John 15:12, NRSV.

[47]John 15:11, NRSV.

Chapter Eighteen

[1]Romans 13:10, NRSV.

[2]First John 4:16, NRSV.

Index